Alternative Nuclear Futures

Alternative Nuclear Futures

*The Role of Nuclear Weapons in the
Post-Cold War World*

edited by

JOHN BAYLIS

and

ROBERT O'NEILL

*This book has been printed digitally and produced in a standard specification
in order to ensure its continuing availability*

OXFORD
UNIVERSITY PRESS

Great Clarendon Street, Oxford OX2 6DP

Oxford University Press is a department of the University of Oxford.
It furthers the University's objective of excellence in research, scholarship,
and education by publishing worldwide in

Oxford New York

Auckland Bangkok Buenos Aires Cape Town Chennai
Dar es Salaam Delhi Hong Kong Istanbul Karachi Kolkata
Kuala Lumpur Madrid Melbourne Mexico City Mumbai Nairobi
São Paulo Shanghai Taipei Tokyo Toronto

Oxford is a registered trade mark of Oxford University Press
in the UK and in certain other countries

Published in the United States
by Oxford University Press Inc., New York

ISBN 0-19-829624-X

ACKNOWLEDGEMENTS

The editors would like to express their gratitude to Dominic Byatt of Oxford University Press for the efficiency and enthusiasm he brought to the production of this book and to Amanda Watkins for all her hard work and support. They would also like to thank Dr Paul Roe for all his help in producing the final manuscript to Dr Mark Smith for his assistance in proof-reading and producing the index, and to Elaine Lowe and Merja Jenkins for their help in typing various sections of the book. The editors are also grateful to Lynne Reinner Publishers for permission to publish the chapter by Colin Gray.

CONTENTS

Notes on Contributors　　　　　　　　　　　　　　　　　ix

Introduction: The Contemporary Debate about Nuclear Weapons
John Baylis and Robert O'Neill　　　　　　　　　　　1

1. To Confuse Ourselves: Nuclear Fallacies
   Colin Gray　　　　　　　　　　　　　　　　　　4

2. The Unavoidable Importance of Nuclear Weapons
   George H. Quester　　　　　　　　　　　　　　31

3. Aspiration, Realism, and Practical Policy
   Michael Quinlan　　　　　　　　　　　　　　45

4. Eliminators, Marginalists, and the Politics of Disarmament
   Lawrence Freedman　　　　　　　　　　　　　56

5. Nuclear Weapons, Prudence, and Morality: The Search for
   a 'Third Way'
   John Baylis　　　　　　　　　　　　　　　　70

6. Nuclear Weapons and the Post-Cold-War Middle East:
   Business as Usual
   Efraim Karsh　　　　　　　　　　　　　　　87

7. The South Asian Nuclear Challenge
   Ramesh Thakur　　　　　　　　　　　　　101

8. Nuclear Disarmament: The Case for Incrementalism
   Harald Müller　　　　　　　　　　　　　125

9. The Elimination of Nuclear Weapons
   Michael MccGwire　　　　　　　　　　　144

10. Reflecting on War in the Twenty-first Century: The Context
for Nuclear Abolition
Robert S. McNamara   167

11. At the End of a Journey: The Risks of Cold-War
Thinking in a New Era
Lee Butler   183

12. Weapons of the Underdog
Robert O'Neill   191

Notes   209

Appendices
1. Prepared Statement on the 'Future of Nuclear
Deterrence'   *Walter B. Slocombe*   238
2. Legality of the Use by a State of Nuclear Weapons in
Armed Confict   *International Court of Justice, The Hague*   246
3. Nuclear Weapons: The ICJ 1996 Pronouncement
Sir Michael Quinlan   247
4. Executive Summary   *The Canberra Commission on the
Elimination of Nuclear Weapons*   250

Select Bibliography of Recent Sources   255

Index   257

NOTES ON CONTRIBUTORS

JOHN BAYLIS is Professor of International Politics and Dean of the Faculty of Economic and Social Studies at the University of Wales, Aberystwyth. He is also a Fellow of The Royal Historical Society. His latest publications include *Ambiguity and Deterrence: British Nuclear Strategy 1945 to 1964* (Oxford University Press, 1995); *The Globalization of World Politics*, ed., with S. Smith (Oxford University Press, 1997); and *Anglo-American Relations since 1939: The Enduring Alliance* (Manchester University Press, 1997).

LEE BUTLER was Commander-in-Chief of the US Strategic Air Command (1991–2) and subsequently the US Strategic Command (1992–4) with responsibility for all US Air Force and Navy nuclear deterrent forces. He was closely involved in the development of US nuclear doctrine. General Butler served as a deputy to General Colin Powell.

LAWRENCE FREEDMAN is Professor, Department of War Studies, King's College London. His publications include *The Evolution of Nuclear Strategy* (Macmillan, 1981); *Britain and the Falklands War* (Blackwell, 1988); and *The Gulf Conflict 1990–91* (Faber & Faber, 1993), with Efraim Karsh.

COLIN S. GRAY is Professor of International Politics and Director of the Centre for Security Studies at the University of Hull, England. Dr Gray has written many books, articles and reports for the US Government on aspects of nuclear strategy. His latest books are *The Second Nuclear Age* (Lynne Rienner, 1999), and *Modern Strategy* (Oxford University Press, 1999). His current research is focused on the relationship between strategy and revolutions in military affairs.

EFRAIM KARSH is Professor and Head of the Mediterranean Studies Programme at King's College, University of London. He has held teaching and/or research positions at Columbia University, the International Institute for Strategic Studies (London), the Kennan Institute for Advanced Russian Studies (Washington DC), and the Jaffee Centre for Strategic Studies at Tel-Aviv University. His many books *include Empires of the Sand: The Struggle for Mastery in the Middle East 1789–1923* (Harvard, 1999); *Fabricating Israeli History: The "New Historians"* (Cass, 1997); and *The Gulf Conflict 1990–91* (Princeton, 1993; with Lawrence Freedman).

MICHAEL McCGWIRE holds honorary appointments as Fellow in the Faculty of Social and Political Sciences at Cambridge University and Professor of

International Politics at the University of Wales, Aberystwyth. As a British naval officer (1942–67), he served as an attache in Moscow, a NATO war planner, and ran the Soviet naval section of British Defence Intelligence. From 1979 to 1990 he was a Senior Fellow at the Brookings Institution in Washington, DC, working on Soviet Defence and foreign policy.

ROBERT S. MCNAMARA was Secretary of Defense under Presidents Kennedy and Johnson. He is a former President of the Ford Motor Company and the World Bank. Since leaving the World Bank he has been active in economic and development efforts across the globe and in the areas of arms control and nuclear non-proliferation.

HARALD MÜLLER is Director, Peace Research Institute Frankfurt; Professor of International Relations, Frankfurt University; Visiting Professor, Johns Hopkins University Center for International Relations, Bologna, Italy; and member of the Advisory Board on Disarmament Matters of the UN Secretary General.

ROBERT O'NEILL is the Chichele Professor of the History of War at All Souls College, University of Oxford. An Australian, he served in the Australian Army 1955–68, including a year in the Vietnam War. He was Director of the International Institute for Strategic Studies 1982–7, and a member of the Canberra Commission on the Elimination of Nuclear Weapons, 1995–6. He is currently a member of the Tokyo Forum on Nuclear Non-Profileration and Disarmament.

GEORGE H. QUESTER is a Professor of Government and Politics at the University of Maryland, where he teaches courses on International Relations, American Foreign Policy, and International Military Security. He has taught previously at Cornell and Harvard Universities, at UCLA, and in the Department of Military Strategy at the National Qar College. From 1991 to 1993, he served as the Olin Visiting Professor at the United States Naval Academy.

MICHAEL QUINLAN, lately Director of the Ditchley Foundation, spent his main career in the UK Civil Service, mostly in the defence field; his last post was as Permanent Under-Secretary of State, Ministry of Defence. In several posts he was closely involved with nuclear-weapons policy, both national and NATO. He has written numerous articles on nuclear issues (including ethical aspects) and in 1997 published *Thinking about Nuclear Weapons*, in the RUSI Whitehall Paper Series.

RAMESH THAKUR is Vice Rector (Peace and Governance) of the United Nations University in Tokyo. Educated in India and Canada, he was formerly Professor and Head of the Peace Research Centre at the Australian National University in Canberra and Professor of International Relations at the University of Otago in New Zealand. He was a member of the National Consultative Committee on Peace and Disarmament in Australia, having previously been a member of the Public Advisory Committee on Arms Control and Disarmament in New Zealand. He is the author/editor of over a dozen books, the most recent being *Keeping Proliferation at Bay* (1998), *Past Imperfect, Future UNcertain: The United Nations at Fifty* (1998), and *Nuclear Weapons-Free Zones* (1998).

Introduction

The Contemporary Debate about Nuclear Weapons

John Baylis and Robert O'Neill

Since the end of the cold war nuclear weapons have receded somewhat in the policy debates between the United States, Russia, and China. The process of relegation began with the 1987 INF Treaty banning ground-based theatre nuclear weapons in Europe, which was followed in 1991 with an agreement between President Bush and President Gorbachev to eliminate shorter range, tactical nuclear weapons. The START I and II Agreements were also signed in 1990 and 1993 respectively, which, if fully implemented, will reduce the number of American and Russian strategic weapons from around 20,000 to 3,500 on each side by 2007. Other recent positive developments have included the May 1994 decision by the United States and Russia to stop targeting each other's territory (although not to take their strategic missiles off alert), the indefinite extension of the Non-Proliferation Treaty in 1995 and the signing of the Comprehensive Test Ban Treaty in September 1996 after nearly thirty years of sporadic negotiations.

By contrast with this process of de-emphasizing nuclear weapons, it has become clear by the late 1990s that the five long-standing nuclear powers (the United States, Russia, China, Britain, and France) and the two recent nuclear powers (India and Pakistan) appear to have no intention of completely giving up their nuclear capabilities. The nuclear tests by India and Pakistan in May 1998, in particular, have highlighted the continuing perceived utility of nuclear weapons as instruments of vital national security in the post-cold-war era. It seems highly likely that Israel will also continue to maintain its covert nuclear capability, given the contemporary problems with the Middle East peace process, and that several other 'aspiring' nuclear states (and perhaps non-state groups) will pursue their search for nuclear, as well as, chemical and biological weapons, as we move into the twenty-first century.

In response to the apparent contrast between the easing of world tensions that followed the end of the cold war, and the stated desires of the nuclear powers to maintain these weapons as essential elements of their armed forces, a major debate has emerged in recent years which centres on the future role of nuclear weapons in world politics and international security. This debate has both private and public aspects: it takes place within the councils of governments, both of nuclear weapons states and of non-nuclear weapons states; more recently it has emerged onto the public stage. The Stimson Center in Washington, DC, has published two major and radical reports on the future of nuclear weapons. The Canberra Commission on the Elimination of Nuclear Weapons produced its report in 1996. Several other bodies have also reinforced calls for a fresh approach to the question of nuclear weapons. As we write this introduction another major body, The Tokyo Forum on Nuclear Non-Proliferation and Disarmament is in the mid-stages of preparing a further report, which will be released in the second half of 1999. It is also significant in this debate that the traditional 'left-wing' versus 'establishment' officials divide that was characteristic of discussion during the cold war has largely disappeared, with a growing number of senior military and defence officials, and governments allied with the United States, openly advocating the abolition of nuclear weapons.

This important post-Cold War debate centres on a wide range of old and new questions which form the main framework for this book. These include:

- Is the total abolition of nuclear weapons now desirable? If so, is it feasible?
- Did nuclear weapons help to keep the peace during the cold war?
- What are the moral and prudential cases for and against retaining nuclear weapons in the post-cold-war world?
- Are the risks of nuclear weapons accidents greater or less than during the cold war?
- How serious are the new dangers of nuclear proliferation?
- Is proliferation inevitable?
- Would this be a bad outcome?
- What problems arise for the command and control of nuclear weapons when nuclear weapons states disintegrate?
- What is the significance of the May 1998 nuclear tests by India and Pakistan? Should India and Pakistan now be accorded the status of the other nuclear weapons states with regard to the Non-Proliferation Treaty? If not, how are they to be treated—as international pariahs?
- Is the spread of nuclear weapons in the Middle East now probable?
- Has the 'Revolution in Military Affairs' made nuclear weapons less necessary by giving conventional weapons increased destructive power, accuracy, and flexibility?
- Is nuclear deterrence still relevant to the long-term security of the post-cold-war world?

- If so, are the requirements of nuclear deterrence still the same as during the cold war?
- Are nuclear weapons useful in deterring chemical and biological weapons?
- Are nuclear weapons incompatible with 'co-operative security'?
- Is there a future for strategic arms control?
- Does the marginalization of nuclear weapons represent a viable and preferable 'third way' between 'traditionalist' and 'abolitionist' approaches to nuclear weapons?[1]

The primary aim of this book is to highlight the key themes which have emerged in this debate and to provide the main alternative answers which have been given to these questions. We, the editors, hope that this book will make a contribution to the analysis of the role of nuclear weapons in world politics and thereby help in advancing a wider debate about a subject which, despite the changes that have taken place since 1989, continues to be of supreme importance for the future of the human race.

The authors have been deliberately chosen, partly because of the significance of their contribution to the debate, and partly because of their positions within the debate. We were also anxious to make sure that a number of different national perspectives were represented. No attempt has been made to summarize the arguments presented in each of the chapters. The editors want the authors to speak for themselves. We hope that after reading the volume, others may feel more strongly motivated to join the discussion on the basis of a deeper understanding of the points raised on all sides of the debate.

1

To Confuse Ourselves: Nuclear Fallacies

Colin S. Gray

This chapter is designed to filter judgements broadly on nuclear ideas and policy. So much of the professional literature today barely lifts its level of concern from the weeds of the erstwhile marshes of southern Iraq, or ventures beyond the containing walls of nuclear reactors, that major effort is required to escape capture by technical and diplomatic detail and local context. This author is concerned lest these early years of the second nuclear age (understood as the years since the ending of the cold war in 1989–91) should be squandered by a transnational, extended Western defence community which is not equipped theoretically to understand the strategic history that is to hand, let alone the strategic history that may be.

The main body of the discussion here comprises exploration of what is labelled, undeniably with malice aforethought, as 'eight nuclear fallacies'. The choice of eight is not significant. What is significant, however, is the spirit of the analysis and discussion. This spirit is sceptical, irreverent, unapologetic, and yet deeply serious about the emerging perils to national and international security posed by weapons of mass destruction (WMD). The nuclear fallacies discussed below are fallacies about today and tomorrow: they have some minor resonance for all nuclear history, but they have major resonance for this second nuclear age.

The fallacies identified and discussed below comprise a mix of beliefs and arguments, some of which are advanced explicitly in the literature (e.g. on nuclear abolition, on virtual arsenals, and on a nuclear taboo), while others either are implicit in public debate (e.g. the reliability of deterrence, the unfeasibility of defence, and the ability of the current international security system to cope well enough with a small nuclear war) or at least—in my opinion— loom as important topics likely to attract attention before very long. Whether the extant literature on a 'fallacy' is large or small, the belief in question inherently is important, either because it addresses a matter structural to this second nuclear age, or because it attracts adherents who might succeed in influencing nuclear policy in significant ways.

1.1. *Fallacy One: A Post-Nuclear Era has Dawned*

Neither the non-proliferation regime that has the NPT as the jewel in its crown, nor strategic trends of other kinds (e.g. keyed to the political, ethical, or technological, dimensions of strategy), are in the process of aborting the nuclear character of this second nuclear age. Nuclear deterrence is not at present actively intended in great power relations, but it remains a background element. It is useful for Sir Michael Quinlan to distinguish between a policy towards nuclear deterrence that has shifted comprehensively into generality—'to whom it may concern' as the unnamed addressee[1]—and one that absolutely renounces nuclear war. As Sir Michael notes, most countries' armed forces, most of the time, are not specifically 'addressed' as threats to particular putative foes. However, the popular notion of general deterrence, and especially general nuclear deterrence, can be over-appreciated.[2] After all, American nuclear weapons do help frame, or backstop, US diplomacy for the (pre-)containment of China, they are obviously a factor in any Russian speculation about the staging of some return of imperium, and they would be inalienably on the board of statecraft in roles supporting any US military intervention against regional foes. The US policy stance today is decidedly unenthusiastic about nuclear weapons,[3] probably unduly so, but no matter how bland and general that policy is, actual or potential enemies of the United States have to ask the question, 'What do US nuclear weapons mean for us?'

Identification of this first fallacy is not intended to invite an argument about current trends. Most trends are reversible. The political and military-technical tide certainly would seem to be leaving nuclear options 'on the beach'—with apologies to the late Nevil Shute for the reference to his apocalyptic novel.[4] The indefinite extension of the NPT at the latest review conference (1995) assuredly was a great success for the non-proliferation regime, and at least apparently was a boost to the norms promoted by that regime. Moreover, the surge in precise military lethality that is allowed by the clutch of capabilities developed for information-led warfare would seem to place nuclear weapons at a discount. One can argue that the quest for precision in bombardment has been motivated in part by the strong desire to escape from the grip of military rationales for nuclear weapons.[5] All that appears to beckon, however, may not really be on offer.

The numbers of nuclear-weapon, and nuclear-threshold, states, remain much lower than proliferation pessimists were predicting in the 1950s and

1960s.[6] There is no question but that the pace of proliferation has been slow and at present shows no thoroughly convincing signs of a prospect for other than a distinctly steady acceleration. But, this trend, if that is what it is, of a deliberate pace in proliferation, is vulnerable to nuclear learning from any crisis, anywhere, that seems to demonstrate a strategic necessity for nuclear arms. The trend that has produced only five NPT-'licensed' nuclear-weapon states—which happen to be the Five Permanent Members of the UN Security Council—three unlicensed nuclear-weapon states (Israel, India, Pakistan), at least one near-nuclear-weapon threshold state (North Korea), and three would-be nuclear-weapon states (Iraq, Iran, Libya), is indeed impressive. Also it is impressive that, *inter alia*, Sweden, Switzerland, Japan, Argentina, Brazil, Egypt, and Taiwan, have stepped back from active pursuit of the military nuclear option.[7] More noteworthy still was the renunciation in 1990 of actual, as opposed to virtual, nuclear weapons by a South Africa whose internal and external security condition has been transformed by and large for the better,[8] and by the distinctly insecure extra-Russian legatees of part of the erstwhile Soviet nuclear arsenal.

Unfortunately, the problem is not with the fact of a slow pace of nuclear proliferation. The problem, rather, lies in knowing what that fact means. Are we witnessing a trend in nuclear reduction towards zero—a high policy goal embraced formally, if insincerely, by the extant nuclear-weapon states—towards an existentially post-nuclear era? Or, does what we see signify nothing in particular about the strategic salience of nuclear weapons? Just one unde-terrable, or deterrable but not deterred, nuclear act, could revolutionize the terms of debate over nuclear policy in several countries.

Quantity and quality should not be confused. The small number of nuclear-weapon, and near-nuclear-weapon, states is less important than is their iden-tity, the potential for, as it were, infectious further proliferation that they bear, and the implications for character of conflict that they carry. The principal reason why nuclear proliferation is dangerous, even if, occasionally, it can make a net positive contribution to regional peace with security, is exactly the reason why arms control usually disappoints. The global non-proliferation regime cannot handle the hardest of hard cases. Even if there are only a handful or fewer of predictably near-threshold states, that short short-list happens to include polities with exceedingly serious security problems— which is, of course, a leading reason why they resist the force of the control regime. The polities in question are, at present, *only* North Korea, Iraq, Iran, and perhaps Libya. In 1998, India and Pakistan left the realm of 'threshold' states to enjoy the uncertain mixed blessings of full-blown nuclear-weapon standing.

A significant reason why this second nuclear age is not in the process of radical transformation into a post-nuclear era has been identified with some hyperbole by Martin van Creveld. 'By the time the cold war ended, any state in possession of even a halfway modern conventionally armed force was also capable of manufacturing, begging or stealing nuclear weapons.'[9] Van Creveld exaggerates, but not by much, and the exaggeration is merited because it highlights a point of the utmost importance. The new-found effectiveness of regular Western conventional arms is the very reason why those who are conventionally challenged find NBC (nuclear, biological, and chemical) arms of great interest.

1.2. *Fallacy Two: Nuclear Abolition is Feasible and Desirable*

Two problems with nuclear weapons have the effect of acting like forces of nature. The first problem is the persistence of the strategic (i.e. force-related) element in human history; the second is the elemental fact of 'the nuclear discovery'.[10] The synergy between these two 'problems' creates the condition this essay analyses. One can imagine a world wherein the undesirable and admittedly irreversible fact of the nuclear discovery would be entirely unimportant, but the kind of world that generates no policy demands for nuclear arms is not a world likely to be on offer any time soon. For reasons both of general humanity and particular Western interest, the desirability of attempting to 'marginalize' nuclear weapons as a central thrust to our security policy is fairly obvious.[11] The difficulty with 'marginalization', though, is that it cannot succeed if, to repeat, those security communities who are conventionally challenged logically see in NBC arms the prospect of a great equalizer. One need not master the finer points of Sun Tzu's *Art of War*,[12] or even invest much time in the design of cunning plans, in order to appreciate that the highest of high roads to success lies in attacking the enemy's strategy. In 1991 the United States taught would-be regional hegemons a master class in why nuclear armament is not a dispensable luxury if one chooses to act in ways strongly deplored by Americans.

Marginalization may warrant classification as a fallacy, certainly it is a candidate fallacy, but at least it has the merit of being desirable for the United States, and it may even be feasible in a few cases that matter to the United States. That judgement is not intended as a ringing endorsement of the thesis that nuclear weapons can and should be marginalized in local, regional, and world politics, but it notes that this modest notion has some modest strategic utility. The contrast with the abolitionist position could hardly be more stark.

Two linked arguments on the feasibility of nuclear abolition should render any subsequent discussion about desirability moot. First, the nuclear discovery of 1945 means that for all time nuclear weapons cannot really be abolished. Only if one toys with the notion that somehow, as with the formula for the Byzantines' wonder weapon, 'Greek fire',[13] human beings will lose the nuclear knowledge, could one speculate about abolition. But, unless knowledge even of the fact of the erstwhile nuclear discovery also was mislaid, why would nuclear rediscovery not occur? 'Virtual nuclear arsenals' by definition would lack physical presence, but they would comprise nuclear arsenals possible in the future.[14] (The distinctive fallacy of purposefully virtual arsenals is discussed below.)

The second argument against the empirical and logical integrity of the abolitionist thesis is the persisting and reliably predictable fact of policy and strategy demands for the services of nuclear arsenals. Notwithstanding Peter R. Lavoy's interesting emphasis on the manufacture of 'nuclear myths'[15] —defined by Lavoy as unverifiable, rather than necessarily as false, beliefs— by key individuals, strategic history shows that proliferant polities 'go, or approach, nuclear', for a mix of deeply serious reasons. Whether or not Western would-be nuclear abolitionists find these mixes of reasons deplorable, or on balance imprudent, is beside the point.

If nuclear abolition were politically feasible, it would not really be necessary. For a global security regime, perhaps an anti-security regime, wherein there was robust (lasting? everyone who mattered?) consensus on the irrelevance of nuclear weapons—and biological and chemical (BC) weapons also, of course—there should also be a no-less robust consensus on the irrelevance of weapons of any kind, save those necessary for local security. With respect to nuclear weapons, in principle one can conceive of a world wherein the nuclear revolution is rendered obsolete, not merely obsolescent, by transformational changes in technology. That is a less than compellingly persuasive thought, one must hasten to add. There are strategic historical precedents for whole classes of weapons being abandoned—at least by the practitioners of 'civilized' and regular warfare—because they have ceased to be effective. It is difficult to imagine how nuclear weapons writ large and various—which is to say not only as deliverable by ballistic or air-breathing vehicles—might be rendered globally obsolete, but one should have sufficient respect for the power of history to offer surprises as to recognize the distant possibility. However, this author does not recognize even the distant possibility of a global community that does not need to be a strategic security community because it has come to embrace all possible earthly security communities. Such a global community is more likely to be achieved in the form of a dictatorial world empire than by the effect of some stain-like spread of a zone of political peace.

Nuclear abolition is impractical because, unless time travel becomes feasible, 'the nuclear discovery' by the Manhattan Project in the Second World War cannot be undone. To argue for a policy that is inherently and permanently impractical has to be foolish, given that it can raise public expectations that cannot be fulfilled, it wastes scarce intellectual effort, and it can serve as a counsel of perfection that destabilizes more sensible nuclear policy.[16] The idea, or standard, of abolition is not merely irrelevant to the security challenges that attend nuclear armament, however, it is irrelevant in ways that could damage security. Readers may recall that, although the Intermediate-range Nuclear Forces (INF) Treaty of 1987 was overtaken rapidly by the political events of the meltdown of the Soviet empire, during the years of its negotiation it was a menace to the political legitimacy of NATO's nuclear-dependent defence doctrine.[17] Given that arguments for nuclear abolition plainly are impractical, and that many of those who have associated themselves with abolitionist sentiments are genuinely nuclear experts, one is at a loss to know how to characterize those people's views other than uncharitably.[18] Experts, those whose reputations for expert knowledge lends credibility to a debatable cause, should not advocate a process that looks to accomplish complete nuclear disarmament when they know that that process must fail.

1.3. *Fallacy Three: Virtual Arsenals*

'The thinking person's' variant of nuclear abolition is the proposal for a transition to virtual nuclear arsenals.[19] Recognizing the permanent force of the nuclear discovery, and indeed leaning upon its dissuasive power, at least the virtual nuclear warriors would not be seeking impractically to reverse strategic history by declaring nuclear facts to be non-facts. As with many of the fallacies treated in these pages, this idea of movement towards virtual nuclear arsenals is not bereft of all merit.

Lest there be any misunderstanding, '[v]irtual arsenals would identify as a goal a situation in which no nuclear weapon is assembled and ready for use'.[20] Rephrased, '[f]or nuclear-weapon states, creating such a cushion [of time between a given stage of nuclear technology and a deployed nuclear force] means banning the existence of assembled, ready-to-use nuclear weapons'.[21] Virtual and opaque nuclear-weapon status should not be confused. If India and Pakistan prior to spring 1998 were adherents to the former, then Israel plainly enjoys the latter. A virtual nuclear arsenal is an arsenal that could be used in action quite soon. An opaque nuclear arsenal is a nuclear arsenal that is probably entirely real, but one whose owners choose to leave formally unannounced or not yet verified authoritatively.

The proposal for virtual nuclear arsenals does have its attractive features. For example:

(1) Disassembled nuclear weapons cannot detonate.
(2) A move towards virtuality in nuclear arsenals should help marginalize nuclear weapons as a consequence of removing them from active military inventories. Any measure of nuclear marginalization must

enhance the prospective potency of the conventional weaponry in which the West currently enjoys a long lead. Military planners must discount the political availability of 'weapons' that policy has insisted must be only virtual.

(3) Nuclear virtuality should reinforce the NPT regime, by disarming the world's active military inventories of nuclear weapons.

(4) Virtual nuclear weapons would be 'weapons' unready for prime time in the hands of terrorists, criminals, or dissident generals.

(5) An only virtual nuclear arsenal would be an arsenal whose 'mobilization' lead-time (i.e. assembly and perhaps transport) might serve usefully to slow down the pace of a crisis slide towards catastrophe.

None the less, having granted its apparent attractions there is much that is unattractive about this proposal. A first-order problem with virtual nuclear deterrents is that their post- (perhaps pre-) existentiality is most vitally dependent upon the ability and willingness of policy-makers in popular democracies to spot evil intention and armament in time to prepare to thwart it. A virtual nuclear arsenal has the attractive quality that it will not explode as it were by accident, or be stolen in a ready-to-use condition. But if the problem of nuclear accident leading to holocaust effectively is slight, and the risk of theft is minimal, why chance paying a significant price in deterrence forsworn when the benefit to security from virtuality is arguable at best?

The case against virtual nuclear arsenals is not impregnable, but it is strong.

1. Existing nuclear-weapon states—the P5 members of the UN Security Council, plus India, Pakistan, and Israel—have judged the risks to be disproportionate to the highly theoretical benefits. That list comprises an impressive assembly of opinions on nuclear policy.

2. The vital temporal quality and quantity of delay that makes for virtuality represents political and military opportunity for the foe. A near-nuclear-armed state is not quite a nuclear-armed state.

3. When pressed beyond the level of concept, the practical problems with a policy of nuclear virtuality assume huge proportions. For example, strategic history shows that democracies have severe political difficulties coping even with unmistakable evidence of malfeasance on the part of authoritarian polities.[22] There are problems at every relevant level of assay. Specifically: what is going on? What should we do about it?

The argument for negotiation of virtual nuclear arsenals is quite clever, and not without some appeal, but it fails the tougher tests that strategic history requires one to apply for policy adoption. Virtual nuclear arsenals must be unattractive to policy-makers habituated to real nuclear arsenals, and virtuality implies a range of gratuitous vulnerabilities.

The reasons why the proposal for virtual nuclear arsenals amounts to a fallacy are intensely practical. Above all else, perhaps, the proposal is likely to appear inherently foolish to established nuclear-weapon states. There are several strands to this argument. With respect to politics, none of the existing NPT-licensed, nuclear-weapon states would be strategically comfortable moving from the now familiar condition of being more-or-less ready for nuclear action, into some zone of only near-nuclear armament. With reference to military strategy, the virtual nuclear-weapon states would worry about the prospective military effectiveness of nuclear forces that had been critically disaggregated until a time of acute crisis triggered the process of operational nuclear constitution or reconstitution. The case for a virtual nuclear arsenal would be an extremely difficult 'briefing' to give in Washington, DC, Moscow, Beijing, London, Paris, Islamabad, or New Delhi. This author would not even attempt to deliver the briefing in Jerusalem.

This may sound a little strange, coming as it does from the pen of a fully licensed professional academic, but there are some ideas in strategic studies that are too clever, eccentrically brilliant, or just eccentric, to be real contenders for policy or strategic adoption. Whereas a skilful strategic theorist will always find something to say in praise of any idea, especially for the nuclear field, concerning which so little truly is known, strategy is a quintessentially practical realm. The proposal to move towards virtual nuclear arsenals, whatever the intellectual merit in the idea, suffers from the same malady as did Thomas C. Schelling's appallingly insightful notion of a 'threat that leaves something to chance',[23] and as also did the official US plan announced in 1982 to deploy MX ICBM's in a 'dense pack' basing mode.[24] Virtual nuclear arms sound silly, or at least gratuitously perilous; the taking of risks that purposefully leave something to chance sounds dangerously irresponsible, not to mention culturally opposed to policy-makers' desire for control; while 'dense pack' basing affronted the widespread view that one should disperse forces for survivability, not concentrate them as a clustered target.

Carl von Clausewitz wrote that '[e]verything in strategy is very simple, but that does not mean that everything is very easy'.[25] Anything in strategy, and especially anything bearing upon nuclear strategy, that appears to be distinctly odd or extremely subtle stands little chance of policy adoption. Most politicians, senior civil servants, and senior military officers, are not practising defence intellectuals. Ideas for nuclear policy that need to drive minds in the official audience far down unfamiliar paths, are all but doomed to failure. The core reason is hard neither to locate nor to explain. If contingent nuclear use is the *ultima ratio regis* (as well possibly as the *reductio ad absurdum* of strategy) in the defence of basic national security values, it follows that the nuclear force posture and strategy should be guarded in a most conservative—or dare one say, prudent—spirit.

1.4. *Fallacy Four: Deterrence is Reliable*

Deterrence is never reliable, and this general truth applies with particular force today in the second nuclear age. In the most vigorous and rigorous assault to date on the smellier orthodoxies of both expert and popular beliefs about deterrence, Keith B. Payne offers an uncompromising view of the pertinent realities.

In the second nuclear age, several factors are combining to change the strategic environment of effective deterrence policies: the apparent increase in threats posed by rogue states such as Iraq, Iran, Libya, Syria, China, and North Korea; the retraction of US forward-based armed forces; and the proliferation of WMD. Given these features of the second nuclear age, in comparison with the cold war, US deterrence goals will have to be expanded: the list of players to be deterred has to be expanded, as do the types of behavior to be prevented.[26]

Why is it that deterrence, even nuclear deterrence, is unreliable? Sir Michael Quinlan penetrates to the heart of the matter when he writes: '[d]eterrence is a concept for operating upon the thinking of others. It therefore entails some basic presuppositions about that thinking'.[27] Deterrence, therefore, is a relational variable; it is an effect upon, or influence over, behaviour, achieved and achievable only with the co-operation of the intended deteree. Deterrence is structurally unreliable for precisely the same leading reason why friction in war cannot be eliminated by wonderful new technologies:[28] specifically, there are human beings in the loop for deterrence and for the conduct of strategy in war. An individual policy-maker, or a group of policy-makers, may decide not to be deterred. Literally, there can be no such thing as '*the* deterrent', nuclear or otherwise. Whether or not a nuclear arsenal deters is a matter for decision by the recipients of would-be deterrent menaces, not by the owners of the putative deterrent.

At issue here is not so much the core logic of some long-appreciated deterrence theory, but rather the application of that theory to strategic historical practice and the judgements offered in explanation of strategic history. What we know, as contrasted with what we believe, about the record of deterrence in the first nuclear age of the cold war, appears less and less impressive as the archives open, as oral histories burgeon, and as scholars seriously entertain second thoughts about 'nuclear history'.[29]

The logic of deterrence, as propounded quite formally in a small library of books, articles, and studies since the mid-1950s, most probably is eternal and universal. But, the application of that logic, indeed even knowledge of when to apply that logic, is ever potentially catastrophically variable. To understand a problem in general terms is not necessarily the same as to understand how to solve or alleviate it. The United States in 1990 was led by a generation of cold-war trained would-be practitioners of deterrence, could draw upon an historically unparalleled measure of scholarly expertise in deterrence theory, and happened to be at the peak of its military prowess. And yet, Saddam Hussein was not deterred from seizing Kuwait.[30] If the US, indeed the Western defence community of 1990 was proud of anything, it was proud of its presumed achievement in deterrence over four decades of cold war.[31]

Deterrence, *per se*, is not the source of difficulty. The last thing the world needs is another great tome on deterrence *theory*. The problem, rather, is that deterrence is inherently unreliable because actual locally encultured human beings, deciding for any of the reasons that may move we humans, can decide that they will not be deterred. It is probably true, indeed it is very probably true, that nuclear deterrence is much more reliable than is non-nuclear, at least (extra-NBC) conventional, deterrence, but even the tilting of the playing field in favour of deterrence with the WMD qualification cannot guarantee success. For once, Sir Michael Quinlan is not entirely to be trusted when he judges that '[o]nly a state ruler possessed by a reckless lunacy scarcely paralleled even in pre-nuclear history would contemplate *with equanimity* initiating a conflict that seemed likely to bring nuclear weapons down upon his country'.[32] Sir Michael's intended reassurance has the reverse effect of that intended. If the rhetorical qualification, 'with equanimity', is deleted, the fragility of Sir Michael's claim is exposed.

Forty-plus years of superpower-led cold war may tell us really rather little about the working of deterrence, and especially about the requirements for its successful functioning. If deterrence works at both a general and an immediate level, with the former helping to shape the course of events that might plausibly bring the latter into play, was either side specifically, which is to say 'immediately', deterred (from doing what over which issues?) in the cold war? And if deterrence is believed to have worked 'immediately', just why did it work? These are questions so hard to answer with high confidence of historical accuracy that scholars must qualify their responses. The necessity for such qualification makes the point which drives this fourth fallacy. If one is irreducibly uncertain as to why particular deeply undesired events did not occur during the cold war, even though one knows the course of relevant strategic history, how much more uncertainty pertains to putative deterrent relations in the future?

Nothing, repeat nothing, can render intended deterrent effect entirely reliable. Prudent and sensibly fearful policy-makers certainly should be appalled to the point of co-operation by some not-totally-incredible prospect of suffering damage utterly disproportionate to the prospective gains from an adventurous policy. But 'should' is not 'will', and even if policymakers genuinely are appalled by the risks that they believe they are running, they might decide to run those risks anyway. Western scholars who place confidence in the practice of the theory of stable deterrence are wont to neglect to factor in the political dimension of strength of motivation for inimical behaviour.[33] The key problem is that even if every roguish regime in the world is deterrable over every issue concerning which they are contemplating bold moves, there is no way that an American would-be deterrer can be certain that they would know the specific requirements of deterrence for all those cases.

A United States that, for example, wishes to achieve such deterrent effect in Beijing as may be necessary is entirely uncertain over how much, and over some questions even whether, deterrence is needed. To a significant degree the deterrence needs of the United States *vis-à-vis* China currently are unknowable. Some readers may be discomforted by such an open-ended argument regarding China, but that open-endedness is the very core of the difficulty that one must recognize. A China hugely in a condition of domestic turmoil is distinctly possible for the next several decades. How the desperately insecure leaders of such a China could be deterred from taking action—in a bid for national unity—over Taiwan, we cannot know reliably, and even those insecure Chinese leaders themselves cannot know reliably. Ultimately, deterrence is like that.

1.5. *Fallacy Five: Stable Deterrence Works Today*

This fallacy has two important aspects. First, it misunderstands current conditions, and, second, it all but invites misunderstanding of some chaotically non-linear futures.[34] At the level of general deterrence, US military power casts a shadow of global domain over the cunning plans of any and every would-be 'rogue'—or regional 'aggressor'—in the world. But each would-be regional revisionist polity has to interrogate its specific circumstances, and its understanding of American affairs, to inquire whether that general deterrence has any plausible, let alone probable, relevance to the adventure that it contemplates. Unfortunately for reliability of scholarship, if the general deterrence delivered by the US armed forces has practical effect in immediate deterrence, we are unlikely to know about it. When lines are not drawn in the sand, there are unlikely to be footprints for scholars to photograph.

It is a common failure of the strategic imagination to recognize how difficult it can be to deter those who are truly desperate, those who are overconfident, and those who are fatalistically resigned to submit to 'History's command' or the 'will of Allah', and so forth, according to cultural predilection.[35] For most of the time the absence of conditions of acute crisis and war will not be (negative) evidence of the successful functioning of some mechanism for stable deterrence. The leading problems of evidence for scholars are that they cannot know how much dissuasive influence US military power produces for a general deterrence that discourages those would-be aggressors who rule out certain forms of challenge to a US-backed regional order; and they cannot know or discover whether or not a regional power declines to be heroic in face of immediate US deterrence, having first decided to be brave in face of general US deterrence.

Argument by illustrative analogy is not widely favoured by American scholars, but this author will defy that fact. Because the Soviet leadership in 1989–91 decided not to fight for the Soviet imperium, the Soviet empire, or even, utterly unpredictably, for the USSR itself—even the Turkish empire, 'the sick man of Europe' for the better part of a century prior to 1914, resisted its demise more vigorously—it is widely believed that stable deterrence throughout the cold war must have been easily achievable. After all, if Soviet leaders would not even contest, *à l'outrance*, their political patrimony at home, how formidable really were they over matters of relative influence much further afield? This is not the place to debate the decline and fall of the Soviet empire; indeed, such a mission would exceed the domain of the enquiry.[36] But the author is concerned lest false conclusions be drawn from the relatively painless demise of Soviet authority. A group of Soviet leaders different from that led by the unfortunate and incompetent Mikhail Gorbachev could well have decided that their sacred ideological duty mandated a brutal response to the thoroughgoing challenge posed by local opposition to Soviet imperium in East–Central Europe in 1989. Admittedly, this is counterfactual argument, but it would not have been excessively difficult for different Soviet leaders to have licensed, one need hardly add motivated, East–Central European satraps to suppress popular dissent. 'Tiananmen Square' easily could have happened in Berlin in 1989 (e.g. 'Alexanderplatz'). If it had happened, the Soviet imperium of the great socialist empire might well have been preserved, albeit in politically and morally severely damaged condition.

The point of the above pseudo-analogy is to emphasize that the fall of the Soviet empire probably tells us nothing of great importance about deterrence, stable or otherwise. On the basis of the perilously limited evidence available to date, one has to conclude that the East–West deterrence relationship played scarcely, if at all, in the demise of the Soviet empire. To make the point unmistakably, one needs to specify the contrary hypothesis. Specifically, Gorbachev could have asked, 'Can we suppress (shoot down, and so forth) the dissenters?' wherever and whenever they needed suppressing. Had Gorbachev decided to roll tanks over anti-Soviet protesters throughout East–Central Europe, and had the United States and NATO decided to try and discourage such action, then we would know more about the relative ease with which the USSR could be deterred. The problem for strategic theorists is that they do not know whether the manner of, and conclusion to, the demise of the USSR, is, or is not, attributable to the suasive effort of nuclear-led deterrence.

1.6. *Fallacy Six: Carry On . . . Small Nuclear Wars?*

Modern chaos theory alerts us to the possibility, even probability, of discontinuities in strategic history.[37] Whereas the gunpowder revolution took more than a century, from the 1320s to the 1410s,[38] to take substantial effect, the atomic age occurred apparently after the fashion of a light being switched on. That is in some sense an exaggeration, but still it is true to claim that the atomic age exploded into political and strategic reality between the surrender of Germany and the surrender of Japan in 1945, only a three-month period. A similar shock to popular and official consciousness undoubtedly will be administered by the next episode of nuclear use in war.[39] This author suggests, in the guise of yet more fallacies discussed below, that anti-nuclear taboos and assumptions about a persisting non-use of nuclear weapons, are apt to disappoint and mislead. The principal problem with beliefs about such anti-nuclear taboos and assumptions—apart from the plausible fact that they may be perilously fictitious—is that they encourage Westerners to disarm themselves against significant potential dangers. If one believes, and wants to believe, that there is a tolerably authoritative universal taboo against nuclear threats, and especially against nuclear use, one is unlikely to expend many scarce resources worrying about, let alone preparing against, actual nuclear use. This is not to claim that scholars who write about a nuclear taboo are dismissive of the possibility of it being defied. On the contrary, they emphasize the importance of the normative proscription of the taboo precisely because of the danger of nuclear war. Such scholarship, though no doubt well intended, confuses a limited truth—that nuclear weapons carry some normative stigma—with a social proscription of great significance. As we shall see, the idea of a nuclear taboo is both empirically somewhat valid, yet all but irrelevant to international security.

This sixth nuclear fallacy is especially poignant because it illustrates with exemplary clarity how the path to hell can be paved with good intentions. Paradox is the problem here. The more settled the expectations of a future that excludes nuclear (or other WMD) use, the more shocking must be the events of blunt nuclear threat, or of actual nuclear use. In principle this need not be the case, but in practice when anti-nuclear preferences influence strategic culture, as has happened in the West, readiness to cope with the stigmatized nuclear events is likely to have fallen early victim to the virus of hope. No one knows the probability of occurrence of nuclear war, but we all should know that

Whenever there is a possibility of a nuclear detonation, a vital interest is created. Whatever the prior security commitments or stakes in a particular conflict, few events would rock national, regional or global security more than even one nuclear detonation. While a war involving small nuclear powers need not necessarily raise such apocalyptical scenarios as those developed for a superpower war, with the spectre of a true end to history, *the concept of a 'small' nuclear war has yet to be developed.* Any nuclear use still moves us into the area of unimaginable catastrophe.[40]

A small nuclear war is an oxymoron. While most probably it is true that a nuclear war between regional powers would have the effect of encouraging extra-regional actors to keep their heads down, it is not likely that a 'small' nuclear war between regional rivals would have negligible, or world-system supporting, consequences. Scholar-theorists like Kenneth N. Waltz probably are correct when they point to the readily confinable domain of a regional nuclear conflict. In Waltz's brutally realistic words: '[i]f such [relatively weak] states use nuclear weapons, the world will not end. The use of nuclear weapons by lesser powers would hardly trigger them elsewhere.'[41] No one wants to be a player (target) in other people's nuclear wars. But to argue that a small regional nuclear war is going to remain small and regional is to risk missing the point. The historical event of a nuclear war, no matter how small and tactically contained, *must* demonstrate the non-sense in the assumption that nuclear non-use is the 'rule of the road' in world politics.

The principal concern behind this sixth nuclear fallacy is that theoreticians and policy-makers should not discount the strategic effect of small nuclear wars, either because such wars are geostrategically distant or because they are small relative to large. The sounder proposition is the claim that nuclear war is nuclear war. Unfortunately, it is improbable that a benign resolution to many human security dilemmas would follow from the experience of a small nuclear war. All things are possible, but they are not all equally probable. Man's strategic condition and proclivities, in short his (and her) humanity, have remained constant throughout history; it is, therefore, unlikely that a small nuclear war in south Asia, or indeed anywhere, would prompt an end to strategic history *per se*.

The occurrence of a small nuclear war is entirely possible, though, of course, not certain. Moreover, such an event would be eminently survivable for most of the planet: it would be 'Apocalypse now', but only in one or two neighbourhoods, albeit leading to much peril downwind (*à la* Chernobyl, only probably much worse). The nuclear event, far from proving the exception to a taboo on nuclear use, probably would consign the taboo to mankind's well-stocked museum of impracticable beliefs.[42] One can argue that a small nuclear war, for all its horror, actually because of its horror, would serve usefully to underline all of the long-known, but perhaps now blandly over-familiar, reasons why the non-proliferation regime is of extraordinary importance. In other words, a small nuclear war would be a generally readily survivable and isolatable event that, on balance, probably should reinforce the NPT regime and its associated norms. That is possible, but one argument may not suit all cases. By way of contrast to the relatively optimistic view just cited, a small nuclear war might:

(1) Demonstrate the political and military value of nuclear arms, both against a regional foe and as a means strategically to cancel out extended deterrent menaces by a superstate would-be protector.[43]

(2) Remind all interested polities that efforts to marginalize nuclear weapons are a forlorn hope.

(3) Suggest plausibly, if not quite conclusively, that the non-proliferation regime largely has been an exercise in self-deception by parties so self-interested in restricting proliferation that they have deceived themselves over the attractiveness of NBC weapons to others.

For all the speculation that the subject of this sixth nuclear fallacy could attract, at least three interdependent claims merit close attention. First, too little thought is being given to the consequences of a nuclear war, small or otherwise. Much of the world, certainly much of the Western community of defence experts, appears unwilling to face the persisting problems of a permanent nuclear era. A sense of nuclear incredulity renders many people, experts not excluded, disinclined to think prudently about nuclear (biological and chemical) *war*. Much as most civilian strategic theorists will wallow happily in ideas about security, strategy, and war in the abstract, but shy away from the decidedly ugly 'face of battle',[44] so they are profoundly uncomfortable with discussion of events beyond, or through, the veil of deterrence and crisis as they relate to nuclear (and biological/chemical) war. If one's energies are focused upon the restricting or reversing of NBC proliferation, and if need be upon (extended) deterrence of NBC-led menace in regional conflicts, it is humanly understandable, though not professionally praiseworthy, for one to be reluctant to venture into a future zone of policy failure.

The second claim about this fallacy is that, in Freedman's words, 'few events would rock national, regional or global security more than even one nuclear detonation'. If a major aeroplane accident, a large earthquake, or even just a handful of Tomahawk cruise missiles on Iraqi targets, can command global attention as shaped by media coverage, what kind of notice would a 'small' nuclear war attract? The question all but answers itself. One cannot predict in detail what the many consequences of a small nuclear war would be for the course of, and eventual conclusion to, this second nuclear age, but one can be certain that the shock of the nuclear event would score extremely high on the strategic Richter scale. Even if much more forethought had been devoted to anticipation of such a nuclear event than is the case to date, still the shock would be profound. Some experts may expect a small nuclear war or two over the course of the next several decades, but it is unlikely that a large fraction of the general public, their opinion-shapers in the mass media, or their political leaders, would share that 'expert' expectation.

Third, tragedy in one arena can, though need not, sound an alarm that is heeded elsewhere. The successive tragedies that overwhelmed Czechoslovakia in 1938, Poland in 1939, and much of Scandinavia, the Low Countries, and France in 1940, delivered a cumulative and salutary wake-up call which Britain eventually heeded. It seems most probable that a small nuclear war would not change much of the structure of the global political context, but it would change radically the terms of debate over strategy around the world, including the United States. Following some no doubt hysterically 'abolitionist' immediate reaction to the fact of nuclear use in war again, Americans and many others would realize that what they would just have witnessed by way of nuclear tragedy actually could have been precluded, or at least rendered far more difficult to effect, by military counter-force, offensive and especially defensive.[45]

One can predict that the wake-up call to deploy active anti-missile defences most probably, and sadly, will have to take the form of real historical demonstration that nuclear weapons are weapons that can be used. This second nuclear age will wake up to the necessity for treating nuclear weapons as weapons only after the nuclear-armed belligerents in some regional conflict have sounded the bell of danger as clearly as did Germany's actions from 1938 to the spring of 1940.

1.7. Fallacy Seven: Defence does Not Work in a Nuclear Age

Of all the highways and byways of nuclear-related policy and strategy, none is so harassed by mythical perils, yesterday's anxieties still promoted long past their sell-by date, and general ideological baggage, as is the subject of ballistic missile defence (BMD). One of the less well appreciated reasons why BMD options failed to crack the consensus barrier in the United States during the cold war was because the prospect of actual nuclear war was denied psychologically. When the massively undesired is denied as a plausible future—it is too awful to think about—it is hugely unlikely that scarce assets will be allocated to prepare to alleviate the consequences of catastrophe. There were always some grounds for technical argument over the probable effectiveness of the BMD technologies then in contention for adoption, but the military-technical debate over BMD in the 1960s, 1970s, and especially the early to mid-1980s, offers rich pickings to those in quest of barely concealed subtexts.[46] Many arguments were not quite what they seemed to be. There was no BMD deployment, no matter how sophisticated or ample in relevant redundancy and mass, that cunning offensive-force planners could not defeat, at least in theory, with their deadly vu-graphs.

This text has no interest in reopening old debates over BMD. Suffice it to say, as this seventh fallacy claims, that it is an error simply to argue that 'defence does not work in the nuclear era'. In this second nuclear age the challenge is to be able to defeat missile threats far more modest in scale and sophistication than was the case in the 1970s and 1980s in the great cold war. Both the strategic theoretical and the military-technical-tactical referents for this subject have been transformed since 1989. Some of our arms control experts appear still to be trapped in a cold war time-warp which prevents them from thinking about BMD in a rational manner. If America's arms control experts would elevate their eyes to scan the political context that provides the meaning for their professional endeavours, they would notice that, notwithstanding the START process, there is no political context of real antagonism in Russo-American security relations. Much of the contemporary cottage industry of US arms control activity proceeds with a blithe indifference to the overwhelming political fact *that there is no Russo-American 'strategic balance' today.* To risk overstatement of what should be obvious, no one cares, or should care, how US strategic nuclear forces stack up against Russian strategic nuclear forces, because such military comparison lacks political referents of antagonism. When there is no political content worthy of the label in dispute between two great powers, their military relationship is apt to be a topic only for relaxed contemplation.

Of course, Russia today resents the American-led Western victory in the cold war; that is not at issue. It follows that today's Russia easily is seduced into a political flirtation with China, another power resentful of the contemporary US hegemonic condition. None of this means, however, that there is, or is likely to be again, a Russo-American strategic balance of much significance. Strategic history is governed by political history. It is not impossible that the new Russian Federation should *reprise* the role of the Soviet problem for Eurasian and US security, but it is distinctly improbable. At this time of writing, at least, Russia appears as a still noteworthy, and still unusually nuclear-well-armed, power, but one which is set solidly on the path of an enduring decline. Moreover, there are persuasive reasons of broad political context why Russian nuclear-armed forces should not be the proximate US problem either in the remainder of this second nuclear age, or in a third such age. Of course one cannot be sure, but when contrasted politically and geostrategically with the China of the twenty-first century, the Russian Federation looks like yesterday's menace. This is not to deny that the brief, troubled era of Russian–American co-operation now has passed. More to the point, however, is the fact that early twenty-first-century Russia will have security problems far more serious than those stemming from resentment of a United States that is hegemonic after the cold war.

Active defence in the nuclear era would have had great difficulty working against, say, 'the Soviet threat' of 1980–5 vintage, but that tactical judgement cannot hold *vis-à-vis* regional missile threats today and tomorrow. Because the United States could not have limited damage usefully in the context of a Soviet missile attack in 1970 or 1980—if that is true—it does not follow that the (ballistic and cruise) missile threats posed by regional powers, not excluding China, could not be defeated early in the twenty-first century. There is no technically compelling connection between claims from the early 1980s that the (Soviet) missile assault will always get through,[47] and parallel claims today that BMD will not work in the future.

While there can never be any absolute guarantees, it is as certain as anything can be in this friction-fraught realm that a multi-tiered US BMD architecture would defeat militarily any missile menace from regional powers. None the less, there are particular tactical problems posed by regional foes which would stress BMD competencies. Regional nuclear wars will register short times of flight for missiles dispatched to strike targets in-theatre. Short ranges translate as minimal, potentially even sub-minimal, reaction times even for optimally alert and well-positioned active defences. Almost regardless of the degree of technical sophistication of the defence, short-range ballistic missiles, and some medium-range ballistic missiles, could pose a genuinely intractable challenge to the defence. That limiting thought aside, BMD today and tomorrow can pose a politically and militarily lethal menace to the suasive power of missile threats.

The Russian–American agreement at the Helsinki Summit meeting on 21 March 1997 to prohibit the development, testing, and deployment of space-basing for interceptors for theatre missile defence (TMD) is profoundly atavistic.[48] In order both to help sustain the ABM Treaty regime, and to hinder the pace of TMD programmes, for the first time TMD is subject to explicit international control. The rationale for this backward-looking policy *démarche* is that allegedly there is urgent need to demarcate TMD from the so-called strategic missile defences that are constrained by the terms of the ABM Treaty. It is difficult to appreciate the strategic wisdom in placing entirely new constraints upon BMD developed to defeat the WMD that regional powers might deliver by missile, when that mission is urgent, technically feasible, and fraught with awful consequences should it fail. The difficulty increases when one finds that a leading reason for the agreement is to spare possible Russian anxieties over the survivability in flight of their long-range ballistic missiles, when, to repeat, the United States is not, and is unlikely to be, in a condition of strategic balance or imbalance with the new Russia. One might observe of a United States that remains officially still committed to expansion of constraints upon BMD in a world of growing WMD menace—on official US assay, please note—that those whom the gods would destroy, they first make mad (or is it MAD?).[49]

Although this author is strongly persuaded of the cause for BMD, and has debated the subject for nearly thirty years, he is not contemptuous of views different from his own (appearances to the contrary notwithstanding, perhaps). Of course, there is a case against BMD; there always was. The point is that that case is not sound. Critics can argue, correctly, that today's BMD options are not militarily very impressive. That is true, but beside the point; it argues for more effort and better programmes. Also, one can argue, again correctly, that intelligent adversaries will attempt to swamp or evade US BMD prowess. Again, that is true, but irrelevant because obvious and expected. If the United States declined to build any force that foes would try to thwart, we would not build anything. The issue is not, 'Will they try?' but rather 'Are they likely to succeed?' Also, one could seek to oppose BMD with the distinctly sensible argument that foes thwarted with respect to missile delivery will seek to evade such active defences by means of 'irregular' insertion of WMD into the United States. As a matter of strategic logic that argument is sound.[50] It is not sound, however, to argue that because there are several ways to deliver WMD (e.g. by ballistic and air-breathing vehicles, and by sea and across land frontiers), we should grant ballistic missiles a free ride.

Missile defence should not be analysed in isolation. This text treats BMD in the context broadly of counter-force, in company with offensive military action against missile forces. Even when BMD is treated properly within a mix of active offensive and defensive options, still it remains a subject curiously stapled to counsels of military perfection. The strategic truth of the matter is that BMD may well prove useful for deterrence and defence, but no defensive measures literally can guarantee the tactical negation of the offence. If deterrence is unreliable, as strategic history in general, but not cold war strategic history, shows, then the case for active defence against proliferant powers' most probable weapon of choice, the ballistic missile, is strong indeed.[51] Reflection on the decades of cold war yields a less than ringing endorsement for the thesis that nuclear-era deterrence is robustly reliable. Both sides of the argument over the military-technical perils of the East–West nuclear stand-off can register telling blows in debate. Does the record of a non-war outcome to the cold war, notwithstanding the facts of many accidents and much mutual miscalculation,[52] reveal the reliability of nuclear deterrence, simply the authority of luck, or some indeterminate mix of the two? Because there was no Soviet–American nuclear war, it does not follow that the case against BMD stands proven. Alas for scholarly rigour, the absence of nuclear war proves nothing in particular about the merit in opposing views during the recurrent debates over BMD. US BMD deployment might have added complications for a rational would-be Soviet attacker that could prove definitively dissuasive, or—improbably, but who really knows?—Soviet strategic anxiety at the prospect of impending US deployment of multi-layered missile defences might have triggered desperate action on the Soviet part. We are in the realm of strategic fiction, or perhaps prudent forecasting.

Much less fanciful than the above small venture into counterfactual history, however, is consideration of the merits in BMD today.

1. The unreliability of deterrence that must attend strategic relations between a US superpower and some regional polity strongly motivated to assert itself in its immediate neighbourhood, renders actual defence more important than it was for East–West strategic nexuses during the cold war. Readers may recall that a significant asymmetry that helped structure the American phase of the Vietnam War was the contrast in intensity of commitment between Washington and Hanoi. Basic punitive deterrence on the grand scale, though perilous in the extreme if challenged, let alone tripped into consequential military action, probably is robust in the face of broad threats to national values. But, if the political will of the US superpower is challenged over some matter of only arguably vital national interest—the continued independence of the Republic of China on Taiwan, for instance—vast threats of nuclear punishment are less than self-evidently deterring.[53] In confrontation with regional powers, the United States, acting as protector of a regional order, has a need to be able to deny tactical, and hence strategic, success to the aircraft and missile-deliverable NBC weapons of those regional powers. Multi-tiered and mobile forward-deployable theatre missile defence (TMD), backstopped critically by a national missile defence (NMD) capability—to minimize the option for terroristic efforts at blackmail—should help enable the superpower to extend protection, even by extended deterrence.

2. US deployment of complementary tiers of BMD—and extended air defences—devalues the currency of missile threats. Given that missiles have no close substitutes as terrifying, tactically reliable, and swift delivery vehicles for WMD (even though they are less than ideal for delivery of BC agents that must work in aerosol form), the strategic benefit to regional order from US BMD is considerable. One should not advance this argument too far. There is no question but that US BMD should be able to defeat the offensive missile force of any regional polity, but the workings and anticipation of friction, the enemy's cunning plans, bad luck, and strategic prudence, all would function in practice to diminish the leverage that BMD and air defence deployments should yield.

3. The ability of the world's 'ordering' powers, the G-7 club, to function responsibly in extended deterrence and defence roles, requires that they should not be hostage to any polity, faction from a polity, eccentrically motivated military unit, accident-prone military unit, or roguishly criminal body, that can brandish a tactically credible threat to deliver a few NBC weapons by plane or missile. Active missile defences cannot banish all menace of NBC weapons. But such defences can carry a plausible promise to defeat a threat

that typically would number only in the tens of vehicles, at most. There are some NBC delivery threats that BMD cannot answer: weapons of very short range, for example, or weapons that arrive in backpacks, by car, or by boat. None the less, what BMD and air defences certainly can do with high assurance is strategically—not to say morally—well worth doing.

4. Finally, with the arguable possible exception of the residual, though still modernizing, Russian strategic nuclear arsenal, there are no missile-armed groups in the world today, or prospectively tomorrow, whose WMD capabilities should prove beyond defeat by US offensive, *and especially defensive,* counter-force means. It is not obvious on military-technical or economic grounds why the United States should be obliged to settle again for the potentially strategically paralysing reality of *mutual* assured destruction nexuses with regional polities.[54] Acting strategically as a distant protecting power for regional security, the United States needs to deny leverage to regional owners of WMD. If both the United States and a regional foe rely heavily on a punitive deterrence, the probable asymmetry in vitality of rival interests at stake will leave the United States with a politically lethal deterrence deficit. US BMD and extended air defences can help deny hostages to US behaviour compliant with the wishes of regional foes. Moreover, the United States and its principal allies could commit to deploy active defences that would stay either ahead of, or at least tactically competitive with, regional missile-borne threats of action by WMD. But so long as the ABM Treaty regime is permitted to prevent orbital deployments of BMD-dedicated interceptor missiles, or of BMD weapons based on 'other physical principles', the prospects for really effective missile defences are short of glittering.

1.8. *Fallacy Eight: Nuclear Weapons have Come to be Stigmatized by a Taboo Against their 'Use'*

Reference has been made already to a nuclear taboo. Although the proposition of a nuclear taboo is both plausible and attractive, it is perilously flawed in a way that is likely to set damaging ambushes for those who have been imprudently optimistic. The idea of a nuclear taboo hovers somewhat uneasily between fact and value. Widespread endorsement of the desirability of social demotion and general denigration of all things nuclear work to hinder prudent thoughts and action on the subject of how best to cope with the permanence of nuclear facts. Commitment to the worthy idea of a nuclear taboo is wont to encourage effort devoted to strengthening the non-proliferation regime—activity that generally is sensible, praiseworthy, and often worthy of the energy expended—rather than planning to deal effectively with the enduring nuclear dimension to security.

The case of a nuclear taboo is one of those instances where a sound idea, as well as a culturally inescapable, but not thoroughly effective, proscriptive norm, has the potential to function to unanticipated dangerous consequences (the law of unintended consequences). The proposition that the global non-proliferation regime has come to be supported and is to a degree propelled forward by a nuclear taboo, is an astrategic rationalization by generally unintentionally hypocritical Westerners. The fragility of Western theory about a nuclear taboo is easily demonstrated. Supported by the structurally discriminatory NPT regime, the majority of declared nuclear-weapon states simultaneously reaffirm the nationally vital security functions of their WMD, while condemning WMD in the hands of others: not all others, one must hasten to add. Israel's nuclear arsenal attracts little negative comment from the West, while the newly demonstrated and declared nuclear-weapon states of India and Pakistan have attracted more expressions of understanding than condemnation from other polities outside the West. It is only the third tier of would-be nuclear-weapon states, deemed irresponsible, not to say roguish, for their rejection of Western norms of civilized international (and domestic) behaviour, that falls under the heavy censure of spokespeople for a nuclear taboo.

The policy inclinations fairly attributable to Iraq, Iran, North Korea, and Libya, hold no appeal for this author. However, that said, one should not risk gratuitous damage to international security by fooling oneself with parochial nostrums. While arguably it is true to claim that a nuclear taboo has grown which deglamorizes and delegitimizes nuclear arms, such a taboo has proved itself no reliable barrier to further nuclear proliferation. If there had ever been some danger that states capable of acquiring nuclear arms somehow would slip, as it were naturally, into actual nuclear capability, then the taboo argument would have much more force. But, for all its popularity, inherent attractiveness (at least to us in the West), and apparent political sophistication, the operation and significance of a nuclear taboo is not all that it may seem to be. One should not presume causal connection between the phenomenon of a very slow pace of nuclear proliferation and the international popularity of a nuclear taboo. The latter probably has some relevance to the former, but nowhere near as much as often is implied or claimed.

Similarly, one should not presume a causal connection between nuclear non-use and a nuclear taboo. One of the major studies of weapon taboos, for example, inadvertently illustrates the weakness of the evidential base for taboo claims. Null hypotheses are notoriously difficult to prove. For example, Richard Price and Nina Tannenwald overreach severely when they claim that '[t]he strengths of the nuclear taboo and the odium attached to nuclear weapons as weapons of mass destruction renders unusable all nuclear weapons, even though certain kinds of nuclear weapons could, from the perspective of Just War theory, conceivably be justified'.[55] This is just not so. The arguments for the historical functioning of a nuclear taboo advanced by Price and Tannenwald cannot bear the strategic traffic that is run over it. In their analysis, normative proscription—taboo-related injunctions—assumes a residual value that is methodologically unfeasible. The 'taboo' argument tends to degrade under pressure into a residual culturalist explanation that is advanced as an unduly pervasive explanation. The problem is that a taboo does exist, but its worth as an explanation for the non-occurrence of some undesired events is not at all powerful.

Before proceeding further into a critique of the hypothesis of a nuclear taboo, it is important to outline the apparent context of that hypothesis. A taboo is a socially-sanctioned prohibition which may, or may not, carry the force of law.[56] Contemporary discussion of nuclear-weapon issues is ambivalent on the question of whether or not a nuclear taboo is extant. It is significant, for example, that in a well-regarded 1991 study, Lewis A. Dunn wrote aspirationally that '[t]he goal here should be to reduce to an absolute minimum the role of nuclear weapons *and to bring about a global nuclear taboo*'. He proceeded to refer favourably to the prospect that '[a] commitment to reducing the role of nuclear weapons *and fostering a global nuclear taboo against their use* would also contribute across the board to containing the scope of nuclear proliferation and its consequences.'[57] To quote Dunn again, a global taboo against nuclear use would:

(1) 'Reduce the prestige of going nuclear';
(2) 'Greatly help to ensure the long-term extension of the NPT';
(3) 'Influence thinking among new nuclear powers';
(4) 'Provide legitimacy for great power or UN Security Council actions to defuse or contain the threat of regional nuclear wars.'[58]

There is much to be said in praise of the taboo hypothesis. Unfortunately, the proposition that an international political taboo against the 'use' (i.e. the threat or the employment) of nuclear weapons has coalesced, is coalescing, or might coalesce, has about as much validity as the proposition that major war is, is becoming, or soon will be, obsolete.[59] In the decent opinion of truly civilized folk the use of nuclear weapons (let alone chemical or, heaven forbid, biological weapons) may well be far beyond the pale of acceptable options for statecraft; that, however, can never be the relevant issue. Most probably there is today extant a political taboo against nuclear weapons, *per se*, and certainly against the use of nuclear weapons, which is authoritative for most people and most polities. If ruling notions for all of world politics were determined by a crude head, or political unit, count, then indeed it would be true to point to the power and influence of *a*, or *the*, nuclear taboo.

The reality of world politics in this second nuclear age is, alas, far removed from that just fantasized. Self-helping security communities cannot be influenced very usefully by a nuclear taboo, especially when the principal articulators of this taboo are citizens of contentedly and prospectively permanently nuclear-armed states. To put this concept in some context, there are social (and legal) taboos against incest (everywhere) and spitting in public (in some societies), but in neither of these cases are taboos able to cope with the truly hard cases ('necessity knows no proscriptive norms', to misquote Theobald von Bethmann Hollweg[60]). The idea that embattled polities with the most serious of security problems could be influenced conclusively by a Western-led nuclear taboo is close to absurd. Less absurd is the proposition that the stigmatization of nuclear arms that is largely implicit in the global non-proliferation regime which is capped by the NPT, might help inhibit the pace of further nuclear proliferation. A general delegitimization and 'deglorifica-tion' of nuclear arms should facilitate the efforts of those who seek to impede the path of would-be nuclear proliferants. That granted, the superordinate dif-ficulty remains that supply-side anti-proliferation measures cannot succeed, unless success is claimed merely for delay.

The central problem with the hypothesis of a nuclear taboo is that it endeavours to deny needs both of the logic of policy and the grammar of strat-egy, to resort to Clausewitzian phrasing.[61] American adherents to the hypoth-esis of the importance of a nuclear taboo should explain why this taboo can carry authority, given that it is flatly and robustly contradicted in key senses by the strategic beliefs and policies of eight nuclear-weapon states. There is a nuclear taboo which stigmatizes nuclear threat or employment. But policy-makers in the eight nuclear weapon states do not equate such stigmatization— or singularization, for a less pejorative rendering—with unusability. Nuclear weapons may be weapons of last resort—for us, at least—but last resort should not be confused with 'no resort'. More to the point, perhaps, is the question of how a nuclear taboo possibly can contribute usefully to world peace with security, when this second nuclear age provides a buyer's market for fissile material, skills in nuclear-weapon design and industrial fabrication, and certainly for ballistic and air-breathing means of nuclear-weapon delivery?

To show the absurdity of the hypothesis of a nuclear taboo is akin to demonstrating the folly in the United Nations. Neither critique really is fair, because neither subject can command the merit in its destiny. Practical demo-lition of the value in the hypothesis of a nuclear taboo and thoroughgoing criticism of the United Nations ultimately are futile exercises, because both are shooting at straw targets. The United Nations cannot reform until its members reform their approaches to world politics. Similarly, a nuclear taboo cannot assume solidly reliable significance until political-military conditions are permissive, in which case it will not be needed. It is just naïve to believe that nuclear arms, or other WMD, can be rendered morally unfashionable to a point of policy insignificance.

Occasionally a strategic topic arises that is so basic that it is unusually chal-lenging of the ability to communicate pertinent considerations. This author is legally Anglo-American, and is typically entirely unsympathetic to the regional uses to which sundry 'roguish' proliferants might commit a nuclear arsenal, but still he is troubled by the ethnocentrism that suffuses the idea of a nuclear taboo. I have no difficulty whatsoever understanding, even applauding, policy decisions for a putatively permanent *nuclear* future for *my* polities. It follows that I have no difficulty comprehending why Iraqis, Iranians, North Koreans, and Libyans, expect to register worthwhile security benefits from nuclear acquisition. If the Western-authored hypothesis of a nuclear taboo impairs our (Western) ability to empathize with non-Western incentives to acquire NBC weapons, it will have done us poor service.

This author has striven to avoid writing scenarios of nuclear use. One of the more important reasons why this essay attaches importance to BMD—and indeed to all variants of counter-force, offensive and defensive—is because the author believes that this age may well register an actual regional nuclear war. Whether or not there is 'a global nuclear taboo against their use', is a question of no great interest. What is of interest is whether or not nuclear-armed, nuclear-threshold (almost nuclear-armed), or opaquely nuclear-armed, security communities would sanction nuclear threats or employment. Given that the eight declared currently nuclear-weapon states have no difficulty answering that question in the affirmative, what plausible confidence can repose in the hypothesis that a nuclear taboo can severely modify the answer? Thus is the nuclear taboo revealed as a toothless proscription; somewhat true, but not true enough.

Because the theory of the nuclear (and BC) weapons taboo is neither wholly correct nor incorrect, it is exceptionally difficult to provide fair judgement upon the writings of the handful of scholars who have pursued this idea to date. Since it may well be impossible for this author to do full justice to the nuanced views of those scholars, he can at least be clear in the presentation of his own views. The recognition that nuclear weapons provide cause *usefully* to be stigmatized by a taboo, is—in my opinion—a fallacy because:

(1) although there is a very widespread taboo which stigmatizes nuclear weapons—possession, threat, and use,
(2) that normative proscription cannot handle arguments and assertions of security necessity.
(3) Recognition, let alone celebration, of the fact of this widespread taboo, helps disarm us psychologically, politically, and militarily, so that we are less able to cope with WMD realities than we might be in the absence of notice of this taboo.

In addition to the logic advanced above that is critical of the taboo theory, two more general complaints also need airing. First, 'nuclear tabooists', if I may call them such, have yet to demonstrate that they have thought very deeply about the true scope of normative influences upon political and strategic behaviour. In other words, the nuclear taboo as a normative proscription is apt to be offset in its impact upon political behaviour not only by the impulse of security necessity, but also of competing norms. Second, as one who has ventured into the perilous waters of theory about 'strategic culture', I must attest to some uneasiness about the open-ended influence allowed nuclear (*et al.*) tabooist, which is to say 'culturalist', explanations, especially of nuclear *non*-events.

1.9. *Conclusions*

Most of the discussion in this essay has been devoted only to the analysis of nuclear, among NBC, issues. Generally, though not invariably, such problems as have been identified for Western society as likely to flow from nuclear pro-liferation are considerably worse when treated in the context of chemical and biological perils. BC weaponry is harder to isolate and detect than is nuclear (e.g. many insecticides are nerve agents[62]), but is probably tactically easier to deliver—though not to deliver in a condition of reliable lethality. The only good news of strategic importance is that BC—and especially biological—weaponry can be difficult to employ to useful effect as weapons.

There are four 'working conclusions' to this essay. First, there can be no serious dispute about the assumption that the nuclear era is with us forever. This apparently self-evident point, though obvious, none the less meets with resistance. The nuclear discovery of 1945 settled the matter, as it were pre-emptively, for all time. Nuclear use may be deterred, evaded, putatively defeated, or otherwise sidelined, but it cannot be removed from the board of world politics. The contemporary literature on nuclear abolition needs aug-mentation by the reminder that that which has been abolished could, after a while, be reassembled (with no need for reinvention).

Second, nuclear non-proliferation, anti-proliferation, and counter-proliferation ultimately will not work. Policy approaches that address the supply side to profound matters of security invariably fail. One could mod-erate this negative judgement, in praise of the additional multi-dimensional costs, including loss of time, that the NPT regime and adjunct measures often can impose on would-be proliferants, but one should not blur the issue and risk misleading people. Eliot Cohen is exactly correct when he writes: '[o]f course it makes sense to pursue marginal remedies [fundamental remedies for proliferation being unavailable] as energetically as possible . . . But both tech-nically and politically they can achieve only limited success.'[63] The regional security demand for some WMD-offset to contemporary US conventional prowess, the diffusion of nuclear (biological and chemical) knowledge, and the post-Soviet relative ease of access to necessary technologies and skills, all add up to mission impossible for non-proliferation. Sensible defence planners certainly should buy such time as they are able at a reasonable cost before an

Iraq or an Iran acquires an 'Islamic bomb' to add to BC arsenals, but the challenge for the future is more to learn how to cope with proliferation, and especially how to defeat the more malign of its possible consequences, than to devise new (and futile) ways to stem or reverse it.

The third conclusion is that the United States and her friends and allies are unlikely to be persuaded by anything short of the dread event of actual WMD use to take the problems of WMD security really seriously in this second nuclear age. The US defence community appears still so hoist with self-regard for the presumed success of its deterrence policy during the cold war, that it has yet to notice that it has adopted no policy or strategy to date likely radically to alleviate, let alone resolve, the principal military security challenges of the early twenty-first century. Deterrence is wonderful, if achievable. While many leaders of newly proliferant polities are likely to be as risk-averse as Waltz and Quinlan affirm *all* nuclear-menaced folk to be,[64] only an irresponsible optimist would extrapolate from the decades of the cold war an uncritical paean of praise to the all-purpose marvels of deterrence. It would take only one leader who was not as nuclear risk-averse as textbooks on nuclear deterrence say he or she ought to be, or only one policy decision that erroneously was believed to be prudent, but transpired to be otherwise, for the second nuclear age to register a 'small' nuclear war.

The fourth working conclusion is that the unreliability of deterrence, in a political context where the United States continues to act as the sheriff for regional order around the world, mandates rapid acquisition of active missile and extended air defences as components integral to a multi-layered 'war-fighting' approach to regional NBC challenges. Admittedly, BMD will have an impossible task against truly short-range threats, while extremely low-flying NBC-armed vehicles also will stress defensive competence. There is no single magical solution to all the military threats that proliferant polities and extra-state groups technically could pose. Moreover, no matter how multi-tiered is the US answer to proliferation and the peril of hostile NBC use in war, Stanley Baldwin's somewhat accurate claim that 'the bomber will always get through' should be assumed to be a probable strategic truth for our NBC future. 'Zero tolerance' of tactical, operational, strategic, and political failure is the right attitude, the correct vision, with which to approach nuclear and BC threats, but it should not be the authoritative expectation. Furthermore, the typically defence-inattentive general publics in democracies, reared on official faith in deterrence, probably excessive confidence in US military power, and deeply incredulous about WMD disaster, most likely would be shocked into panic reactions by the utterly unexpected arrival of a 'small' regional doomsday. If that oxymoronically modest doomsday were to engulf a Western expeditionary force, then truly would we see a policy and strategy debate on this subject of how to live prudently in a nuclear era that we cannot annul.

2

The Unavoidable Importance of Nuclear Weapons

George H. Quester

Can nuclear weapons be eliminated, or will nations still find them desirable and important? Can we eliminate such weapons by refusing to assign any importance to them?

It may be that Americans, and the citizens of most other democracies, will now indeed wish that nuclear weapons had never been invented.[1] But, for all the years of the cold war, citizens of the NATO countries obviously had more mixed feelings on this question. Nuclear weapons could produce a Third World War that would mean the end of life as we know it. But the threat of such a thermonuclear holocaust might also be harnessed as the 'great equalizer', when the Soviet Union had the geopolitical advantages of being based at the centre of Eurasia, able to strike in so many different directions, when the Soviet Union had acquired so many conventional forces to exploit this geopolitical position, possessing more than 80,000 tanks at the end of the cold war. The United States, in its policies of extended nuclear deterrence and 'flexible response', was thus over some four decades attempting to harness the threat of nuclear escalation (an escalation that would be a disaster for all concerned if it ever had to be executed) as the means to deterring Moscow from exploiting its military advantage in conventional weapons.[2]

With the break-up of the Warsaw Pact in 1989, and of the Soviet Union itself in 1991, Moscow still retained the geopolitically central position, but had to withdraw its forces from its forward base at the heart of Germany, all the way to the east of Ukraine and Belarus. Rather than holding the advantage in numbers, Russia was now actually to be outnumbered in manpower by the United States alone, while former members of the Warsaw Pact were petitioning to become members instead of NATO. And the technologically advanced weapons demonstrated by the United States in the Desert Storm liberation of Kuwait suggested that the conventional balance now favoured the United States and its democratic allies. If anyone were now to be looking for a 'great equalizer' in the application of threats of nuclear escalation, it was not thought likely, after 1989, that this would have to be the United States or its allies.[3]

Leaving aside the polarity of which side of the old cold war confrontation would welcome or regret the influence of nuclear weapons, most people in the world have almost certainly now come to the conclusion that they do not want to see these weapons spread ('proliferate') to many more separate national arsenals. This was indeed one of the earliest points of agreement between Moscow and Washington on military matters, as the two super-powers jointly presented the Nuclear Non-Proliferation Treaty (NPT) in 1968, and have worked quite closely together in backing it ever since.[4]

Some 'realists' and other sceptics about arms control have painted the NPT as simply self-serving, in terms of raw national power interests, on the part of the two superpowers. Possessing substantial nuclear arsenals themselves, Moscow and Washington, in this view, would 'naturally' not want other states to get them, because this might entail a greater sharing of power thereafter. The 'haves' will want to disarm the 'have-nots', in a picture endorsed by Indian government spokesmen and by other critics of the treaty.[5] Yet a powerful case can be made (perhaps very well demonstrated in the open-ended extension of the NPT in 1995, which was achieved much more easily than pessimists had predicted) that most of the other countries in the world, even the countries capable of producing nuclear weapons and denied this option by the terms of the NPT, find this treaty very much to their own national interests, regardless of whether it also serves the interests of Moscow and Washington.[6]

It is useful to remember that the original 'non-proliferation' effort emerged at the end of the 1950s in the Irish proposal for a 'non-nuclear club'. The Irish United Nations General Assembly Resolution in fact would have imposed no requirements on the existing possessors of nuclear weapons, but amounted instead to nothing more than a mutual compact among other countries by which they would abstain from acquiring such weapons themselves.[7] Perhaps the Irish and other parties to such a commitment were thus sending a 'common sense' signal that nuclear weapons were unimportant, or bad in general. Perhaps rather the consensus would have been that, since the super-powers' nuclear arsenals were already effectively deterring each other, there would be no reason for other countries to acquire such weapons.

The subsequent evolution of the Nuclear Non-Proliferation Treaty (NPT) may thus have muddied the waters somewhat, by writing in obligations for the current possessors of nuclear weapons. The obligation of Article I not to share such weapons with other states made perfect sense. The Article VI obligation to undertake 'to pursue negotiations in good faith on effective measures relating to cessation of the nuclear arms race at an early date and to nuclear disarmament, and on a treaty on general and complete disarmament under strict and effective international control' will seem to make sense for the advocate of total nuclear disarmament, but it raises the broader questions this book seeks to analyse, on whether nuclear weapons can really be eliminated.[8]

And Article VI unfortunately sets the stage for an assessment by which the potential nuclear-weapons states are all 'giving up' something in following the suggestion of the Irish resolution, making a 'sacrifice' in terms of their own inherent national interests, for which they somehow have to be compensated by the superpower nuclear-weapons states. The reality of the nuclear world may well be that such weapons in the arsenals of Russia and America make them indeed unimportant or undesirable in the arsenals of Australia and Japan, or Brazil and Argentina. But if there had been no such weapons already under the control of Moscow and Washington, would the option of a non-nuclear club have seemed as attractive and logical in Dublin?

The classic goals of arms control, as defined by Thomas Schelling and Morton Halperin[9] almost four decades ago, were: reducing the likelihood of war, reducing the destruction if war occurred, and reducing the burdens in peacetime of being ready for war. By these measures, it is easy to outline an argument against nuclear proliferation, for the national interests of Australia and Japan, or of Argentina and Brazil, or (less convincingly for the peoples involved) even for Pakistan and India.

One might imagine some ways in which the proliferation and wider deployment of nuclear weapons may decrease the risks of war, as nuclear deterrence reinforces conventional defences that might have been insufficient. But one can also generate scenarios where the reverse would hold true, as the temptations of first-strike and pre-emption were revived in local confrontations, the temptations that so much worried the world in the earlier Soviet–American confrontations of 'bomber gaps' and 'missile gaps'. The outside world, and the countries directly within a region, will have to be very nervous about the transition periods where countries are coming into the possession of such weapons, and can deploy only rudimentary delivery systems, thus tempting an adversary to strike first in a preventive war.

If the impact of nuclear proliferation on the likelihood of war might thus be mixed, the impact on the destructiveness of war will most probably be horrendous, as millions are killed in short bursts of warfare, rather than thousands. The spread of nuclear weapons to any large number of separate countries increases the chances of their coming into use, simply because they are embedded in the military forces that are committed to conflict, and come to be treated as 'just another weapon', but with potentially horrible results where the targets are the cities of south Asia or the Middle East. And yet another possibility, of course, is that a relatively irrational or actually crazy ruler would come into command of one of these arsenals, someone indifferent to the nuclear or other retaliation that his country would suffer, someone thus capriciously launching a local nuclear holocaust.

Turning to the burdens in peacetime of being prepared for war, the spread of nuclear weapons can also poison the political relations in pairs of countries. Consider the normal relations of Brazil and Argentina today, as compared with what those relations might have become if each had acquired a nuclear arsenal, amid all the calculations and discussions of what each could do to the other's cities.

There are thus powerful arguments for why most of the world's nations will not want nuclear weapons to spread, into their own region, or to any new region, to any new countries. And there may be similarly strong reasons for many countries and people to want nuclear weapons to be de-emphasized, to be reined in, in terms of where they are deployed or where plans are made for their use, and to be reduced in the numbers maintained and deployed. But there is the possibility of a fundamental error and illogic here, and of a real disservice to non-proliferation and arms control, if this leads us to go about saying that nuclear weapons are 'not important'. Certain aspects of politics are indeed a form of self-confirming hypothesis, as something becomes true only because people believe it to be true, or because governments go about saying that it is true. But there are limits to how far such a phenomenon can take effect. Merely pretending that nuclear weapons have lost their importance, that they are no more important to international power politics than bars of gold are to the international economy, may indeed miss a great deal of what is at work here, and may become the kind of prediction that afterwards gets written off as foolish 'wishful thinking', rather than as an effective self-confirming hypothesis.

The effective management of the risks of nuclear weapons will require that we thus confront some of the advantages nations may see in the possession of such weapons, and that we then try to box such advantages in, so that they can be overcome by greater disincentives. And a realistic analysis of such advantages will also be necessary if we are not to overstate the possibilities of nuclear disarmament, or to overrate the chances of a world without nuclear weapons. Looming over much of the analysis here will be what the world would be like if *one* other power possessed such weapons, and our country did not.

Nuclear weapons will thus indeed remain very important in face of the possibilities that one or another of the existing nuclear-weapons states might cheat on its commitments to nuclear disarmament, commitments by which all the existing possessors of nuclear weapons are supposed to go to zero, or by which they would have agreed to go to some low levels of finite deterrence.[10]

The risks here will be manifold and iterative, in complicated patterns of mutual expectations and mutual fears. A state might be tempted to cheat, expecting that it could retain some nuclear warheads despite the best surveillance efforts of the International Atomic Energy Agency (IAEA) or any parallel inspectorate. Or such a state might fear such cheating on the part of another state. Or, almost the worst fear of all, our state might anticipate that our political adversary would unjustly expect us to cheat, with that adversary then deciding to protect itself by retaining some nuclear weapons, to which the response of our own state would have to be to retain some of its own nuclear weapons, of course, thus reacting to suspicions by confirming them.

And nuclear weapons will also be very important, as we take steps to reduce the size of the various national arsenals, in face of the continuing proliferation possibility just noted above, the possibility that additional new countries might obtain them, or that such countries might obtain chemical and biological 'weapons of mass destruction'. The commentators who now generally dismiss the importance of nuclear weapons seek to advance a general pattern here, by which what holds for some countries will hold for others as well. The 'power of example' is assigned major significance.[11] If the United States and Russia have chosen to reduce the number of nuclear weapons they are deploying, surely this will influence opinion in Argentina and Brazil as well, reducing the electoral appeal of any candidate who advocates a national programme of nuclear proliferation, spreading instead a 'common sense' by which all the world sees such weapons now as losing importance.

Yet there are powerful reverse linkages as well. Someone advocating a national nuclear weapons programme in these countries, or in Australia or anywhere else, would in the past always have faced the argument that the Soviet and American nuclear arsenals could not be matched, that a small nuclear arsenal in an 'nth' country would be derided and dismissed as puny by comparison.

What would be a puny nuclear arsenal measured against the 'overkill' of the 1980s would hardly be so puny, however, if it were suddenly to appear on the scene in a world which had tried to divest itself totally of nuclear weapons. The tiny American nuclear arsenal of 1945, when no one else had nuclear weapons, was not insignificant or unimportant. And a small venture into nuclear weapons would also not be so unimpressive when every other country had committed itself to a very 'finite' nuclear force, perhaps 200 warheads or so.

A serious debate is under way even today on how we are to control chemical and biological weapons, and (where such weapons somehow none the less slip into the hands of one power or another, of regimes resembling the Iraq of Saddam Hussein) how we are to deter the use of such weapons.[12] If the United States and Russia fully adhere to their commitments to destroy all of such weapons, what retaliation would punish a 'rogue state' that had introduced them into combat, attacking a forward deployment of American forces, or attacking an American city? 'Graduated deterrence', by which each escalation by an adversary is responded to (and thus perhaps deterred by) a matching retaliation in the same category, becomes impossible where these entire categories of weapons have been dispensed with.

For a longer time, the 'common sense' answer for most Americans was that the United States could 'of course' retaliate with nuclear weapons. This was the answer typically offered for the scenario of the Soviets cheating by suddenly attacking NATO with chemical or biological weapons. And this is still often the answer that emerges today, at the prospect of these other weapons of mass destruction being introduced by an entirely different 'rogue state'.

Some advocates of a more total dismissal of nuclear weapons would now shift to a reliance on the most robust and advanced of United States *conventional* weapons, the weapons demonstrated in Desert Storm, weapons based on the American advantage in the application of computers and the latest in information technology, producing what is often referred to as a 'Revolution in Military Affairs' (RMA), or a 'military technological revolution' (MTR).[13]

Yet there are some problems as well with any such reliance on conventional weapons to deter chemical and biological warfare. To begin, the United States may already have to be exploiting these weapons to their maximum of power, as part of repulsing a conventional aggression, so that the question would then loom of 'what else' the US can do, as an additional response to the addition of chemical or biological warfare in the aggression. One could apply a 'brutalized' conventional response, after Iraq had once again invaded Kuwait, and this time had applied weapons of mass destruction, by utilizing conventional weapons to kill large numbers of people in Baghdad, but this would strike many analysts as just as morally reprehensible as the introduction of nuclear or other 'WMD'.

The inherent risk is also that other countries may be able to upgrade their own conventional forces over the next decade or two, reducing the American advantage in computers, so that Washington no longer had such a dominance in this area of weaponry. And finally, one comes back to what Americans themselves were doing with nuclear weapons, in the years of the supposed Soviet conventional force preponderance, utilizing nuclear weapons, and their deployments and threats of escalation, as a 'great equalizer', for we come here to a third way in which nuclear weapons have been very important to the nations contemplating acquiring or retaining them.

Nuclear weapons have been significant in face of an adversary's conventional weapons, and will continue to be so. When the USSR held such a strong geopolitical advantage in its central position in Eurasia, with its investment in mobile armoured forces very much enhancing and exacerbating this advantage, and with Soviet-built tanks being deployed as far forward as the centre of Germany, or within an easy drive of the South Korean capital, Seoul, the United States continually relied on the threat of nuclear escalation as a way of deterring an assault by such tanks. Even today the United States has not yet totally renounced the option of a nuclear escalation where a conventional armoured onslaught could not otherwise be repulsed. Critics of American policy would see this as a foolish perpetuation of the importance and legitimacy of nuclear responses, supposedly now quite unnecessary since the Soviet Union and Warsaw Pact have fallen apart.[14]

But, for the idea of nuclear deterrence of conventional attack to continue to get a hearing, it is hardly required that the United States and NATO be slow in renouncing 'flexible response'. The strategic planners of the world are not so unimaginative that they could not hit upon such a device on their own, without the provision of an American example. Israel, for example, may have been relying for several decades now on the 'bomb in the basement' that it has acquired in the nuclear capability installed at Dimona, relying on the rumours that have been leaked about Israeli nuclear weapons, to deter any Arab dreams of exploiting a temporary advantage in conventional weapons to drive Israel into the sea.[15] If there is anything to geopolitical analysis at all, it certainly suggests that the Israeli frontiers will never be definitively secure. Conventional wars have always been somewhat unpredictable in their outcomes, and an Israel that is only some 9 miles wide where the Arab West Bank territories come closest to the Mediterranean might thus always have invited Arab hopes and dreams of winning one sudden and grand tank battle, to erase the injustice that the Palestinian Arabs remember from 1948. But as any Arab leader has, since the 1960s, also had to factor in the possibility of an Israeli nuclear retaliation, this Arab 'fondest dream' has instead become a nightmare.

One cannot prove that various of the Arab decisions to accept Israel's existence stemmed from the nuclear factor, but there is reason to suspect such a linkage. If the United States were now totally and categorically to renounce the first-use of nuclear weapons, giving up on shielding the NATO countries or South Korea from tank attacks by the prospect of nuclear escalation, would one really predict that this American gesture would terminate any Israeli reliance on the nuclear threat to deter Arab tank attacks?

A case can be made that an American maintenance of 'extended nuclear deterrence' contributes to legitimating such a strategy elsewhere. An American renunciation of such a strategy, matched by a Russian return to what had been a somewhat fleeting Soviet endorsement of 'no first use', that is, a Russian renunciation of recent speculation about 'flexible response', might thus marshal more of the world's moral opinion against any reliance on nuclear weapons as a great equalizer.

Yet there is more in a typical strategic choice than the calculation of the world's moral climate. A country fearing a catastrophic sudden conventional attack by a hostile neighbour will either seek the extension of nuclear guarantees by a powerful ally like the United States, or seek nuclear weapons of its own. Israel has sought its own in face of this kind of threat. Facing a similar threat, with North Korean conventional forces poised within easy reach of Seoul, South Korean governments have sought American extended deterrence, but have at times also moved to narrow the gap to a *de facto* nuclear-weapons capability of their own.[16]

Taiwan is yet another example of a political unit that has to fear the conventional power of a declared adversary, the Communist 'People's Republic of China' governing the mainland. Given that the 'Republic of China' governing Taiwan is accorded no status at all at the United Nations, and goes unrecognized politically by most of the countries of the world, one would have to find other pressures, rather than the mere 'moral pressure of world opinion', to get the Taipei authorities to pass up a nuclear-weapons option. Strong American pressures have sufficed over the past several decades to achieve this, and Taiwan indeed has other means of leverage to apply against Beijing, including the importance of its economic investments on the mainland. But the Taiwan nuclear option has remained in the background, and one could hardly argue that this option will immediately begin to look silly or immoral the minute that the United States gives up extended nuclear deterrence elsewhere.[17]

To return to the very outset of this discussion, Americans remember a cold war where the Soviet bloc was assumed to command a tremendous advantage in geopolitical position and conventional forces, where the existence of nuclear weapons thus had to be regarded by Americans as an antidote to this Soviet advantage, to be coupled to potential war scenarios, to deter Moscow from initiating such wars in the first place. As the cold war ended and the Warsaw Pact was dissolved, and the USSR broke into pieces, Americans could be expected to reverse such feelings about nuclear weapons.

But we then have Russian military journals also reversing polarity here, reopening options of 'flexible response', hence beginning to erode previous declarations of no first use, on the argument that the United States and its NATO allies now have the conventional advantage.[18] An advocate of nuclear disarmament and nuclear de-emphasis might respond that such recent Russian statements may be little more than a mimicking of previous American extended deterrence postures, or that they are provoked by, and amount to a ploy against, the expansion eastward of NATO membership. Perhaps there is thus nothing so very real about Russian 'flexible response' extensions of nuclear deterrence to Belarus in face of the 'NATO threat', or to Kazakhstan in face of the Chinese threat.

It is important to note that this kind of exploitation of nuclear weapons, as a link to the deterring of someone else's armoured advance, has had at least *some* reality in the past, a reality which does not simply get copied from standard and abstract textbooks on arcane 'nuclear strategy', but which has been tied to genuine concerns about national security. One must thus look ahead to a series of possible confrontations where one country can threaten another in conventional terms, and where the militarily weaker power might then see nuclear weapons as its insurance against attack (and, perhaps even more important, its insurance against the political intimidation that would otherwise emerge from the mere possibility of such a conventional attack).

We have already mentioned Israel facing the Arab states, and the problems of South Korea defending Seoul, and Taiwan's confrontation with the PRC. One must guard against excessive pessimism here. There are 'realist' political scientists who, since the end of the cold war, have been predicting a great number of such conventionally imbalanced confrontations, including Ukraine defending its new independence against Russian pressure, etc., arguing that most of the political disputes that were suppressed by the ideological constraints of the cold war will now come to life.[19] If there are other factors that might ease some of these tensions here, for example the surprising growth of trade and investment between Taiwan and mainland China, some of these political disputes will never get to the stage of military speculation. Perhaps the Oslo peace process will be restored between Israel and the Arab Palestinians, and perhaps North Korea can be weaned away from its isolation and hostility toward the outside world.

But one does not need any long list of continuations of political conflict to bring back some importance for nuclear weapons here. We might speculate forward, a decade or two, to see whether Saddam Hussein or any other Iraqi ruler will ever become resigned to the independence of Kuwait, to the seemingly outrageous discrepancy in per-capita incomes which persists between the Iraqis and the Kuwaitis or Saudis.

The wealth will remain outside of Iraq, while the advantage in conventional armed forces will remain on the Iraqi side. Is it really beyond imagination that, if Western commitments to the defence of the oil-rich states were to seem at all weakened, the rulers of Kuwait or Saudi Arabia might elect to invest some of their funds in 'dual-use' nuclear technology, allowing the rumours then to spread, just as Israel and Pakistan have in the past, that nuclear weapons were being secretly acquired?

Finally, quite apart from the deterrence of conventional threats of armoured invasions, the possession of nuclear weapons may play an important psychological and political role in the future, in how we see the national stature of the countries which have them within reach, compared to the countries which do not have them. For example, we would be assessing Russia and China, and Britain and France, as compared with Germany and Japan, or we would be comparing North Korea with Cuba.

When defenders of British nuclear-weapons programmes have been asked to consider a move of unilateral nuclear disarmament (this being seen at the height of the cold war as a way of setting an example for the world, and of showing the error of the American reliance on nuclear deterrence), they often have responded that the retention and maintenance of such a nuclear force has earned Britain 'a place at the high table', that is, it has increased Britain's stature in world affairs.[20] Similar arguments are expressed at times in support of France's investment in nuclear weapons.

The commentators dismissing any 'importance' for nuclear weapons have tended to scoff at this proposition, arguing that the world today accords much more importance to economic power than to nuclear power, that it thus attaches more significance to Japan and Germany, countries without nuclear weapons, than it accords to Britain and France. Yet the obvious comparison would have to be between a non-nuclear Britain and France, and a Germany and Japan that had acquired nuclear weapons. The world would then surely assign even more importance to what evolved in the political processes of Berlin and Tokyo, and even less to Paris and London.

The typical American student, not particularly well-educated on the details of history, might assume that it was by design that the five permanent members of the United Nations Security Council are also the five countries which were, until May of 1998, the only openly acknowledged possessors of nuclear weapons. The historical reality is of course that this identity is more accidental, as most of the drafters of the original United Nations Charter in 1945 were unaware of the impending emergence of nuclear weapons.

The United States introduced nuclear weapons with the bombing of Hiroshima in August of that year, and the Soviet Union in effect established mutual nuclear deterrence in 1949. Britain detonated its first nuclear weapon in 1952, and France in 1960, with the Communist regime in Beijing, not yet accorded the Chinese seat at the United Nations, then exploding its first nuclear device in 1964. India established that it had nuclear weapons by a similar detonation in 1974, however labelling it a 'peaceful nuclear explosive' (PNE), and then waited until 1998 to detonate five more devices within three days, now openly announcing that these were nuclear weapons. Pakistan then quickly matched the Indian 1998 detonations.

Concerns have been expressed that the current membership of the United Nations Security Council may none the less seem to be a reward for the possession of nuclear weapons, given that few people will remember the sequences of history, and will thus serve as an artificial reinforcement for their importance. Proposals were advanced for according permanent membership to Germany and Japan, *before* these states move to acquire nuclear weapons as well, and/or to India *before* it had openly proclaimed itself as having such weapons, thus to erase the linkage that might otherwise be perceived.

Yet the realities of power and importance are what led the United Nations designers to assign a veto to the permanent members of the Security Council in the first place, with this assignment then perhaps being perpetuated by the simple inertia of the difficulties of thereafter amending the Charter. One does not simply make a country important or unimportant by how one chooses to think of it, and similarly one can not make nuclear weapons 'unimportant' by the simple psychology of how one chooses to think of them.

The factors that were known to be in play in 1945 were of real importance. The Charter requirement, that UN Security Council resolutions can only be binding if they are not vetoed by Russia, China, Britain, France, or the United States, similarly enhances the real importance of these countries. And nuclear weapons enhance the importance of the countries possessing them.

One similarly has to ask how much Americans and others would be concerned about developments in Moscow, and about the future political and economic health of Russia, if Russia had not inherited such a large nuclear arsenal from the Soviet Union. Traditional power considerations might have dictated that the United States and the democracies of Western Europe would welcome every possible division in what had been the Soviet empire, welcoming the secession of future Chechnyas, on the old principle of 'divide and conquer', or at least 'divide and avoid the threat of being conquered'.

Because the Soviet Union had acquired nuclear weapons, however, the United States cannot abet or welcome such endless division, and even had to have mixed feelings about the break-up of the old Soviet Union, because Americans could hardly rest easy if it became uncertain who had control over all the nuclear warheads aimed at the United States. What made sense in power-politics terms, in the absence of nuclear weapons, thus might be substantially reversed once such weapons were factored into the calculations. The United States will have to care more about the territorial integrity of Russia, and more about accommodating the feelings of the Russians, because of the Russian nuclear arsenal.

Turning away from the power-politics orientation of the self-styled 'realists', political scientists who styled themselves as 'liberals' would instead be more interested in the support of self-determination and democracy, not favouring the division of any country in the world, no matter how large, unless the component peoples of that country indeed wanted to secede and be governed separately. The liberal instinct is to support democracy, politically and economically. If there were to be a dispute between two components of the former Soviet Union, one of which was more of a practising political democracy, and the other of which was more of an authoritarian dictatorship, the liberal instinct would be to support the democracy.

Yet the enormity of the Western victory in the cold war may have overwhelmed the consciousness of any liberal in the world. During the cold war, there were perhaps only some eighteen political democracies in the world. In the aftermath of the cold war there may be more than seventy, straining the sympathies of anyone and even the ability of people to pay attention to all the elections that have to be held in so many 'governments by consent of the governed'.

A common complaint among the former members of the Warsaw Pact, and former components of the Soviet Union, echoed by all the Latin American republics now freed of juntas, and by the restored political democracies in Africa and Asia, is that Americans do not accord them as much attention, or offer as much economic and material assistance, as might earlier have been anticipated.

It is indeed interesting to speculate about what American and other Western attitudes would have been if only one of the members of the Warsaw Pact had been allowed to break free, for example Hungary, or if only the Baltic Republics, Latvia, Lithuania, and Estonia, had been allowed to secede from the Soviet Union. In response to such a limited and finite expansion of the free world, the response of Western governments and peoples might indeed have been to assign a great deal of attention to making democracy secure and effective in these places. Since the actual spread of political self-government went so much further, it is difficult for Americans or others to muster any comparable amount of attention.

Yet one then comes back to the nuclear factor. Americans are much more likely to recognize Boris Yeltsin by name than the leaders of any of the other new democracies, and are more likely to worry and be concerned that democracy not fail in Russia. Why should Russia be so singled out for attention? History and the sheer size and population of Russia would account for part of this, as we often referred to the old USSR as 'Russia'. But the presence of nuclear weapons accounts for another large portion of this seemingly uneven allocation of liberal attention. Liberals have to care about democracy for its own sake, but also have to care because they share the worry about how nuclear war is to be prevented.

When the Ukraine, Belarus, and Kazakhstan were dragging their heels about relinquishing the Soviet nuclear weapons that had been left deployed on their territory, about returning them to the custody and control of 'Russia' as the one legitimate nuclear heir to the former Soviet Union, the result was that American attention and offers of assistance were addressed to these former Soviet republics, attention that would not go to Uzbhekistan or Khyrgiztan.[21] One does not want to paint the nuclear factor as the only determinant of importance here. Ethnic factors make Westerners pay more attention to Estonia, and considerations of oil supply increase the significance of Azerbaijan. But the central point is that the presence of nuclear weapons, and even a latent potential for nuclear weapons, does indeed change how even a less power-oriented person will see countries.

A further illustration could be found in the disparate treatments that have been accorded the last two regimes in the world striving to stick to a classical Marxist approach in economics, politics, and the dictation of individual human behaviour. The Cuba of Fidel Castro and the North Korea of Kim Il-sung might both have seemed consigned to the dustbin of history, after communism was renounced in the former Soviet Union, and after China shifted to 'Socialism with Chinese characteristics'. But the American approach to these two leftovers of communism has indeed diverged, with some of the difference to be explained by the latent capability for producing nuclear weapons that loomed up in North Korea, with nothing to match it appearing in Cuba.[22]

Concessions were made to North Korea in exchange for the regime's finally adhering to the treaty commitments it had accepted earlier when it signed the Nuclear Non-Proliferation Treaty (NPT). If the rumours had not begun to emerge that Pyöngyang might be developing the plutonium with which to build atomic bombs, Americans and other outsiders might well have been content to let the odious and dictatorial North Korean regime collapse of its own economic incompetence, and trade and assistance could have been withheld, on the argument that there was nothing to be gained by outside subsidies prolonging such a regime.

The latter approach is basically what the United States government has felt appropriate for a similarly odious communist regime in Cuba. But the former approach, looking for a 'soft landing', offering compensation for co-operation on the nuclear non-proliferation front, has been applied to the North Korean regime. While there are always some other factors in play, it would be difficult for anyone, even the most vocal of the sceptics about the significance of nuclear weapons, to deny that the North Korean reactors are a very important part of the picture here.

2.1. *Summary of the Argument*

To return to the basic premises of our discussion, it will continue to be essential, as we now have the cold war behind us, to hold down the probability of war, and at the same time to reduce the destruction if a war were to occur. And it will also be desirable to reduce the costs in peacetime of having states prepared for war. As was the case during the cold war, these goals can conflict with each other, since reducing the destructiveness of a war might make it more likely, because one side sees it as less of a disaster, or because the other side fears that the first will see it that way, and hence will be more tempted to launch a 'nuclear Pearl Harbor'.

Reducing the totals of nuclear weapons will almost surely make sense, as we balance these considerations. But the more difficult question becomes *how*

much they can be reduced, whether the world is safer and better off if the arsenals are reduced to the range of 100, or safer instead at more than 1,000.
And the advocate of zero still has to address the transition to a world without
nuclear weapons, and the issues of verification and cheating, of preventive
wars and temptations to such wars.

Preventing nuclear proliferation will even more surely make sense, as noted,
not just for the countries currently possessing such weapons, but for pairs of
countries opting to abstain from acquiring them. Yet a coherent analysis,
serving any of these objectives in arms control, a prevention of further proliferation, and/or a reduction in existing arsenals, will require a realistic assessment of the ways that one country or another might still find its interests
served by an acquisition and retention of such weapons. We do no good in
telling ourselves that an India or a France or a North Korea gain nothing by
possessing nuclear weapons, if such countries, in their most cool-headed
analyses of the international scene, conclude just the opposite.

In short, success at arms control may well require a more rigorous specification of the particular ways and situations in which nuclear weapons will
indeed remain 'important'. The 'fair-minded' analyst sometimes concludes
that, if nuclear weapons are to be important for Washington and Moscow,
they must also then be so for every country in the world, and that the only
alternative is that they thus be deemed unimportant for every country and
every situation. But the world has never been this fair. The only thing that may
make Russian nuclear weapons less important is an American nuclear force,
and vice versa. And the pairing of these two forces may be needed to make
'nth' nuclear forces less important.

3

Aspiration, Realism, and Practical Policy

Michael Quinlan

The world's schooldays in nuclear-weapon learning were spent in the cold war environment, with the adversarial immediacy and bilateral simplicity which—in a way, salutary—it imposed. The passing of that environment naturally prompted new questioning and challenge to the tenets first evolved within it. The last decade has seen a rich stream of mingled hope, scepticism, conservatism, perplexity, and idealism, with widely different visions of the future of nuclear weapons confidently propounded or fervently urged. Much of this stream has, however, not tried hard enough—or not succeeded well enough—in first distinguishing, within the cold war *acquis*, between what is permanent and general reality and what is peculiar to that specific setting. There are fundamental and enduring realities to be recognized about what nuclear weapons are; about what war is; and about what the former have inescapably done to the latter.

The basic reality about nuclear weapons has two parts. Part one is the well-worn truism that they cannot be disinvented. Whether or not, or in what forms, numbers, ownerships, and deployments, they may physically exist, we know ineradicably how to make them; and exploiting that knowledge will always be within the reach of any substantial and determined state with a strong technological base. Part two is that they provide force of an utterly different order from any other weapon—overwhelming force, virtually (by any human measure) infinite force. Thus it is not appropriate to treat them as though they were just another class of notably disagreeable weapon, such as the international community has over the years sought, with uneven success, to exclude by treaty or otherwise from armed conflict. Biological and chemical weapons are no analogue (and the convention whereby they are commonly lumped together with nuclear weapons under the portmanteau heading 'Weapons of Mass Destruction' has become an impediment to clear thinking). We may speculate on what their capability might by now have become if they had had the same huge investment as nuclear weapons; but they have not in fact been developed and demonstrated as revolutionary transformers of military force. They have accordingly not become cardinal features in the structure of power in the world. It is probably the very fact of nuclear weapons, overshadowing them, that has pushed them hitherto into the strategic background of military power.

Next, the basic reality of war is that it is a contest envisaging winners and losers, and that in a world without a supreme authority able to prevent its outbreak or guarantee discipline in its conduct it cannot dependably be viewed as though it were like a game, a competition constrained by rules. We cannot think it likely, still less take it as a reliable certainty to serve as foundation for security policy, that nuclear opportunity will stay safely in a hermetically sealed box amid the fires of major war—that a nation with its back to the wall on an issue it regards as truly vital will acquiesce in defeat if that could be averted by the use or threat of means which it is capable of mobilizing, even if those means do not initially exist or are formally debarred by treaty, law, or peacetime promise.

And the basic reality of the interaction between the first two realities is that all-out war in its classical form as a trial of military strength is rendered, between contestants who possess or could acquire significant nuclear armouries, strictly irrational. A trial of strength between effectively infinite forces is nonsensical. We have therefore attained the *reductio ad absurdum* of major warfare between advanced states. This is a condition—whether desirable or not—that is not reversible by aspiration, international compact, or legal enactment (and it is incidentally also the reason why in the early nuclear era strategists and military planners often found it so hard to fit and evaluate nuclear weapons—as indeed a few still seem to think apt—within familiar concepts of the conduct of war).

The result of this interaction is that, so far as we can tell, the existence of nuclear weapons and knowledge has had an unprecedented effect in helping to prevent war between technologically advanced states. 'So far as we can tell' because of the impossibility of knowing and proving, especially to those who would rather not be persuaded in a particular direction, just why something that did not happen did not happen. But the absence of war between such states for already over half a century is historically remarkable enough—amid sharp geographical and ideological confrontation, moreover, for most of the time—for any complete dismissal of nuclear weapons from causal explanation to be implausible; and the very fact that most of the governments principally concerned believe in the causative contribution is itself relevant to future policies and possibilities.

These are the realities at the heart of the massive obstacles to securing and implementing agreement to the dissolution of all current nuclear armouries. The obstacles are no doubt usually compounded also of diverse other elements of more debatable permanence or merit, like national-status concerns, domestic political obstacles, institutional conservatism or self-interest, or sheer inertia; but these lie at the core. Their operation is to be seen in both major categories—distinct but not wholly separate—of specific difficulty besetting abolitionist aspiration in the world as it is. The first category concerns the unwillingness of current nuclear-weapon possessors. The second concerns verification.

Under the 1968 Nuclear Non-Proliferation Treaty there are five recognized and legitimated nuclear-weapon possessors: the United States, Russia, China, the United Kingdom, and France. The likelihood is vanishingly low that all or even most of these would genuinely accept and work towards complete nuclear abolition in global political conditions anything like those now prevailing. And the same is true, in one way or another, of three other states: Israel, universally regarded as possessing significant nuclear capability even though its formal avowal is still deemed impolitic; and India and Pakistan, who had both long been believed to have taken nuclear development to a point where an operational capability could swiftly be constructed, and who have recently moved openly closer—if not indeed, before long, all the way—to such a capability.

Even if severe internal political difficulties about ratifying the START II strategic nuclear arms control bargain are overcome, and if hopes thereafter for a START III prove well-founded, Russia will remain a state reeling from profound internal and external upheaval, and conscious also of wide instability and mistrust around her borders. She shares with China—whatever the near-term ebb and flow of their political relationship—an immense frontier along which confident defensive adequacy is unachievable with her conventional forces. Her conventional capability overall is anyway in deep disarray in *matériel*, manning, training, readiness, and morale, as the débâcle in Chechnya demonstrated. For reasons like these Russia has been reshaping defence doctrine in ways that tend to put more emphasis, not less, on nuclear weapons—she has, for example, withdrawn her long-standing declared preference for a no-first-use agreement. Beyond this, the nuclear armoury constitutes the one unmistakable claim Russia retains to special status internationally. It is unreal to suppose that any likely Russian leader—even if economic and political turmoil leaves in place a genuinely democratic one—will be seriously interested in abandoning the sense of underlying security assurance, and of political importance *vis-à-vis* the United States and the rest of the world, which nuclear-weapon status confers.

From President de Gaulle's day onwards the idea of France as a nuclear power has been at the heart of her national self-awareness and self-confidence. France has made a huge investment of political credit, scientific effort, and financial resources (she has spent three or four times as much as Britain, with heavy opportunity costs elsewhere) in building, more or less independently, a capability of which she is deeply proud and to whose maintenance she is deeply attached; the abrasive episode of the final nuclear test series in the

South Pacific illustrated that. France is moreover a great and distinctive nation looking back on more than a century of history which in military terms has seen a painfully large share of defeat and disaster (much of it attributable, as ingrained national perception holds, to being let down by others). Nuclear weapons in French hands are the grand equalizer, the guarantee that France cannot be humiliated again; they have become central to French national self-perception. To construct scenarios, in any world at all like the one we live in now, in which her political leaders give all this up is again beyond reasonable probability.

Russia and France seem the two cases, among the recognized five, where renunciation seems most clearly far-fetched whatever other countries may do. The obstacles in respect of the other three are more obviously (though perhaps not only) of an interactive kind. The United States has world-wide concerns and responsibilities on a scale no other country now approaches—she is, in effect if not in formal recognition, the prime steward of the international system. Whatever long-term view may be taken of US superiority in high-technology conventional capability, it must be out of the question that the United States would surrender nuclear capability so long as it remains in any other hands whatever, whether declared or undeclared. (It is also worth considering, if US technological superiority were indeed to be recognized, as commentators often nowadays suggest, to be pervasively and permanently overwhelming at non-nuclear levels, what that might imply for likely Chinese and Russian readiness to surrender all nuclear capability.) So long as the United States retains capability, China will demand the right to do so. The United Kingdom is, of the five, perhaps the least locked-in strategically by such interactions. But with its major modernizing investment just coming to completion, it cannot be expected that a UK government of any likely political complexion would take a lead in making and sustaining an unconditional promise to abandon that investment or not renew it decades hence irrespective of what the global scene might then be.

The repercussions reach on into the 'unofficial' three. There can be no possibility that India will commit itself to abolition unless China does (and probably also the remainder of the official five). Pakistan will not commit itself if India does not. Israel is a special case, and a particularly illuminating reminder of basic reality because the relevant interactions are not obviously nuclear ones. There can be no expectation that Israel will truly surrender its unavowed capability unless its peaceful existence within settled and secure borders on terms which a stable consensus of its people finds satisfactory is solidly accepted by all its neighbours in the region; and that is a complex and demanding condition whose prospect remains regrettably remote.

The second category of problems about abolition is distinct from but linked to that of political acceptance. It relates to verification. The world community, and especially the present nuclear possessors of whom proven renunciation would be required, could not accept an abolition regime unless it was underpinned by verification and enforcement arrangements of great strength and durability. The standard of assurance needed—and insisted upon by such powerful and sceptical actors as the US Congress—would be higher than has been the norm in most previous arms-control agreements, for two reasons. The first and most obvious reason is the unique impact of a nuclear breach in a non-nuclear world—the specially powerful leverage which a violator would be trying to seize. But secondly (and less often noted) an abolition agreement would, by definition, lack the underlying corrective and deterrent power which the continued existence of nuclear armouries has hitherto provided in tacit support of other arms-control agreements. For example, a state cheating—as the Soviet Union undoubtedly did—on the poorly verified Biological Weapons Convention of 1972 would always have known that Western nuclear power would loom over any attempt to exploit the illegal behaviour. So long as nuclear armouries are still there to overtrump the prohibited sorts of capability if a state does breach its agreements, open democracies can afford to settle—and from time to time in the past have settled—for a good deal less than watertight perfection in agreements to ban other weapons. But a nuclear-abolition agreement would have no such backup, and would moreover remove the nuclear contribution from the underpinning of other agreements.

Supporters of abolition typically accept that their preferred course would require a verification system of exceptional scope, depth, and solidity, embodying an unparalleled combination of demanding features, including powerful provisions for mandatory enforcement. The historical examples of Iraq and North Korea—both of them signatories to the NPT, yet defaulters on it—illustrate the difficulties about aspects of this. The former in particular, even in defeat and disgrace and under explicit UN interdict and surveillance, has proved a remarkably tough nut for arms-prohibiting endeavours to crack. (The reluctance of key UN members to support effective measures to ensure the cracking is moreover a warning, if one were needed, against any assumption that the support of a global nuclear-abolition regime would be seen by all as a duty overriding every other consideration.) In a different way, South Africa's nuclear history offers further cautionary illustration; and all these three seem relatively easy cases by comparison with what would be entailed if misgivings arose about the actions of (say) China, or of a Russia whose political evolution had taken a course different from that for which the liberal democracies of the West have been hoping. To postulate a verification and enforcement system of the universal rigour and permanent effectiveness required for an abolition agreement is not to postulate a set of ancillary technical requirements in support of a bargain; it is to postulate a radically and irreversibly more benign political configuration of the world.

These multiple considerations about political acceptance and about secure maintenance amount to insuperable barriers to the feasibility of abolition in any political setting at all like that now existing or any that seems within reasonable enough probability to serve as foundation for security policy (which is inescapably in the business of insurance, not aspiration). Feasibility is however not the only aspect. It is far from evident that a world substantially like today's except in having had actual nuclear weapons officially abolished would be a safer one. The world's war-prevention structures would have had a major load-bearing component removed, without any dependable assurance that other pillars—whether international political and legal instruments or conflict-resolution achievements—had been correspondingly strengthened. Military deterrence to the threat or use of biological or chemical armouries—always and inescapably easier to create than nuclear ones—would have been attenuated. And if major war, thus made to appear less plainly and immediately irrational, did break out or loom between technologically capable states, there would re-emerge powerful pressures, for perceived self-preservation and as a national duty, to race towards nuclear rearmament. It is romantic to suppose that the political arrangement of a world of continuing nation-states would be reliably transformed by the comfortable afterglow of agreed abolition. The effect might even be to the contrary—the nuclear *reductio ad absurdum* of warfare between major states is the best way yet established of ensuring that amid stress and uncertainty they recognize always that there are no coherent military options for settling deep disagreements, and that political management is the only path available.

The tasks with which the global community must expect to have to deal in the next century include accommodating the likely rise of China towards something like superpower status, and the settling of Russia into a configuration, both internal and external, with which she and her neighbours can live in a better degree of stability and contentment. These tasks—even if no others of comparable kind and scale emerge to complicate the scene and distractingly demand the attention of the international community—will be a formidable challenge to political skills. It is not necessary to impute deep ill-will to China, or to apply gross over-pessimism to Russia, to recognize that purporting to re-rationalize military conflict would not improve the political and psychological framework within which awkward issues will have to be resolved. And since the re-rationalization of military conflict could not in fact be made dependable, the underlying implication of nuclear abolition would be that we were confident of having permanently and irreversibly removed military force or even its shadow from the conduct of relations between advanced states. That would be a remarkably bold claim on which to rest security policy.

But, many abolitionists will say, all this reasoning ignores the proliferation problem. How can a world in which nuclear weapons still exist, yet are legitimated only in the hands of a small number of states determined by history already a third of a century in the past, avoid an inexorable drift into much wider possession, with more numerous and more complex interactions, more precarious arrangements or mindsets, and thus higher risk of appalling events?

Proliferation must of course be a continuing concern, and its constraint therefore a proper preoccupation of international policy. But worries about this do not dissolve the huge impediments to abolition earlier reviewed; nor do they automatically invalidate the arguments that it is undesirable in a still-anarchic world (even if, as is by no means beyond debate, it be supposed that in a purportedly nuclear-free world no fresh temptations of different kinds towards nuclear acquisition could arise). There is no practical virtue in demanding that an infeasible and perhaps undesirable *deus ex machina* dispense us from the task of managing proliferation.

And the difficulty of that task itself is often overplayed. The regime centred on the NPT has been in the round a striking success, long confounding much dark prediction. The Treaty itself, for all its asymmetry, has held unchanged for thirty years, and three years ago was extended indefinitely by full consensus. Over 180 states have ratified it—more than for almost any other treaty in history. Within the past decade Ukraine, Kazakhstan, and Belarus have acceded as non-nuclear states; South Africa has given up the capability it had secretly acquired; Argentina and Brazil, once high among conjectured candidates for nuclear acquisition, have solidly renounced the possibility; and two attempted defections from the regime, by North Korea and Iraq, have both in different ways been tackled by widely supported international action—however the details may play out, neither will in the end be allowed to establish itself as the acknowledged possessor of a significant operational nuclear armoury. The bursts of nuclear testing by India and Pakistan (neither of them a signatory to the NPT) rank on the debit side, but what they have done is in essence to make what was generally recognized as a virtual bilateral capability, and a virtual deterrent stand-off, less virtual. How much further the two countries will go is, at this writing, not yet clear; it is right that the international community should seek to persuade them towards restraint; and diplomatic skill and ingenuity will be needed both to accommodate the now-more-overt India/Pakistan reality without excessively damaging the NPT's formal coherence, and to engage the two countries in dialogue to share the benefits of the practical experience of others in nuclear management without thereby implying over-ready contentment with what has happened. But whatever the outcome in such respects, external reactions to the tests—leaving neither country clearly more secure militarily, more respected politically, or more prosperous economically—scarcely constitute a wholesale encouragement to proliferators elsewhere. There is no plausible train of infection, save perhaps to Iran, on whom international attention had already focused. It remains hard to see any other country—and every other save Israel and Cuba has acceded to the NPT—that must rank as a serious further concern.

Rather like stock markets, the political market-place is vulnerable to fashionable beliefs and tides of sentiment not always rigorously based upon objective analysis. The product of this vulnerability can take on a life of its own that then has to be reckoned with—the perception can itself become a sort of meta-fact, which thereafter risks distorting or over-complicating policy. The international significance of a comprehensive nuclear test ban—which has long since and irreversibly acquired political salience in a degree justified, on cool strategic evaluation, neither by intrinsic importance nor by on-balance merits—is an example. It will be no service to the non-proliferation regime to allow a supposition that it is highly precarious to become another such meta-fact.

In reality, the regime is underpinned not only by well-established and widespread habits of acceptance, approval, and treaty compliance, and by accompanying structures like the Missile Technology Control Regime and IAEA safeguards, but also by basic facts of permanent interest. The NPT bargain is not primarily a favour from the non-nuclear states whereby they issue a temporary licence to five exceptions to persist for a while in bad behaviour. It is at least equally a deal among the non-nuclear states—starting from a five-power nuclear reality which numerous key members among them positively welcome, even if political correctness mostly now precludes their saying so—in their own interest to abstain from local nuclear arms races amongst themselves. The proportion of parties whose mindsets and interests might be in the least likely to tempt them towards incurring the high costs of break-out is, even on the severest worst-case projections, minute.

Article VI of the NPT, with its commitment to nuclear disarmament by the official five, is much appealed to. But the appeal is usually selective, as it seemed to be even in the somewhat inglorious addressal of nuclear issues by the International Court of Justice in 1996 (see n. 1). In the text of Article VI the nuclear commitment is directly partnered by a commitment, binding upon all parties, towards general and complete disarmament. Most of the nuclear five have done a good deal more already to meet their nuclear commitment than anyone has to meet the wider parallel one. The reasons for international silence on the latter relate no doubt to judgement about practicality; but if that be so, there is neither logical nor legal basis for excluding similar judgement from the former and demanding further action on it in ways or time-scales not reflecting political and security reality.

None of what is said in this essay seeks to convey either that nuclear armouries must exist for the rest of time, or that while they do still exist there is no further scope for useful adjustment to their current condition. On the latter front, though a great deal of beneficial change has been made since the frostiest years of the cold war, and increasingly since its end, there remains room for a good deal more. Just for example, there would be benefit in more openness—especially from China—about existing armouries (in which regard the announced outcome of the UK government's 1998 Strategic Defence Review exemplified useful advance); in deeper pruning of, in particular, the bigger armouries; in bringing constraint to bear if possible upon warheads rather than just delivery vehicles, and perhaps upon total holdings, not just operational deployments; in further easing of needlessly high states of operational readiness; in exchanging information and expertise on safety; in constraining more surely the production of special nuclear materials; and in enhancing the MTCR and the IAEA safeguards system. It is not clear that such an agenda of improvement is yet being pursued with sufficient and adequately co-ordinated international vigour.

At the same time, the pursuit of the agenda needs to be informed, and priorities shaped, by a hard-headed appraisal of the real merits of particular candidate items. Not every proposal carrying a disarmament or arms-control label is automatically virtuous or sensible, and candidates need to be coolly assessed for whether they truly will reduce cost or risk, or enhance international security and confidence. We need to beware of creating new meta-facts, and distorting the useful agenda, by letting lip-service or even reticence encourage momentum to build up for particular proposals in ways disproportionate to their real advantage. To take four examples which have some currency at present:

1. 'No-first-use' declarations are a poor idea.[1] We should certainly want to avoid any use of nuclear weapons; we should seek so to arrange matters that we do not face the need to consider initiating it; we may be highly confident of success in that. But formal, permanent, unqualified promises about it are a different matter. No one is going seriously to contemplate nuclear use save in desperate circumstances where every other course seems worse. The notion that a state *in extremis* would accept being driven solely by a distant peacetime promise to accept an alternative course judged *ex hypothesi* even more appalling is manifest fantasy; and security policy should not pretend to rest on such foundations.

2. Ideas for 'minimal' armouries need to be approached warily.[2] The merits of numerical reduction do not increase uniformly as zero is approached. Beyond a certain point (which itself needs to be the subject of careful professional study, and may differ with the circumstances of a possessor state and its role in the international system) war-preventing effectiveness and stability amid crisis may well both suffer; and cost will not necessarily fall much further. If nuclear armouries are to exist at all, it is foolish to damage their deterrent utility by endless pruning at the margin.

3. Ideas for complex international 'de-alerting' schemes also need to be approached warily. Schemes for 'virtual nuclear armouries'[3] or for holding all

weapons in 'strategic escrow'[4] require the international negotiation and implementation of elaborate and novel arrangements, importing questions about (for instance) how to maintain ready-enough availability still to discourage hostile adventurism, and how to maintain symmetry of reconstitution capability among armouries of markedly different composition. Such schemes seek to address perceived problems about risk of accident, misunderstanding, or over-reaction. It is, however, far from evident that risks of these kinds—especially after the various less complex measures of de-alerting already widely taken, in hand or otherwise available—have enough reality to warrant such difficult solutions. (If, as much conjecture though less direct evidence suggests, there is a serious problem about the security and control of the former Soviet nuclear arsenal and its supporting infrastructure, that must be matter for concern; but it would need to be tackled in more basic ways, and in more urgent timescales, than those relevant to VNA or similar schemes requiring complex design and international negotiation.)

4. The concept of nuclear-weapon-free zones is valuable in the right settings, and may well be capable of further exploitation. But it does not fit every setting. Appendix 1 briefly discusses its aptness in Central Europe.

The careful and realistic evaluation of the nuclear-management agenda is made necessary by a further consideration, not always sufficiently remembered: that governmental attention and diplomatic effort are limited resources, the allocation of which needs to be directed to whatever best blends benefit and practicability. In particular, attempts to insist on acceptance of the abolitionist aspiration as though it were a goal actually within reach of policy—and, still more, on the laying-out of a specific and timed set of steps (as some demand) to its achievement—are likely only to distract effort from what can reasonably be done, and to reduce the credit and therefore the influence of their proponents, whether commentators or countries, for the real agenda.

Ultimately, we cannot want, and we need not assume, that actual nuclear armouries should remain in being for the rest of human history. But the route to dissolving them has to lie through the removal of the political conditions which lead states to regard them as necessary. There are two main paths to that, and both of them are essentially matters of political management, not arms control. The first is to resolve or defuse the particular issues which stand to bring states into severe opposition—the Kashmirs, Taiwans, Arab/Israel issues, and the like. The second is to reinforce the authority and efficacy of international institutions and instruments, political or legal, for settling disputes without recourse to war, to the point where even under grave stress all parties can and must accept that their operation has to be accepted and obeyed. Neither of these routes is capable today, whether singly or in partnership, of swift development to the point of assured universal reliance. But until that is far nearer achievement we cannot reasonably expect, and we should not too eagerly want, to dispense altogether with the war-excluding contribution of nuclear armouries. They are healthily less salient and less costly than they used to be, and the world is increasingly preoccupied with problems to whose solution they cannot contribute; they can no more prevent Bosnias, Rwandas, and Somalias or hold back terrorism than they can cure AIDS. But if their effect remains simply to help fend off any risk that advanced states may come to blows, that is a contribution as massively beneficial as it is historically remarkable.

4

Eliminators, Marginalists, and the Politics of Disarmament

Lawrence Freedman

Appeals for international disarmament have a long and largely unsuccessful history. They have suffered from four core problems. First, the link between the incidence and intensity of conflict and the availability of weaponry remains uncertain in practice, whatever might be asserted in rhetoric. There are no iron laws at work here. Second, by necessity these appeals must convince political leaders convinced of the honour of their own intentions and the unthreatening nature of their own arsenals. Third, they must reassure these same leaders that attempts at general restraint, however noble in conception, will not provide golden opportunities to miscreant states who have the greatest interest in, and capacity for, cheating. Fourth, such appeals tend to be stronger when it comes to describing the ultimate destination than the mode of travel. It is easier to depict the putative benefits of a disarmed world, and its superiority to all alternatives, than to demonstrate how the processes of disarmament, with all their potential technical and political distractions, will achieve the desired result.

Military expenditure is often wasteful and arms build-ups can be provocative but they can also be prudent and defensive. The assumption that there is a simple relationship between peace and the size of arsenals does not withstand careful analysis, largely because it ignores the large matter of politics. For that matter disarmament movements themselves are highly political organizations, and not just the instruments of a higher reason as they would like to present themselves. The schemes they propose must pass political as well as technical tests if they are to be implemented, and their impact then needs to be judged against the state of international politics. My objective in this chapter is to explore the politics of the anti-nuclear movement in its past and more recent incarnations.

4.1. *The First Anti-Nuclear Campaigns*

Had it not been for the arrival of nuclear weapons on the international scene, grand schemes for disarmament might have been left totally discredited as a result of the experience of their pursuit following the First World War. The actual disarmament negotiations of this period had often been farcical. Meanwhile the diagnosis behind them—that arms races caused wars and that international law could prevent them—was undermined by the events that led up to the Second World War. This left disarmament associated with futility and a naïve utopianism. Those drafting the United Nations Charter were very careful to avoid extravagant language in this area. The lesson they had drawn from the 1930s was that democratic governments dare not neglect balance-of-power considerations.

The coming of nuclear weapons was such a shocking event that there was a natural reluctance at first to rely on power politics as usual to prevent their further use. They posed a unique challenge, demanding an effort to secure an international agreement even while the cold war was gathering steam. In the event power politics as usual—in the form of the developing cold war—doomed the major initiative of the late 1940s. This was the US Baruch Plan, which envisaged transferring control of nuclear facilities to an international authority. Given that the United States enjoyed a nuclear monopoly at the time it was generous, but at the same time from a Soviet perspective it could soon be interpreted in conspiratorial terms. The plot, according to Moscow, was to get the Soviet Union out of the nuclear business as soon as possible. Then the Western countries would use a decision-making process in which Moscow was denied a veto to find a pretext to allow the United States to hold on to its own arsenal.

After the failure of the Baruch Plan both the superpowers retained a rhetorical commitment to general and complete disarmament until the early 1960s but they had quite different concepts of what this would entail. Moscow wanted to start with nuclear weapons (perceived to be an area of Western advantage); Washington was unwilling to move on nuclear weapons without parallel moves on conventional weapons (perceived to be an area of Soviet advantage). Washington demanded intrusive means of verification; Moscow saw such demands as tantamount to seeking a licence to spy.

While disarmament negotiations were getting nowhere, mass movements in support of nuclear disarmament were gathering pace throughout the world, largely in response to the hazards of nuclear testing and alarm at the destructive power of thermonuclear weapons. The first broadly based movement was the British Campaign for Nuclear Disarmament, which mobilized initially around marches to the government's atomic weapons establishment at Aldermaston, and bequeathed to the world the peace symbol of a circle encompassing a broken cross. The anti-nuclear movements, inspired by some charismatic and often egocentric personalities such as the philosopher Bertrand Russell, the scientist Linus Pauling, and the saint-like Albert Schweitzer, could base their appeal on a natural revulsion at the prospect of global genocide. So long as that prospect was to the fore—as a result of tests or crises such as those over Berlin and Cuba—then the movements could grow. It is worth recalling, however, that they still faced difficulties as a result of the sort of problems that confront all radical groups when they suddenly realize that they have touched a popular chord.[1] These largely result from the need to scale down demands in order to reach out to the moderate majority.

Thus pacifists, especially those who had first been inspired by inter-war groups such as the Peace Pledge Union, could not but support any campaign against instruments of war but still wanted to steer the new movement away from the idea that the problem was only nuclear weapons so that somehow other forms of armed force might be tolerable. Those who came to the campaign out of groups such as the World Federalists and other deep believers in world government were nervous about demands framed in national terms. The most serious problem was that communist parties expected to provide the leadership as well as activists for the anti-nuclear movement while refusing to accept that there was anything wrong with the 'workers' bomb'. So it was that the anti-nuclear movement was afflicted by the cold war. By getting close to communists they risked alienating moderate opinion and being turned into a front organization, peddling the latest Soviet line. Keeping communists at arms length was uncomfortable, giving in to the movement's most vociferous local opponents and often, in the devices required to keep communists out, offending democratic principles. In the event communist involvement undermined the anti-nuclear movement in many countries.

It was not only its own internal divisions, however, that caused the movement to lose momentum. After the scares of the early 1960s the cold war appeared to calm down. The 1963 Partial Test Ban Treaty removed one of the more obnoxious manifestations of the nuclear age, and the associated concerns about fallout. Meanwhile the Vietnam War soon provided another and more immediate rallying point for liberal opinion and activist energies.

4.2. *Arms Control*

A further problem was that the moral strength which provided the anti-nuclear movement with its crusading zeal did not always lend itself to intellectual creativity. From the late 1950s the most important policy ideas came from the arms control community. Contemporary concepts of arms control emerged in the mid-1950s. With the arrival of thermonuclear weapons of apparently unlimited power, busy production lines starting up in the Soviet

Union as well as the United States, mainstream opinion effectively gave up on disarmament and turned instead to arms control.[2] According to this view there was no immediate way out of the nuclear age. Deterrence appeared as the best of a set of bad options for coping with this age, though this needed to be reinforced by measures designed to build on the shared interest of both superpowers in avoiding nuclear war. In a perverse way, the awfulness of nuclear weapons offered a positive opportunity. By presenting political leaders with an unequivocal and inescapable prospect of utter disaster in the event of war they created a great incentive for peace. From this perspective, the objective of international diplomacy was not to remove that incentive by eliminating the nuclear arsenals but rather to develop means of managing the arsenals sensibly so that neither side felt able to catch the other through a surprise attack or triggered a catastrophe by being panicked into premature use. Sensible management also involved taking steps to avoid unauthorized use or a crisis getting out of hand for want of efficient communication, keeping weapons out of where they did not need to be, like Antarctica or outer space, and restricting the number of nuclear powers to as few as possible.

The intellectual strength behind arms control was formidable, captured perhaps best by Hedley Bull's disillusion with the old disarmament philosophy of Philip Noel-Baker and his analysis of the possibilities for an alternative philosophy as set out for a study group of the newly formed Institute for Strategic Studies.[3] For disarmers arms control was dangerous, because it was all about managing the arms race rather than sending it into reverse, but in practice they were hard put to object to many specific measures championed by the arms controllers, such as the Hot-Line agreement, the Non-Proliferation Treaty, and the Strategic Arms Limitation Talks.

The arms controllers at most paid lip-service to the idea of disarmament. More often they criticized its strategic innocence, the simple presumption that fewer weapons would mean more peace, and the inattention to problems of verification. In the world of the 'non-nuclear' the 'just-nuclear' would be king. A dramatic premium would attach to cheating, made possible by the accessibility of key components, materials, and technology. The fact that the knowledge of the science and basic engineering concepts involved with atomic bomb manufacture could not be eliminated created a high risk that it would be resumed as soon as a 'conventional' war broke out. The disinclination to forgo the benefits of peaceful nuclear energy, indeed the readiness to spread these benefits under the 'atoms for peace' programme of the 1950s, meant that there was always some risk of civil facilities being diverted to military purposes. By the start of the 1960s proliferation had been identified as a major problem, and perhaps a secular trend, starting with the more awkward members of the established alliances—France and China.

The exact role of deliberate diplomacy as compared with the core, brutish logic of mutual deterrence in keeping the nuclear peace is hard to discern.

Both were reinforced from the early 1970s by a lack of an obvious dynamic toward a great power confrontation. The revival of international campaigns for nuclear disarmament coincided with the apparent revival of the cold war in the early 1980s. This time the improvement in superpower political relations was seen immediately at the highest level, and not just on the streets, as an opportunity to reduce the role of nuclear weapons in international affairs through actually reducing the arsenals rather than improving the quality of their management.

President Ronald Reagan's Strategic Defence Initiative (SDI), launched in March 1983, was based on a reluctance to rely on nuclear deterrence, as his European allies nervously observed. The intellectual framework developed to support active defences was no different to that supporting radical disarmament, and while disarmament remained a challenging proposition it could look quite realistic when compared with the rather fantastical schemes for space-based directed-energy weapons. Part of the Russian counter to the SDI was to accuse it of taking the arms race into space and threatening conditions for a first strike, but the most potent was to argue that its declared objectives could be met more cheaply and more simply through removing the offensive weapons. Thus Soviet leader Mikhail Gorbachev in April 1985 set a schedule for progressive nuclear disarmament, to conclude effectively with a nuclear-free world by the end of the century. Reagan wanted both disarmament and SDI. So both men worked to put disarmament high on the political agenda, reflecting their fears of where an unresolved cold war might lead. For one heady moment in November 1986, a hastily contrived summit at Reykjavik between President Reagan and General Secretary Gorbachev almost came out endorsing a plan for the total elimination of nuclear weapons.

Until the end of the cold war, the arms control agenda was followed patchily and sporadically, through tacit understandings as much as formal agreements, but at least to some effect. The nuclear age was not brought to a close but it was survived. The institutional and intellectual framework of arms control even allowed for the easing of the core superpower antagonism through more severe strategic arms reductions than had been anticipated, including the as yet unratified START II treaty, the removal of nuclear munitions from general purpose conventional forces, and the conclusion of a comprehensive test ban treaty in September 1996 after decades of effort.

4.3. *A Strategy of Marginalization*

The drive to reduce dependence upon the 'balance of terror' can be traced back to before the end of the cold war, to fears that it might prove to be insufficiently robust to cope with a great power confrontation. However, the risk of such a confrontation was apparently reduced substantially, if not removed altogether, with the end of the cold war. The issue was now less the fragility of the balance of terror and more its irrelevance. This led immediately to studies of the new opportunities for moving to a nuclear-free world.[4]

Irrelevance does not make for political urgency. As political leaders struggled to come to terms with the consequences of the collapse of the European communism, all schemes for world order became suspect. It did not necessarily matter if there was a lack of momentum behind disarmament by design so long as there was a powerful logic building up behind disarmament by default. If nuclear weapons could not be eliminated at least they could be marginalized. Disarmament would be achieved through the influence of its most effective known instrument—finance ministries—who would not take seriously arguments for maintaining surplus inventories let alone further investment.

One precondition for marginalization lay in non-proliferation, for while the East–West antagonism might be over new nuclear powers might still need to be deterred. The importance of this was underlined by the post-Gulf War disclosures concerning Iraqi progress with its nuclear programme and uncertainties surrounding the nuclear legacy of the Soviet Union. While neither set of problems was solved, concerted international action did bring results, in easing Ukraine, Belarus, and Kazakhstan out of their nuclear status, helping Russia maintain a modicum of control over its residual nuclear assets (human as well as material), eradicating the traces of the Iraqi programme and gaining general support for a continuation of the non-proliferation regime and important regional advances in Africa and Latin America, where countries deliberately eschewed the nuclear option. Meanwhile, the number of nuclear warheads was coming steadily down, far fewer weapons were kept on alert, and most were disentangled from conventional forces.

Two events undermined this benign process of marginalization. The first was the 1995 French nuclear test series in the Pacific. The outcry against Paris had an important anti-colonial aspect: if, as was claimed, these tests were so environmentally harmless why not undertake them in France rather than inflict them on a distant region? But this was mixed with outrage that a leading state, especially one so relatively secure as France, could still assign any sort of priority to preparations for a nuclear war, even though this was rationalized as a necessary precursor to a test ban. The result was a boost to those determined to revive the cause of universal nuclear disarmament. A number had already come together in the April of that year in activities surrounding the twenty-fifth review conference of the Non-Proliferation Treaty. The World Court had not quite outlawed nuclear weapons, but made strategies based on their possible use even more questionable to those who took international law seriously.[5] The award of that year's Nobel Peace prize to Joseph Rotblat, president of the Pugwash conferences on science and world affairs, was widely seen as a rebuke to France. Another response came from Australia, one of France's most vociferous critics. This took the form of the establishment, in November 1995, of the Canberra Commission charged with developing 'ideas and proposals for a concrete and realistic program to achieve a world totally free of nuclear weapons'. This they did with some enthusiasm, reporting their findings in August 1996, after meeting four times.

The second event, in May 1998, was the tit-for-tat nuclear testing by India and Pakistan. Neither were true neophytes. Both had been assumed to be nuclear powers for many years. India's first test was in 1974, though claimed as a 'peaceful nuclear explosion', and not long after it became apparent that Pakistan had acquired the relevant technology. Their tests were more political statements than military moves, geared to domestic morale as much as external enemies. A new Indian government was determined to restate its claim to great-power status. None the less, the established nuclear powers did not hesitate to condemn the tests. To this there were obvious ripostes. If they consider their nuclear arsenals to be of great value to their security why should not others reach the same conclusion? If it is the case that deterrence helped keep the peace in a divided Europe during the cold war might it not also work to keep the peace in other divided regions, such as south-east-Asia or the Middle East? Claims that the established nuclear powers had earned the right to possession by demonstrating the requisite maturity patronized the newcomers and served to confirm them in their conviction that it was all about status and international hierarchy. Thus in challenging the newcomers the established nuclear powers unavoidably had to challenge their own nuclear pretensions.

4.4. *A Strategy of Elimination*

Both the disarmament movement and its opponents could use the south Asian tests to support long-standing positions. To the latter it indicated the importance of regional factors in triggering proliferation. For the former it confirmed proliferation's imitative aspect: if the established powers had renounced their arsenals then there would be no excuse for the Indians and Pakistanis to develop their own. This position was also adopted by the Indians and Pakistanis, indicating that by blaming everything on the precedents set by the established powers disarmers can provide a rationale for proliferators.

The disarmers found it difficult to understand how the established powers could justify holding onto their arsenals when the threats that had been used to justify them before had evaporated. How could the cold war end but not the nuclear age? Their response reflected the system of logic with which they had been working for many years. They did not see any need to reconstruct their case and their movement to take account of the post-cold-war world, except to insist that this new world can support the essential preconditions for its long-standing dreams. In this view it has been supported by the readiness of a number of figures once associated with more mainstream strategic thinking to align themselves with proposals for the abolition of nuclear weapons. These include Professor Robert O'Neill, Chichele Professor of the History of War at Oxford University and a former director of the International Institute for Strategic Studies. The most significant convert, at least in terms of his past responsibilities is General Lee Butler, who, until his retirement in 1993, had been in charge of the USAF's Strategic Air Command, and thus in some senses had been the world's leading nuclear warrior.

A number of bodies with well-established interest and expertise in the disarmament business have worked together to promote the cause. Many of the key figures were gathered together to prepare the Canberra Commission Report. Butler, for example, was a key member of that committee and also acted as the leading spokesman for a statement issued by a collection of former military officers who signed a manifesto addressing 'a challenge of the highest possible historic importance: the creation of a nuclear-weapons-free world'. This statement was sponsored by the State of the World Foundation.[6] In addition Butler played a starring role in a book by Jonathan Schell, author of one of the best-selling books of the early 1980s campaign, who has interviewed many of the leading figures in the contemporary disarmament movement.[7] Elsewhere the Stimson Center has a Project on Eliminating Weapons of Mass Destruction, which 'seeks to explore the obstacles to, and implications of, the progressive elimination of all nuclear, chemical and biological weapons from all states and to consider measures that might bring all states closer toward that goal'.[8]

It is perhaps because of this long and distinguished pedigree that the current anti-nuclear campaign feels less like a popular crusade and more like an extended discussion of policy detail. The sense of continuity with past debates is reinforced by the disarmers' seniority. The anti-nuclear movement of the 1950s was led by old men but inspired the young: the anti-nuclear movement of the 1990s has yet to gather a large youthful constituency although its sentiments command wide support. The post-cold-war generation, who were not close to their teens when the Berlin Wall came down and have no memory of the great debates on nuclear issues of the early 1980s, are not being engaged. They are looking elsewhere for their green issues.

Another consequence of this continuity is the assumption that a new nuclear debate need only pick up where the last one left off, except that those in favour of possession are supposed to have lost their best arguments. As a result the disarmers consider their case to be unanswerable and so the hurdles then appear to be largely technical in nature, or else the familiar opponents of the best causes—weary cynicism, old thinking, vested interests, and insufficient political will (that crucial but invariably absent ingredient). There is also the irritating tendency to deny the existence of a middle ground, to assume that those who cannot accept the case for complete disarmament are doomed to argue for nuclear weapons for all. Thus Jonathan Schell insists that the choice is truly stark, between 'on the one hand, condemnation of nuclear weapons and their abolition and, on the other, their full normalization and universalization'.[9] Either nuclear abolition or nuclear proliferation: given the impediments to his own preference, posing such an absolute choice risks a quite irresponsible outcome.

4.5. *Military and Political Utility*

These impediments emerge through a consideration of the Canberra Commission Report. It offers a robust refutation for what it alleges to be the main claims for continued possession of nuclear arsenals: prevention of war between major powers; protecting the credibility of security guarantees; deterring the use of other weapons of mass destruction; conferring political status and influence; providing effective deterrence at lower cost; defeating large-scale conventional aggression. Some of these claims can certainly be dispatched with ease but others are more problematic, especially in the light of the historical record. The Commission inclines to the familiar mistake of anti-nuclear advocates, especially those with a military background, in assessing nuclear weapons against conventional military criteria where they can soon be shown to be worse than useless.

Thus the Commission concludes that the 'only military utility that remains for nuclear weapons is in deterring their use by others'.[10] A statement such as this must be highly conditional. A monopolist nuclear power might find all sorts of uses for an arsenal. So might a state locked in total war with a non-nuclear rival, if other nuclear states had declared themselves wholly neutral or if these other states might otherwise have been inclined to meddle. The classic 'what if' case here is a nuclear-armed Iraq in 1990–1. Western governments may no longer see any value in requiring nuclear threats to make up for conventional disadvantages because the conventional balance has shifted in their direction. Unfortunately, for the very same reason Russians are now much more impressed with this role. Hence the reluctance of the Duma to ratify START II and its readiness to turn non-ratification into a political weapon in the campaign against the enlargement of NATO.

The enlargement debate had a slightly artificial character because the first wave of members are less bothered about a security guarantee, which strictly speaking must include the extension of the American nuclear umbrella, than membership of the Western club. All involved have been anxious to ensure that the nuclear question is not given a high salience during the course of the debate. None the less, this episode provides another reminder of a point that gets lost in disarmament advocacy. However questionable their military purposes, nuclear arsenals can serve a variety of political purposes—from holding together alliances to gaining international attention as well as deterrence and intimidation.

What might have happened had nuclear weapons not existed is the Great Counter-Factual. Some do believe that the fear of a non-nuclear total war would still have been sufficient to prevent a Third World War (although of course that is what had been believed after the First World War, reinforced by the prospect of poisoned gas being used against cities). What is quite implausible is to extract nuclear weapons from contemporary European, Asian, and Middle East history and to assert that everything else would have been the same. Consider some propositions. The Korean truce might have taken longer to arrange in 1953–4. China might have pushed its claims again Taiwan more vigorously in 1955 and 1958. Eisenhower would not have been so reticent about helping the Hungarians in 1956 nor Johnson so wary about pushing the bombing of North Vietnam close to the Chinese border. Germany would have followed France more readily in the mid-1960s. The Sino-Soviet split would not have been so intense yet a war would have begun on the Sino-Soviet border in 1969. Syria might have pushed forward more energetically against Israel in October 1973. Arab leaders would have been less willing to accept the need to learn to live with the Jewish state. Russia would have refused to tolerate the unification of Germany within NATO because it had no response to this dramatic deterioration in the conditions of its security. Iraq would have used chemical weapons during the 1991 Gulf War. Ukraine would not have achieved such high-level international attention as the Soviet Union dissolved. North Korea would not have been given the time of day by Washington in 1994. Less encouragement would have been given to the IMF to support the rouble during Russia's financial difficulties of 1998. Of course many of these propositions are dubious, but addressing them helps to indicate the complexity of nuclear politics over the past half-century. They are part of the warp and weave of contemporary international affairs. To one who has spent some time researching the views of policy-makers during the most tense moments of the cold war, the suggestion that the fear of nuclear war was of scant importance in inducing caution and designing policies is preposterous. On this point the documentary record is clear.

The Canberra Commission believes that the only purpose of one nuclear arsenal is to deter another, in which case then without the established nuclear arsenals there would be no stimulus to proliferation. Leaving aside the moral problem of drunkards demanding abstinence of others, the analytical problem of the relationship between established and nascent nuclear arsenals is complex. States contemplating a nuclear programme will certainly be influenced by the programmes of others, but not always in predictable ways, only as part of a much broader political relationship, and only as one factor among many. To take one example, the French responded to the American nuclear programme by rejecting dependence and the full disciplines of alliance, and constructing their own arsenal, while the Germans embraced dependence and sought to use it to construct an even tighter alliance.

Whatever the problems of deterring chemical use through nuclear threats, it is hard to see Israel, for example, giving up its nuclear capability if other weapons of mass destruction are still held by its neighbours. Moreover, the presumption of a mechanical connection between continuing nuclear possession by one group of states provides a potentially dangerous argument, should the major project of eliminating the core nuclear arsenals fail. As noted above with India and Pakistan, an easy argument for proliferators is provided, instead of them being obliged to justify their actions by reference to their actual security environment. It was, after all, such wider security assessments which led the Ukraine, South Africa, Argentina, and Brazil to conclude that little would be gained by pursuing their nuclear programmes, despite the persistence of nuclear arsenals elsewhere. The Commission says that 'Progress towards a nuclear weapon free world should not be made contingent upon other changes in the international security environment' (p. 51). Perhaps not, but it will be.

The Canberra Commission's erroneous conviction that sets of nuclear arsenals have no purpose other than to deter each other's use reinforces two assumptions. The first is that the solution to the nuclear problem lies in a general agreement to eliminate all sets simultaneously, for their residual rationales would also be eliminated at the same time.[11] Even to a rather amateur political eye this would seem to turn the whole project into a 'no-hoper'. It represents a condition that will be so difficult to obtain that insisting on its inclusion suggests subversion.

4.6. *Out of the Nuclear Age?*

The problem with planning for a non-nuclear world is similar to all those that overcame those other 'architectural' studies which followed the end of the cold war. To set a desirable end-state against an unacceptable present tends to produce tortuous discussions of the processes of transition. The problem was summed up by Maynard Keynes in his assessment of Bertrand Russell, a great campaigner for nuclear disarmament:

Bertie in particular sustained simultaneously a pair of opinions ludicrously incompatible. He held that in fact human affairs were carried on after a most irrational fashion, but that the remedy was quite simply and easy since all we had to do was carry them on rationally. A discussion of practical affairs on these lines was really very boring.[12]

So it is that to turn dream into reality the Commission must assume that other good things will happen, for example in dealing with other weapons of mass destruction, to create the political conditions for success. Sir Michael Quinlan has complained that 'non-nuclear advocates often apply all the optimism to their alternative, all the pessimism to the other one. They typically assume away the hard realities, postulating a world liberated of almost every feature awkward for their preference.'[13] Alternatively, when such assumptions appear far-fetched, particular obstacles are described as difficult and therefore requiring years of patient work to overcome but not of decisive importance.

We are stuck in the nuclear age for some time to come. The Commission itself wisely avoids setting a firm timetable for its goal being achieved.[14] In addition there are very real technical limits on the speed with which warheads can be decommissioned. It is notable that even the more optimistic scenarios still present a level of nuclear weapons capable of leading to an utter catastrophe.[15] It is not even clear what constitutes zero when it comes to nuclear weapons. Schell considers the distinction between technical zero (when the weapons are truly dismantled and can not be covertly reconstructed) and political zero (when nuclear use has been completely disavowed).

It is hard to see how either zero could be guaranteed as a permanent condition of humankind, but it is possible to chart movements in the right direction. The most committed abolitionists are wary about concepts of virtual nuclear arsenals, according to which weapons exist but can not be launched except with a great degree of noisy and prolonged preparation,[16] as they still legitimize the idea that nuclear weapons might have a purpose. Moreover, as the nuclear capacity of nuclear-weapon states is reduced to an embryonic form, other states whose capabilities have not progressed beyond this stage suddenly acquire an equivalent status. Yet if we take as our starting-point a situation in which there remain real concerns about unauthorized launches or accidents, especially in Russia, this would seem to be an area where the best could be the enemy of the good.

Schell sees political zero as an issue for international law because he is looking for means of institutionalizing a renunciation of nuclear use. He is searching for some consensus international position, negotiated on behalf of humanity, to which governments might just be persuaded to sign up. With these grand schemes large problems soon emerge: the design of regime that is both transparent and enforceable, the resources and time required for safe decommissioning, the possible role of ballistic missile defences as a form of reassurance, worries about biological weapons, the current mood in Russia, the real insecurities in south Asia and the Middle East. When these schemes are being promoted there is always a tendency to handle such problems by a well-turned phrase or else they are side-stepped altogether or placed deftly into some quite separate negotiating basket to be sorted out later.

There is another approach to political zero, which would focus more on strengthening the 'norm of non-use', constantly demonstrating the irrelevance of nuclear weapons to most conflicts and working hard on conflict resolution where a lingering relevance has been identified. This does not offer a definitive solution, a durable blueprint for a non-nuclear world, but such a quest may be a distraction. By comparison with the grand goal, immediate problems—such as the maintenance and control of the Russian arsenal or the developing Indo-Pakistani relationship—seem trivial, yet they require urgent attention.

The alternative to abolition as a crusade is recognition that we are stuck with the irritating, pragmatic questions of priorities and consequences. The potential effects of nuclear explosions on physical structures and living organisms may be the same but the political circumstances in which they might come about have changed. The risk of all-out nuclear exchanges, perhaps culminating in some global black-out, has receded. The major powers no longer integrate nuclear weapons into their general purpose forces, inventories have been cut and new weapons are barely being developed. In South Africa and Latin America countries have decided against nuclear strategies.

At the same time in tense parts of the world nuclear strategies retain some attraction, as in the Middle East and south Asia. The argument that the prospect of nuclear war renders political leaders cautious may be universally valid,[17] but during the cold war there was a dangerous learning process before mutual deterrence appeared at all stable, as both sides explored the possibilities for decisive first strikes and allowed themselves to become excessively dependent upon the quality of their early warning systems and their capacity to control their forces at times of crisis. The past half-century contains many hair-raising stories of false alerts, straying aircraft, and temperamental technologies. It took some time before all the reassuring paraphernalia of hotlines and confidence-building measures were in place. It may not be so easy to persuade India and Pakistan to relinquish their new nuclear status, and that, having done so, covert capabilities are not still being held. It might at least be possible to help them appreciate their responsibilities for the care and maintenance of their nuclear arsenals, and for strict controls. These responsibilities can tax the most advanced state.

The Russian experience warns that even cutting back nuclear forces through decommissioning missiles can be a slow and expensive process.[18] Despite the responsibility shown by the Russian authorities in attempting to haul in all its small nuclear weapons and render the rest of its arsenal safe the combination of a country suffering such inner turmoil and a large, decaying nuclear establishment remains truly frightening. The situation is not helped by the Russians concluding that they now need nuclear deterrence more than ever, as their conventional forces suffer from financial cut-backs, poor morale, and administrative chaos. A serious debate is developing on the potential threat that might be posed by biological weapons, perhaps even deployed by sub-state groups. As NATO countries have eschewed both biological and chemical systems there is at least an argument that there is some role for nuclear deterrence here, for which the Desert Storm provides some tenuous support.

As political arrangements in East Asia become more tense following the economic collapse that began in 1997, and with continuing uncertainty about the modalities of Korean unification or exactly what China might do to regain Taiwan, there is an issue concerning the relationship between American nuclear capabilities and current Asian security arrangements that could suddenly come to the surface with an unnerving rapidity.

So as with other abolitionist tracts, the Canberra Commission directs its considerable fire against a bad case which is now rarely made—an essentially unreconstructed nuclear strategy—instead of engaging with a good case which is often inchoate: marginalization combined with intensive trouble-shooting. The eliminator may say to the marginalist that so long as nuclear weapons exist there is an intolerable risk of something going terribly, catastrophically wrong and that a policy of benign neglect is no answer—to which the marginalist can only agree, but point out that this is likely to be a risk the world will run for some time to come. We are left with little choice but to contain and manage it the best we can.

5

Nuclear Weapons, Prudence, and Morality: The Search for a 'Third Way'

John Baylis

One of the most interesting and encouraging things about the post-cold-war era is the way the rigid debate about nuclear weapons which characterized the cold-war period has given way to a more tolerant and less ideological discussion. There are still those who adopt 'traditionalist' and 'abolitionist' positions, as a number of the chapters in this book demonstrate, but there is also a wide-ranging discussion about what might be described as a 'third way'. Although there is no clear agreement about precisely what a 'third way' might entail, those writers who fit into this category all share a common desire to marginalize nuclear weapons in world politics. At the same time, they remain largely unconvinced that, in the short term at least, it is practical to seek the total abolition of nuclear weapons. Some see abolition as a desirable and possible longer term ambition, others are more sceptical on both accounts. The main purpose of this chapter is to consider a number of 'third way' approaches which have been put forward (including further arms control measures, minimum deterrence, and 'virtual nuclear arsenals') in the context of the contemporary debate about prudence and nuclear ethics. The first section looks at the prudential and ethical foundations of the search for a 'third way'. Section 5.2 focuses on the post-cold war debate about the need to de-emphasize nuclear weapons as instruments of state policy. The third section looks at this debate in the context of the prevailing nuclear trends. The following sections then consider the ideas of arms control, minimum deterrence, and 'virtual nuclear arsenals' in some detail as possible 'third way' approaches.

5.1. Nuclear Weapons, Prudence, and Morality

The important process of what has been called 'cooperative denuclearization', which characterized the early post-cold-war period, reflected a particular concern about the destabilizing consequences of the war-fighting nuclear strategies which had been adopted by the United States and the Soviet Union and their respective alliances during the later stages of the cold war.[1] These countervailing strategies helped to accelerate the arms race and contributed to a widespread questioning of the dangers of nuclear deterrence both by the general public and, significantly, within the strategic studies community itself.[2] In turn this helped to reopen the debate about the morality of nuclear weapons which began with the dropping of the first atomic bombs on Hiroshima and Nagasaki in August 1945 killing more than 200,000 people.[3] The main characteristic of this debate, not surprisingly, has been the fundamental disagreement which has existed between different schools of thought on the moral implications of nuclear weapons.

For some realist writers, the laws of morality cannot be applied to nuclear weapons or indeed to any weapons of war. Given the cultural diversity of the world in which we live and the lack of consensus on a universal moral code, ethical issues are regarded as being irrelevant to policy decisions about the use, or threat to use, nuclear weapons. According to this Machiavellian view, a nation's national interests are—or should be—all that it considers in its interactions with other nations. Prudence is seen as having a higher priority than morality.[4]

Amongst those who hold the perhaps more sustainable view, that nuclear weapons do raise important moral questions, the most interesting and profound debate has been waged between deontological and consequentialist approaches.[5] The deontological school classes actions in terms of their 'kind', regardless of their consequences. According to this view, the use of nuclear weapons, with their immense destructive capability and lingering genetic and ecological effects, is morally unacceptable under all circumstances. Nuclear deterrence, as a form of 'hostage-taking', is regarded as just as immoral as nuclear use. This is summed up in Jefferson McMahon's comment that 'what is immoral to do, is immoral to threaten'.[6] Those supporting this deontological view tend to regard total nuclear disarmament as the only moral approach to adopt.

Although there are different strands of consequentialist moral thinking, and different judgements about nuclear use, there tends to be general support for nuclear deterrence on the grounds that it helps to keep the peace. Prudence is seen, not in opposition to morality, but as an important moral good in its own right. During the cold war this was reflected in Henry Kissinger's frequently expressed comment that 'Peace was the supreme morality'.[7] Similarly, Michael Walzer also justified deterrence, in moral terms, on the grounds that it was 'the supreme necessity'.[8]

In the context of the post-cold-war era, this consequentialist view begs the very important question of whether deterrence did actually keep the peace between 1945 and 1989. This has been the subject of a very lively debate since the end of the cold war. For writers like John Mueller, nuclear weapons were largely irrelevant.[9] The 'long peace' was more likely to have been the result of the fear of repeating the immense destruction of the Second World War rather than any particular anxiety over nuclear weapons. Other writers, like John Gaddis, have taken issue with this view, arguing that nuclear weapons have been a unique and indispensable element in creating caution between the great powers.[10] This is a very popular, some would say 'common-sense', view and it is one which is very strongly supported by the nuclear powers themselves.[11]

The problem with this debate is that it is based on educated guesses and not on certain knowledge. It is very difficult to establish precisely which of the two arguments is true. Consequences are after all inevitably uncertain when viewed in advance. What supporters of deterrence tend to argue is that because it is impossible to *disprove* that nuclear weapons are indispensable in helping to keep the peace, it would be morally irresponsible to throw away the major apparent benefits of such weapons by prematurely trying to abolish them. They also point to tentative empirical studies, like the one recently published by Lebow and Stein, which suggests that the existence of nuclear weapons—as opposed to particular nuclear strategies—probably did help to keep the peace in various crises during the cold war.[12] These are arguments which are very difficult to dismiss.

But how do we square them with the powerful deontological arguments against nuclear deterrence—especially the moral problems associated with what Richard Falk describes as 'the terrorist logic' of making threats against innocent civilians?[13] One interesting answer, provided by Steven Lee in a recent study, is that a proper moral and prudential understanding of the role of nuclear weapons in world politics requires that *both* consequentialist and deontological arguments are taken into account.[14] The conclusion which arises from this more complex view of nuclear ethics is a rather paradoxical one. It is that there are strong reasons both for continuing the policy of nuclear deterrence *and* for abandoning it. Both sets of arguments are of roughly equal persuasiveness and there is no clear objective criteria for judging between them. That leaves us with a very real moral dilemma with which to wrestle. For those who hold this view the only way to extract themselves from this predicament is to search for an alternative policy which secures most of the moral advantages of deterrence, while at the same time avoiding most of the moral disadvantages. This suggests the need to search for a concept of deterrence which is rather different from the war-fighting nuclear strategies adopted during the cold war.

In order to consider what form this alternative concept of deterrence might take, it is useful to look at the post-cold-war critical debate about nuclear weapons which has contributed to the growing consensus in favour of denuclearization. This debate which has been far less public than in the past has centred on four key issues: nuclear safety, nuclear non-proliferation, the growing power of conventional weapons, and US–Russian relations. Each of these will be looked at in turn.

5.2. *Contemporary Arguments in Favour of a 'Third Way'*

A number of studies were published in the immediate post-cold-war period by nuclear historians who, for the first time, had access to the documents on nuclear decision-making. As the veil of secrecy over cold war nuclear mishaps has lifted it has become possible to see more fully the consequences which can arise from human error, equipment failure, and questionable practices by governments. Research by Bruce Blair in the early 1990s on the command and control of American and Soviet nuclear forces produced convincing evidence that the dangers associated with nuclear deterrence were far greater than had been appreciated at the time.[15] According to Blair there were a number of occasions in the cold war when there was a distinct possibility that nuclear war could have broken out as a result of either the unauthorized use of nuclear weapons or by accident.

This new evidence about nuclear accidents by Blair and others raises afresh important prudential and moral questions over the risks and uncertainties inherent in deterrent policies. There are now over 100 incidents involving nuclear mishaps which have been documented. Apart from Chernobyl, with its genetic legacy of thousands of deformed children, there have been a number of accidents with nuclear weapons which have come very close to catastrophe.[16] These have included aircraft crashing onto nuclear weapons storage facilities, fires which engulfed nuclear weapons, and the explosion of the fuel tanks of missiles with nuclear warheads connected.[17] One of the most worrying of these incidents occurred in 1962 when an American B-52 bomber broke up in mid-air releasing two nuclear weapons. One of these was a 24 megaton bomb which was later found hanging from its parachute with five of its six safety catches tripped. Some have seen this as a vindication of the effectiveness of the electronic safety devices used to prevent premature explosions. Others have argued, with more justification, that a major disaster was avoided more by luck, than technical ingenuity.

Worries about nuclear accidents and miscalculation are not confined to the cold-war period. Evidence emerged in July 1998 that President Yeltsin activated his 'nuclear briefcase' for a retaliatory attack on the United States in January 1995 when Russian early warning stations picked up what they thought was an approaching American Trident ballistic missile. Moscow apparently began a ten-minute count-down to launching their own missiles. At six minutes into the incident, according to Bruce Blair, the Russian military 'actually issued orders to the Strategic Rocket Forces to prepare to receive the next command which would have been the launch'. In fact, the Russians had mistaken a Norwegian weather research rocket for a Trident missile. Eventually, the Norwegian rocket crashed into the ocean 600 miles from Russian territory and the incident ended 'successfully'. According to one Russian source, however, the incident underlined the poor state of the early warning system and the potential dangers posed by Russian missile forces.[18]

Anxiety about the 'limits of safety' have also been highlighted in research published by Scott Sagan.[19] Sagan points to a number of concrete examples during the Cuban Missile Crisis in 1962 and the Indo-Pakistan War in 1990 when military forces by-passed normal political control over nuclear weapons.[20] The main thrust of Sagan's research is that military establishments in general are prone to pre-emptive strategies and with the proliferation of nuclear weapons to countries with limited civilian control over the military, this poses a great danger for the future. Contrary to those like Kenneth Waltz, John Mearsheimer, and more recently of David Karl who have argued that nuclear proliferation was likely to bring greater caution, Sagan is much more pessimistic about the consequences of the spread of nuclear weapons.[21] The very primitive and dangerous designs for a nuclear weapon found by the UN inspectors in Iraq after the Gulf War,[22] the belligerent rhetoric associated with the surprise nuclear tests carried out by India and Pakistan in May 1998, and also the growing fears about the theft of weapons-grade materials in Russia seem perhaps to support Sagan's pessimism.

These worries about nuclear proliferation have been important in helping to establish the growing post-cold-war consensus on the need to de-emphasize nuclear weapons. It was one of the major reasons why the influential Canberra Commission came out in favour of the total abolition of nuclear weapons in their report published in 1996.[23] Significantly also, a number of quite hard-headed strategists and defence chiefs, who were strong supporters of nuclear deterrence during the cold war, have gone on record arguing that nuclear proliferation posed major new dangers which required an urgent change of policy.[24] In December 1996, sixty retired generals and admirals from seventeen countries added their voices to the call for the elimination of nuclear weapons. These included three former Supreme Allied Commanders in Europe, with responsibility for NATO nuclear policy, and also General Lee Butler, who in the early 1990s, was head of US Strategic Command and therefore a key figure in American nuclear planning.[25] In their declaration, these highly experienced senior officers, argued that nuclear proliferation was the most serious danger facing the world at the end of the twentieth century and could only be combated if nuclear weapons were abandoned by the nuclear powers.[26]

A third set of arguments have been put forward by other influential members of the strategic studies community, including Paul Nitze, the doyen of American nuclear strategy during the cold war. Nitze has argued that, with the 'Revolution in Military Affairs' that has taken place in recent years, conventional weapons are now so powerful and accurate that nuclear weapons are no longer needed.[27] Getting rid of nuclear weapons is seen as being very much in American interests because of its clear superiority in the kind of high-tech conventional weapons demonstrated in the Gulf War. Significantly, Nitze bases his argument not only on American interests, but on the same kind of moral arguments traditionally used by anti-nuclear supporters. He argues that the idea that the future peace and well-being of the world should rest on the threat of nuclear annihilation of large numbers of civilians is morally unacceptable.

Apart from these questions of nuclear safety, the dangers of nuclear proliferation, and the growing power of conventional weapons, the recent process of denuclearization has also been supported by those who worry about the effects of the cold-war 'nuclear legacy' on attempts to build a new, more co-operative security relationship between the United States and Russia. Fred Iklé—a former American defence official—and Sergei Karaganov—a high-ranking Russian foreign policy official—have warned recently that the positive progress towards greater co-operation between the old cold-war adversaries, which has taken place in recent years, could be undermined if both retain threat-based, deterrent strategies as an insurance against the other.[28] According to this view, the continuing determination of the United States and Russia to retain nuclear weapons and to pursue common security policies, at the same time, is fundamentally contradictory and ultimately will undermine the *rapprochement* which has taken place.

The key question, which seems to arise from this contemporary debate, is how far the process of marginalizing nuclear weapons can, and should, go. Should marginalization lead to total abolition? Is such a move feasible or desirable? Are there any other concepts of deterrence worth considering? To answer these questions we need to look in more detail at what has been happening in the nuclear field in recent years.

5.3. *Nuclear Trends*

Overall, the evidence is rather ambiguous. Some trends suggest progress towards total disarmament. Other trends, however, suggest that nuclear weapons are likely to remain a feature of international politics for a long time to come. This ambiguity can be seen particularly in American nuclear policies in recent years. The Clinton administration first came to power in 1993 amidst expectations that it would undertake a radical reorientation of its nuclear strategy. Many of the top-ranking foreign and defence officials were on record as supporters of the need to take steps to deal with the dangers associated with nuclear weapons.[29] Part of this promise was fulfilled with the adoption of the 'Co-operative Threat Reduction Program' in the early 1990s, designed to forge a new strategic partnership with Russia, with the marginalization of nuclear weapons as its central objective. This was reflected in the important role played by President Clinton in achieving the indefinite extension of the Non-Proliferation Treaty and the signing of the Comprehensive Test Ban Treaty.

At the same time, however, it became increasingly clear half-way through the administration's first term of office that there were limits to its denuclearization policy. In September 1994 the Defense Secretary, William Perry, unveiled the government's 'Nuclear Posture Review' which revealed an uneasy compromise between those within the administration who wanted to maintain the legitimacy of nuclear weapons and those who wanted to move towards total abolition. Perry characterized American policy as one of 'leading and hedging'. By 'leading', he meant that the United States had a duty to play a leadership role in continuing the reduction in nuclear weapons. By 'hedging', he meant that the US had to be cautious about the reversal of reforms in Russia. This part of the policy reflected powerful pressures from Congress and from America's allies who were concerned about the weakening of the American nuclear guarantee in an uncertain world.[30]

What 'hedging' meant in practice was a determination by the administration to maintain a significant operational nuclear capability: in effect to maintain the *status quo*. This was reflected in what became known as the 'Stewardship Program' designed to preserve a nuclear research, development, and production complex which could, if necessary, reconstitute an expanded nuclear force. The latest purchase of super computers by the Livermore Laboratory and the development of the new Hydrodynamic and National Ignition Facilities are designed to allow safety checks and improvements in warhead design to be made even after the Comprehensive Test Ban Treaty comes into force.[31]

Strong rumours have also circulated that information from American computer simulation of nuclear testing has been promised to Britain, France, and Russia to secure their support for the Comprehensive Test Ban Treaty.[32] This, together with the nuclear policies pursued by these traditional nuclear states since the end of the cold war (as will be shown below), suggests that they all have plans to retain their nuclear forces well into the next century.

Much the same appears to be true of India and Pakistan. India refused to sign the Comprehensive Test Ban Treaty in September 1996 on the grounds that it would not lead the nuclear powers to give up their nuclear weapons as they had promised under Article VI of the NPT Treaty. India retained a covert nuclear capability following its first nuclear test in 1974 and in May 1998 shocked the international community by conducting six further tests and declaring itself a fully fledged nuclear power. Despite intense international opposition, Pakistan responded a few weeks later with its own nuclear test series, completing the nuclearization of south Asia, and opening the prospect for a future nuclear arms race in the region.[33]

Continuing anxiety in Israel, fuelled in part by the Scud missile attacks during the Gulf War and problems in the Middle East peace process, suggest that they will also maintain a potent, if undeclared nuclear capability.[34] Attempts by Iraq and possibly Iran to develop nuclear capabilities, together with worries about the possibility that its enemies can easily develop and conceal chemical and biological weapons, have left the Israeli government, they believe, little alternative but to provide themselves with 'weapons of the last resort'.

If total abolition, therefore seems unlikely, the key question for the future of nuclear weapons is whether the process of marginalization can be taken a significant stage further. Can a different balance be struck between power, prudence, and morality than the one that exists at present?

5.4. *The Prospects for Further Arms Control*

There appear to be a number of possible ways forward in the search to reduce the salience of nuclear weapons in international politics. The first is concerned with continuing the relatively successful process of unilateral and multilateral arms control which characterized the late 1980s and early 1990s. After the understandable disillusionment with the arms control measures of the 1970s, which did very little to slow down the arms race, it is now possible to argue that arms control can, under certain conditions, be a vehicle to accomplish and maintain peaceful change, rather than merely codifying the *status quo* as it did in the past.[35] Taking this process further would involve the full implementation of the exisiting START II treaty and successful negotiations leading to a START III treaty. This process has been delayed by the failure of the Russian Duma to ratify START II, partly because it will require the expensive development of a new single warhead missile to replace multiple warhead missiles which are to be phased out. The need for negotiations, leading to a START III Treaty, were accepted at the Helsinki Summit meeting between Presidents Clinton and Yeltsin when it was agreed to try and reduce the numbers of strategic weapons to 2,500 on each side by 2007.[36] Until recently the American position has been that a follow-on treaty cannot be negotiated until START II is ratified. American officials, however, have indicated that it might be possible to negotiate a framework agreement on lower levels (which would preclude the need for expensive missile developments) to encourage the Russian Duma to ratify START II and move on to a full START III treaty. It has been argued by Harold Brown, a former US

Secretary of Defense, that the numbers of strategic weapons could, in due course, be reduced to a 1,000 or less without damaging the security of either state.[37]

There is also growing official interest in negotiating a Fissile Material Production Cut-off Treaty. In August 1998 agreement was reached at the sixty-one-nation Conference on Disarmament in Geneva to begin negotiations in early 1999 after Israel, India, and Pakistan agreed to abandon long-standing objections. If such a treaty can be negotiated over the next couple of years it would make an important contribution to the reinforcement of the non-proliferation regime by limiting the amount of weapons-grade fissile material available.

However, welcome and important as these measures would be, even if they were implemented, the nuclear framework which characterized the cold war would still be largely in tact. Reduced numbers have not, so far, significantly changed operational nuclear planning. Nor is an end to fissile material production likely to have much effect on the existing nuclear powers who have more than enough. It must also be said that the nuclear tests carried out by India and Pakistan in May 1998 have significantly undermined the non-proliferation treaty regime and reinforced the arguments of those who argue that arms control is seriously flawed as an approach to national security. This is probably unfair because, despite its limitations, arms control, both unilateral and multilateral, still has an important role to play in enhancing international stability and further marginalizing the role of nuclear weapons in international politics. Nevertheless, apart from sustaining and developing the existing regime of arms control measures, there would seem to be an argument for considering other more radical approaches which would retain some of the benefits of deterrence while continuing to reduce the salience of nuclear weapons even further.

5.5. *Minimum Deterrence*

One approach which has been put forward is to go well beyond the present START II agreement (and even the proposed START III treaty) and at the same time to change the operational plans for the use of nuclear weapons. According to Iklé and Karaganov, the total abolition of nuclear weapons, recommended by bodies like the Canberra Commision, is unlikely to be achieved in practice. The best that can be expected is to reduce nuclear weapons to a minimum level of around 200 and make them as unthreatening as possible. Their argument is based not solely on what they believe to be possible and realistic. They see the maintenance of small numbers of nuclear weapons as having a residual prudential benefit in helping to keep the peace in the unpredictable post-cold-war world.

Supporters of Minimum Deterrence, like Iklé and Karaganov, argue that the vast number of nuclear weapons built up by both sides during the cold war was wholly unnecessary as a means of keeping the peace. They believe that just a few hundred or, at most, a few thousand of such weapons, capable of unimaginable destruction, would be sufficient to deter conflict. McGeorge Bundy has even argued that cold-war experience suggests that just a few weapons are enough to secure the necessary caution. In his view, the simple existence of nuclear weapons were, and are, sufficient to deter. In the context of the Cuban Missile Crisis, Bundy has argued that 'if even one Soviet weapon landed on an American target, we would all be losers'.[38]

Those, like Bundy who hold such views, believe that it is highly dangerous to adopt a war-fighting concept of deterrence because it is based on a logic which requires the continuous accumulation of weapons. This, in turn, breeds constant uncertainty and poses grave dangers of miscalculation. Reflecting this view, Lebow and Stein argue that: 'Too much deterrence, or deterrence applied inappropriately to a frightened and vulnerable adversary, can fuel an arms race that makes both sides less rather than more secure and provoke the aggression that it is designed to prevent.'[39] In contrast, their analysis of the 1962 Cuban Missile Crisis and the 1973 Middle Eastern Crisis led them to the conclusion that finite, or minimum, deterrence can contribute to peace and stability by inducing caution amongst adversaries. Applying deterrence 'appropriately' involves tearing up the kind of elaborate contingency plans for nuclear war-fighting maintained by the super powers during the cold war and maintaining a small force for countervalue retaliatory purposes only.

Minimum Deterrence would seem to have a number of advantages as an alternative approach to traditional nuclear-weapons policies. Smaller numbers of nuclear weapons deployed in a less threatening manner are likely to be much less dangerous in terms of accidents and also less provocative to potential adversaries. Because Minimum Deterrence is finite ('enough is enough' to deter) there is no need to constantly match the capabilities of others. Apart from the considerable savings in terms of costs, this would help to overcome some of the dangers of miscalculation associated with deterrence based on a war-fighting concept, which involves 'launch-on-warning' procedures. Such significant reductions in the numbers of nuclear weapons which it would entail would also help to reinforce the non-proliferation regime at a time when it has been eroded by the nuclear tests by India and Pakistan. A gesture by the major nuclear powers to reduce their arsenals may be one of the few ways to encourage the south Asian nuclear powers to restrain their future nuclear developments or to persuade other potential nuclear powers from following them down the nuclear road. At the same time, Minimum Deterrence would ensure that nuclear weapons continue to perform their traditional role of maintaining caution in a world which has become less predictable than during the cold war.

Critics of Minimum Deterrence stress a number of different problems. Many 'traditionalists' argue that to be effective nuclear deterrence requires credible plans for nuclear use. According to this view, small numbers of nuclear weapons, even if they are targeted on the cities of potential adversaries, are unlikely to provide robust deterrence under all conceivable circumstances. Enemies might call the state's bluff by initiating low levels of aggression which would not justify retaliation against its cities. Or they might build up massive superiority in nuclear forces and use them to blackmail the weaker state. 'Existential Deterrence', it is suggested, is likely to be even less effective because it does not involve any specific contingency plans for nuclear use. To achieve credibility, 'traditionalists' argue, deterrence requires a wide spectrum of flexible nuclear capabilities which can demonstrably be used in a war-fighting role.

Supporters of Minimum Deterrence respond by arguing that the requirements for successful deterrence are a matter of judgement. They believe that the lessons of cold-war crisis confirm that the detailed war-fighting contingency plans which existed played no part in preventing war. The key to successful deterrence was the reluctance of statesmen to take the kind of risks which would have led to any nuclear weapons being used. They also argue that war-fighting strategies significantly undermine the search for stability, whereas Minimum Deterrence opens up opportunities for dialogue and co-operation.

'Abolitionists' have different concerns about Minimum Deterrence. They argue that, despite the reduction in nuclear weapons, the dangers of nuclear accidents and miscalculation remain. They may be less than those associated with war-fighting strategies, but they are still present in any security policy which has a nuclear dimension. 'Abolitionists' also have two further concerns. First, they argue that, by maintaining the continuing utility of nuclear weapons, Minimum Deterrence is likely to make proliferation more likely. Secondly, despite what supporters of Minimum Deterrence say about the opportunities for dialogue, they suggest that because deterrence of any kind is based on threats, it is likely to undermine attempts to achieve stable relations between potential or actual adversaries. Minimum Deterrence, therefore, for 'Abolitionists', is likely to remain 'part of the problem rather than the solution'.

Supporters of Minimum Deterrence accept that any form of deterrence poses dangers and problems. Their response is that there is no realistic way to escape this tragic predicament. They also argue that the dangers and problems associated with Minimum Deterrence are, in their view, relatively less than those inherent in seeking total abolition. The attempt to try and escape from the nuclear dilemma is therefore neither practical nor desirable. The problem cannot be transcended, they believe, only mitigated. But are there other forms of mitigation which deal with some of the concerns of 'Abolitionists'?

5.6. *The Concept of 'Virtual Deterrence'*

In 1984 Jonathan Schell, one of the leading opponents of nuclear weapons during the cold war, proposed an arrangement which would ban completed nuclear weapons while allowing nations, as he put it, 'to hold themselves in a particular defined state of readiness for nuclear rearmament'. Schell called this idea 'weaponless deterrence' and he argued that a world of dismantled nuclear weapons would be a much safer world. Under such a system, 'factory', he said, 'would deter factory, blueprint would deter blueprint, equation would deter equation'.[40]

Schell's work was largely ignored by the strategic studies establishment in the 1980s but with the end of the cold war interest in his ideas has been revived. A major study of 'weaponless deterrence' was carried out by Molander and Wilson of the RAND Corporation in the early 1990s.[41] And it was they who coined the phrase 'virtual nuclear arsenals' which was subsequently taken up by Manning and Mazarr in two recent, well-publicized studies.[42]

The idea of 'virtual nuclear arsenals' represents an interesting new approach to nuclear disarmament. It rests on the assumption that, because of the spread of civilian nuclear power and the advances of nuclear technology in general, the aspirations normally associated with nuclear disarmament—that is, the total elimination of all the capability to build nuclear weapons—appear not to be feasible. It may be a cliché but nuclear weapons cannot be disinvented. Even if total nuclear disarmament took place, some form of nuclear deterrence would continue to exist, because the knowledge to produce nuclear weapons would still exist. If this is accepted, a more practical solution may be to aim for a 'virtual arsenals regime' which would involve an agreement banning the existence of all assembled, ready-for-use nuclear weapons. The idea is that warheads and delivery vehicles should be decoupled, electronically tagged, and placed at separate storage sites under international control. Stansfield Turner has coined the term 'strategic escrow' to describe such designated storage areas.[43] Supporters argue that this process would clearly take time—possibly ten to fifteen years—and it would need to be done in a number of distinct phases, designed incrementally to build confidence. Reducing the alert status of nuclear weapons and Minimum Deterrence would be phases along the way, but 'virtual nuclear arsenals' would clearly have a different end-point in view.

This clearly represents a rather different view of disarmament than the way it has been traditionally conceived. The idea behind 'virtual arsenals' is that dismantled weapons would not be available for immediate use but existing nuclear states would still retain the reassuring knowledge that they could be reassembled if attempts were made by 'rogue' states to 'break out' of the regime. A form of 'existential deterrence', or what might be described as 'background deterrence', would therefore continue to operate.[44]

As an approach to disarmament, the idea behind this proposal is that nuclear weapons capability is not one of 'either-you-have-it-*or*-you-don't'. It is one of degree. As many as forty countries now have the knowledge to develop nuclear weapons. The key question is how long will it take states or even non-state actors to produce nuclear weapons? The concept of 'virtual nuclear arsenals' is designed to respond to this reality.

There would seem to be four main advantages with a regime of this sort. First, 'virtual arsenals' would be a significant further step in marginalizing nuclear weapons in world politics. Like Minimum Deterrence they would go way beyond the existing START II and recent START III proposals which will still leave many thousands of weapons in existence and many thousands in reserve if, and when, they are implemented. The act of disassembling weapons, as Michael Brown has shown recently, would require significant changes in traditional strategic planning—away from some of the more provocative, 'launch-on-warning' nuclear doctrines of the cold war, which in some respects are still retained.[45] This clearly would be a step forward.

Secondly, they would help to eliminate the day-to-day risks of nuclear accidents which are a continuing possibility, even with reduced numbers of nuclear weapons held by the nuclear powers. If nuclear weapons were dismantled, this would dramatically reduce the risks posed by operational nuclear forces, even minimum ones. There is little doubt that nuclear safety has been improved as a result of the end of confrontation between the United States and the Soviet Union during the cold war. The dangers, however, remain very real.[46]

Thirdly, 'virtual arsenals' would help to reinforce the non-proliferation regime and possibly provide an element of stability in regions like south Asia. George Perkovich, an expert in this area, writing in 1993, advocated a similar system of 'non-weaponized deterrence' between India and Pakistan.[47] At present serious dangers exist because of the May 1998 nuclear tests carried out by both countries. The continuing conflict over Kashmir and the prospects of a nuclear arms race between them has raised major international concerns. Clearly more stability would be achieved if both sides recognized the futility of engaging in an expensive arms race and agreed not to deploy completed nuclear weapons. In such circumstances they are likely to be more secure, especially if they both accept greater transparency and agree to some form of international inspection to verify their pledges. They would retain what they perceive as the benefits of deterrence against each other without creating the dangers associated with the current situation.

And finally, 'virtual arsenals' provide a more realistic approach to disarmament than total abolition. In the uncertain world in which we live, it seems highly unlikely that nuclear states will give up their nuclear weapons completely. They have, however, been prepared to adopt wide-ranging measures to marginalize these weapons since the end of the cold war and debates have taken place within governments about the merits of disassembly. It is not beyond the realms of possibility, therefore, that they might be prepared, cautiously, to take this process a stage further, providing some form of 'background deterrence' remains as a safety net.

Overall, a move in the direction of disarmament through disassembly would seem to represent an important means of reducing the dangers to humanity posed by nuclear weapons while retaining some of the benefits which seem to accrue from deterrence. At the same time, however, it has to be acknowledged that there are a number of significant obstacles which would have to be overcome if this form of redefined disarmament is to become a serious policy option.

Perhaps the most intractable difficulty is that the nuclear powers themselves would have to believe that taking the process of marginalization a significant stage further would be in their national security interests. So far, we have seen earlier, despite the process of 'cooperative denuclearization' which has been taking place, all the signs are that the United States, Russia, China, Britain, France, India, and Pakistan intend to keep their nuclear capabilities. The situation is complicated by the fact that Russia and China have put even more emphasis on nuclear weapons in recent years.[48] In the case of Russia this may be reinforced even further as a result of NATO's expansion of its membership to include Poland, Hungary, and the Czech Republic.[49] In February 1997 the US Under Secretary of Defense, Walter Slocombe, set out the American position very clearly. He argued that: 'whatever would be desirable, there is, in fact, no reasonable prospect that all the declared and de facto nuclear powers will agree in the near term to give up all their nuclear weapons. But as long as one state refuses to do so, it will be necessary for us to retain a nuclear force of our own.' Unilateral abolition was ruled out by Slocombe, and multilateral abolition, although a possibility in the long term, was not regarded as being likely in the 'foreseeable future'.[50]

Whether the nuclear powers would be prepared to take marginalization a stage further will depend a great deal on domestic politics. The Republican Congress in the United States, for example, has already put a significant brake on the process of denuclearization by raising the proposed number of ICBMs planned by the administration in its Nuclear Policy Review.[51] As indicated earlier, the Russian Duma is also currently holding up the ratification of the START II treaty because it believes it discriminates against Russia.[52] It also seems that the decisions made by both India and Pakistan to publicly test nuclear weapons in May 1998 was driven, as much as anything else, by domestic considerations.[53]

Apart from these domestic pressures, support for a 'virtual arsenals regime' is also likely to depend on the answers to a number of other important questions. One of these is whether a monitoring and inspection regime can be devised which would provide sufficient confidence against cheating. As David Kay has shown recently, it would have to be extremely intrusive and it is likely to be very costly. It is true that one of the great breakthroughs in the disarmament field in recent years has taken place with intrusive on-site inspection, but a 'virtual nuclear arsenals' regime would represent the most daunting verification challenge so far.[54] Inspectors would have to monitor each of the separated components of nuclear weapons—some of which might have to be kept at sea. The difficulties of UNSCOM in Iraq show what an intractable problem this can be. Michael Mazarr, a strong supporter of the 'virtual nuclear arsenals approach', has argued that verification is the single most important issue in determining the feasibility and desirability of this approach to disarmament.[55]

Another problem arises from the danger of rapid nuclear rearmament in a crisis. In some ways, reassembling nuclear weapons as tensions increased might be even more destabilizing than the current situation. Dangers could arise from uneven rearmament and anxieties would certainly exist that nuclear weapons could be used in a future adversarial international environment to make the most of a fleeting nuclear monopoly by one of the states. It remains unclear whether a regime of this sort could actually survive a new phase of confrontation between the great powers in the future.[56]

Finally, and perhaps most importantly, there are also problems arising from other weapons of mass destruction. Some analysts have hesitated to endorse the idea of disarmament because they see nuclear weapons as an essential hedge against biological and chemical weapons which are so easy to produce and to conceal. This would be particularly true of countries like Israel with their recently expressed fear of the production of VX nerve gas by Syria and also anxieties emanating from the Iraqi deployment of biogical weapons during the Gulf War.[57] There are currently more than twenty states that are rumoured to have a chemical and biological weapons capability and, although Biological and Chemical Weapons Conventions were signed in 1972 and 1993, it remains very difficult to detect violations. As a result, the nuclear powers continue to believe that operational nuclear weapons are a useful deterrent against the proliferation of these weapons, just as some non-nuclear states continue to believe that chemical and biological weapons provide them with security against the nuclear powers.[58]

5.7. *Conclusion*

Given these formidable difficulties, what can be said in conclusion about the future role of nuclear weapons and the prospects for a 'third approach' which maintains the caution which nuclear weapons seem to have brought to international politics while at the same time reducing some of the problems which such weapons create?

What we have seen since the end of the cold war are two distinctive but contradictory trends. There has been a very distinctive process of 'cooperative denuclearization' and a broad consensus has developed in favour of international norms designed to restrict the spread of nuclear weapons. At the same time, there appears to be growing support for the total abolition of nuclear weapons. Significantly, unlike the very public campaigns for nuclear disarmament in the past, much of the running this time has been made by experienced strategists and military officials who have traditionally been supporters of deterrence.

At the same time, however, despite the partial marginalization of nuclear weapons which has taken place, it must be said that there appears to be very little evidence of official government support at present for total abolition. Nuclear weapons remain firmly embedded in the security thinking and the strategic policies of the nuclear states. The decision by two of the former 'threshold' nuclear states to develop overt nuclear capabilities also raises new fears about the dangers of accelerating nuclear proliferation. At the same time, the search for nuclear, chemical and biological capabilities by a number of other states and possibly by non-state terrorist groups continues as well—encouraged both by the continuing determination of the established nuclear powers to hang on to their nuclear weapons and by the contemporary processes of industrial and technological globalization.

The idea of moving to Minimum Deterrence or to 'virtual nuclear arsenals' is designed to deal with the prudential and moral complexities and uncertainties of global security in the post-cold-war era. Trying to combine both reassurance and deterrence simultaneously undoubtedly creates conceptual problems, but it does reflect an interesting and creative attempt to deal with the requirements of a messy and far from perfect world in which contradictions, paradoxes, and ambiguities abound. Both ideas reflect the attempt to achieve a compromise, albeit an uneasy compromise, between prudence and morality.

Remarkable things happened with the end of the cold war. The process of denuclearization which has taken place has gone further than anyone would have dreamt ten years ago. As a result the total abolition of nuclear weapons cannot be wholly ruled out. For the moment, however, nuclear weapons will remain with us for the foreseeable future. Although at lower numbers, 'traditional' approaches continue to be in the ascendancy.[59] Minimum Deterrence and 'virtual nuclear arsenals', although not perfect solutions, represent an alternative nuclear future which is at least worth exploring and taking incremental steps to move towards. Amongst all strands of thinking there is a consensus that the further marginalization of nuclear weapons is necessary and practical.[60] For the moment, the best that policy-makers can, and should, do is to continue the search for a better balance between prudence and morality than exists at present. This will involve intellectual tolerance in considering new ideas designed to reduce the dangers associated with weapons of mass destruction, and taking calculated risks. After all, there are no risk-free or morally pure options available in the diverse and complex world in which we live.

6

Nuclear Weapons and the Post-Cold-War Middle East: Business as Usual

Efraim Karsh

The Indian and Pakistani nuclear tests in the spring of 1998 dealt yet another blow to the expectations that the end of the cold war would usher in an era of international peace and stability in general, and real progress towards non-conventional arms control and disarmament in particular. Such expectations were particularly high with regard to the Middle East, where local conflicts had often been viewed as corollaries of superpower rivalry, destined to wither away in its absence. It was also reasoned that if during the cold war local players could exploit the global polarization to their advantage, the dissolution of the Soviet empire would leave them at the mercy of the 'only remaining superpower', the United States, which would be readily able to impose a *Pax Americana,* with its attendant arms control regimes, on the Middle East.

6.1. *The Quest for Nuclear Weapons in the Middle East*

The allure of the Bomb has always appealed to Middle Eastern leaders. Given Egyptian President Gamal Abdel Nasser's unbridled ambition for regional hegemony, it was only natural for him to toy with the nuclear idea. Already in 1955, before any other Middle Eastern actor, Egypt founded its own Atomic Energy Commission and two years later inaugurated a Centre for Nuclear Research. By 1961 Egypt had acquired a small nuclear research reactor from the Soviet Union, and began training a cadre of physicists. Several attempts to acquire larger reactors came to nought, but a technical and scientific infrastructure in the nuclear field was nevertheless established, and Egypt initiated a survey searching for uranium and thorium.

Another leader whose nuclear ambitions date back to the 1950s was the Iranian Shah Muhammad Reza Pahlavi. In 1957 he signed an agreement on the exchange of nuclear information with the United States, and in the early 1970s launched a far more ambitious nuclear programme, with West European and American support, which he boasted would allow Iran to produce twenty-one nuclear plants in two decades.

Though the Shah lost no opportunity to underscore the peaceful nature of Iran's nuclear programme, few believed his pure intentions. Why should a country like Iran, with immeasurable oil and gas resources, need to seek alternative energy sources? Why should the Shah invest some $100 billion in nuclear infrastructure at a time when most of his subjects were still struggling for their daily existence? Besides, the Shah had never concealed his hegemonic, indeed imperialist aspirations. He viewed twentieth-century Iran as successor to the ancient Persian empires, and himself as a present-day Cyrus. He transformed his country into an overbearing military power and fashioned himself as the 'guardian of the Gulf'. Nuclear power, in his perception, was the ultimate confirmation of Iran's regional prowess.[1] This strategic rationale was maintained by the ayatollahs who in 1979 seized power in Iran following the Shah's dethronement. While disowning the Shah's policies and practices, Ayatollah Ruhollah Khomeini, father of Iran's Islamic revolution, carried the hegemonic ambitions of his hated predecessor a step further. He would not content himself with recognition of Iran's political supremacy, or with territorial gains of sorts. He aimed at nothing less than the subversion of the regional *status quo* and its replacement by an Islamic order. 'We will export our revolution throughout the world', the aged Ayatollah pledged, 'until the call "there is no god but Allah and Muhammad is the messenger of Allah" is echoed all over the world.'[2]

The political manifestation of this hegemonic world-view was a sustained terrorist and subversive campaign against the Gulf monarchies and an uncompromising effort to overthrow Saddam Hussein's personal rule in Iraq. Its strategic expression was the continuation of the Shah's nuclear development programme, and its substantial acceleration after the end of the Iran–Iraq War. Notwithstanding the enormous economic dislocation occasioned by this eight-year conflict, Iran has continued to pour substantial sums of money into its nuclear programme, and there is strong consensus among Western intelligence services that she is aggressively seeking nuclear weapons. While reports that Iran has obtained nuclear bombs from a former Soviet republic have yet to be confirmed, Iran is known to have been shopping for nuclear know-how and *matériel* in the West, the successor states to the Soviet Union, not least Russia (from which Iran has acquired two reactors of 400 megawatts thermal each), and selected Third World countries, such as Brazil, North Korea, and China, which is already involved in the Iranian programme.[3] For their part the ayatollahs have made no secret of their interest in the Bomb, at least until they came under heavy American pressure to bridle their nuclear ambitions. 'It was made very clear during the [Iran–Iraq] war that chemical, bacteriological and radiological weapons are very decisive', stated Ali Akbar Hashemi-Rafsanjani, then speaker of the Iranian parliament and commander-in-chief of Iran's armed forces, shortly after the war. 'We should fully equip ourselves both in the offensive and defensive use of chemical, bacteriological, and radiological weapons.'[4]

It was, indeed, the magnitude of the Shah's nuclear ambitions that triggered Iraq's nuclear development programme in the mid-1970s. Having been subjected to Iranian military intervention in their domestic affairs, mainly through support to the Kurdish uprising in the north of the country, Iraq's ruling Ba'th regime was all too aware of the Shah's regional ambitions. It was prepared to acquiesce in them, as demonstrated by the March 1975 Algiers Agreement which involved significant territorial concessions to Iran and recognized the latter's supremacy in the Gulf, but at the same time Iraq sought to blunt Iran's marked edge by initiating its own non-conventional weapons programme.

There was another side to the ledger. To Iraq's strong-man-turned-absolute-ruler, Saddam Hussein, the moving spirit behind his country's non-conventional ambitions, nuclear weapons have always meant much more than the 'great equalizer'. They have been a personal obsession: a symbol of Iraq's technological prowess, a prerequisite for regional hegemony, the ultimate guarantee of the survival of his personal rule.[5] Hence, the fatal blow to Iraq's nuclear programme by the Israeli destruction of the Osirak reactor in 1981 only enticed Saddam into doubling his efforts to nuclearize. By the time of the 1990–1 Gulf conflict few doubted that Iraq, despite being a signatory to the Nuclear Non-Proliferation Treaty (NPT), was actively developing nuclear capabilities; following the war it transpired, mainly through revelations by Iraqi defectors, notably the former Minister for Military Industries and Saddam's son-in-law, Hussein Kamil Hasan, who had long been in charge of his country's non-conventional arms programmes, that the Iraqi nuclear programme had been far more advanced and extensive than previously assumed.

Nor have other Arab states shied away from the nuclear genie. Algeria has purchased two reactors, one of which is apparently capable of manufacturing weapons-grade uranium sufficient for the production of at least one bomb per year, while Syria has shown a keen interest in the nuclear sphere. It ordered a 30 KW research reactor from China; and even though the deal was approved in 1992 by the International Atomic Energy Agency (IAEA), which is also supposed to inspect Syria's compliance with its obligations as a signatory to the NPT, the reactor has the capacity for producing fissionable material for at least a bomb per year. In addition, Syria has been actively seeking to purchase a larger reactor from Argentina, probably owing to its failure to buy one from Russia.[6]

While the Arab and the Iranian quest for the Bomb has thus far fallen short of obtaining fully fledged nuclear capabilities, Israel is believed to be more successful. Painfully aware of the Jewish state's fundamental inferiority *vis-à-vis* the Arab world in terms of human, material, natural, and financial resources, its founding father and first prime minister, David Ben-Gurion, sought in the early 1950s to secure European and/or American guarantees to Israel's survival. As his overtures were rebuffed by the great powers, Ben Gurion saw no choice but to opt for the Bomb as a weapon of last resort—when all other options for securing Israel's existence failed. With French help and know-how, Israel started building a nuclear reactor near the southern Negev town of Dimona, and within a decade had reportedly managed to assemble its first crude bombs. And while Israel has never acknowledged the possession of nuclear weapons, reverting instead to the ambiguous formula that it would not be the first to introduce them into the Middle East, but would not be the second either, it is generally accepted that it has a sizeable and sophisticated arsenal.[7]

6.2. *Obstacles to Nuclear Arms Control*

Arms control efforts in the nuclear sphere have not been more successful than the wider failure to control the flow of other types of conventional and non-conventional weapons to the Middle East. Despite a long-standing Soviet–American unanimity on the need to control the spread of nuclear arms, they have been unable to impose the NPT—the global non-proliferation regime agreed upon in 1968—on their Middle Eastern allies. Those Middle Eastern states that have joined the NPT, notably Iraq and Iran, have unscrupulously violated the treaty. For its part Israel has declared that it would not be the first to introduce nuclear weapons into the region—its official position to this day—but has consistently refused to join the treaty. The deficiencies of this global regime are by now well known, particularly in those instances where verification is most critical. In the case of the Middle East, these limitations have been compounded by a cluster of interrelated factors, notably geopolitical, strategic, and military complexity; external interference; and endemic regional volatility.

6.2.1. Geopolitical and Strategic Complexity

Unlike the bipolar nature of the cold-war military balance, the Middle East is laced with a multitude of strategic balances which, in turn, makes a regional arms control regime virtually impossible, and subregional arrangements very difficult to attain and to preserve. There is a high degree of political permeability and strategic vulnerability between the system's constituent elements—the Arab states, Israel, Iran, and Turkey—for reasons of geography, history, society and culture, giving rise to constant instability. This in turn heightens the role of external powers; especially given the proximity of southern Europe, the former Soviet republics, and south Asia, and, additionally, the global role and cold-war legacy that have introduced the United States as a key player in regional affairs.

The same factors also create numerous linkages throughout the Middle East, exposing the strategic balance in any of its subsidiary or subregions— such as the Arab–Israeli arena, the Persian Gulf, or the northern tier—to new pressures and threats whenever changes take place elsewhere in the wider system. Such linkage drives, and in turn is driven by, a regional arms competition that has developed an ominous momentum of its own. In the course of the past few decades, the Middle East has witnessed the militarization of its societies and economies, acquisition of massive conventional weapons arsenals, proliferation of ballistic missiles and weapons of mass destruction, and growth of indigenous military R&D and production capabilities.

There are, moreover, many current and foreseeable threats to regional stability. Relations between Iraq and its neighbours remain volatile, and the prospect of an Iraqi break-up and Kurdish independence can only disturb the balance of power and trigger a competition for influence between them. The Iranian military reconstruction programme alarms Saudi Arabia and other Arab states, especially as it includes an effort to develop both ballistic missiles and a nuclear capability. Yet despite their concern and the momentous events of the Gulf crisis and war, strains among the Gulf Co-operation Council (GCC) states impede its transformation into a viable collective security agency, while Saudi–Yemeni tensions too may eventually result in further violence. Iranian support for the Hizbullah in southern Lebanon and other radical Islamic operations elsewhere in the Middle East is yet another indication of the intricate linkages between the various conflicts in the region.

Further afield, Libya is under international siege, while Islamist forces pose an increasing threat to government authority throughout north Africa and in Egypt. A confrontation has also built up between Egypt and the Islamist government in Khartoum, while to the south new secessionist wars loom in the Horn of Africa. Syria feels threatened by Turkey and Iraq, while Jordan has good reason to worry about all its neighbours: Syria, Iraq, and Saudi Arabia. On the other side of the Mediterranean, the Yugoslav wars of dissolution threaten to activate Aegean tensions at a time when Turkey is adopting an increasingly assertive stance towards Syria and Iraq. Finally, regional stability in the Middle East is also liable to be adversely affected by tensions between the former Soviet republics, in-fighting in Afghanistan, and Turkish–Iranian rivalry in Central Asia.

Hence, a diminution of the intensity of the Arab–Israeli conflict may not necessarily lead to a reduction in the regional arms build-up. Egypt, though at peace with Israel since 1979, has not reduced its order of battle; on the contrary, it has enhanced its military capability over time by shifting to Western equipment. The improved relationship between Jerusalem and Amman has been accompanied by American promises to sell advanced F-16 jet fighters to Jordan. Similarly, one of the primary reasons for Syria's participation in the current peace process is its desire to get access to American weaponry. All this is unlikely to induce Israel to relinquish its nuclear weapons.

6.2.2. Strategic and Military Complexity

The control of the nuclear race in the Middle East has been further complicated by the existence of formidable chemical (and to a lesser extent biological) weapons arsenals in the region. To be sure, such weapons arrived in the Middle East well before the advent of the nuclear era (e.g. Turkey received mustard gas from its German ally during the First World War), and their strategic rationale has been predominantly non-nuclear, as evidenced *inter alia* by their repeated use in regional, often low-intensity conflicts. Yet they have come to be widely associated with the nuclear factor, as their owners, notably the Arab states, have justified their refusal to eliminate their non-conventional arsenals on grounds of Israel's alleged nuclear capabilities. And while chemical weapons have apparently failed to live up to the description of being the 'poor man's atom-bomb', *biological weapons* present a different problem altogether. The many uncertainties surrounding biological warfare, associated with the lack of experience with regard to their employment and the wide variety of biological munitions potentially available, render predictions in this field extremely difficult to make. Whatever the case, Middle Eastern countries have shown great interest in at least investigating the military utility of such substances. Iran and Syria are thought to possess or to be involved in the development of biological warfare munitions; according to American intelligence sources, a recent collaboration agreement with Russia has enabled Iran to enhance its biological warfare capabilities to such an extent that their operational effect, should they he used, would be similar to that of nuclear weapons.[8] Egypt and Israel, for their part, are sometimes mentioned as either possessing biological weapons or at least having the capability to develop them.

Notwithstanding the failure of successive UN inspection teams to find any evidence of Iraqi attempts to develop munitions to carry the micro-organisms and disperse them on the battlefield, American intelligence sources insisted that a biological weaponization programme had been going on clandestinely.[9] But even they were taken aback when the real enormity of the Iraqi programme transpired in the summer of 1995, following Kamil Hasan's defection. According to the report submitted to the UN Security Council by Rolf Ekdus, Executive Chairman of the United Nations Special Commission

(UNSCOM) established in accordance with Security Council Resolution 687 (1991) to supervise the dismantling of Iraq's non-conventional arsenal, Iraq possessed an offensively geared extensive biological weapons programme. Thus, it was revealed that during the 1991 Gulf War Iraq had at least twenty-five Scud missile warheads carrying about 5,000 kilogrammes of biological agents, including powerful Botulism poison and Anthrax germs. An additional 15,000 kilograms of biological agents were loaded in 175 bombs, to be dropped from aeroplanes, or held in reserve for other weapons.[10]

Indeed, the proliferation of ballistic missiles capable of carrying nuclear, chemical, and biological warheads has substantially added to the regional military complexity since the 1980s. This is so because no defence is available, for the time being, against incoming missiles. The MTCR, a suppliers' global regime established in 1987, has only limited impact on the spread of missile technology, while the Global Protection System (GPS) against missiles, suggested by the Bush administration, is still on the drawing board. The effectiveness of Israel's Arrow anti-missile missile, though at a relatively advanced stage of development, is still a matter of conjecture.

In the past, there have been tacit understandings between Arabs and Israelis to limit use of missiles to the battlefield. In other parts of the Middle East, such as the Gulf and the Saudi Arabian peninsula, missiles have been used with less constraint. After the 1991 Iraqi missile attacks on Israeli population centres, a certain taboo was broken in the Arab-Israeli arena, leaving Israel, the party most sensitive to civilian casualties, at a disadvantage. Hence, Israel has been quite eager to impose some limits on the procurement and use of missiles in order to minimize the vulnerability of its home front. It even joined the MTCR in 1992. The Arab states, however, regard missiles as a way to overcome Israeli air superiority and escalation dominance. Missiles coupled with chemical and biological warheads constitute the perceived Arab countervalue option to Israel's missiles and primarily its nuclear potential.

Finally, it is not simply the strong incentives to acquire nuclear weapons that help underline the difficulties in ensuring agreement about arms control, but the asymmetry in motivation that underpins proliferation. In Israeli strategic thinking these weapons are means of last resort, the so-called 'Samson's Option', designed to offset Arab massive conventional superiority in a situation where Israel's quality can no longer match enemy quantity. In addition, they are vital elements in deterring enemy non-conventional weaponry—a task that, in the Israeli view, cannot be entrusted to inevitably imperfect arms control schemes. Conversely, Arab and Iranian non-conventional weapons programmes, which are only in part responses to the Israeli arsenal, have not been developed for purely deterrent or 'last resort' purposes. They are also an instrument to be used both in intra-Arab and Iranian–Arab hostilities and against domestic threats to the survival of the regime.

As Israel approaches the historical juncture of significant territorial concessions in return for peace, it is unlikely to surrender its ultimate weapons,
particularly since they may he viewed as a trade-off for the loss of strategic
depth. But even if it did the unthinkable and unilaterally surrendered its non-
conventional weaponry, it is doubtful whether others in the region would
follow suit. Quite the reverse in fact: it is arguable that such a move would
only enhance the desirability of non-conventional weapons amongst other
regional states, particularly those opposed to the peace arrangements between
Israel and its Arab neighbours, as there would be no comparable system to
deter the deployment, and even employment, of such weapons.

6.2.3. External Interference

In the field of arms control the role of extra-regional weapons suppliers is
highly important, if only for the simple reason that they are the main suppliers of both conventional and non-conventional weapons and technological know-how. Despite the growing capacity for indigenous military
production in several Middle Eastern countries, all regional armies are heavily
dependent on arms procurement from abroad. How the end of East–West
confrontation will affect the pattern of arms supplies to regional actors is difficult to tell. The major suppliers were, and remain, the United States, Western
Europe, and Russia. Western Europe and Russia have strong strategic and economic interests in the Middle East, and thus will not allow the region to
become an exclusively American sphere of influence. Though Russia is
presently preoccupied with domestic problems, it nevertheless remains a
major actor with respect to arms supply; it is in great need of foreign currency
and is willing to sell even its latest model equipment and technological know-
how at bargain prices. Similarly, West European producers will fight hard to
maintain their share in the lucrative weapons market. Hence, the prospects of
the West Europeans and the Russians joining a comprehensive arms control
effort that would stabilize the region are not very promising. Nor is it at all
clear whether the United States would be willing and able to throw its full
weight behind a thrust towards regional arms control. As vividly demonstrated by the Somali and the Yugoslav civil wars, even in the era of perceived
American hegemony in world affairs there are limits, both external and internal, to how far the United States can affect regional conflicts.

Indeed, a vivid illustration of the lukewarm great-power attitude to the idea
of a Middle East arms control regime was afforded by President George Bush's
stillborn initiative of 29 May 1992. Enunciated in the euphoric period attending the successful ejection of Iraq from Kuwait by a US-led international coalition, the presidential arms control scheme included a heavy focus on weapons

of mass destruction; it called for an international ban on chemical and biological weapons; a verifiable ban on the acquisition and production of plutonium and enriched uranium which could be employed in the production of chemical weapons; an attempt to constrain the supply of the most dangerous conventional weapons; and a freeze leading to an eventual ban on the testing, manufacture, and purchase of surface-to surface ballistic missiles. While these proposals soon received firm backing from the five permanent members of the UN Security Council and a wide variety of other international forums and bodies, it had no impact on the flow of non-conventional weaponry to the Middle East which continued apace, and in the case of Syria and Iran even gained fresh momentum.

6.2.4. The Politics of Violence and the Problem of Verification

Nor does the violent political culture which has plagued the contemporary Middle East since its inception in the wake of the First World War augur well for the prospects of arms control. Whatever the reasons for the immediate collapse of the fragile democratic systems established by the colonial powers, the Arab and Muslim states of the Middle East, with the partial exception of Turkey, have been governed by at best authoritarian regimes and/or rulers; at worst, by some of the most totalitarian regimes in today's world. In such a political system where power is often concentrated in the hands of a tiny minority group (e.g. the Alawites in Syria or the Sunnis in Iraq); where no orderly mechanisms for political participation and peaceful transfer of power exist; and where the goal of regime survivability supersedes everything else, the military and the security forces have become the primary mainstay of the regime, and physical force the foremost mode of political discourse. Examples of this behavioural pattern abound—from civil strife, to interstate wars, to domestic repression. Suffice it to mention here the 1930s massacres of the tiny Assyrian community in northern Iraq, the long-standing repression of the Iraqi and Turkish Kurds, the Lebanese and the Algerian civil wars, in which hundred of thousands of innocent civilians perished, and the Hamma massacre of February 1982 in which some 20,000 Syrian civilians were killed by their unelected government.

Nor have the pro-Western 'conservative' regimes in the Middle East fared much better in this respect. Shah Muhammad Reza Pahlavi of Iran, America's foremost regional ally, predicated his personal rule on his armed forces and the security apparatuses. Even the affable and Western-educated King Hussein of Jordan did not shy away from slaughtering thousands of Palestinians during the eventful month of September 1970 (dubbed 'Black September'), when his throne was endangered by the Palestinian guerrilla organizations. All this means that arms control verification in the Middle East is bound to be extremely difficult, if not impossible. Leaving aside the region's complexity which renders verification far more difficult than in the East–West context, no local regime would dare antagonize its military and security forces, the only guarantors of its survival, by cutting defence allocations; nor would it forego the procurement and preservation of whatever weapon systems deemed necessary for its survival. Thus, for example, having received a Saudi $2 billion cheque in lieu of his participation in the 1991 Gulf War, Asad preferred to pour this money into a new large-scale arms deal with Russia rather than invest it in the development of the Syrian economy.

Hence, no international body, however distinguished, is likely to receive real support and collaboration from the Middle Eastern regimes in its verification efforts, for the simple reason that their very existence hinges on their military might.

6.3. *Iraq: The Limits of Arms Control*

Indeed, the severe limits of verification have been vividly illustrated by the failure of the international community to dispose of Iraq's non-conventional arsenal following the 1991 Gulf War. It was a long-time member of the NPT, yet it had consistently sought to develop nuclear weapons in flagrant violation of the treaty to which it was a signatory and under the very nose of the international organization that was supposed to prevent this from happening. And while it is generally accepted that Baghdad's nuclear development project suffered a devastating setback following the Gulf War, it is highly doubtful whether the international non-proliferation effort has succeeded in completely and permanently removing Iraq from the list of developing states intent upon acquiring nuclear weapons.

Moreover, given the centrality of these weapons in Saddam's Hobbesian world-view, on the one hand, and his keen awareness of the shortness of international memory, exemplified *inter alia* by the deep divisions within the war coalition over its Iraq policy, on the other, Saddam can be expected to continue his cat-and-mouse game with the Security Council over Iraq's non-conventional disarmament *ad infinitum*. Salvaging whatever he can from his deadly arsenal is, in his eyes, a matter of life and death.

While accepting the UN ceasefire resolution 687 of 3 April 1991 in a desperate bid to save his tottering personal rule, Saddam had not the slightest intention to abide by its provision that Iraq destroy, unconditionally and under international supervision, all its nuclear, chemical, and biological stockpiles and research facilities, as well as its ballistic missiles with a range greater than 150 kilometres, and undertake not to 'use, develop, construct or acquire' any such weapons or subsystems related to their production. In the same month as he accepted the UN Resolution, Saddam issued a presidential directive ordering his subordinates to lie to UNSCOM and the IAEA about Iraq's mass-destruction capabilities. Non-conventional-related materials were accordingly turned over to the Special Security Organization (SSO) and Special Republican Guard (SRG). These two organizations, among the most secretive of Iraq's security forces, were originally established to protect the president, but were charged in the 1980s and 1990s with safeguarding Saddam's non-conventional weapons programme.[11] Their relentless commitment to this task following the Gulf War, overseen by Abed Hamid Mahmoud, the presidential secretary, resulted in years of repeated tussles with the Security Council, led by the United States, over the implementation of the ceasefire resolution. In a series of quarrels Iraq has never given an inch rhetorically but has always left enough wriggle room for last-minute concessions whenever an ultimatum has been issued so as to deny any pretext for military action.

Thus far this 'cheat and retreat' strategy has worked impeccably for Saddam. It required eleven inspection visits to Baghdad by teams of the International Atomic Energy Agency (IAEA) before Saddam relented and agreed to the destruction of al-Athir, together with the neighbouring al-Hatin high explosive complex, and his scientists have been less than forthcoming with regard to all procurement details of components, materials, and design know-how. This could form the basis of a later programme or be sold or transferred to other countries in the region or elsewhere. No wonder that in June 1992, the Deputy Head of the IAEA, Maurizio Zifferero, expressed the fear that while 'for the time being our inspectors have cut the head off efforts to turn Iraq into a nuclear threat[, the Iraqis] have got the know-how and the people, so it is only a matter of time before they could try to make a bomb'.[12] Indeed, according to Scott Ritter, a veteran arms inspector for UNSCOM, who in the summer of 1998 resigned his post in protest over the commission's being held back by the US administration at a time when it was on the verge of a major breakthrough in uncovering Iraq's concealed weaponry, Iraq is in possession of three implosion-type nuclear devices, which would become bombs once Iraq obtains the fissionable material.[13]

While Ritter's assessment, like many of its precursors, has been virtually ignored in the West,[14] Middle Easterners are unlikely to take a similarly relaxed view. For them, the possibility that Baghdad is still holding back on technology is disturbing not only because it contains the seeds of a revived Iraqi programme, but also because it casts a heavy doubt on the efficacy of future verification and arms control regimes. If anything, the revelations attending the Gulf War, particularly those of Hussein Kamil Hasan, have underscored how little the international community knows about the scope and capacity of the highly secretive Middle East non-conventional weapons programmes, including members of the NPT regime.

The unprecedented international co-operation in dismantling Iraq's non-conventional weapons was made possible by a unique convergence of regional and international conditions, which are rather unlikely to recur in the future. These ranged from the brutal nature of the Iraqi regime, manifested in domestic repression and external aggression, to the unprecedented nature of the occupation and elimination of Kuwait as a sovereign state, to the strategic and economic importance of the Middle East and the Persian Gulf, to the momentous events in Eastern Europe and the Soviet Union and the consequent diminution in great-power rivalry in the Third World. And yet, even this exceptional measure of global co-operation, forged during the Gulf conflict of 1990–1, and maintained—with great difficulty and diminishing efficiency—in the wake of the war, has encountered formidable obstacles and its result has been far less than complete. Is it realistic to assume that a regional arms control arrangement, operating under far less favourable circumstances, would be able to identify and monitor similar nuclear violations by members of the NPT, such as Iran?

6.4. *A Brighter Future?*

This grim record notwithstanding, the nascent Arab–Israeli peace process seems to have somewhat improved the prospects of some non-conventional arms control measures in the Middle East. Nuclear weapons are on the agenda of the Arab–Israeli peace negotiations under the rubric of the multilateral group on Arms Control and Regional Security (ACRS); and while the two nuclear aspirants, Iran and Iraq, are not participants in the multilateral track, Israel seems better disposed than ever before to deal squarely with the issue, though it prefers to delay concrete moves until the attainment of a comprehensive peace.

There are four main reasons for this guarded optimism. First, and most importantly, the inability of Arabs and Israelis to impose their own solutions after half-a-century of recurrent violence has already resulted in mutual, if asymmetric, disillusionment with the use of armed force and may well drive the two sides to other avenues for pursuing their national goals. This consideration is related directly to domestic factors and changing political agendas in many Middle Eastern countries, including the non-Arab states.

Second, the advent of the 'New World Order' appears to have given a certain boost to the above-mentioned process of regional disillusionment with the use of force, by helping push some Arab states to the final realization that their goal of eradicating Israel is unattainable. Israel, for its part, while a beneficiary of this latter development, is presently in a position where its traditional deterrence policy has been rendered very problematic due to a unique combination of factors: the perceived diminution in its value as an American ally; Arab perceptions concerning Israel's war-waging capability; the enhanced Arab ability to inflict damage on Israel's population centres; the growing doubts about the Israeli resolve to use force; and the constraints on Israel's freedom of action as a result of both the peace process and its desire to maintain good relations with the United States.

Third, the introduction of non-conventional weapons and delivery systems has considerably raised the cost of military conflict. Both sides, the Arab states and Israel, fear that a continuation of an unrestricted arms race will be detrimental to their causes. While Israel fears the development of an 'Arab nuclear bomb', the Arab states apprehend that an overt Israeli nuclear capability will force them to turn their inter-Arab rivalries into a nuclear competition as well. Some of the regional candidates for nuclearization, notably Iraq and Iran, are more threatening to the rest of the Arab states than Israel, which has never threatened its neighbours with a nuclear attack, and its handful of opaque allusions to the nuclear factor have always been defensive in nature and related to the core interest of national existence. Therefore, some form of co-operative security arrangements may become desirable to prevent the high risks.

Finally, the international community has in recent years increasingly stressed the importance of global security regimes in the area of arms control. Because of their dependence on the West, regional actors must consider and respond to this. The Chemical Weapons Convention (CWC), the renewal of the NPT, the Missile Technology Control Regime (MTCR), the Comprehensive Test Ban Treaty (CTBT), discussions about a freeze in the production of fissionable materials, have all been on the international agenda. Yet the regional actors will evaluate such regimes in light of not only the present circumstances, but also past experience.

The key point here is to get the priorities right, first and foremost, to recognize the pre-eminence of political solutions over arms control arrangements. As has been demonstrated in the context of East–West relations, significant reductions in armaments followed superpower *détente, not* the other way round. Where hostility is intense and distrust is great, the prospects for massive reductions in weaponry remain slim. In the case of the Arab–Israeli conflict, or for that matter the Iraqi–Iranian rivalry, the political aspects of the disputes need to be seriously addressed before investing significant efforts in getting the parties to reduce their arsenals. The greater the diminution in mutual threat perceptions, the stronger the readiness to control the proliferation of non-conventional, and conventional, weaponry.

As the Arab–Israeli peace process advances, effort should be made to establish demilitarized zones, peace-keeping forces, enhanced surveillance, and verification measures, as well as Israeli–Palestinian and Israeli–Syrian security regimes. Once a stable and comprehensive settlement to the Arab–Israeli dispute has been reached, comprising the second tier of protagonists such as

Iraq, Libya, Algeria, and (non-Arab) Iran, and given ample time to prove its endurance and to produce a genuine sea-change of sentiments and attitudes at the grassroots level, far-reaching arms control regimes in the Middle East can be negotiated and established. But this may take a generation or more. The different rationales of non-conventional weaponry and programmes in the strategies of the various protagonists, the deeply entrenched distrust between them, and the lack of confidence in verification procedures mean that the Middle East may be one of the last regions to negotiate away its nuclear weapons.

7

The South Asian Nuclear Challenge

Ramesh Thakur

The tit-for-tat nuclear tests of May in south Asia destroyed the Indian summer of complacency induced by the indefinite extension of the nuclear Non-Proliferation Treaty (NPT) in May 1995 and the adoption of the Comprehensive Test Ban Treaty (CTBT) in September 1996. Not only did the 'in your face' tests represent the first substantial breach in the non-proliferation regime established by the NPT in 1968; they also called into question the tools available to great powers for protecting their hegemonic political status, and the modalities for converting international community norms into enforceable regimes.

In this chapter, after sketching the background to the tests, I propose to discuss the south Asian nuclear developments by answering four questions. Why did the two countries resort to open testing? Why were they wrong to do so? How can the fallout be contained? What is the south Asian–global nuclear nexus? The answers will be helpful in drawing appropriate lessons.

7.1. Background

Both India and Pakistan were threshold 'nuclear-weapon states' (NWS). They neither claimed nor admitted to possession of nuclear weapons; had not forsworn the nuclear-weapon option; had produced significant amounts of their own nuclear material or equipment; and refused to accept international control over them. But there were two significant differences between the Indian and Pakistani programmes. India's was driven primarily by civilian applications of nuclear technology and was always under the firm policy control of the civil bureaucracy and government; Pakistan's was begun principally with military goals in mind and operated mainly under the control of the military. In May 1998 India's tests were planned and carried out by civilian operatives, Pakistan's were controlled by the military.

Independent India searched for nuclear self-reliance as a matter of conviction. The Atomic Energy Commission (AEC) was established in 1948, and eight years later Canada and the USA agreed to help India to build a nuclear research reactor for power generation without requiring oversight by the International Atomic Energy Agency (IAEA). India took a militantly anti-NPT stance from the beginning for dividing the world into the nuclear haves and have-nots; Pakistan followed India's example in rejecting the treaty. Possible blurring of the line between nuclear power and nuclear-weapon capability was demonstrated by India's 12 kt 'peaceful nuclear explosion' (PNE) on 18 May 1974 (now dubbed 'Pokhran I'). Punitive economic and nuclear energy measures instituted by the West after the test complicated and delayed, but did not abort, India's search for nuclear self-sufficiency. The delay was an acceptable price for refusing to submit to full-scope international safeguards. By the 1980s, India was among the very few countries in the world, and the only developing country, to have mastered the complete nuclear fuel cycle, backed by a significant research and industrial infrastructure.

The subcontinent became a much-touted region for nuclear-weapons proliferation in the 1980s. Both India and Pakistan were assumed to have nuclear-weapon *capacity*, but not nuclear-weapon-power status.[1] The knowledge that China had acquired nuclear weapons made it an attractive option for India; a reasonable supposition that Pakistan was acquiring the capability and material to make nuclear weapons made it imperative for any Indian government to make the bomb too. India's PNE may equally be said to have made it imperative for Pakistan to acquire the forbidden fruit of nuclear knowledge for the immediate protection of Pakistan's honour and the greater glory of Islam. Yet in fact Prime Minister Zulfikar Ali Bhutto had ordered the Pakistani nuclear capability to begin in 1972, that is, two years earlier.[2] The decision flowed from India's role in the secession of East Pakistan in 1971; India's 1974 PNE merely confirmed Bhutto in the correctness of his decision.

Pakistan followed a two-track nuclear acquisition policy: a network of espionage and smuggling through front organizations and intermediaries in Western Europe and North America, and collaboration with China. In January 1972 Bhutto directed the cream of the country's nuclear physicists to build the bomb, and Pakistan set up a world-wide ring to buy, copy, or steal nuclear-weapon technology.[3] Reports of Pakistan's clandestine nuclear programme and successful enrichment of weapon-grade uranium gave fresh momentum to the debate in India. In 1986, army chief General K. Sundarji assured his soldiers that India was aware of a possible nuclear threat from potential adversaries and, in the event of a war, it would not be required to fight at a disadvantage.[4] In an interview with the Indian journalist Kuldip Nayar in 1987, the Pakistani scientist Abdel Qadir Khan claimed that Pakistan had already made nuclear weapons. He dismissed such a thing as a 'peaceful' nuclear programme, and boasted that, whereas it had taken India twelve years to assemble the bomb, Pakistan had done it in seven. In the context of the US threat to cut off aid, he insisted that testing was not necessary.[5]

The Khan interview was probably directed at three different audiences. To the domestic Pakistani constituency, it signalled determination to resist being browbeaten by outsiders on an issue of national security. To Washington the statement conveyed the hint that, as a necessary conduit for the successful pursuit of US policy on Afghanistan, Pakistan had sufficient leverage to be able to afford to be independent in its nuclear policy. The final target of the disclosure was India. Pakistan feared that the Indian Army's Operation Brass Tacks exercises being carried out at the time could be the prelude to an invasion. Khan effectively upped the ante to the nuclear level. India responded by announcing that the emerging nuclear threat from Pakistan had made it imperative for it to review its own nuclear options.

US intelligence sources were reporting that Pakistan had recently completed a 'workable' nuclear bomb. The development presented the USA with a 'hideous dilemma' in regard to the statutory requirement for a presidential certification that Pakistan did not possess 'explosive nuclear devices'.[6] Because non-proliferation concerns were subordinated to the policy of inflicting a bleeding wound on the Soviets in Afghanistan, intelligence evidence of Pakistan's nuclear-weapon programme was ignored and presidential certifications duly issued. Seymour Hersh has claimed that India and Pakistan were on the brink of a nuclear confrontation in May 1990. Pakistan had put together between six and ten nuclear weapons, and the US-supplied F-16s were prepositioned and armed for delivery—ready to launch on command. The crisis was defused with the dispatch of a high-level, blunt-talking US crisis management team to Islamabad and New Delhi.[7] In October 1990, following the stand-off and after the Soviet withdrawal from Afghanistan, the Bush administration was unable to certify Pakistan's non-nuclear status.[8]

The nuclear option became a party-political issue in India's elections. On 24 September 1989, the manifesto of the Bharatiya Janata Party (BJP) opted for 'optimum defence preparedness, including production of nuclear bombs and delivery systems'.[9] The BJP has been the party to gain the most in all elections since then. Its share of seats in the Lok Sabha (House of the People, India's lower house of parliament) jumped from 2 to 85 in 1989, and then again to 119 in 1991, 161 in 1996, and 178 in 1998.[10]

The 1995 NPT extension, opposed by India, had two further consequences. The next most important item to come on the agenda of global arms control was the CTBT. India suddenly realized that the CTBT would, in practical effect, severely circumscribe its long-held nuclear option. It would pose a technical barrier to the acquisition of new generations of weapons by the nuclear powers, but also to anything beyond India's existing rudimentary nuclear capability. Thereafter, India had four options: to become an overt NWS; to reject the NPT but sign the CTBT; to renounce the nuclear

option; or to maintain the threshold status while keeping open the nuclear
option.[11]

7.2. *Why the Tests were Understandable*

India and Pakistan were thus caught in a self-ratcheting nuclear capability
spiral which culminated in matching nuclear tests: five by India on 11 and 13
May 1998, and six by Pakistan on 28 and 30 May.[12] Pakistan's tests were conducted in the Chagai hills of Baluchistan near the Afghan border, India's at
the old testing ground in Pokhran in Rajasthan (hence 'Pokhran II'). Pakistan's
tests were almost guaranteed after India's (although, in order to draw Pakistan
inside the circle of international isolation, Indian cabinet ministers helpfully
issued some inflammatory statements on Kashmir between 13 and 28 May).
It will be useful, therefore, to examine India's calculations before looking at
the resulting pressures on Pakistan.

Why did India put itself on the wrong side of history? Unless we conclude
that almost all Indians are irrational, it is important to try to come to terms
with the strategic rationale behind India's tests. Advocates argued that nuclear
weapons would enhance India's international status, ensure its strategic
autonomy, erode great power hegemony, reinforce India's leading role in the
Third World and the Non Aligned Movement (NAM), expand its diplomatic
choices in global affairs, and stabilize relations with China and Pakistan. The
nuclear option was perceived as a cost-effective 'political force multiplier'
against China's nuclear-weapon status and conventional superiority. The
destabilizing effects of India's nuclear option on relations with Pakistan were
regarded by New Delhi as regrettable but acceptable 'collateral damage'.

7.2.1. Domestic

Explanations for the tests can be discussed at three levels of analysis: domestic, regional, and global. Domestically, the Vajpayee government had little to
lose and much to gain by tapping resurgent nationalist sentiment. The uneasy
coalition of a dozen parties had been lurching from one crisis to another in
negotiations before and after the formation of government. Its collapse often
seemed imminent, threatening yet another election. The tests enhanced the
government and prime minister's authority and bought a period of political
stability. Instant polls showed 91 per cent approval rating against 7 per cent
disapproval, even though 80 per cent of the people also believed that Pakistan
would follow suit.[13] The BJP argued that only it had the courage of nuclear
convictions that previous Congress and other governments demonstrably
lacked.

Domestic politics therefore cannot be discounted. But nor should their importance be exaggerated. The quest for nuclear self-reliance was begun by Jawaharlal Nehru; the nuclear option was kept open by all successive governments; the 1974 PNE was ordered by Indira Gandhi; the infrastructural preparations for weaponization were authorized by Rajiv Gandhi in the late 1980s;[14] P. V. Narasimha Rao decided upon a test in December 1995 only to retreat under intense international pressure; and the CTBT was rejected by I. K. Gujral in 1996. The continuity across governments has been underpinned by a broad and durable national consensus. 'Had the tests been motivated simply by electoral exigencies, there would have been no need to test the range of technologies and yields demonstrated in May. In the marketplace of Indian public life, a simple low-yield device would have sufficed.'[15] In the immediate aftermath of the tests, the more telling criticism was not that the tests had been conducted in 1998, but that they had not been conducted in 1995–6 when China and France were doing the same. Criticisms directed at India (and Pakistan) under those circumstances would have been substantially more muted and refracted.

While the frame of reference for India's nuclear option includes the global strategic configuration and China as well as Pakistan, the latter's tends to be far more unidimensional. Once India tested, therefore, no government in Islamabad could afford not to provide a matching riposte unless it wished to commit instant political suicide. Opposition leader Benazir Bhutto of the Pakistan's People Party alternately goaded Prime Minister Nawaz Sharif for not having the courage to match India,[16] and called upon Washington to launch punitive air strikes on India for its rogue behaviour.[17] The world tried to counsel restraint through a mix of carrots and sticks. The imposition of sanctions on Pakistan would be as swift and thorough as on India, it was made clear. But if Pakistan abstained from testing, a considerably enhanced package of economic and military assistance would be forthcoming.

However, pressure mounted on Sharif from the public, opposition politicians, and the military. A whispering campaign was begun, questioning whether Pakistan had nuclear capability after all. The nuclear scientists joined generals in assuring the people that they could match India's tests within days; the government just had to give them the order. President Bill Clinton made several phone calls to Nawaz Sharif, and sent high-level delegations to Pakistan. On 16 May, Sharif sent a letter to the economic summit of the G-8 expressing dismay at their lukewarm reaction to India's tests. A delegation was sent to Beijing, but reportedly failed to win positive security assurances against India. Delhi increased the pressure on Islamabad on 18 May when Home Minister Lal Krishna Advani (in charge of Kashmir) declared that Pakistan should come to terms with the new geopolitical reality and cease its militancy in Kashmir.[18]

In the face of such provocation from across the border and the lack of effective international action against India, the government was unable to withstand the domestic pressure despite international blandishments and threats. On 28 May, the government announced that Pakistan had conducted its first set of nuclear tests. Pakistan, said Sharif, had settled the score with India. On 11 June, following India's lead of 21 May, Pakistan formally announced that it too was imposing a unilateral moratorium on further testing.

7.2.2. Regional

If Pakistanis relied on strategic logic rather than emotion, they would realize that the pursuit of the nuclear option by India in itself was the firmest evidence of the lack of Indian designs on Pakistan. For Pakistan can achieve parity with India only through nuclear weapons. India faced strategic encirclement through nuclear-missile collusion between Pakistan, China, and North Korea.[19] Condemnations of Pakistan's tests were tinged with appreciation of its dilemma after India's tests. In effect, India was penalized for its 34 years of restraint (1964–98) *vis-à-vis* China while Pakistan received understanding for its inability to abstain for more than a fortnight. After the signing of the CTBT in 1996, Delhi faced the cruel choice of 'use it or lose it' on its long-held nuclear option. The threshold nuclear-weapon status did not allow India to match China's conventional or nuclear capability. But it enabled Pakistan to neutralize India's conventional military superiority. Pakistan's test of the Ghauri missile on 6 April 1998 destroyed India's natural strategic depth and produced much crowing in Pakistan about having achieved parity with India.[20]

The missile, of North Korean origin, was but the latest in a long series of proliferation-sensitive assistance from China and North Korea to Pakistan. In 1983 a US State Department report, based on CIA information, concluded that there was 'unambiguous evidence', including a secret blueprint for a nuclear bomb, that Pakistan was actively pursuing a nuclear-weapon programme. Moreover, 'China has provided assistance to Pakistan's program to develop a nuclear weapons capability'; Pakistan's blueprint was in fact made in China.[21] After the suspension of US aid in 1989, Pakistan built seven to twelve nuclear warheads 'based on the Chinese design, assisted by Chinese scientists and Chinese technology'.[22] According to unclassified data compiled by the US Senate Governmental Affairs subcommittee on international security and proliferation, China sold proliferation-sensitive weapons technology to Iran and Pakistan at least nine times between 1995 and 1997.[23] But Washington simply refused to act, always looking to fudge the issue because of uncertainty over just what could be done to rein in China and from a desire to avoid damaging the lucrative trade relationship. The sale of sensitive dual-use technology by and to firms that contributed generously to Clinton's re-election campaign only increased the cynicism in India about Washington's ability or willingness to see, let alone address, India's rapidly worsening geostrategic environment.

India had almost institutionalized its position as the world's permanent nuclear dissident. The 'strategy of ambivalence'[24] permitted the effective development of nuclear-weapon capability without incurring the adverse international penalties of open acquisition. The threshold stance was politically sustainable because it appeased the nuclear hawks without arousing the ire of the nuclear pacifists. It was militarily sustainable because it was viable as a policy of minimum deterrence based on calculated ambiguity—a reversal of the standard deterrence theory which rests on the credible certainty of nuclear retaliation.

As the nuclear calculus changed dramatically in the 1990s, Delhi decided to break out of the dead end of an unexercised nuclear option. Domestically, the political costs of *renouncing* the option climbed steeply. Internationally, the costs of *exercising* the nuclear option climbed equally steeply. With the end of the cold war, financial and political incentives increased to co-operate with the West, constrain nuclear programmes, and avert an arms race. But in the mean time, the costs of *maintaining* an unexercised nuclear option also mounted. Few were fooled by the pretence of an entirely peaceful nuclear programme; the rhetoric merely conveyed the impression of deviousness. In return for these escalating costs, India failed to gain military parity with China. Instead it paid the price for an option which helped Pakistan to level the military killing field with India. The *status quo* of maintaining the option without proceeding to a programme of tests and weaponization had become an unsustainable absurdity. For this reason, while the consensus behind the old option ensured that the equilibrium was a stable one for over three decades, by 1998 the equilibrium supporting India's policy of 'maintain but don't exercise' the nuclear option was dangerously unstable.

Without further testing but with the maintenance of the nuclear option, India in effect vindicated the Western world's policy of bracketing it with Pakistan, its traditional military counterweight. The pre-tests nuclear-weapon capability ensured that the reach of India's military power was confined to the subcontinent and that its nuclear ambitions were held in check by Pakistan. To achieve a reliable, effective, and credible retaliatory deterrent against China, a limited series of tests was necessary. On most objective measures, India should be paired with China, not Pakistan. The scale of differences between India and Pakistan is vastly greater than that between India and China. Of the three countries, India is also the least militarized (see Table). Maybe there are good reasons why India should accept a permanent second-class status *vis-à-vis* China and agree to being relegated to a mere subcontinental power while China is accorded the status of a major power globally. If so, the case has to

TABLE *The China–India–Pakistan Triangle, 1996*

	China	India	Pakistan
Population (mn)	1,222	967	137
GDP (US$ bn)	616	371	64
Defence personnel (000)	2,840	1,145	587
Defence expenditure (US$ bn)	38	10.4	3.7

Source: *The Military Balance 1997/98 (London: IISS, 1997).*

be made. So far, not only has the case not been made; it has not even been asserted, merely assumed.

From the perspective of an Indian security planner, the world was firmly in a denial mode on two vital questions. Why was China providing such assistance to Pakistan in the 1990s? The most likely answer is that China wished to constrict India to the status of a subcontinental power. What was India to do? By testing three different types of nuclear weapons (fission, low-yield, and fusion, with yields of 12, 0.2–0.5 and 45 kt respectively), India confirmed levels of scientific, technical, and organizational abilities that until then were merely suspected. Delhi sent three different signals to Pakistan and China. Pakistan's indigenous nuclear capability is still considerably behind India's (although its borrowed technological sophistication may be in advance of India's[25]). Delhi can yet, if it chooses, match China on the nuclear world stage. And the collusion between Beijing and Islamabad will not go unanswered forever. In this context, it is worth noting also that on 11 August 1998, the government approved the second phase of the development of the 2,500 km-range Agni missile, last tested back in February 1994.

7.2.3. Global

While the world had grown increasingly weary of India's tiresome complaints on the need for a timetabled framework for the elimination of all nuclear weapons, Indians had become increasingly more militant. There is more logical merit to India's complaint than was conceded by the five NWS, while their own assumptions are strongly ahistorical. The NWS are trapped in the fundamental paradox that while they justify their own nuclear weapons in national security terms, they seek to deny such weapons to anyone else for reasons of global security. Not a single country that had nuclear weapons when the NPT was signed has given them up. The circuit-breaker in the countervailing nuclear-weapon capability spiral is the United States. Because it insists on retaining nuclear weapons, Russia cannot reduce its stockpile to zero, China cannot be asked or expected to eliminate its stockpile, India will not surrender the option of acquiring nuclear weapons, and Pakistan did not buckle to outside pressure or reason. With the world's most powerful military arsenal at its disposal, Washington claims the right to deal with diffuse and uncertain threats since the end of the cold war with nuclear weapons. But it insists that India and Pakistan must forgo the nuclear option despite facing clearly identifiable threats to their security.

The gravest nuclear danger after the end of the cold war was not war between Russia and the United States, but the spread of nuclear weapons technology and materials to others beyond the five NWS. But the danger of horizontal proliferation could not be contained indefinitely by maintaining the *status quo* of five NWS. The post-CTBT equilibrium was a dynamic equation. Without concrete disarmament on the part of the NWS, the world was bound to slip back into real dangers of horizontal proliferation. The choice was between progress and reversal, not between progress and the *status quo*: a progression down to zero for the existing NWS, or the spread of nuclear weapons to other states.

This is not wisdom with hindsight.[26] The Canberra Commission had argued that the case for the elimination of nuclear weapons was based on three propositions: their destructive power robs them of military utility against other NWS and renders them politically and morally indefensible against non-NWS; it defies credulity that they can be retained in perpetuity and never used either by design or inadvertence; and their possession by some stimulates others to acquire them.[27] Its conclusion has been vindicated.[28] As argued by Jaswant Singh, the government's senior defence adviser, in a world of nuclear weapons, India's national security 'lies either in global disarmament or in exercise of the principle of equal and legitimate security for all'.[29] India's old posture of nuclear ambiguity was increasingly seen as a sham. Delhi was already paying the price through embargoes on high or dual-use technology transfers. It seems to have concluded that the marginal costs of additional sanctions are outweighed by the real gains in national security and pride.

The world tried to corner India through a constitutional trick by which the CTBT was rescued from the deadlocked Disarmament Conference in Geneva and approved by the UN General Assembly in New York. The resulting hardening of India's nuclear stance was predictable: 'Faced with US-led UN coercion, an isolated, sullen and resentful India is more likely to respond with an open nuclear programme, including a ... series of nuclear tests.'[30] General Sundarji changed his mind as a result of the UN manœuvre. With the indefinite extension of the NPT and the CTBT being 'bulldozed through', he joined the calls for India to conduct 'a few more tests'.[31] K. Subrahmanyam, a retired high-ranking defence official and another influential commentator, argued that the UN vote was evidence, not of India's international isolation, but rather of the inability of almost all others 'to defend the principle of sovereignty of nations against the onslaught of nuclear hegemons'. He too concluded that 'The time has therefore come for India to declare itself as a nation with an operational nuclear deterrent capability.'[32] I. K. Gujral, prime minister at the time of India's rejection of the CTBT, and an opponent of the 1998 nuclear tests, nevertheless explained the tests with reference to the CTBT manœuvre. In a speech in Paris on 25 September 1998, he argued that testing 'was practically forced on to India by the decision of the Nuclear Weapon States to force us against our will, and through an illegitimate stratagem, to be parties to the Comprehensive Test Ban Treaty'.[33]

7.3. *Why the Testing was Wrong*

Impressed by the oft-repeated argument that nuclear deterrence was responsible for the long peace between the cold war rivals, Indian and Pakistani strategists see no reason why the subcontinent should not enjoy a similar afterglow of weaponization. The theoretical argument on the beneficial effects of 'the measured spread of nuclear weapons' was made by Kenneth Waltz. In essence he argued that the likelihood of war decreases as deterrent and defensive capabilities increase, and that the newer NWS can and will be socialized into the responsibilities of their new status.[34] Stability-enhancing features of nuclear deterrence in general are given particular cogency in the case of Indo-Pakistan hostility by features distinctive to their relationship. For example, propinquity and the pattern of population distribution would leave either India or Pakistan vulnerable to fallout from its own weapons used against the other, thereby producing a measure of self-deterrence.[35] The wars between India and Pakistan have been exceptional in the degree of restraint shown by both sides. Neither has chosen to bomb civilian targets. A posture of threshold-NWS had already stabilized the *status quo*.[36] The tests merely 'brought into the open the nuclear reality that had remained clandestine for the past 11 years'.[37]

The putative benefits of universalized deterrence notwithstanding, India's security interests suffered substantial derogation in the aftermath of the nuclear tests. Its claims to nuclear-weapon status and permanent membership of the UN Security Council were dismissed. Instead of breaking free from the subcontinent, India found itself bracketed even more tightly with 'arch-rival'[38] Pakistan. The issue of Kashmir was internationalized as never before and Pakistan did its best to keep Kashmir on the world's front pages. Far from China being accepted as the point of departure for India's nuclear security policy, Beijing was actively courted by Washington as a co-manager to contain the nuclear situation in south Asia.[39]

This might suggest perhaps that Pakistan gained from the twin sets of nuclear tests. Such a conclusion would be erroneous. The tests by Pakistan set in train a chain of consequences whose net effect was to bring to a head the cumulative crises of governance and economy. Pakistan appeared set to become south Asia's first failed state. With insecure borders to the east and north, it was also being torn apart by armed sectarian and subnational groups whose violence threatened not just rival gangs but the nation as a whole. The agencies of law and order were delivering neither justice nor order. Costs were spiralling out of control, basic necessities were becoming unaffordable for ordinary people, the government was structurally incapable of reforming the tax system and collecting taxes and debts from the politically powerful, and international donors and creditors were leaving. That is, the economy had outspent itself, the state was inadequate to the tasks of governance, and people-centred 'human security' had collided head-on with state-based 'national security'.[40] Pakistan had become 'a nuclear country with a begging bowl'.[41]

The nuclear crisis compelled Western policy-makers to focus on the India–Pakistan security relativities in a way that they had not done before, with the result that for the first time the disparities began to register on their consciousness. They began to gain an inkling of why India is better paired with China than Pakistan. The latter's economic frailty was in sharp contrast to India's resilience. Pakistan's foreign exchange reserves were a paltry $1 billion against almost $30 billion for India. International sanctions severely dampened Pakistan's economic activity and risked its default on $30 billion debts. The China–Pakistan chain of proliferation as the central cause of security concern for India began to be acknowledged. There is no satisfactory answer from Washington as to why an authoritarian country with an unimpressive human rights record that has been the major proliferator of nuclear technology, expertise, and components to south Asia should be allowed to buy US satellites and other high technology[42] that is denied to the world's largest democracy with stringent export control regimes and no leakage of equipment or technology. Prime Minister Atal Behari Vajpayee went so far as to claim, in a major foreign policy address to the Asia Society in New York on 28 September, that India and the USA were 'natural allies' as the world's most populous and powerful democracies. However, the relationship was often damaged by Washington's unwillingness to 'appreciate and accommodate India's interests and concerns'. On south Asian issues, 'where our supreme national interests are involved, we encounter policy approaches from America that go contrary to our basic, irreducible security needs'.[43]

The deaths of a significant number of Pakistanis in the US air strikes on terrorist camps in Afghanistan in September further validated Delhi's long-standing complaints about active Pakistani involvement in cross-border state-sponsored terrorism in Kashmir.[44] Washington began to understand the complexities of linking Kashmir to any solution to the nuclear stand-off. Where outsiders had worried that Kashmir would be the flashpoint for the

next nuclear conflict, it transpired that nuclear testing had become the catalyst for raising the temperature over Kashmir.[45] In other words, while over the
short term India suffered the setback of being bracketed with Pakistan, over
the long term Pakistan risked the world waking to the realization that the two
countries are in different leagues.

7.3.1. The Flaws of Subcontinental Deterrence

The biggest immediate anxieties were of two types. First, there was fear of the
widening of the breach in the non-proliferation normative barrier in east Asia
(North Korea), west Asia (Iraq, Iran), and north Africa (Libya).[46] The repercussions for the drive to establish a nuclear-weapon-free zone in Central Asia
were also negative.[47] If south Asia's geostrategic environment was already bad,
it could only get worse with the proliferation of nuclear weapons more widely
around the region.

The second set of anxieties stemmed from the flawed analogy with the cold-
war deterrence. To begin with, cold-war deterrence was itself more unstable
than realized at the time. In the 1962 Cuban Missile Crisis, for example, the
US strategy was based on the best available intelligence which indicated that
there were no nuclear warheads in Cuba. In fact there were 162 warheads
already stationed there, including 90 tactical warheads, and the local Soviet
commander had taken them out of storage to deployed positions for use
against an American invasion.[48] The thought of India–Pakistan relations being
as stable as the cold-war deterrence is not very reassuring.

The geostrategic environment of the subcontinent had no parallel in the
cold war. India and Pakistan share a long border; the US–USSR did not. This
dramatically shortens the timeframe within which either country would have
to decide, in the midst of a tense crisis or war, whether or not to use nuclear
weapons. Contiguity permits India and Pakistan to meddle inside each other's
territory in numbers and on a scale that was not an option during the cold
war. The entire province of Kashmir is in dispute; the US–USSR had no direct
territorial dispute. India and Pakistan have fought three wars; Moscow and
Washington fought none. India shares a long border with nuclear China which
too is disputed. This introduces a three-way territorial conflict into the strategic equation which was never the case during the cold war.

The infrastructure of cold-war nuclear rivalry was underpinned by a
theory of deterrence. India and Pakistan are yet to develop doctrines that
would provide the rationale for numbers, types, location, dispersal, or use of
nuclear weapons.[49] The stability of cold-war deterrence rested on credible
second-strike retaliatory capability. Stockpiles, command and control centres,
and the military-political leadership were protected against a surprise
attack that could destroy all of them in one strike. Neither India nor Pakistan

has the most rudimentary survivable basing, command, control, communications and intelligence (C3I) systems in place. C3I systems are necessary for monitoring developments by the adversary through a widely dispersed and reliable surveillance and early warning system, establishing a fail-safe chain of command for the launch of nuclear strikes, protecting the nuclear arsenal against unauthorized or inadvertent use, and constructing a secure defence communications system that is robust enough to withstand an enemy first strike with all functions intact and co-ordinate a retaliatory launch. Civilian defence infrastructure will also have to be created. All this will take many years to develop and install. Moscow and Washington spread their stockpiles across land, sea, and air-based delivery platforms. The three-pronged dispersal added to detection and strike difficulties for the enemy and so buttressed second-strike capability. India and Pakistan lack this stabilizing triad of weapons platforms. India's challenge is the greater since, by its own account, its primary point of reference is China; yet Pakistan cannot be ignored.

Because of the lack of survivable forces and command centres, both countries are vulnerable to a pre-emptive first strike. But there is an inherent asymmetry in risk calculation. Pakistan cannot match India's conventional superiority. But a successful first strike could destroy India's nuclear capability and paralyse its conventional superiority, thereby allowing Pakistan to avenge the 1971 defeat and wrest Kashmir from India: or so a government in Islamabad might conclude.[50] Conversely, a government in Delhi might conclude that since reciprocal nuclear capability rules out their actual use by either country, it is safe to launch a military strike against Pakistan in punishment for its provocations in Kashmir. There is nothing in the history of the US–Soviet relationship to indicate the eventual outcome of such an adventure.

All these worries are exacerbated by political volatility and instability in both countries. Pakistan's government faces economic meltdown and political challenges from Islamist groups and the military. The Indian government is an unstable coalition of an intensely nationalist party sourcing legitimacy in religion and mythology, and a number of disparate parties pursuing different, and sometimes incompatible, regional agendas.

7.3.2. Economic Growth as the Currency of Power and Influence

India and Pakistan could find themselves in an unstable nuclear arms race which, as well as further entrenching the cold-war mentality in the two countries, drains scarce resources from economic development. In the fiftieth year of India's independence, India has the biggest number of poor and illiterate in the world. This gave rise to a distinctively Indian black humour: 'No food, no clothing, no shelter? No worry—we have the bomb'; or 'No water for the people to drink? Never mind, give them heavy water'. Nuclearization entails opportunity costs for development projects. Only the West and the major multilateral institutions dominated by the West (for example, the International Monetary Fund and the World Bank) can provide the necessary amounts of aid, credit, and investment. Both countries need US money, business, and technology to maintain the momentum of economic liberalization and modernization.

Claims of an economically inexpensive strategic posture that would produce miraculous tension reductions are dubious. Weaponization could prove to be a major cost-multiplier if India found itself competing with the nuclear powers. India's tests were surplus to requirements for defence against Pakistan. To catch up with China, India would have to conduct many more tests and establish the entire supporting infrastructure of a NWS. India's missile and space developments give it a substantial delivery system capability. Missiles can carry less explosives and are far less accurate than fighter bombers. But they are more difficult to intercept, and so can breach enemy defences more readily and rapidly than non-missile alternatives. Because of their lesser payload and accuracy, they are an expensive extravagance unless mounted with weapons of mass destruction; they are not intended to deliver 'bouquets of flowers'. India has ambitions in designing and building multistage ballistic rockets, remote sensing and communications satellites, and monitoring and guidance systems for putting different types of vehicles into space orbit. Developing these capabilities and adapting them to a nuclear posture will be expensive.

Nuclear weapons do *not* provide defence on the cheap; India's and Pakistan's direct costs (even before counting the opportunity costs) have barely begun. A recently published Brookings Institution study concluded that between 1940 and 1996, the US spent $5.5 trillion (in 1996 prices) on nuclearization (fifteen times India's GDP). In the distribution of these costs, of the total expenditure, only 7 per cent was on the weapons; another 7 per cent was on dealing with the effects of tests, storing radioactive wastes, and cleaning up the environment; and 86 per cent was on building delivery and C3I systems.[51] In a 1992 study, Brigadier Vijay K. Nair put the total projected cost over a ten-year period at Rs 6,835 crores, of which Rs 3,500 was C3I-related.[52] The most recent, post-south Asia tests and post-Brookings study analysis projects a total cost, at current prices, of Rs 40,000–50,000 crores over ten years, or Rs 5,000 crores per year.[53] Can India (let alone Pakistan) really afford to spend $1.2 billion just on nuclear weaponry and associated infrastructure per year for the next ten years? A 10 per cent increase in the defence budget in real terms over the next decade would be a crippling burden for any country. It will likely be even worse for Pakistan, where almost one-third of central government expenditure already goes on defence.

7.3.3. Diminished Prestige

I have argued elsewhere that fifty years after independence, India in the world was neither rich enough to bribe, powerful enough to bully, nor principled enough to inspire. India should renounce the nuclear option, I suggested, and concentrate on regaining international influence as a moral exemplar of a stable and prosperous democracy.[54] India could then aspire to great-power status like Japan and Germany through economic prowess and market power. The examples of North and South Korea are very instructive. Nuclear brinkmanship earns North Korea neither prestige, power, nor friends; an unambiguous non-nuclear status has not prevented South Korea from doing better on all three. Outsiders' negative images of India and Pakistan were not based on their non-nuclear status, but on daily power shortages, crowded roads, congested seaports, user-hostile airport facilities and personnel, almost non-existent sewage and sanitation facilities, child brides, dowry deaths, sectarian warfare, and so on.

Kanti Bajpai has identified several domestic costs of the nuclear option for India.[55] Relying on secrecy and obfuscation, a nuclear programme undermines the tradition of democratic accountability and contributes instead to a culture of lies and evasions. Shielding the programme from public scrutiny hides the inefficiency, malpractice, mismanagement, and dangers—and nuclear technology is unforgiving when things go wrong. The nuclear programme encourages excessive centralization of political control as well as obsessive secrecy. In turn both exacerbate bureaucratization and militarization. In addition, the scale of the peaceful nuclear energy programme is such as to have produced grave safety and environmental concerns.

India's and Pakistan's relations with other south Asian countries will be seriously aggravated with nuclearization. The regional security environment will deteriorate greatly, accompanied by a rise in levels of fear and distrust. The other countries could come to fear and loathe the two powers that cast the shadow of the mushroom cloud over south Asia. In the mean time, India's developing 'normalization' with China suffered a severe setback.

India's political credibility has been damaged in the wider Non-Aligned and Third World. India causes deep offence to many countries by implying that somehow everyone else has been duped by the nuclear powers. For example the South Pacific nations, having campaigned against French testing for thirty years,[56] do not believe that the CTBT is illusory. It will end totally and forever testing and the associated health and environmental risks. In insisting on marching to a nuclear tune that no one else wants to hear any more, India and Pakistan risk the CTBT being dead on arrival in the US Senate. Having been the targets of criticism at the annual meeting of the ASEAN Regional Forum (ARF) in Manila in July, India and Pakistan found themselves on the defensive also at the NAM summit meeting in Durban and the annual session of the UN General Assembly in New York in September. The Durban experience was particularly galling for India, the principal founding member of the anachronistic association.[57]

7.4. *What can be Done to Contain the Challenge?*

The nuclear tests by India and Pakistan raised the spectre of nuclear warfare that many thought had ended with the cold war. They also dashed hopes of progress towards universal disarmament. The world could not allow India and Pakistan to defy the anti-nuclear norm with impunity. But what to do?

7.4.1. Sanctions

The instinctive response was to impose sanctions. Under the Glenn-Symington Act, Washington had to apply sanctions on credits and credit guarantees, loans from US banks, and military assistance; and oppose loans from the IMF and the World Bank. Japan, the subcontinent's biggest donor, also suspended all foreign aid. Other Western countries followed to varying lesser degrees. Unfortunately, sanctions faced three sets of difficulties: the historical record, moral equivalence, and practical calculations.

The case against comprehensive generalised sanctions, based on a mass of historical evidence, appears to be very strong. They were discredited in the 1930s when imposed on Italy in punishment for its invasion of Ethiopia, and again when applied against the Ian Smith regime in Rhodesia in the 1960s. Sanctions do not work because the target country can choose from a range of sellers in the international market-place: it is virtually impossible to secure universal participation in embargoes.[58] It is difficult to police their application even in countries that have agreed to participate. The incentive to make large profits by circumventing sanctions is usually more powerful than the motive for enforcing them, and a variety of means and routes exist to camouflage sanctions-busting contacts. Sanctions can damage producer-groups in the countries imposing them, for example farmers. They can inflict considerable pain upon innocent countries in the neighbourhood. And the besieged country itself can actually emerge stronger overall, or in strategic sectors like defence, by pursuing a determined policy of import-substitution. Even the moral premises of sanctions are open to serious question. The imposition of sanctions is frequently accompanied by sentimentality and sanctimony. Yet sanctions are neither effective, non-violent, nor clean as a diplomatic tool. Rather, they are blunt and crude. They do cause death and destruction, sometimes on a large scale, through 'structural violence': starvation, malnutrition, the spread of deadly diseases, and the lack of adequate supplies of medicine. Their primary victims are innocent civilians, mainly women and children.

The five nuclear powers, who preach non-proliferation but practice deterrence, have no moral authority to impose sanctions. Their stockpiles are in defiance of the World Court's opinion of a legal obligation to nuclear disarmament; India and Pakistan breached no international treaty, convention or law by testing. For the five NWS to impose sanctions on the nuclear gate-crashers is akin (on this issue) to outlaws sitting in judgement, passing sentence, and imposing punishment on the law-abiding. The whiff of hypocrisy in statements from those who have nuclear weapons, or shelter under them, robs their condemnation of much value in shaping the nuclear choices of India and Pakistan.[59]

Outsiders' self-interest lies in assisting south Asia's economic growth. Pakistan's predicament after India's tests was better understood than India's before. Therefore there was little enthusiasm to impose sanctions on Pakistan. Yet it was far more vulnerable. India's size, resources, and depth give it enough resilience to withstand sanctions to a much greater extent than Pakistan. Rajagopala Chidambaram, Chairman of India's AEC, argues that India is self-reliant, understood 'not as self-sufficiency per se but as providing immunity against technology-denial. I don't think sanctions will have too much of an effect.'[60] Moreover, at a time when the world community was mounting emergency rescue efforts in countries besieged by currency and stock markets collapse, it made little sense to try to push Pakistan towards the same precipice of economic, social, and political meltdown.

The dilemma faced by outsiders was this. A moderate response would be self-negating. The nuclear hawks would feel vindicated, saying that India was now being treated with respect because it had nuclear weapons, so these should be openly deployed in numbers. To accept India and Pakistan as NWS would reverse three decades of non-proliferation policy and victimize many countries that had signed the NPT and CTBT on the understanding that the number of NWS would be limited to five.[61] A harsh response would be self-fulfilling. The hawks would argue that a friendless India that is the target of hostile international attention needs an arsenal of nuclear weapons to defend its interests.

7.4.2. Leading by Example

The preaching of exhortations and the coercion of sanctions need to be buttressed with the force of example. It is difficult to convince some states of the lack of utility of nuclear weapons when all who have such weapons insist on keeping them. By eliminating its stockpile of nuclear weapons, the United States would prove that national security and foreign policy independence can be preserved without nuclear-weapon capability. Other NWS could then follow, and potential proliferators would be most impressed by such a levelling down of the security field. Conversely, the spread of nuclear weapons to other countries would erode the US advantage as the world's dominant power, and multiply the number of potential trouble spots where the United States might be called upon to intervene. As Thomas Schelling noted many years ago, 'the best way to keep weapons and weapons-material out of the hands of non-governmental entities is to keep them out of the hands of national governments'.[62]

In present circumstances, there are some security arguments for the United States, Russia, and China to keep nuclear stockpiles even while working more seriously to reduce their numbers. But the continued possession of nuclear weapons by Britain and France seems to be driven more by historical pride and a quest for status than by genuine national security concerns. A dramatic gesture by either of these states towards genuine nuclear disarmament might be able to reverse the nuclearization trend before India and Pakistan come to blows. The colloquial response in the subcontinent was that Britain should put up or shut up. Either nuclear weapons do confer power and prestige, in which case sovereign states are entitled to pursue this option. Or they do not, in which case Britain would not lose anything by giving up its nuclear weapons.

7.4.3. The UN Card

India has long campaigned for a permanent seat on the UN Security Council and has justified its nuclear programme by pointing to the total coincidence of nuclear-weapon status with permanent membership of the Security Council. Ironically, India has itself broken the link: there is universal agreement that India's prospects of becoming a permanent member have nose-dived as a result of the nuclear tests. Britain could complete the break by becoming non-nuclear. Its moral authority in the world would be greatly increased. Conversely, in the absence of such leadership, more questions will be raised as to why Britain should remain a permanent member, since the possession of nuclear weapons is no longer a sufficient criterion.

An alternative solution to the impasse would be to tie India's permanent membership to renunciation of the nuclear option.[63] Diplomatically and economically, non-aligned India was on the margins of the defeated and the losers in the cold war. India's very prickliness on sovereignty issues—nuclear and economic nationalism—is evidence of fragile self-confidence and low world esteem. Permanent membership of the Security Council could tip the balance between incentives and disincentives in India's nuclear option calculus. It would confer global status. Without in any way diminishing national security, it would enhance India's international prestige. From the point of view of the world community, the gains would include widening the representational credentials of permanent members, separating the status of great power from the possession of nuclear weapons, and achieving significant progress in non-proliferation objectives: all without any corresponding cost.

There would be many advantages to India in signing the NPT as part of a package deal. Joint accession of the NPT by India and Pakistan would freeze the military balance more or less permanently in India's favour. Renouncing the nuclear-weapon option would allow India to reclaim the moral high ground in moves towards nuclear arms control and disarmament. It would also facilitate access to nuclear technology for peaceful purposes. It would make it possible for the Indian government to finesse nuclear hawks while delighting the nuclear doves by joining the NPT regime. It would also please the hawks, for permanent membership of the Security Council would put Pakistan in its place while giving India a seat alongside China at the high table in the UN system.

7.5. Lessons

In their addresses to the annual session of the UN General Assembly in September 1998, the prime ministers of India and Pakistan expressed a qualified willingness to sign the CTBT and accede to the non-proliferation regime. The contours of a possible agreement are taking shape. The nuclear new deal will be based on six crucial lessons.

First, no matter how dominant, economics has not totally replaced geopolitics. Strategic calculations, raw politics, and emotions have driven the nuclear policies of India and Pakistan even at the cost of economics. The old hard questions of nuclear proliferation, nuclear conflict, and nuclear disarmament are back on the international security agenda.

Second, the vital interests of key actors have to be accommodated in any security regime, otherwise it will unravel. The world was dismissive of India's security concerns in drafting the clauses of the CTBT and of Pakistan's security dilemma once India tested. Outsiders underestimated India's and Pakistan's ability to break out of the attempted strangulation of the nuclear-weapon option, and overestimated their own capacity to coerce them into submission. International regimes, if they are to avoid falling into the feel-good trap, must rest on conjunctions of interests. If the possession of nuclear weapons is accepted in the arsenals of some states, then non-proliferation cannot be forced on those who reject the treaties underpinning it: 'India cannot accept a semi-colonial and inferior status as a nation whose security prescriptions are determined for it by others.'[64]

Third, non-proliferation and disarmament are two sides of the same anti-nuclear coin. If India and Pakistan are committed to a nuclear-free world, as they claim, then they need to be told clearly that their tests were a major setback to the anti-nuclear cause. The five nuclear powers have also to be called to account for their complacency and go-slow tactics on nuclear disarmament. On 26 September 1988, the US conducted a fourth subcritical nuclear test to assure the safety and reliability of its nuclear stockpile. The US Energy Department announced that it plans to conduct two more subcritical tests in 1998 and more in 1999.[65] Washington continues to argue that because no self-sustaining nuclear chain reaction is triggered, subcritical tests are not tests of nuclear explosive devices and do not violate the CTBT. Anti-nuclear groups around the world, including in the USA, respond that they do violate the anti-testing 'norm' and do undermine the legitimacy and authority of the CTBT. Through subcritical testing under the benign–sounding, $4.5 billion per annum 'Stockpile Stewardship' programme, new 'nuclear weapons can be developed while avoiding politically unpopular nuclear explosions'.[66] The 1998 NAM summit meeting, noting the complexities arising from the nuclear tests in south Asia, underlined the need to work even harder to achieve the objectives of disarmament, 'including the elimination of nuclear weapons'.[67] The norm is anti-nuclear, as embodied in the NPT, including Article VI; the CTBT is the anti-testing expression of the broader norm; the self-serving conflation of the anti-nuclear norm into an anti-testing norm by the five NWS does not withstand critical scrutiny. This is also the core of the abolitionist case. Even if we concede that nuclear weapons confer some security gains, these have to be assessed against the costs, risks, and alternatives. In particular, the likelihood of the usability of nuclear weapons must be weighed against the costs of the political chain reaction of nuclear-weapon status. That is why a group of eight non-nuclear countries, in contradistinction to the G-7, issued a joint foreign ministers' declaration to the five NWS *as well as* to India, Pakistan, and Israel calling for an end to nuclear arms.[68]

Fourth, the consequences of the tests have finally registered the reality of what many have been arguing for years: nuclear weapons confer neither power, prestige, nor influence. Domestic support for the tests has been steadily waning since the initial outbursts of euphoria.[69] South Asians are less secure today than before May 1998. History and geopolitics make the south Asian nuclear equation more unstable than deterrence between Moscow and Washington during the cold war. Nuclear weapons are not going to help Islamabad and New Delhi combat internal insurgency, cross-border terrorism, or parasitical corruption. Their economic programmes have been disrupted. Nuclear weapons cannot help India and Pakistan solve any of their real problems of poverty, illiteracy, and malnutrition.

Fifth, sanctions are too blunt to be useful diplomatic instruments. The contrast between the policy of constructive engagement with China and destructive disengagement with south Asia was painfully obvious. Having imposed sanctions, Washington finds itself imprisoned in the classic termination trap:[70] how to lift sanctions without appearing to back down, on the one hand, or rewarding 'bad' behaviour on the other. Often, sanctions are maintained because policy-makers cannot decide on the best time to lift them. Having already paid the international price for testing, India sees no reason to revert to the *status quo ante* on high-technology access in return for signing the CTBT and joining the global non-proliferation regime. Washington would find it difficult to lift the restrictions on access to advanced technology without appearing to reward India for the tests.

Sixth, in the clash between new strategic realities and selective puritanism, the latter has to give way: that which has been tested may be detested, but cannot be de-tested.[71] The government's official paper tabled in parliament on 27 May declared simply but firmly: 'India is a nuclear weapon state. This is a reality that cannot be denied. It is not a conferment that we seek; nor is it a status for others to grant'.[72]

7.6. Conclusion

The new deal will have to be based on these six lessons. The challenge is 'to reconcile India's security imperatives with valid international concerns regarding nuclear weapons'.[73] The proliferation deed is done. Instead of demanding the impossible feat of untesting, it is better to accentuate the positive. Having come out of the nuclear closet, India and Pakistan can move from moralizing about nuclear disarmament by others to engaging each other in meaningful arms control negotiations.

The one-dimensional nature of Pakistan's security policy means that its nuclear posture lacks ballast and texture. The sense of nuclear drift in India is being replaced with a stress on responsibility and restraint. The rudiments of its strategic posture have begun to emerge since the shock tests of May: an acknowledgement of the nuclear reality *vis-à-vis* Pakistan; a 'minimum' deterrent against China based on a 'recessed' or 'virtual' deployment of nuclear weapons; unilateral promises of no use of nuclear weapons against non-nuclear states and no first use against nuclear adversaries; unilateral moratorium on any further testing; a willingness to convert this into a binding obligation under the CTBT in return for a satisfactory outcome of discussions with 'key interlocutors', meaning largely the United States; and a commitment to work towards a universal, non-discriminatory nuclear weapons convention.

Difficulties remain. Just what is a 'credible minimum deterrent' that would dissuade nuclear blackmail and coercion and permit second-strike nuclear retaliation? The history and logic of nuclear weapons show little respect for minimalists. Can the contradictions between 'recessed/virtual deterrence' and 'no first use policy' be resolved? The latter requires a credible second-strike retaliatory capability—the capacity to absorb a first strike by enemy forces and still be able to launch delivery missiles and precision munitions at designated times on critical targets, such as command and control centres and communication and energy nodes. India will need to develop the Agni missile and extend its range from 2,500 to 5,000 km. In the strategic triad, the best platform for achieving such a capability is strategic submarines. This is especially relevant for India because of historical and geopolitical realities. Britain ruled India because Britannia ruled the waves.

The genuine security concerns of India and Pakistan can be met without overt nuclear deployment: tested capability is enough to assure deterrence. Two important firebreaks can be constructed in the form of separating warheads from delivery systems, and storing delivery vehicles separately from launch sites. In return for a tacit acceptance of the new reality and the lifting of sanctions, both India and Pakistan must sign the CTBT: unilateral moratoria are less helpful than legally binding accession. If they want the full range of dual-technology assistance, they can sign the NPT as well.

Renouncing the nuclear option would enable India to focus its energies on economic growth as today's currency of power and reclaim the disarmament moral high ground. Ironically, India could probably maintain the nuclear option at greatly reduced political cost from within the NPT. The flow of enabling technologies, *matériel,* and expertise in the nuclear power industry can be used, through strategic prepositioning of materials and personnel, to build up 'virtual' nuclear-weapon capability that can be weaponized quite rapidly following the political decision to do so. That is, a non-NWS can, within the constraints of the NPT, build up the necessary infrastructure to provide it with the 'surge' capacity to upgrade to nuclear weapons within the timeframe of a crisis degenerating into conflict.

The anti-CTBT consensus in India rests on a deliberate, but very successful, campaign of disinformation which discredited the regime. The domestic political difficulties are thus of the Indian government's own making. Unlike the NPT, the CTBT is universal and non-discriminatory. Having carried out the tests, India need no longer have security worries about signing the CTBT. Both A. P. J. Abdul Kalam, head of the Defence Research and Development Organisation (DRDO), and AEC Chairman Chidambaram have publicly said that further nuclear tests are not necessary from a scientific and technical perspective, and that signing the CTBT would not pose any problem for India's nuclear status.[74] The treaty is not linked to a timetabled commitment to total nuclear disarmament. But non-proliferation is worth pursuing in its own right. In doing so the CTBT does not jeopardize nuclear disarmament. It will permit the nuclear powers to keep their existing arsenals but prevent them from developing new generations of nuclear weapons. By insisting on linkage, India ensures that the best (a nuclear-weapon-free world) becomes the enemy of the good (an end to vertical plus horizontal proliferation).

The world matched India's folly of testing with a reciprocal foolishness of instant condemnations. There was no serious analysis of either principles or justice, on the one hand; or efficacy and realism, on the other. In terms of principles, India's complaints are unanswerable. One would not think that the person saying that nuclear-weapon capability 'is not necessary to peace, to security, to prosperity, to national greatness or personal fulfilment'[75] is the president of the country that has conducted by far the largest number of nuclear tests, maintains by far the largest stockpile of nuclear weapons, and insists on a continued programme of subcritical testing.

In terms of realism, condemnations that wilfully refused to acknowledge India's and Pakistan's minimum security requirements in their immediate geostrategic environment were always likely to aggravate rather than ease tensions. India's nuclear tests resulted, in addition to domestic political calculations, from the actions of China and Pakistan in the region, the inaction of the five NWS globally, and a craving for international recognition. In these circumstances, for the UN Security Council, dominated by the five permanent members who are also the five NWS, to condemn eleven Indian and Pakistani tests—when not one of the over 2,000 previous tests had ever been so condemned by the Council—inflamed opinion in the subcontinent. The official Indian response was to point out that no other NWS had supported the World Court advisory opinion on the illegality of nuclear weapons; that India's record of restraint on export of nuclear technologies and commodities was better than that of some of the five NWS; that unlike India's unconditional commitment to a nuclear weapons convention, the five NWS were not prepared to commit themselves to decisive and irreversible steps towards nuclear disarmament; that instead they were all engaged in programmes of modernization of their nuclear arsenals; and that India's tests had been restricted to 'the minimum necessary to maintain what is an irreducible component of our national security calculus'.[76] The Security Council's presidential statement of 14 May, strongly deploring India's tests, was rejected by Delhi as 'completely unacceptable to us'.[77] Security Council Resolution 1172 of 6 June 1998, condemning India's and Pakistan's tests and demanding that they stop, was similarly dismissed by Indian spokesmen as 'coercive and unhelpful in respect of the objectives it seeks to address'.[78]

The world has to decide whether to engage with India as a responsible NWS or a rogue regime and, if the latter, then to accept the risk of a self-fulfilling prophecy. If China, India, Pakistan, and the US understand each other's bottom lines, and respect each other's legitimate concerns on national security, regional proliferation, and global disarmament, then we may still pull back from the nuclear brink yet again.

8

Nuclear Disarmament: The Case for Incrementalism

Harald Müller

8.1. *Introduction*

The present controversies surrounding nuclear weapons do not only express different interests of nuclear-weapon states and some non-nuclear-weapon (and threshold) states, but they are also expressions of two different strategies towards nuclear disarmament: a plea for prompt, far-reaching measures such as a nuclear-weapons convention or a time-bound framework for nuclear disarmament that would fix the final date for arriving at a nuclear-weapons-free world here and now; and a preference for a step-by-step approach that would start from an understanding that nuclear disarmament is the final objective, but would not try to impose a time-scale to arrive there. Both prompt disarmers and incrementalists start from the same assumptions:

1. Nuclear weapons should be abolished because, their intended, accidental, erroneous, or unauthorized launch is a matter of time as long as they are around.

2. They fulfil plainly the criteria for inhumane weapons that must be banned, such as their inherent incapability to discriminate between combatants and civilians and their causing unnecessary and irreparable pain to humans, namely through long-lasting radiation damage.

3. The legal obligation to abolish them exists, in Article VI of the NPT as interpreted by the Principles and Objectives adopted 1995 when this Treaty was extended permanently, and by the 1996 legal advice of the International Court of Justice.

4. The existence of nuclear weapons implies a discrimination that cannot be maintained in the long term: the logic of non-proliferation is also a logic of nuclear disarmament. If the latter fails, the former will become unviable.

8.2. *The Strategy of Prompt Nuclear Disarmament*

Those who derive from this argumentation the request for immediate and unambiguous prescriptions, such as the prompt negotiation of a nuclear-weapon convention or a time-bound framework for nuclear disarmament point to additional facts to strengthen their case.

First, the past record of the nuclear weapon states has not been too encouraging of the hope that the relatively vague stipulations of the NPT would lead to the objective of complete nuclear disarmament. For almost twenty years, the trend was more rather than less nuclear weapons, including qualitative improvements. Likewise, the present stagnation of the START process is a sign that, without an unequivocal commitment that would force certain timelines, real progress cannot be hoped for.

Second, the considerable enhancement of the quality of the commitment of the non-nuclear weapon states that rests in the indefinite duration the NPT assumed in 1995 makes the asymmetry of obligations even more unbearable. The nuclear-weapon states have now to strengthen the quality of their commitment in an equivalent way.

Third, the recent tests of the south Asian *de facto* nuclear-weapon states have revealed that the non-proliferation regime is under considerable stress. Without quick and determined disarmament measures, proliferation will again become the main trend.

8.3. *The Case for Incrementalism*

Those who plead for an incremental strategy towards nuclear disarmament see a major difference between nuclear weapons and other types of arms that have been prohibited so far: nuclear weapons have become so well integrated into the military structures, security policies, and, most important of all, processes of thinking about security in the world's major powers, and even many of their non-nuclear-weapon-states allies, that it is politically and socially virtually impossible to remove the nuclear factor from this security policy overnight. There are several factors which contribute to the petrification of this situation.

There is, first of all, a genuine sense that nuclear weapons have prevented war in the past and are essential for providing national and/or international security in the future. The following security functions are claimed:

(1) to provide a deterrent against nuclear attack (this function is proclaimed by all five official nuclear weapon states and at least two of the threshold states)

(2) to provide a deterrent against non-nuclear attack by weapons of mass destruction, notably biological weapons. This may include a deterrent umbrella over intervening armed forces 'out of area', as in the Gulf War.[1]

(3) to provide a deterrent against massive and overwhelming conventional attack (this purpose was the motivation of the Western alliance to maintain strong nuclear forces, not only at the strategic, but also at the tactical level; it appears to be behind the recent change in Russian nuclear doctrine and is more extensively discussed in Russia in the context of NATO enlargement, and presumably plays a role in the considerations of the threshold countries).[2]

This feeling is not confined to the narrow circles of security experts, strategists, military officers, and policy-makers; polls taken in nuclear weapon states (and threshold countries) usually show large majorities for the maintenance of national arsenals, though there appears sometimes a readiness to throw them away if all nuclear possessors do so. One can make a case against each of these three supposed functions of nuclear weapons (see below). The point is, however, that there are people who believe genuinely in these functions.

The second factor is an understanding that the national status depends on nuclear possession. In the light of the experiences of the nuclear age, this notion is highly contestable. To the nuclear-weapon states, their arsenals have not afforded great additional powers (with the exception of the USA, all the present P-5 had their permanent seats before acquiring nuclear weapons). Bi-polarity during the cold war rested largely on conventional resources of power: geography, population, technological prowess, economic strength, organization, conventional armed forces, and power projection. Nuclear weapons neutralized each other, not more. The former Soviet Union did not survive a change in the correlation of technology, economic strength, conventional armed forces, even though nuclear arsenals did not vary. And nuclear arms have not helped Britain or France to enhance their status, prestige, and real influence; their special position depended very much on their past as world powers, and their particular position in integrating Europe.

The same applies for the proliferants. Israel's position is mainly dependent on its impressive and repeatedly proven conventional superiority over its Arab neighbours. India's weight in world politics has rather diminished than grown after 1974, when it tested a nuclear device. Its recent resurgence has rested on domestic economic reforms and its capability of regional power projection, not on its nuclear capabilities. Pakistan has gained nothing at all by its nuclear activities, but has rather been marginalized through the end of the Soviet presence in Afghanistan. The powerlessness of nuclear weapons to acquire influence for their possessors and to protect their core values, though, has been demonstrated by South Africa's apartheid regime.

Conversely, the two countries that have most gained in terms of international status and influence over the last decades, Japan and Germany, stand out by their renunciation of weapons of mass destruction. They have focused instead on developing economic and environmental skills. Also, the international position of South Africa, Argentina, and Brazil has risen markedly after the former dismantled its nuclear arsenal (which had done nothing to diminish international contempt for the apartheid regime) and the latter two took an unequivocally non-nuclear position. For these reasons, it can be argued that the 'status' value of nuclear weapons is in decline.

The third factor consists of the vested interests of the nuclear-weapon complexes, where thousands of jobs and careers depend on the production, or at least the maintenance, of those horrifying arms. In democratic systems, local constituencies and their representatives add to the intra-bureaucratic lobbying power of these complexes. One should keep in mind that this vested interest is normal for every industrial, scientific, and bureaucratic formation. We should not be surprised or offended that we find it in this sector as well. The right answer is to devise alternative perspectives for the people and organizations concerned.

The point here is not to state that, for these reasons, complete nuclear disarmament is impossible. Rather, it should be emphasized that it is facing serious and formidable obstacles that must be overcome. Given that nuclear arms are embedded in structures of established politico-strategic thinking, and in social complexes with vested interests, it becomes clear that a merely legal approach to the problem will not be crowned by success. The suggestion that national delegations just sit down and negotiate a nuclear weapons convention that will do away with the arsenals tends to ignore the resistance existing in precisely those political centres that will be required to make the biggest changes away from the *status quo*.

In addition, the history of arms control negotiations shows that they do not usually follow preset timetables. This might be possible for relatively simple, straightforward measures, but nuclear disarmament, for the reasons elaborated above, is a complex issue. Pleasant and (more probably) unpleasant surprises, delays, and, possibly, even unexpected accelerations are likely to occur. Setting strict timetables is thus not only unrealistic, it makes even more sure that commitments will not be kept—nuclear disarmament may suffer rather than profit from such time-induced breaches of obligations.

The key is that populations, experts, strategists, and policy-makers in nuclear-weapons and threshold states must be convinced that the conditions are ripe for the dismantlement of the arsenals. At least, enough of them must feel this way if a 'winning coalition' in the domestic debate is to be formed. In other words, the concerns, arguments, and interests on which their present position rests must be taken seriously, and must be addressed one by one to win them over. This is a far cry from the attitude of those who call for immediate negotiations on abolition. This call does not take seriously the positions of those who must be turned around. It is trivial, but still needs to be recognized, that nuclear disarmament can go forward only *with* the nuclear-weapon states, not *against* them.

8.4. *The Key for Abolition: Tackling the Security Equation*

The key issue remains, of course, security. Nuclear weapons are a strategically important part of the whole cobweb of security relations, and their abolition cannot be sensibly envisaged without a thorough reshaping of this cobweb.

8.4.1. Conventional Prevention Against Nuclear Rule-Breakers

Security needs would be fulfilled if and when a state, a protector allied to this state, or, alternatively, the international community within a credible collective security framework, possesses the conventional means to prevent a rule-breaker from exploiting its nuclear assets for political or military purposes. This presumes that the defending state, its ally, or the international community will be able to:

(1) acquire timely intelligence on the location of weapons, materials, and facilities well before they can be put to use;
(2) procure reliable and timely tactical intelligence on the intention to use, or to weaponize and use, or to produce, weaponize, and use.

The time tolerance for such intelligence varies with the status of the respective nuclear weapon programme. It is very short for ready-made weapons, more relaxed for weapon-grade material that must be put into a weapon before it can be militarily employed, and still more relaxed for a situation where the proliferator has yet to produce such material. This suggests that time-lags for intelligence acquisition will be shortest for former nuclear-weapon states that might have hidden a few remaining warheads in the process of disarmament; middle-level for the same states (because they might also have hidden some weapons-usable material), countries with large fuel cycle activities, and countries where operating enrichment or reprocessing facilities are discovered; and most relaxed towards countries where the construction of such facilities is discovered well before they enter the operational phase, such as is presently the case with North Korea. The international climate surrounding the alleged rule-breaker, in such a situation, would be uncomfortable, to put it mildly. It is likely that vast intelligence resources would be focused on the country, with the purpose of detecting traces of nuclear weapons, and to detect in advance any signs of an intention to use them. Military means for quick intervention would be on high alert on a permanent basis, in order to:

(1) take the necessary decisions, in accordance with international law, particularly the Charter of the United Nations, to act against the targets;
(2) deploy the conventional assets necessary to conduct such military action;
(3) mobilize military manpower trained and capable to fulfil the mission;
(4) conduct such action against armed resistance with a reasonably good prospect of success;
(5) avoid intolerable collateral damage to the innocent civilian population, and trans-border consequences which such action might engender.

Obviously, this is a very tall order. It is questionable whether these conditions will ever be met with sufficient confidence. The question is not so much whether, in reality, the defender possesses these necessary qualities, but whether he will have faith in his capacity to get the job done. As will be explored in more detail further below, the psycho-political factor tends to be more important than 'hardware' aspects as we approach a non-nuclear world.

Starting with a scenario that a former nuclear-weapon state has succeeded in hiding a few nuclear weapons, the challenge to intelligence would be considerable. Nuclear weapons cannot be hidden in the pocket, but they are not all that bulky either, depending on the type. It is doubtful that without human intelligence (defectors) either the existence or the location of such weapons could be identified with any degree of confidence. Even if such human intelligence is available, hints of defection might force the rule-breaker to move the weapons to another location and then to open up for inspection. Panic movements may not go without detection, but, on the other hand, coolly planned and conducted movement may meet success, if it is realized early enough after defection for the other side to have no opportunity to reallocate and reinforce intelligence.

Hidden weapons must be deployed to their launchers, presumably after some movement. If the rule-breaker had to expect requests for prompt inspection, it would be unwise to store the weapons too closely to the delivery vehicles, because that is where inspectors would presumably start their search. Moving hidden weapons, mounting them on the launchers, and preparing them for launch is a complex task that would consume enough effort and time to be detected by national means of intelligence, including human intelligence on the ground, high-flying reconnaissance aircraft, and satellite. Unfortunately, such intelligence, even if available, is no guarantee of detection. The experiences of the Gulf War, with, after a few days, unchallenged air superiority by the alliance, show that even under such favourable circumstances the location of mobile ballistic missiles and aircraft that can be moved between airfields and shelters is a difficult task that will be accomplished over the course of several weeks or months of combat, but not at the speed and with the reliability needed to deal with such time-critical targets as nuclear weapons.

The crux of the matter is that hardly anything could re-establish full confidence once allegations based on human intelligence of this kind were made. On the other hand, the authenticity of such intelligence could also not be verified in many cases without some doubts remaining—unless convincing photographic, documentary, or tape-recording material accompanied defectors' contentions. People can have all kinds of motivations to blame their former employers. Thus the verification of alleged human intelligence might be a 'Catch-22' and neither establish the knowledge needed for the preparation of prevention nor provide enough evidence to discard the necessity for such preparations.

Military prevention to deal with ready-made nuclear warheads will be an option that will be inevitably discussed and considered when evidence for such an act of nuclear rule-breaking obtains in a non-nuclear world. But given the doubts surrounding such actions, such military action will be an undesirable last resort, to be taken out of despair, and not a well-thought-out strategy for the non-nuclear community.

The second possibility to be prevented is the possession by suspect states of weapons-grade fissile material. Such material may be accumulated through not disclosing stocks during the disarmament phase, by clandestinely or openly diverting it from the civilian fuel cycle, or by producing it in clandestine facilities not discovered by international inspection and verification.

Starting with the latter two assumptions, the main task for the international community would be to make sure that a verification regime was strict enough to prevent both the diversion of material from the fuel cycle and the operation of clandestine facilities. This would require intrusive inspection and continuous surveillance which might not be easy to achieve in closed and centralized societies. As for the sudden change of a civilian into a military fuel cycle plant, the obvious solution would be to prevent the existence of such plant in the territory of suspect states. It has to be emphasized that this implies the readiness to employ force against supposedly civilian nuclear energy plants.

There is no ready-made recipe for dealing with hidden weapons material other than strict surveillance of the kind required to detect the matching of weapons to launchers. While it is possible to intercept the movement of components to weaponization facilities, it is much harder to acquire the necessary intelligence, particularly if the rule-breaker abandons the usual safety standards applied to military and civilian fissile material transport.

The third possibility is the construction and operation of clandestine facilities to produce weapons-grade fissile material and to form it into warheads. Obviously, time tolerances are higher here since the lag between the start-up of such a project and the completion of combat-ready weaponry must be measured in years. For this reason, the intelligence task is somewhat easier, since more time is available for looking at strategic warning indicators. Improvements in IAEA verification stated in the Additional Protocol have enhanced the tools available to international verification efforts. At present, it is too early to propose a final judgement as to whether this new set of instruments for the job will suffice.

It must be assumed, on the other hand, that in conflict-prone regions a lingering doubt will remain as to whether or not such activities can be detected clearly enough to take action to prevent the production of nuclear material. Once such material had been produced, it would be difficult to assure that all such material in a country would be revealed through inspections. Operational records of plants can be faked or destroyed if search is imminent. Conversely, a cheater could not be certain of deceiving the international community: for North Korea, the discovery by the IAEA that Pyöngyang had diverted undeclared plutonium came as a bad surprise.

If illegal facilities are discovered in a timely manner, and international pressure has not dissuaded the rule-breaker from continuing his efforts, then preventive action is easier to accomplish than in the other cases. Facilities are immobile, and they are not easy to defend presently against determined attack using all assets available for such a mission: counter-electronic warfare, tactical surprise, stand-off precision munitions, and/or high precision cruise missiles. The international community may feel confident that it can destroy nuclear-weapons-related facilities if such action is taken. Two caveats are in order, though.

First, if the rule-breaker is an industrialized state with high military capabilities, and if present efforts at tactical anti-ballistic missile defence bear fruit, then such an attack will be more difficult to accomplish and less promising of success than just suggested. Second, if the attacked facilities are running, rather than being destroyed before start-up, the resulting radioactive damage to the innocent civilian population, and maybe even in neighbouring countries, could well be prohibitive. This must be weighed by multiplying the expected damage resulting from the rule-breaker's employment of nuclear weapons by the probability that it would use such weapons in armed conflict.

This discussion has tried to explore to what extent the possibility of military prevention offers the international community and its members sufficient assurance against rule-breakers to tolerate the uncertainties of a non-nuclear world. The outcome has been ambiguous for three reasons. First, the daunting task of ascertaining compliance by verification and intelligence cannot be accomplished with full certainty. Better verification systems and improved intelligence than that which existed at the outset of the Gulf War are possible and even likely, but doubts cannot be removed entirely. Second, the employment of military force, if such fears are realized, does not provide sufficient certainty of success to force preclude the possibility that the rule-breaker will retain some nuclear weapons. Where success is more likely, as against facilities producing fissile material, other considerations counsel caution. Third, in all cases, the possibility of the attacked rule-breaker retaliating by using his remaining nuclear assets, or his conventional means against sensitive targets (e.g. civilian nuclear plants or chemical facilities) must be thoroughly weighed against the probability of complete success. There can be no certainty, and the dilemmas will be so haunting that it seems reasonable to exclude this option as a convincing strategic policy for reining in a non-nuclear world. Besides, the amount of intelligence needed and the high level of conventional weaponry on permanent alert do not bode well for this world to be a much friendlier one than the nuclear one in which we live today.

8.4.2. Conventional Deterrence Against Small Nuclear Arsenals

If we take from the preceding discussion the conclusion that prevention is an unpromising proposition as a generalized security strategy for non-nuclear weapon states in a non-nuclear world against rule-breakers, then conventional deterrence comes to mind as an alternative.

In his sophisticated discussion of conventional deterrence[3] Mearsheimer arrived at the conclusion that the intrinsic deterrence value of a conventional posture lies in its distinct capability to force protracted attrition onto the aggressor rather than to permit him immediate victory. Conventional deterrence, in that analysis, required denial of a quick victory of the *Blitzkrieg* vintage. Once an aggressor faced the prospect of prolonged combat, his prospects of early and probable victory receded, the discount rate for a victorious outcome increased, and the net present value of aggression decreased.

Unfortunately, this hopeful proposition does not hold in our case. In Mearsheimer's scenario, the threat of nuclear attack was countered by the threat of retaliation in kind. In a non-nuclear world, this is not available. This means that retaliation by conventional means cannot focus on attrition. The attrition value of even a few fissile weapons is higher than that of a prolonged conventional war. The only alternative is the threat to destroy an equivalent target set by conventional means.

While at first sight this proposition appears fairly absurd, this feeling might well be an inheritance of our familiarity with a world where nuclear deterrence was the rule of the game. It is quite conceivable that, with improved accuracy and enhanced firepower of conventional means of destruction, large-scale damage can be done to the military and civilian infrastructure of a nuclear aggressor. This is certainly a lesson that can be drawn from the Gulf War. In fact, if the coalition had not been constrained by respect for the laws of war and the rule of proportionality of means to ends, it could have completely annihilated Iraqi society.

There are limits, however. To achieve the effects required for conventional deterrence against nuclear weapons, several challenging conditions must be met. First, the defender must possess equivalent firepower against a nuclear attacker even after sustaining a nuclear attack. Second, it must dispose of the capability to bring this firepower to bear on pre-selected enemy targets, again even during or after an attack. Redundant command and control structures, top-of-the-line attack aircraft and missiles containing most modern intelligent munitions with high lethality, and extremely disciplined and well-trained soldiers who would be able to conduct retaliation after the stunning experience of suffering a nuclear assault are required. This can, if at all, only be expected from a great power facing an otherwise inferior enemy.

Alternatively, a collective security system could provide the necessary means of retaliation. This looks far more promising, of course. The combination of the world's great and middle powers, with all their conventional military assets whose posture would indeed be shaped by the need to participate in collective retaliatory action, should be capable of threatening a devastating conventional counterblow. This proposition would be valid if the nuclear aggressor did not possess the means needed for all-out attack against the militarily more capable members of the international community.

Here, we are facing the dilemma of all collective security action: the asymmetry of interest between the attacked and the community of protectors. The victim's interest in retaliation and—if at all possible—reliberation seems obvious. Not so for the protectors. If retaliation can be afforded at relatively low risk, as in the Gulf War, debate will still rage—as documented in the lively Congressional dispute in January 1991—but retaliation might still follow. If, however, the risk of a nuclear blow to the wider community rises, the calculation begins to change. We are facing a well-known dilemma of collective security. The states which have pledged mutual assistance may have second thoughts in a specific conflict. Geopolitical interests vary, and an attack on one of them might not seem crucial enough an infraction of national interests of members whose participation would be essential to compel them into action. This recantation of earlier promises in specific conflict situations is all the more likely the higher the danger of being drawn into a costly dispute with uncertain outcome. It is obvious that taking a stand against a nuclear-armed enemy entails major risks. Intervening troops might suffer losses that cannot be defended domestically—remember some of the arguments in the Western debates before the Gulf War, notably the assessments of possible losses to chemical attacks. Risks loom even larger if the aggressor possesses means of long-range delivery, or is suspected to do so. The situation contains an asymmetry that favours the attacker despite its apparent numerical isolation. The attacker can threaten focused retaliation against any single member of the collective coalition. Whether it will eventually make good on such threats or not is unimportant. By concentrating threats against each new potential entry into a coalition the aggressor might be able to prevent the agglomeration of a sufficient force to threaten effective conventional retaliation, even if, theoretically, the combined conventional power of all potential coalition partners surpassed by far the destructive capability of the few nuclear warheads the rule-breaker might possess.

So far, we have discussed an aggressor with only few warheads at its disposal. The deterrence balance is weakened the more nuclear weapons the rule-breaker possesses. Because of the extraordinary damage entailed in nuclear warheads and the psychological momentum a nuclear threat would contain even for conventionally clearly superior forces, a conventional counter-threat is rapidly devalued with each additional deliverable warhead. This poses again an enormous intelligence dilemma to the defending coalition: how to ascertain that a given assumption about the nuclear arsenal of the enemy is valid? How could one be sure that this arsenal was not larger than intelligence indicators suggested? Remember that governments would have to evaluate intelligence in an acute crisis situation, and in the light of enemy propaganda that would offer incentives to exaggerate the other side's fears and to exacerbate its worst-case scenarios.

The dilemma grows stronger if the proliferator is known to operate a weapons-production programme, since it is obvious that the conventional deterrent will rapidly decay with time, as the arsenal to be deterred would grow out of control with time. At this point, conventional deterrence would then have to change into prevention in order to maintain its validity, and we would be back to the set of prevention scenarios discussed above.

As a result of this discussion, it seems unlikely that conventional deterrence against substantial nuclear threats would offer sufficient reassurance for peaceful coexistence. Besides, as in the prevention scenario, the need to maintain tremendous offensive conventional capabilities to credibly threaten damage equivalent to small-scale nuclear arsenals does not bode well for a peaceful world.

8.4.3. Virtual Arsenals as Deterrent

Jonathan Schell, in a most inventive discourse on alternatives to nuclear arms racing,[4] proposed a posture of mutual nuclear surge capabilities short of actual weapon deployment. States would abolish their nuclear weapons, but at the same time hold, on a standby basis, means to reconstitute a minimum nuclear deterrent.

Schell arrived at this proposal since he acknowledged—largely corroborating this analysis—that in a non-nuclear world, even with fairly strict verification systems in place, lingering doubts would, and possibly justifiably, persist between rivals in global or regional conflicts that the potential enemy might cheat. His proposal also was derived from the insight that conventional answers to nuclear cheating would presumably not be seen as sufficient.

Yet, on a second glance, the kind of world resulting from mutual nuclear surge deterrence is not all that appealing. If it is believed that nuclear weapons might be hidden, or that nuclear weapons might be prepared clandestinely, the surge capabilities that would be acceptable would be fairly close to the last turn of the screw. Small stockpiles of nuclear-weapons-grade material would be available. Non-nuclear parts of nuclear weapons and trained nuclear weapon manpower would be held on standby status. Nuclear-capable delivery vehicles would stand ready to be matched to weapons. Their crews would regularly exercise launch procedures. Emergency targeting plans would be repeatedly updated. Conventional means to defend nuclear assets during the transition period to weaponization would be on permanent high alert. Nuclear-focused intelligence would be needed.

I hesitate to call such a world non-nuclear; for me, this is cheating on the label. All ingredients of the past are there. The whole structure of the nuclear-weapon state would be preserved: anything short of that would seriously compromise the purpose of a surge nuclear deterrence capability. This preservation of all but one structural element of the nuclear weapon world would have grave consequences for interstate relationships. The nervousness over possible cheating would be far higher than in past arms control agreements—where it was bad enough—because the relative consequences of an error would be far greater in terms of the power balance. This situation is ripe with misperception and misreaction. Misread signals on alleged cheating of another party would immediately trigger the surge.

Even worse: in the surge world, the norm of non-proliferation could not be upheld in its present discriminatory form. Since this world pretends to be a non-nuclear one, surge postures would acquire generalized legitimacy. A proliferation of threshold status in the new sense, that is, countries possessing surge capacity, would ensue. If misperception (or actual cheating) triggered weaponization, there would not just be a commensurate response by the balancing nuclearization of a single rivalling state. Rather, a mushrooming of nuclear weapon states would follow. Status problems and multi-pronged conflict structures would trigger such a chain reaction. Instead of a world with a fairly limited number of nuclear-weapon states, we would be left with a truly nuclearized planet.

8.5. *Countering Other Weapons of Mass Destruction and Conventional Threats*

The notion of countering chemical and biological threats by nuclear weapons is based on the alleged effectiveness of this counter-threat during the Gulf War. However, in terms of chemical weapons at least, this proposition is patently unconvincing. A chemical arsenal that could be developed under the auspices of the verification system of the Organization for the Prohibition of Chemical Weapons (OPCW) would, by necessity, be somewhat imperfect in military terms. Against such a chemical posture, overwhelming conventional power could be marshalled; the conventional deterrent could not be knocked out by pre-emptive chemical attack. Against otherwise superior, defensively well prepared armed forces, chemical warfare would not be enough to win a war. A strong conventional coalition is thus sufficient for deterring, preventing, and, if it comes to that, retaliating against, chemical weapons use.

With biological weapons matters are more difficult for two reasons. First, verification will be much more exacting, if possible at all. Second, the damage resulting from biological weapons could be much more horrifying, and given the versatility and variability of bio-agents, protecting one's own forces might prove impossible. A crucial question then is whether an emerging biological weapons programme could be detected early enough, with improved transparency and verification measures, to make conventional pre-emption a viable option. Given that the signatures of biological weapon programmes are much weaker than in the nuclear case, the answer might be a reluctant no. The second question, then, is whether credible conventional retaliation can be maintained in the face of a persistent biological weapons threat, and could be effectively and consistently pursued even after the forces acting in the name of the international community have absorbed a biological weapons attack. Whether the jump from a very few nuclear weapons to zero will be possible might, in the end, well depend on the answer to this question.

This answer depends on fairly complex calculations, involving the effectiveness of a conventional, long-range air campaign—implemented from bases far from the perpetrator turned target—against a determined air defence; would such a campaign be enough to jeopardize the values vital to the leadership of the biological weapons attacker, one which might respond to quite a different value system than the international community? It appears to me that the answer might be yes, and also that transparency in the biological sector could be vastly improved by international co-operation; but it will take a long and hard look, and in-depth analysis, to arrive at a position that commands sufficient support in those countries most important for nuclear disarmament, namely the five nuclear-weapon states and the threshold countries. Fortunately, the whole issue becomes virulent only during the last phase of nuclear disarmament and should not hamper determined steps at present leading towards this goal.[5]

Countering conventional superiority is, in comparison, a far less exacting mission for purely conventional forces. The perceived need to provide a nuclear deterrent to a conventionally stronger force results from a double *faute de mieux* situation:

(1) The failure to achieve a regional balance of conventional forces.
(2) The failure to provide for adequate collective security arrangements or, alternatively, countervailing coalition-building procedures.

The need for a rough regional balance can be achieved by a strong effort at arms control.[6] The Conventional Forces in Europe (CFE) treaty plus supplementary arrangements and the arms control rules pursuant to the Dayton agreements give clear examples how this could be done. While such arms control measures might not in every case result in a fully satisfactory balance, and may, in such cases, need some external underwriting to create the necessary confidence among the parties concerned that their security can be maintained, they go a long way to reducing untenable asymmetries of conventional military power which push weaker, but technically proficient states towards considering a national nuclear deterrent. This consideration supports the connection made in the NPT preamble and Article VI between nuclear and conventional disarmament. While a treaty on complete disarmament might prove unachievable, nuclear disarmament is likely to necessitate a network of regional and, possibly, global conventional arms control arrangements that help enhance a feeling of mutual trust and security, and shape a balance situation that would make a successful attack much less likely.

A rough conventional equivalence would be all the more useful as it would facilitate countries providing external support—be it in the form of a mutual defence coalition built on Article 51 of the UN Charter, or be it in the shape of a collective security action under Chapter VII—in dissuading a state poised to dare an assault on its neighbour from really attacking, in repelling an attack where it occurs, and to invoke retaliation by conventional means that would deprive the attacker of its power structure. The risk, effort, and expense for the supporting extra-regional parties would be reduced, and their willingness to lend the necessary support to threatened or attacked regional countries would be greater.

However, given the imperfection of regional balances achieved by means of arms control, coalition-building and/or collective security arrangements must be in place in order to underwrite a nuclear-weapon-free world. This does not only apply to the latter (conventional superiority) scenario, it applies also to the dangers that weapons of mass destruction are held or produced illegally by rogue actors, and are used for threat, or even employed, in a political conflict. It is unviable to leave these situations to national self-defence. Apart from the problem that only a handful of countries could hope to withstand such a threat or attack anyway, left to national means alone almost any government that would be uncertain about such a possible threat in the foreseeable future would certainly consider going nuclear, or, to put it differently, the nuclear-weapon-holders would hardly be willing to lay down their nuclear deterrents.

These arrangements must work much better than they do at present. As for collective defence, NATO and, to a certain degree, the United States' Pacific arrangements provide reasonable confidence to their respective allies, but they have the tendency to alienate or even threaten—at least in perception—other actors; the Russian protestations against NATO enlargement and the Chinese objections to a regional missile defence system in east Asia are cases in point. The collective security structure in the UN Security Council, on the other hand, probably gives too little confidence to reliably secure a non-nuclear world. The support of one permanent member for a country whose government tries to backtrack from legally binding obligations under a peace treaty; the protestations of a second P-5 state against the request of the war criminal court in The Hague to detain suspected leading war criminals in Bosnia; the extensive territorial claims of a third permanent member to vast areas of sea territory far from its own shores: all these undermine confidence in the capability of the UNSC to deal with the respective conflicts as long as the veto obtains. Hesitation to come to the assistance of threatened or attacked parties has been far too obvious in the recent past. Thus, collective security must be improved significantly in order that a nuclear-weapon-free world will be seen as a reliable security environment by a considerable number of states that rely now, directly or indirectly, on nuclear umbrellas.[7]

8.6. *Required Conditions for a Non-Nuclear World*

Throughout these considerations, two factors of pivotal importance have been repeated time and again. The first is the assumption that conflict will persist which might degenerate into violent clashes between states. The second is that the structure of international relations and the internal structures at least of some players in the game, create considerable uncertainty regarding political intentions and the development and use of nuclear capabilities. In fact, these two basic conditions of the present world dominate completely the more narrow strategic, military, and technological factors discussed so far. This makes it imperative to tackle these conditions in parallel with the incremental steps we take towards a nuclear-weapons-free world.

8.6.1. The Impact of Co-operative Conflict Solution on Non-Nuclear Prospects

The first variable is the level of conflict world-wide, in a given region, or just between two neighbouring states. The so-called realist approach to international relations contends that the conflict is inevitable in a world shaped by nation-states and without higher enforcement authority.[8] If we accept this approach and the premise that military options offer little insurance against an unwelcome nuclear surprise in a non-nuclear world, then the prospects of moving towards a nuclear-weapons-free world are nil. As nuclear disarmament proceeds, proliferation incentives for states in acute conflict increase as the protection granted by extended deterrence—explicitly or implicitly—fades away, and the margins of danger offered by the appearance of a previously clandestine nuclear-weapon threat increase.

Experience shows, however, that the probability of conflict can tend towards zero even without world government. North America, Scandinavia, and EU Europe, and largely also Latin America, are regions where interstate conflict has become highly unlikely, not because regional powers hold each other in check by threat of retaliation, but because the subjects of disputes are of marginal value as compared with the gains provided by broad co-operation, and because alternative, low-cost means exist to settle disputes where they exist. Germany, for example, does not feel threatened by French nuclear weapons because there is complete disbelief that Paris could ever decide to strike at its friendly neighbour. Likewise Canadians might not be fond of US nuclear might, but they hardly feel threatened by it. We can conclude that in a world where relations between countries are predominantly friendly and co-operative, and alternative processes of conflict solution are available, margins of tolerance do exist. We can further conclude that, contrary to so-called 'realist' predictions (I have always had difficulties in calling an approach realist that defies reality in so many regards) such worlds exist at several places at the regional level.

8.6.2. Democratic Structures and the Problem of Uncertainty

The second problem we have confronted is uncertainty over intentions and capabilities. Again, the so-called 'realists' believe that this is the equivalent to a natural law in international relations. Yet, we find in practice that uncertainty over capabilities is at zero level in Western non-nuclear-weapon states, due to the combination of open nuclear energy policy debate, public licensing processes, parliamentary investigations, transfer registers, and joint ventures between nuclear companies of different nationality. Uncertainty over intentions is close to zero, after some doubts about the direction Germany would take after unification were laid to rest by the solid continuity of German foreign and security policy.

Two conclusions can be drawn. First, the institutional co-operation among states, in the security field and beyond, already mentioned in reducing inter-state tension is also conducive in mitigating uncertainties. Second, and more important, the internal structure of states is the decisive variable influencing whatever degree of certainty or uncertainty exists over their intentions and capabilities. Countries with divisions of power, open discursive decision processes, a distinction between economy and politics, free movement within, and accessibility of all parts of, the country, and the right of parliament, the courts, media, and citizens to investigate executive action independently and critically leave little room for governments to operate large-scale secret pro-grammes. The most ingenious institution of democracy, the leak, closes most remaining loopholes.

There is also an important lesson regarding intentions to be borne in mind. Procuring nuclear weapons in a non-nuclear world is a sign of intentions at coercive policies. For what other purposes would such a drastic breach of rules be risked by a government? Such intentions are less likely in a democratic welfare state as compared to non-democratic states. First, in refraining from requesting their government to 'go nuclear', citizens must calculate that benefits from co-operation outweigh those from the application of violence, or prey; they must have something to lose that they would not desire to put at risk. This condition applies in modern welfare states where social well-being exists for a considerable part of the population. Second, the citizenry must have the means to make its view relevant to government. That requires demo-cratic process and the ability to remove leaders who do not follow mainstream demands for a low-risk, conflict-avoiding, co-operation-seeking policy. Again, it is democracy that best realizes these conditions.

The history of imperialism has taught us that relatively democratic states do not necessarily refrain from using force. It was a low-risk enterprise for countries under economic strain to seize a colonial prey. As democracies develop into welfare states, the balance of incentives moves them away from taking risks. In more recent times, democracies were capable of acting harshly to non-democracies, but learned to resolve their disputes with their fellow democratic partners peacefully in a co-operative institutional framework.[9] Their nuclear programmes lie open, and their constitutional conditions make it virtually impossible to pursue secret programmes to acquire nuclear weapons.

The structure of democracies contains an additional reassuring feature: the particular relationship of international norms and the democratic process. In the transition to a non-nuclear world, the norm which rejects nuclear weapons will lose all ambiguity and become a firm part of international law and a part of world political culture simultaneously.[10] In democracies, the

norms of international law are being internalized into national decision structures through constitutional process. Once they are breached by the executive,
they represent an assault on the constitution as well. Moreover, international
norms gain the support of interested citizens in pluralistic societies. Nuclear
disarmament has found its advocacy in peace movements and arms control
communities, both permanent pains in the necks of military establishments.
Once a non-nuclear world was established, such advocacy and watchdog
organizations would become far more powerful. Non-nuclearism would
become part of the national political cultures, and attempts of the executive
to violate this norm would meet enormous outrage and resistance, which, in
turn, would serve as strategic warning to the country's neighbours.

The decisive advantage of non-nuclearism in this world is that it can live
without enormous conventional armament. Some defensive forces and some
mobile units for contributing to collective defence arrangements will be there,
but they will be limited by mutual agreement and integrated into joint
structures. The rather unpleasant overhang of many conventional swords of
Damocles in the previous scenarios could only make fears and distrust in that
world worse. The relatively limited military assets prevailing in the world of
co-operating democracies, in contrast, reinforces mutual trust and thus helps
to maintain confidence in the validity of a non-nuclear security posture.

8.7. *Conclusions*

In a world where democracies live alongside totalitarian states, nuclear proliferation is a distinct possibility. Because of the genuine distrust in the intentions of a Ghaddafi, Saddam Hussein, Hitler, or Stalin, and uncertainties over
the capabilities of non-democratic countries, the mere chance of clandestine
weapons or weapon production will dissuade states in such a mixed-state type
of system from accepting the risks of the non-nuclear world. Conventional
prevention and deterrence options are not without promise, but this promise
is not one of assured success in all or most conceivable circumstances. Hence,
the international community will probably wish to keep a nuclear deterrent
reserve, however small and in whatever institutional form (national, multilateral, or global).

This sombre assessment becomes brighter when we imagine a long transition to the abolition of nuclear weapons world-wide. As in the case of the
East–West relationship, nuclear disarmament is interdependent with political
evolution. The reasoning in the last part of the paper makes it plausible that
denuclearization, democratization, and growing international co-operation
are three aspects of the same process.

If the trend towards democracy continued, and if new democracies were
successful at economic development and thus increased their citizen's

demands for low-risk foreign and security policy, the norm of non-nuclearism would take deep root in the minds of people everywhere. Accordingly, the probability of violent conflict and the uncertainty over possible nuclear-weapon programmes in 'black sheep' states would disappear. In a world of interdependent, mutually interlocked, totally transparent democracies where the executive is checked by a division of power, the media, and an attentive public, and where this public is strongly devoted to the non-nuclear norm, then public trust in the validity of non-nuclear security might grow large enough to make it viable.

For these reasons, incrementalists argue, nuclear disarmament means devising and marching on a feasible path towards abolition; this requirement forces us to rebuild, step by step, our global and regional security structures. Striving for a non-nuclear world means enhancing mutual confidence and transparency among the nuclear-weapon states immensely; it means setting up regional arms control regimes in the most war-prone regions of the world; it means enlarging the verification potential of international organisations by several orders of magnitude; it means the strengthening of collective security structures far beyond the brittle means available presently at UN level. Achieving these various objectives would reduce the risks of international war to the extremely rare exception of a state consciously breaking out of these legal constraints and thereby risking complete isolation internationally, and most probably a forceful response. The development that began with the Charter of the League of Nations would come to its completion, not on paper, but in the form of viable, practical arrangements. This would not mean the end of history: break-out would, unfortunately, remain a possibility, and its realization would be a historical event of sorts; likewise, internal war, the most terrible scourge of present times, would not be contained by the measures taken, and even terrorism by WMD means could not be excluded. But we would have built an order that would give humankind a chance to survive the next century, an objective that is in doubt if the present disorder persists, and if everybody is left to their own—and the great powers'—devices. Complete nuclear disarmament is not another simple step, but a great long-term project for reforming global security.[11]

9

The Elimination of Nuclear Weapons

Michael MccGwire

Is it desirable? Is it feasible? The case for eliminating nuclear weapons requires a 'yes' to both questions. In practice, the focus of the first question needs to be sharpened to ask 'Is it preferable?'. The subjects for comparison are the *likely outcomes over time* of alternative courses of action: (1) persist with existing policies; or (2) adopt the 'firm and serious policy goal' of a nuclear-weapons-free (NWF) world.[1] Neither course of action is risk-free. It is therefore misleading to differentiate between *traditionalists* and *eliminators* by saying the former are 'realists'. The latter's view of international relations is equally, if not more jaundiced.

The labels are only relevant in the sense that so-called realists tend to be short-term pessimists and long-term optimists. So-called idealists tend to the opposite view and therefore seek to structure the future in such a way as to improve the odds. In the view of eliminators, the traditionalists are dangerously complacent about future developments in the international system. More serious, their policy prescriptions are based on a superficial and Western-centric reading of the history of the cold war.

Returning to the initial questions, one could expect 'Is it feasible?' to be the more problematic, but that is not the case. For more than fifty years nuclear weapons have been promoted as the bedrock of Western security and they now have honorific status.[2] This means that the primary focus of this chapter is on the desirability of eliminating nuclear weapons. It then turns briefly to demonstrating that, given the political will, the goal of an NWF world is entirely feasible.

9.1. *The Categorical Imperative*

The benefits of eliminating nuclear weapons are several, but there is one overriding imperative.[3] We need to adopt the goal of an NWF world because:

(1) Nuclear weapons make nuclear war possible.
(2) Of humankind's many enterprises, a major nuclear war has the unique capacity to destroy civilization as we know it and to jeopardize the survival of the human race.
(3) Human fallibility means that a major nuclear exchange is at the very least highly probable and, for all practical purposes, ultimately inevitable.

The *aims* of such a policy would be:

(1) To reduce the probability of a major nuclear exchange to zero
(2) To reduce the probability that nuclear weapons will be used by anyone in any way to as low a level as possible.

These aims are specific, limited, and achievable. Achieving those aims will bring ancillary benefits, but the elimination of nuclear weapons is a 'good' in its own right.

Objections to the eliminators' argument fall into three main categories:

(1) Nuclear deterrence means that a nuclear exchange is extremely unlikely.
(2) An NWF world would create the new danger of nuclear break-out.
(3) Nuclear weapons are needed to keep the peace.

The validity of these objections is discussed in the sections which follow, the third of which evaluates key historical arguments underlying the traditionalist's case for retaining nuclear weapons. A fourth section summarizes the eliminator's argument, outlines ancillary benefits that would flow from adopting the goal of an NWF world, and compares the cost/benefit calculus of the alternative policies. The fifth section considers the question of feasibility.

9.2. *A Nuclear Exchange is Extremely Unlikely*

In this category, the traditionalists make three kinds of claim:

(1) The possibility of accidental or inadvertent nuclear war is very low, if not negligible.
(2) If there were to be war between nuclear powers and nuclear weapons were used, reciprocal constraints on escalating the conflict would come into play.
(3) History shows that nuclear weapons prevent nuclear war.

In addressing these claims, I take as one of my texts the recent monograph by Michael Quinlan.[4] His central contention is that the *reductio ad absurdum* of nuclear war is needed to deter major states from using military action to settle disputes.

9.2.1. Inadvertent War is Unlikely

Quinlan considers the possibility of a nuclear exchange stemming from a technical malfunction or procedural error as 'absurdly far-fetched'.[5] He does not, however, mention or rebut the detailed studies based on well-informed empirical analysis of the US and (to a lesser extent) Soviet experience during the cold war.[6] The conclusion of those analyses is that the risks of nuclear accident and accidental war during the cold war were even higher than had been claimed by critics at the time. Particularly in a crisis, a significant and unavoidable danger of 'nuclear inadvertence' was inherent in the complex and tightly coupled command and control structures associated with opposing strategic nuclear forces.

Quinlan chooses not to discuss the danger of inadvertent war (resulting from an unfortunate combination of background circumstances, mutual misunderstanding, and an unforeseen chain of events), but argues that if the military balance underlying deterrence is properly maintained, mutual deterrence will not fail.[7] He mentions the 'Soviet adventure in Cuba' as one example of 'occasional surface perturbations' of that deterrent balance, which he says was never a real risk during the cold war.[8]

The implication of Quinlan's conclusion is different to what emerged from the series of research conferences on the Cuban crisis. This brought together former officials who had personally participated in the decision-making processes of the three countries directly involved and had the benefit of archival research. It is not clear whether Quinlan is aware that decisions in Washington, Moscow, and Havana 'before and during the crisis had been distorted by misinformation, miscalculation and misjudgement', and that the scene was set for the use of Soviet tactical nuclear weapons against invading US forces, with incalculable results.[9]

Quinlan seems unaware of the scope for misunderstanding or accident that was inherent in NATO's hybrid command structure on the central front in Europe.[10] Nor does he mention the disturbing incident in November 1983, during a NATO command-post exercise, at a time of high East–West tension and a few weeks before the bitterly contested deployment of Euromissiles. Newly delegated nuclear release procedures being exercised by NATO for the first time were misinterpreted by the Soviets, and the General Staff instituted nuclear alert measures. Fortunately, the West did not pick this up, a lucky intelligence failure that saved us from the dangers of alert escalation. This was at a time when the lines of authority in Moscow were blurred by the mortal illness of Yuri Andropov, while the Soviet political and military establishments were uncertain of US intentions and extremely concerned about the danger of inadvertent war brought about by US brinkmanship.[11]

Quinlan's relaxed approach to the danger of inadvertent war is so far removed from that of Robert McNamara and General Lee Butler that they might be living in different worlds. And to a large extent they were. Quinlan's focus was on the European theatre, a heavily armed but highly stylized encounter zone, where formulation of nuclear doctrine was in the hands of 'a systematic and active collective mechanism' and was 'tested by study, debate and challenge'.[12] Compare this with Butler's description of the nuclear arena as 'a world beset with tidal forces, towering egos, maddening contradictions, alien constructs and insane risks'.[13] American strategic forces were a world apart from NATO, as were US global interests and operations, and their inter-action with the Soviets.[14]

The fact that we avoided inadvertent and accidental war during the East–West confrontation provides no grounds for assuming that we will be able to do so in the future. Besides the laws of probability, it will be seen that the circumstances of the past fifty years were unusually benevolent in terms of historical evolution, weapons development, and the character of the key protagonists.

9.2.2. Escalation is Not Inevitable

Quinlan accepts that, if conflict were joined, there is good reason for fearing escalation to large-scale nuclear war, although he emphasizes that the risks are not necessarily odds on and considers the idea of inexorable momentum in a developing exchange as implausible.[15] He outlines scenarios showing how escalation might not necessarily occur in all circumstances, but also talks of plans to 'exploit escalation risk most effectively'.[16] Again, one has the sense that he is thinking primarily in the context of Europe. He accepts that nuclear deterrence is not possible without grave escalation risks, but claims in mit-igation that these risks are inescapably present in any significant armed con-flict between nuclear-knowledgeable powers.

The claim is disingenuous. In a nuclear world, such as exists today, the com-batants would already possess arsenals of operational weapons numbered in thousands. In the event of major conflict in an NWF world, there would be a race to re-establish a nuclear capability. By comparison with the present situ-ation, the initial arsenals would be tiny and time for mediation and reflection would be of a quite different order.

Besides highlighting the contradictions and paradoxes underlying much of deterrence theory, Quinlan's exposition alerts us to the disjunction between the theory as generally understood, and the realities of US strategic weapons procurement and employment policies and practices.[17] It also exposes the scope for miscalculation through misperception. Take, for example, the silent assumption that Soviet leaders would have based their actions and escalatory responses on the cool image of Western policy projected by Quinlan's version of deterrence theory. It seems more probable that the Soviets would have used

a worst-case assessment of likely Western behaviour derived from their cumulative analysis of the generally hostile and punitive US strategic debate, melded
with the hard evidence of US force structure and assertive operational
behaviour.

And there is the explicit assumption that, if the Soviets had launched a conventional offensive on the central front, the only vital interests involved would
have been NATO's. Western leaders could therefore assume an asymmetry of
resolve in their favour, which the Soviets would surely recognize when considering escalation.[18]

In reality, the asymmetry ran the other way. If the Soviets had ever launched
such an offensive, it would have signalled their momentous assessment that
the chain of events meant that world war (which they absolutely wanted to
avoid, but could not afford to lose) was now inescapable. To lose such a war
would result in the overthrow of the Soviet state. In order not to lose, the
Soviets had to defeat NATO in Europe and evict US forces from the continent,
while holding the USA deterred at the strategic level. To defeat NATO in
Europe required a standing-start *Blitzkreig* offensive. The *vital* interests lay
with the Soviet Union. Even if the USA were forced to withdraw from Europe,
it would only have suffered a defeat. It would not have lost the war.[19]

These points illuminate one of the more disturbing aspects of the cold-war
deterrence regime that is now being proposed as an acceptable model for the
future, namely our limited understanding of Soviet strategic priorities and the
nature of their political and military objectives in the event of world war.
Because the doctrine of nuclear deterrence was premised on a Soviet urge to
aggression, Western officialdom focused on the worst-case analysis of their
offensive capabilities, paid no attention to Soviet interests and requirements,
and actively eschewed any analysis of their intentions, which were a 'given'.[20]
This ensured the worst of two worlds: dangerously confrontational policies in
peacetime; and should war come, fallacious expectations about the Soviet
response to Western nuclear escalation or attempts at war termination
through 'militarily significant action', i.e. nuclear strikes.

If that is the best we were able to achieve with respect to the Russians, with
whom we had been enemies or allies for some 200 years and who were our
priority intelligence target for the last forty-five, what hope is there of carefully graduated escalation when dealing with unfamilar cultures in a multi-
polar world in the future?

9.2.3. Nuclear Weapons Prevent Nuclear War

The third of these claims is a subset of the more general assertion that nuclear
weapons are needed to keep the peace and is covered later, when addressing
that category of objections. Discussion at this stage is limited to noting ways

in which nuclear weapons and the associated theories actually *increased* the danger of nuclear war. We start with the truism that without nuclear weapons there could be no nuclear war.

A more substantial point concerns deterrence theory.[21] There were many variants, but they shared common features that help explain the pernicious effects of the central doctrine: an abstract style of reasoning derived from axiomatic disciplines such as mathematics and economics, rather than empirical ones like psychology and international politics; an absence of serious Sovietologists from the strategic debate; and the central assumption that the Soviet Union had a persistent urge to aggression that could only be checked by the threat of nuclear devastation. A dogma, more than a doctrine, it was fundamentally punitive in tone, and the will to inflict punishment was as important as the capability to do so.[22]

The doctrine encouraged exaggerated, moralistic rhetoric directed as much at domestic constituencies as at opponents, and it was easier to inflame hostility than assuage it. Add the need to make the threat credible and it was inevitable that policies based on deterrence would favour intransigence and discourage serious negotiations and the search for compromise. Meanwhile, the theoretical approach to ensuring stability fostered complacency in crises and concealed the danger that lay in the dynamic of events over which there could be no control.[23] Focusing exclusively on the possibility of Soviet aggression, the dogma obscured the reality that war itself was the greatest danger and that measures to enhance deterrence often made war more likely.

The dogma encouraged arms racing. A long-established feature of international relations, the nuclear variant had a dynamic of its own, combining the crude logic of conventional advantage with the sophistries of deterrence theory. The requirement for an assured second strike, combined with traditional targeting criteria, justified an ever-increasing number of warheads and diversity of delivery systems.[24] As we saw in the 1970s, attempts at *détente* were undermined by the relentless build-up of weapons. Obeying the dictates of cognitive dissonance, threat perceptions followed suit, leading to calls for increased military strength. These were reinforced by doctrinal elaborations, which provided additional rationalizations for new weapons programmes: escalation dominance, intra-war bargaining, war termination; and the need to prevail in a protracted nuclear conflict.[25] In the 1980s, deterrence doctrine was used to justify plans to weaponize space.

The doctrine not only drove the arms race, it legitimized it as an instrument of policy. Emphasizing above all else the *stability* of deterrence (a malleable concept), the theory favoured large and varied weapons' inventories. Contrary to common perceptions, it saw no danger in arms racing *per se*, which was valued as a way of increasing the Soviet defence burden. That it undoubtedly did, but for the Soviets it also epitomized the US drive for military dominance.[26] Seen in the context of contemporary American pronouncements,[27] it confirmed the Soviet military in its deeply pessimistic assessments of the imminence of war in 1981–4.[28] This, and the particular quality of nuclear-missile systems, magnified the danger of operational misjudgements as the Soviet leadership reacted to increasingly assertive probes of their defence perimeter.

As evidenced by the very sharp rise in support for peace and antinuclear movements in NATO member countries, large sections of the public in Western Europe and North America shared the Soviets' assessment of the heightened danger of war. But NATO officialdom knew better. Drawing on the logic of deterrence theory, it claimed that its confrontational policies made war less, rather than more likely, and ridiculed the idea that the Soviets could be genuinely worried, let alone have justifiable grounds for concern.[29]

9.3. *The Danger of Break-Out*

Traditionalists claim that an NWF world would create the new danger of 'nuclear break-out', which would allow one state to hold the rest to ransom. That objection is best answered by a comparative assessment of risk.

9.3.1. Break-Out from an NWF World

Risk is the product of the consequences of a calamity and the likelihood of its occurrence. In a nuclear world (of the kind we have known this half-century), the worst case is a *full-scale nuclear exchange*, which would destroy civilization as we know it. In an NWF world, the risk would be nuclear break-out, leading in the very worst case to the *limited use* of nuclear weapons.

Opinions will differ on how the probability of break-out from an NWF world compares with the probability of accidental or inadvertent war in a high or even a low-salience nuclear world. But in terms of *risk*, we can be certain that if there were to be a significant difference between the probabilities, the disparity would not be sufficient to balance the incomparable calamity of a nuclear exchange.

That said, how likely is break-out from a properly verified NWF world? Postulated treaty evaders fall into three categories: two of them (the rogue and the high-tech state) secretly develop new nuclear devices; the third category secretly holds back a significant arsenal from the weapons dismantling process. Given sufficient ingenuity and resources, evasion is at least theoretically possible—but to what purpose?

A comparison of the costs and benefits argues that there would be little political-military incentive to break out from an NWF world.[30] This is partly because it has yet to be discovered how to translate the notional power of a nuclear monopoly into practical gains, but also because the certain costs are so high.[31] The possible exception is the irrational rogue state, but while the probability may be somewhat higher, the calamity factor of such a break-out is by far the smallest of the scenarios considered.

9.3.2. Break-Out from the Non-Proliferation Treaty

Break-out from an NWF world is just a special category of the more general problem of preventing the proliferation and use of nuclear weapons. This points up the fact that the proper comparison of risk is not between two 'situations' (the current post-cold-war hiatus and some future NWF world), but between *two unfolding processes*. The question at issue is which course of action is potentially the least dangerous and most likely to bring the greatest benefits in the foreseeable future?

What are the risks of break-out from the existing NPT regime?[32] There is a strong argument that the difficulty of preventing nuclear proliferation will inevitably increase over the next ten to twenty years, leading to recurrent crises, withdrawals from the treaty, and the steady spread of nuclear weapons. This is because an effective non-proliferation regime must rely in large part on voluntary compliance, and this requires that almost all non-nuclear states believe that the regime serves their long-term interests and that the terms of the treaty are fair. It is clear that agreement on those questions is by no means unanimous. Meanwhile, there are other possibilities. For example, will Japan always be satisfied with the security of an American umbrella?[33] And if the sense of Muslim identity develops a stronger political vector, might Pakistan choose to share its know-how with other Islamic states?

This deteriorating situation would be fundamentally transformed if the policy-goal of an NWF world were adopted. Dissatisfaction over the imbalance between the respective obligations and responsibilities of nuclear and non-nuclear states would be assuaged. And because halting proliferation would be essential to the process of achieving an NWF world, enforcement of the NPT would become a matter of universal concern, rather than being seen by many non-nuclear states as a dispute between the haves and have-nots.

In sum, current nuclear policies face an increasing danger of break-out from the NPT; if we adopt the goal of an NWF world, that danger will diminish over time, both for political reasons and as the heavy investment in verification bears fruit. This unfavourable balance must be included in our risk assessment of current policies. To the gross disparity of risk once the NWF threshold has been crossed must be added the steadily growing disparity in the intervening period.

9.3.3. A Multi-Polar Nuclear World

Implicit in the above is the possibility that current signatories will withdraw from the NPT. There are now seven declared nuclear states (plus Israel) and, while the treaty was unexpectedly successful in the past, its two-tier nature and the selective approach by some of the five 'nuclear weapon states' to the spirit and the letter of the original treaty and its extension in 1995 are the cause of growing dissatisfaction.

In other words, beyond the possibility of individual break-out from the NPT lies the possibility of treaty erosion or even breakdown. Earlier in this chapter, it was shown that, in the bi-polar nuclear world of East–West confrontation, the danger of inadvertent war remained significant, despite twenty-five years' attention to the problem. In a multi-polar world with more limited experience of the relevant command and control mechanisms and procedures, the dangers would increase exponentially.

9.4. *Nuclear Weapons are Needed to Keep the Peace*

Underlying this category of objections is the belief that, if it had not been for nuclear deterrence, the Soviets would have attempted to seize Western Europe, leading to the Third World War. This has been generalized to claim that, during the cold war, nuclear weapons were responsible for keeping the peace. Elements of this claim are present in most arguments that favour retaining nuclear weapons.

When the claim is challenged on the grounds of historical evidence, the traditionalists fall back on the defence that it cannot be proven one way or another and then argue 'better safe than sorry'. But that defence is only true in a trivial pseudo-scientific sense. In practical terms of historical analysis, there is a great deal of solid factual and circumstantial evidence which tilts the balance decisively against such a claim. That applies equally to Quinlan's variant of this objection, although his is more thoughtful and carefully qualified.

9.4.1. Quinlan's Argument

He starts from the important observation that major conventional war between advanced states is not only appalling in itself but also the likeliest route to nuclear war. Without postulating an inherent urge to military expansion on the Soviet part, Quinlan then argues that nuclear weapons probably played some part in what he sees as 'the remarkable maintenance of peace through over forty years of East–West confrontation'. To continue with his own words: '[H]ad [nuclear] conflict not been so manifestly intolerable the ebb and flow of frictions might have been managed with less caution, and a slide sooner or later into war . . . might have been less unlikely.'[34]

At first sight, this modest claim is not unreasonable, even though Quinlan ignores the fact that the imperatives of nuclear strategy and the dictates of deterrence generated many of the 'frictions' in the first place, Cuba being a prime example.[35] There are, however, three problems with his argument.

One is the silent assumption that nuclear deterrence does no harm. It is only because Quinlan tacitly assumes that deterrence is cost-free that he is able to suggest that the speculative and rather minor benefits he identifies (involving two 'mights' and a 'less unlikely') justify such a policy. But it has already been shown that deterrence incurred substantial costs. It had a corrosive effect on Soviet–American relations, fuelling the arms race and undermining *détente*. Its single-minded emphasis on 'credibility' led to the débâcle in Vietnam. It favoured containment and punishment over negotiating and compromise, and saw heightened international tension as a normal, even desirable state of affairs. Deterrence stunted the development of US foreign policy, had a damaging effect on domestic attitudes, and drove military strategy from the so-called strategic debate.[36] It is *not* cost-free.

And there were other, less tangible costs. By claiming to have solved the problems of nuclear weapons, deterrence theory dissipated the sudden urgency that this awesome new capability had brought to the post-war search for ways of managing interstate relations. Threatening a greater evil than it sought to prevent, the dogma echoed the communist line that ends justified means. The 'means' were the military capability and political will to devastate the Soviet Union. And, as nuclear arsenals grew, so this explicit threat to the Soviet Union evolved into an implicit threat to the survival of the human race. Deterrence dogma made it 'moral' to put the world at risk, as the West pursued the chimera of total security.

The second problem with Quinlan's argument is the contradiction between his claim that the possibility of nuclear conflict induced caution, and the almost universal Western assumption that deterrence would not (could not) fail. It was that assumption which underlay Henry Kissinger's approach to crisis management as US Secretary of State, which (by his own showing) was anything but cautious.[37] Crises were seen, not as something to be avoided, but as an opportunity to make gains by manipulating risks and escalating threats with no danger of losing control.[38] This highlights a second assumption at the core of Western deterrence policy, namely that war could only come about through some *Soviet* initiative, and the need for caution lay only with them. Both these dangerous assumptions underlay the confrontational policies of the first Reagan administration.[39]

Meanwhile, confidence that mutual deterrence would not fail cut both ways. In the early years of Soviet involvement in the Third World, military intervention was constrained by concern that interaction with US forces would provoke nuclear strikes on Russia.[40] In 1984, faced by growing US intolerance of pro-Soviet regimes, Moscow set caution aside and decided on an assertive policy of supportive intervention, confident that Washington would be deterred from escalating to an intercontinental exchange.[41]

The third problem with Quinlan's heavily qualified claim is that a more satisfactory explanation already exists. There are three reasons, one systemic, one ideological, and one experiental, each of which on its own go a long way to explaining the last fifty years of partial peace. Taken together, they provide a more than sufficient explanation for the absence of war during forty-plus years of East–West confrontation, and one that is supported by the historical evidence.

The systemic explanation lies in the tidal change in the nature of international relations between 1850 and 1950,[42] a change that was largely obscured by the carnage of the First and Second World Wars. By the middle of the nineteenth century, the long-established 'great powers' were mainly 'satisfied' in respect to the European region,[43] and by the end of the century their drive for overseas possessions had peaked, although the process was not checked until the Second World War. There had, however, emerged in the second half of the nineteenth century three new 'western' nations—Italy, Germany, and Japan—who were *not* satisfied. Arriving late on the scene, they called for their share of the spoils, and it was these ambitions that led to the 'Forty Years War' that ended in 1945.

This war, which reached unprecedented levels of destructiveness in 1915–18 and 1941–5, masked a fundamental shift in the factors of international power and the relative utility of different instruments of national policy. For most of the 500 years which saw the quarrelsome nations of Europe move out and effectively take over the world, national wealth and political prestige were largely associated with control of territory, trade, and raw materials. These were finite resources, competition was zero sum, and the utility of military force as an instrument of political and economic policy was high.

By the middle of the nineteenth century, these factors of power were already changing.[44] By the beginning of the twentieth century, it was being argued that war between major industrial states was surely dysfunctional, a prognosis that was proven correct by the First World War and finally assimilated after the Second World War. For industrially advanced nations, the world of military capabilities and geostrategy has now been replaced by a world of economic strength and geofinance, in which national power derives from export industries and currency markets. This change is exemplified by Germany and Japan, which secured through their economic exertions in the post-war period much of what they sought through war in the 1930s and 1940s.[45]

A second reason for the absence of war was the nature of the ideological conflict. The West tended to define it in absolute terms, as a struggle between good and evil, freedom and slavery. The Soviets defined it in evolutionary terms, a struggle between an outmoded system of capitalistic imperialism and the emerging system of world socialism. Central to Marxist theory was the idea that socio-economic forces shaped history. Military power was required to counter attempts by the capitalists to suppress these forces, but the revolution could not be spread on the swords of a socialist jihad. Unlike the military challenge posed by the Axis Powers to the established Western order, the Soviet challenge was one of ideas based on theory, and the progressive shift in the correlation of forces after 1917 and the steady spread of socialism following the Second World War appeared to confirm that history was on their side.[46] Historical inevitability justified a long perspective and, unless the security of the homeland was at risk, the Soviets were always ready to cut their losses in the competition for world influence.

A third reason was the experience of two world wars and their aftermath. The Second World War gave renewed impetus to the establishment of a global organization designed to help resolve conflicts and prevent war, and prompted the idea of a European Union. The United Nations metastasized into an ever-growing family of international agencies, organizations, and regimes (and an even larger number of NGOs), which worked to reinforce the tidal change in international relations and the nascent concept of some kind of 'world order'.

The Second World War also brought the Americans face-to-face with the Soviets in Europe and, within a few years, most of the advanced states had been corralled into one of two alliances, each of which kept the peace between its members.[47] Worst-case analyses ensured that there was ample evidence to support each side's perceptions of the other's aggressive intentions. Both sides sought to deter the other, and by 1953 Western threat perceptions had become encased in nuclear deterrence theory. This was premised on a Soviet urge to invade Europe, with the ultimate goal of military world domination, and Western strategic analysis focused entirely on enemy capabilities, with aggressive intentions being taken as given.[48]

The systematic nature of Marxist-Leninist military science meant that Soviet doctrine continued to evolve and by 1959, the threat of premeditated Western attack had been discounted. The possibility of world war remained inherent in the antagonisms of the two social system, but the danger was now inadvertent or accidental war. This might be avoided, but could not be deterred.

Soviet policy was therefore shaped to avoid crises and military confrontation, unless the survival of the Soviet system was at risk. That threat resurfaced at the end of the 1970s and became steadily more serious in the first half of the 1980s. It was fortuitous (and fortunate) that Mikhail Gorbachev, elected general secretary in March 1985 on the grounds of his domestic skills as a party apparatchik and economic manager, had the detachment to recognize the dangerous absurdity of the hyper-armed action–reaction confrontation.

It was the theoretical nature of the Marxist-Leninist view of international relations and the systematic approach to military doctrine that allowed the Soviets
in 1987–8 to redefine both in such a way as to justify walking away from the
arms race and withdrawing their forces from Eastern Europe, thus signalling
the end of the cold war.[49]

These interdependent explanations and their ancillary consequences
provide a persuasive reason for what Quinlan calls the 'remarkable maintenance of peace' during the East–West confrontation, but there remains one
ambiguity. Recognizing that the Soviets (at least) were constrained by the
danger of inadvertent war, did that only apply to the *reductio ad absurdum* of
nuclear war (as Quinlan suggests) or did it extend to include major conventional war?

A review of the post-war period shows that the pattern of war avoidance
was set well before the 1960s, when the strategic nuclear arms race took off.
The American case is particularly instructive because there were strong incentives to resort to war in the 1946–56 period and the possibility of war with
the Soviet Union was part of public discourse. By the second half of 1946, it
was often spoken of as inevitable, while in 1947 the idea of preventive war was
common currency and the option of bombing Moscow was openly discussed.
At least three senators proposed dropping atomic bombs on Russia to enforce
compliance with US policies.[50]

There were three main incentives for going to war: the deep ideological
aversion to communism; the idealistic objection to Soviet domination of
Eastern Europe; and the requirement for national security, newly defined in
expansive terms.[51] By the summer of 1946, the dominant body of official
opinion in Washington was that the very existence of the Soviet Union
threatened American security,[52] and by March 1947, the idea that Soviet communism was bent on world conquest had been firmly implanted in the American mind.

Except for losses of men and military *matériel*, America had come through
the Second World War relatively unscathed, with its industrial base expanded
and intact. It had developed a culture of strategic bombing and enjoyed a
nuclear monopoly.[53] But despite this overall military advantage, the continuing 'acceptability' of war as an instrument of policy, and strong incentives to
go to war, America chose not to do so. In 1948, it established an air bridge
rather than risk an armoured thrust to Berlin. In 1951–2 it kept secret the
involvement of Soviet-manned aircraft in the Korean War. And despite brave
words about 'roll back', it stood back from the East German riots in 1953 and
the Hungarian uprising in 1956.

One can argue about the particular mix of factors that led to each of those
decisions, but two things are certain. In the first three cases, fear of nuclear
escalation could not have been a factor, because the Soviet Union lacked an
effective nuclear capability of any kind.[54] In all four cases, the danger of

becoming embroiled in a conventional war with the Soviet Union was a major factor, and probably the determining one.[55]

At this same period (as discussed below) the Soviet Union had neither the urge nor the capability to invade Western Europe. For both sides, the Second World War had reaffirmed that serious war between major states was not a rational instrument of policy and must be avoided at almost any cost. The pattern of war avoidance was established well before the threat of bilateral nuclear escalation emerged. Since then the costs of conventional war have risen to include the devastating results of enemy attack on chemical plants and nuclear power stations.

In sum, even if nuclear deterrence were cost-free (which it isn't), our experience since the Second World War provides no grounds for arguing that the fear of nuclear escalation is needed to deter advanced military powers from resorting to major war as a way of settling their differences. They are well aware that major war is dysfunctional, that the components of power have shifted, and that economic strength is now the crucial factor.

9.4.2. Cold-War Perceptions

Turning to the more general claim that nuclear weapons have kept the peace, this can only be applied (at best) to the superpowers and their allies in Europe. But before dissecting that claim, we should register a case where nuclear weapons did not keep the peace, namely the Korean War (1950–4), in which China was not deterred by the US nuclear monopoly from entering the war when the 'UN' forces crossed the 38th Parallel.

In order to validate their claim with respect to Europe, the *traditionalists* must show that (1) the Soviets had both the urge and the capability for military aggression in Europe, and (2) they would not have been deterred from such action by the prospect of fighting a conventional war. Given the devastation of the Soviet homeland and the level of military and civilian casualties in the Second World War, this second point is inherently implausible. Nor is the first point any easier to demonstrate.

If the Soviet Union had this urge to territorial expansion, why did it withdraw its forces from so many strategic areas in the wake of the Second World War and again in the 1950s?[56] Second, where was the *incentive* for the Soviet Union to go to war? In the course of evicting the Axis invaders, it had regained the territories it lost in 1918–21 and restored the old imperial boundaries.[57] In 1947–8, when Moscow came to perceive the more immediate threat of a capitalist-initiated war within five years, the *de facto* front line was 500 miles west of Soviet territory and ran across the narrowest part of the continent, making it easier to turn Eastern Europe into a military and ideological glacis. And third, where was the Soviet *capability* to go to war? In 1946–7, the time when US threat assessments swung to portraying Soviet communism as set on military world domination, the Soviet Union could barely feed its people and had adopted the expedient of removing the second track of German railways to help restore the rail system in Russia.[58]

These historical facts contradict the Western portrayal of Soviet capabilities and intentions in 1947–53, the period when mutual perceptions of threat crystallized into East–West confrontation.[59] Such 'worst-case' assumptions may have been justified as the basis for the military contingency planning that shaped Western policies in Europe at that time. But those fallacious assumptions cannot now be promoted to 'truths' and used to argue that, having kept the peace in the past, nuclear weapons must be retained for that purpose in the future.

Furthermore, nuclear deterrence did not always yield the results predicted by theory. In 1967, NATO adopted a policy of 'flexible response', designed to make nuclear deterrence more credible and hence war *less* likely. In practice it led to the opposite result. In the event of war, the so-called 'conventional pause' provided the Soviets with the opportunity to neutralize NATO's theatre delivery systems by conventional means, which would remove the first rung of the escalation ladder.[60] Should war seem inescapable, the new possibility of finessing nuclear escalation in the European theatre would reduce the constraints on launching a pre-emptive conventional attack, making it just that much *more* likely that the Soviets would cross the threshold from peace to war. This was the opposite to what the West had intended. So much for the theory. On the ground, the wholesale restructuring of Soviet forces to exploit this conventional opportunity coincided with the redirection of US military attention from Vietnam to the European theatre. Combined with other factors, this heightened Western perceptions of threat and sharply increased international tension, increasing the danger of inadvertent war.

9.5. *The Argument for Elimination*

It clarifies the argument to invert the order of the previous discussion and start with the traditionalists' case and the problem with their claims.

9.5.1. The Traditionalists' Case

There are two main variants of this argument, both based on perceptions of the cold-war years. The strong argument assumes that Soviet communism was set on military world domination and they were only prevented from seizing Western Europe (the essential first step) by the threat of nuclear devastation.

The historical evidence shows that in 1947–60 the Soviets lacked the urge, incentive, and capability to invade Western Europe. In respect to the procurement, structuring, and deployment of Soviet forces in the 1947–87 period, the only hypothesis that explains the totality of the evidence is that Soviet military requirements were shaped by the very real possibility of world war, a war the Soviets absolutely wanted to avoid, but could not afford to lose.[61]

The weak variant of the argument claims that, even assuming the Soviets had no urge to conquest, the possibility of conflict escalating to nuclear war engendered caution in decision-makers and probably played some part in the maintenance of peace, despite the East–West confrontation. There are at least three problems with this rather meagre claim: (1) the assumption that nuclear deterrence could not fail encouraged risky behaviour rather than caution; (2) a fully persuasive, multi-causal explanation for the absence of East–West conflict is already available; and (3) no account is taken of the costs of deterrence.

Ancillary arguments are advanced by traditionalists to justify the retention of nuclear weapons, even if (like Quinlan) they would not acquire them *de novo*.[62] There are the pragmatists, who think the weapons may 'come in handy'; the sceptics, who argue 'better safe than sorry', without counting the costs of deterrence; the agnostics, who acknowledge the logic of an NWF world, but favour 'the devil they know', without thinking how it could mutate and grow in the next twenty to thirty years; and the optimists, who think marginalization is already under way, without considering the dying embers of a forest fire, where a change of wind can re-ignite a major conflagration; so too can a change in the international climate reignite a new and more deadly arms race.

The present low-salience nuclear world is a transient phenomenon, a consequence of the Soviet Union's disintegration. The dynamics of nuclear deterrence mean that high-salience is the equilibrium low-point (the 'sink') to which a nuclear world will naturally gravitate in the absence of some external impulse, such as the drive for an NWF world.

9.5.2. The Eliminators' Case

Their central contention is that the combination of human fallibility and nuclear weapons means that a nuclear exchange is ultimately inevitable. This judgement is supported by a significant body of empirical research, which concludes that 'nuclear inadvertence' was inherent in the structure of the opposing strategic forces during the cold war, and that there was considerable scope for misunderstanding or accident in the NATO command structure on the central front in Europe. There has yet to be any public challenge to the underlying analysis, which was published in 1989–93.

The evidence adduced in this chapter indicates that there was also a significant possibility for inadvertent conflict through mutual misunderstanding of the other side's reactions, interests, and objectives during the forty-plus years of East–West confrontation. The danger of escalation to unintended war was inherent in those situations and was exacerbated by deterrence doctrine, with its emphasis on condign punishment.

A deterrent strategy invariably reinforces and often generates an inherent bad-faith model that is immune to evidence that contradicts preconceived motivational assumptions. This provides fertile ground for misperception, confrontation, and possibly conflict. Meanwhile, deterrence theory increases the danger of inadvertent war by encouraging misplaced confidence in the ability to manipulate risk in crises. During the cold war, the manipulation of risk by the West sometimes yielded dividends, but that was because the Soviets' historical perspective allowed them to cut their losses and because 'they had the fear of war in their bones'.[63] The future is unlikely to be so simple.

9.5.3. A Comparison of Costs and Benefits

The two courses of action to be evaluated are: (1) persist with present policies; and (2) adopt the firm and serious policy goal of an NWF world. The assessment focuses on three aspects: the situation after the NWF threshold is crossed; the period between the adoption of such a goal and reaching the threshold; and the potential role of nuclear weapons in national policy.

First, once the NWF threshold is crossed, the possibility of break-out from the regime will exist. However, as a precondition for taking the final step, that possibility will be low and will diminish over time through the continued improvement of verification measures, the consolidation of the NWF regime, and the decay of 'tacit knowledge'.[64] 'Break-out' does not necessarily imply the use of nuclear weapons but should that occur, the calamity factor would be comparable to a localized natural disaster.

Second, retrospective analysis shows that in the bi-polar circumstances of the cold war there was a significant possibility of accidental or inadvertent nuclear war. In twenty to thirty years' time, failing the adoption of the goal of an NWF world, the probability of a significant exchange of nuclear weapons will have increased exponentially. Any such exchange would be a calamity of unprecedented dimensions. It could destroy civilization as we know it and jeopardize the survival of the human race.

As discussed later, adopting the goal of an NWF world would have a beneficial effect on international relations in general and the problem of preventing nuclear proliferation in particular, especially as regards verification and enforcement. Persisting with present policies, which perpetuate the two-tier system of the NPT, will not only generate further challenges to the regime, but will encourage attempts to evade the Chemical and Biological Weapons Conventions. And because enforcement will be suboptimal, the danger of nuclear terrorism will be higher. Meanwhile, dissension among the privileged 'nuclear-weapons states' will increase, as will the temptation for weapons-capable states to withdraw from the treaty.

Third, in terms of an improved international climate and a reduced risk of a nuclear holocaust, the benefits of adopting the goal of an NWF world are clear. What are the costs in terms of policy options foregone by giving up nuclear weapons? Traditionalists used to describe five tasks that needed a nuclear capability;[65] they now claim only two, but neither withstand scrutiny. As already discussed, historical analysis does not support the notion that the possibility of nuclear escalation is needed to deter major states from resorting to war. And in an NWF world, there would be no requirement to deter attacks by other nuclear powers.

The wider role of nuclear weapons is discussed in the final chapter of this book by Robert O'Neill, the aptly titled 'Weapons of the Under Dog'. He emphasizes the importance of *status* as a reason for possessing nuclear weapons and notes that the less powerful a state, the greater the gain from nuclear status. This inverse relationship applies also to the weapon's role as the great equalizer. That role is not, however, relevant to any of the three Western nuclear powers, and the question of status does not enter into Washington's calculations. Nor should it carry any weight in London and Paris when comparing the risks inherent in their existing nuclear policies with the risks of an NWF world.

9.5.4. Ancillary Benefits

If the nuclear weapon states were to adopt the 'the firm and serious policy-goal' of an NWF world, significant benefits would accrue to the international system. For example:

1. The number and variety of co-operative policy measures that would be involved in moving towards the goal of an NWF world would necessarily have a significant impact on national leaders and their electorates, and on the structure of the evolving international system.

2. The treaty-making process would help bridge the gap with the non-aligned nations and be a force for compromise and co-operation within the international community. By renouncing their nuclear capability, the most powerful nations would commit themselves to the greatest concessions. The transparency required to ensure control and verification of the NWF regime would apply to all.

3. Adopting the goal would defuse dissatisfaction with the Nuclear Non-Proliferation Treaty.

4. The policy goal would make it easier to police the Chemical and Biological Weapons Conventions and to monitor the Comprehensive Test Ban Treaty.

These benefits flow *from* the goal of an NWF world and begin to take effect from the moment of its adoption. The logic is that of the 'functionalist' approach to conflict prevention and international security, which has been demonstrated so powerfully in the genesis of the European Community. The EC grew out of the European Economic Community (founded in 1957 with just six nations), itself an extension of the European Coal and Steel Community (1950), which was the product of a policy decision to avoid further Franco-German conflict by intermeshing their heavy industry.

Although less tangible, the transformative effect of adopting a 'firm and serious policy-goal' was demonstrated by Mikhail Gorbachev's 'new political thinking about international relations', which he publicized with increasing vigour throughout 1985. Within two years, the adoption by a superpower of that clearly articulated policy, reflecting as it did the principles underlying the UN Charter and the conclusions of the Palme Commission Report, was largely instrumental in bringing about a relaxation of international tension from the heights it reached in the first half of the 1980s. This relaxation was achieved *without* noticeably softening Soviet policy towards America (that shift took place in spring 1987); *before* the first concrete evidence of the change in Soviet military doctrine (the asymmetrical INF treaty signed in December 1987); and *despite* Gorbachev's 'new political thinking' being dismissed in Washington and London as utopian propaganda.[66]

9.6. *The Feasibility of an NWF World*

There is a growing body of authoritative literature on the practical steps needed to achieve an NWF world,[67] but for the purpose of this truncated discussion, the feasibility of eliminating nuclear weapons is considered under three headings: adopting the goal; verification and compliance; and the elimination process.

9.6.1. The Goal

The policy-goal of an NWF world became a live issue in the wake of the Gulf War in 1991. This demonstrated America's global reach and overwhelming conventional capability, while highlighting the potential threat to that preponderance from 'the great equalizer', nuclear weapons. This led influential members of the US national security community to argue that elimination would be in America's interests, if it were possible. Russia (in the shape of the Soviet Union) had reached a similar conclusion in the mid-1980s (albeit for very different reasons), and China had long favoured an NWF world, because of its conventional potential.

As this window of opportunity began to open in Washington, it began to close in Moscow as a result of the disintegration of the Soviet Union and the new threat to Russia posed by NATO enlargement, which was announced in January 1994. The nuclear debate within the US administration had meanwhile been resolved in favour of the traditionalists and of a policy of punitive 'counter-proliferation' (of the kind applied to Iraq in late 1998), which would exploit the full potential of the impending 'revolution in military affairs'.

The United States is obviously the key to the whole process, and this development could be seen as a setback. But the concept of an NWF world had been legitimized and the debate has been joined by an increasing number of extremely authoritative and well-informed voices. The argument has yet to be won, but one of the strengths of the American political system is its openness to grass-root pressures and the readiness of individuals to band together to bring about fundamental change in public perceptions.

9.6.2. Verification and Compliance

The effectiveness of verification and compliance measures will obviously be critical to the acceptability and success of an NWF regime but, given the investment of sufficient resources, this is unlikely to be a problem. The discipline has made immense strides in the last ten years, but it is still low on its learning curve and there is significant scope for further advances. The full array of measures do not have to be in place before the signing of a treaty of serious intent, initiating negotiations on the shape of the regime, or starting the dismantling process, which is already in progress under START.

9.6.3. Elimination

The process of dismantling and eliminating the nuclear arsenals is expected to take some twenty to thirty years and will require the sustained political and financial commitment of the kind that drove the strategic arms race during the cold war. Given that commitment, the mechanics are perfectly feasible. The problems will lie with the policy process.

The goal of obviating the high probability of a global catastrophe means that there would be a quite unusual coincidence of interests among the various participants in the treaty-making process, and (as we have seen) there would be other advantages from adopting that goal. But problems arise before that goal can even be adopted.

Timetabling. One problem concerns disagreement over timing. It can be assumed that the elimination process would be mapped out in differing degrees of detail, starting with an overall conceptual plan setting out the main phases of arms reductions, with each phase subsequently divided into stages and, ultimately, each stage broken down into successive and/or concurrent steps. The argument is whether this process should conform to a rigid timetable (be 'time-bound') or be advanced as circumstances allow?

The issue is not one of method but of trust. The declared nuclear states made no attempt to meet their solemn commitment under the 1970 NPT to work for the elimination of nuclear weapons; they then refused to be tied down on this point at the Review and Extension Conference in 1995 and the subsequent negotiations on a CTBT. Having little political leverage, the demand for a time-bound commitment was a bargaining response by those who saw the NPT and CTBT as further enshrining the advantage of the declared nuclear states, while making no progress towards an NWF world.

In practice, the physical scale of the requirement, the complexity of the issues (political, military, legal, administrative, technological, and scientific), the number of unknowns, and the cybernetic effects of the process, make it both impractical and counter-productive to establish a fully time-bound schedule for eliminating nuclear weapons, even if it were acceptable to all members of the top tier.

Nevertheless, the question of 'good faith' *must* be addressed. An essential step would be for the main nuclear powers to make a caveat-free commitment to an NWF world, backed by a 'treaty of intent' and a sustained public education programme on the urgency of that goal and its feasibility. Equally important, this political commitment would be reinforced by agreed (and inviolable) procedures for continually establishing new targets and deadlines and for signing interim protocols and agreements. These procedures would be designed to drive the process inexorably towards that ultimate objective to be achieved at some unspecified time in the future. However, while there would be no predetermined deadline for the final stage of elimination, a continuous series of successively agreed interim deadlines would be an essential feature of the process.

Geopolitical preconditions. Concerned by the calibre of support that the argument for an NWF world is attracting, traditionalists now argue that any move towards nuclear disarmament can only be made as part of a wider move towards regional and global stability and security. This merely restates their traditional argument in a different form.

A more serious problem is presented by those who strongly favour an NWF world but, on the grounds of 'political reality', contend that the final stage of elimination requires the resolution of regional conflicts and the wide-ranging renunciation of the use of force.

The reality in question is American domestic politics; an electorate that has been brought up on the merits of nuclear deterrence; and pressure groups with a strong interest in its preservation. It is understandable that American advocates of elimination should make the process seem as evolutionary as possible. An NWF world would come about as the consequence (rather than the cause) of a fundamental change in the nature of international relations. Nuclear weapons would be progressively marginalized, and the process would be more one of atrophy than elimination.[68]

The problem with this politically realistic scenario is that it ignores other kinds of 'reality' which are outside American control. One is the international system. There is no reason why, in the absence of some major new initiative, the conflictual pattern of world affairs should not continue into the future and quite likely worsen. A major attraction of a decision to eliminate nuclear weapons is that it would provide such an initiative. Because nuclear weapons are mainly in the possession of nations with great-power status or pretensions, a voluntary decision by such states to join with others in removing this threat to humanity would have far-reaching consequences and could start a virtuous spiral towards a more harmonious international system.

Attempts to specify or even postulate geopolitical preconditions for various phases of eliminating nuclear weapons are unnecessary and misleading. As the elimination process unfolds, national leaders will make their own judgements as to what is militarily prudent and what is politically practical, while the specification of geopolitical preconditions will favour the obstructionists. They are misleading because they posit constraints that are amenable to change. The 'reality' of domestic politics has the unique advantage that it can be shaped by effective national leadership and public education.

9.7. *Conclusion*

The elimination of nuclear weapons is not only desirable, it is essential if we are to obviate the high probability of a nuclear catastrophe. The main obstacles to adopting the goal of an NWF world are complacency and fatalism: complacency that, having avoided an inadvertent nuclear exchange in the past, we will continue to do so in the future; fatalism that nuclear weapons cannot be disinvented and there is nothing to be done about it.

In practical terms (science and technology, organization, administration), the elimination of nuclear weapons is eminently feasible. In political terms, it requires vision, courage, and leadership by the five original nuclear-weapon states, the Western three in particular. Vision is needed to project the alternative courses of action twenty to thirty years ahead, to face up to the long-term consequences of current policies, and to visualize the ancillary benefits of adopting the goal of an NWF world in terms of international relations in general and the rule of law in particular.

Courage is needed to admit to Western electorates that things other than nuclear weapons were responsible for the avoidance of major war during the years of East-West confrontation, that deterrence doctrine actually increased the danger of unintended conflict with the Soviet Union, and that a significant danger of nuclear inadvertence was inherent in the posture of the opposing nuclear arsenals. Leadership is needed to ensure that once the goal of an NWF world is adopted, it continues to receive overriding priority in terms of political attention and resource allocation, until it is finally achieved.

At a time when the West is striking moral attitudes about genocide and other crimes against humanity, it would be ironic if its 'leaders' were unable to contemplate foregoing weapons that have no demonstrable utility, but whose very existence threatens the survival of civilization as we know it and even the human race.

10

Reflections on War in the Twenty-First Century: The Context for Nuclear Abolition

Robert S. McNamara

Peace . . . will require greater understanding and respect for differences within and across national boundaries. We humans do not have the luxury any longer of indulging our prejudices and ethnocentrism. They are anachronisms of our ancient past. The worldwide historical record is full of hateful and destructive behavior based on religious, racial, political, ideological, and other distinctions—holy wars of one sort or another. Will such behavior in the next century be expressed with weapons of mass destruction? If we cannot learn to accommodate each other respectfully in the twenty-first century, we could destroy each other at such a rate that humanity will have little to cherish.[1]

In this quotation the Carnegie Commission is saying, in effect, that the end of the cold war in 1989 did not, and will not, in and of itself, result in an end to conflict. We see evidence of the truth of that statement on all sides. The Iraqi invasion of Kuwait, the civil war in the former Yugoslavia, the turmoil in northern Iraq, the tension between India and Pakistan, the unstable relations between North and South Korea, and the conflicts across the face of Sub-Saharan Africa in Somalia, Sudan, Rwanda, Burundi, Zaïre, Sierra Leone, and Liberia. These all make clear that the world of the future will not be without conflict, conflict between disparate groups within nations and conflict extending across national borders. Racial, religious, and ethnic tensions will remain. Nationalism will be a powerful force across the globe. Political revolutions will erupt as societies advance. Historic disputes over political boundaries will endure. And economic disparities among and within nations will increase as technology and education spread unevenly around the world. The underlying causes of Third World conflict that existed long before the cold war began remain now that it has ended. They will be compounded by potential strife among states of the former Soviet Union and by continuing tensions in the Middle East. It is just such tensions that in the past fifty years have contributed to 125 wars causing forty million deaths.

So, in these respects, the world of the future will not be different from the world of the past—conflicts within nations and conflicts among nations will not disappear. But relations between nations will change dramatically. In the post-war years, the United States had the power—and to a considerable degree we exercised that power—to shape the world as we chose. In the next century that will not be possible. Japan is destined to play a larger role on the world scene, exercising greater economic and political power and, one hopes, assuming greater economic and political responsibility. The same can be said of Western Europe, following its major step toward economic integration.

And by the middle of the next century, several of the countries of what in the past we have termed the 'Third World' will have grown so dramatically in population and economic power as to become major forces in international relations. India is likely to have a population of 1.6 billion; Nigeria 400 million; Brazil 300 million. And if China achieves its ambitious economic goals for the year 2000 (they are likely to be exceeded), and then maintains satisfactory but not spectacular growth rates for the next fifty years, its 1.6 billion people will have the income of Western Europeans in the 1960s. It will indeed be a power to be reckoned with: economically, politically, and militarily.

These figures are of course highly speculative. I point to them simply to emphasize the magnitude and pace of the changes that lie ahead and the need now to adjust our goals, our policies, and our institutions to take account of them. In particular, they should make clear that neither the USA nor Japan has even begun to adjust its foreign policy to relate properly to the China it will face in our children's lifetime. While remaining the world's strongest nation, in the next century the USA will live in a multi-polar world, and its foreign policy and defence programmes must be adjusted to this emerging reality. In such a world, need clearly exists for developing new relationships both among the great powers and between the great powers and other nations.

Many political theorists, in particular those classified as 'realists', predict a return to traditional power politics. They argue that the disappearance of ideological competition between East and West will trigger a reversion to traditional relationships based on territorial and economic imperatives. They say that the United States, Russia, Western Europe, China, Japan, and perhaps India will seek to assert themselves in their own regions while still competing for dominance in other areas of the world where conditions are fluid. This view has been expressed, for example, by Harvard Professor Michael Sandel, who has written: 'The end of the Cold War does not mean an end of global competition between the Superpowers. Once the ideological dimension fades, what you are left with is not peace and harmony, but old-fashioned global politics based on dominant powers competing for influence and pursuing their internal interests.'[2] Henry Kissinger, also a member of the 'realist' school, has expressed a similar conclusion:

Victory in the Cold War has propelled America into a world which bears many similarities to the European state system of the eighteenth and nineteenth centuries. . . . The absence of both an overriding ideological or strategic threat frees nations to pursue foreign policies based increasingly on their immediate national interest. In an international system characterized by perhaps five or six major powers and a multiplicity of smaller states, order will have to emerge much as it did in past centuries from a reconciliation and balancing of competing national interests.[3]

In contrast to Sandel and Kissinger, Carl Kaysen, former director of the Institute of Advanced Studies at Princeton, has written that: 'The international system that relies on the national use of military force as the ultimate guarantor of security, and the threat of its use as the basis of order, is not the only possible one. To seek a different system . . . is no longer the pursuit of an illusion, but a necessary effort toward a necessary goal.'[4]

Kissinger's and Sandel's conceptions of relations among nations in the post-cold-war world are, of course, historically well founded, but I would argue that they are inconsistent with our increasingly interdependent world. No nation, not even the United States, can stand alone in a world in which nations are inextricably entwined with one another economically, environmentally, and with regard to security. I believe, therefore, that for the future the United Nations Charter offers a far more appropriate framework for international relations than does the doctrine of power politics.

I would argue also that Kissinger and Sandel's emphasis on balance-of-power politics in the twenty-first century assumes we will be willing to continue to accept a foreign policy which lacks a strong moral foundation. I am aware that the majority of political scientists, particularly those who are members of the political realist school, believe morality—as contrasted with a careful calculation of national interests, based on balance-of-power considerations—is a dangerous guide for the establishment of foreign policy. They would say that a foreign policy driven by moral considerations promotes zealousness and a crusading spirit, with potentially dangerous results.

But surely, in the most basic sense, one can apply a moral judgement to the level of killing which occurred in the twentieth century. There can be no justification for it. Nor can there be any justification for its continuation into the twenty-first century. On moral grounds alone, we should act today to prevent such an outcome. A first step would be to establish such an objective as the primary foreign-policy goal both for our own nation and for the entire human race.

The United States has defined itself in highly idealistic and moral terms throughout our history. We have seen ourselves as defenders of human freedoms across the globe. That feeling was the foundation of Woodrow Wilson's support for normative rules of international behaviour to be administered by a League of Nations. Our moral vision has had an impact on the world. It has led to the formation of a score of international institutions in the economic, social, and political fields. But it remains under attack both within and outside the USA—by those who put greater weight on considerations of narrow national interest.

Many of the most controversial foreign-policy debates have found both sides basing their arguments on moral considerations. US policy towards Cuba today is justified on moral grounds by its supporters who say it is immoral to support dictators who abuse human rights. And it is attacked, on moral grounds, by its critics who say it leads to suffering by the mass of the Cuban people. Similarly, a US policy toward China which placed primary emphasis on support of individual civil rights might well weaken the Chinese government's ability to increase the access of the mass of its population to advances in nutrition, education, and health.

Nor do moral considerations offer a clear guide to action in many other foreign-policy disputes: for example, the conflicts today in the Middle East or in the former Yugoslavia. And even where the moral objective may be clear—as in Rwanda and Burundi where all agreed the killing should stop—we may lack the capability to achieve it. We are learning that external military force has limited power to restore a failed state. Moreover, peoples of different religions and different cultures, confronting common problems, often arrive at different moral judgements relating to conflicts between individual and group rights, between group rights and national rights, and between the rights of individual nations.

So, while there is general acceptance in the USA of the proposition that our foreign policy should advance the welfare of peoples across the globe in terms of political freedom, freedom from want, and preservation of the environment, those objectives are so general that they provide little guidance to addressing the problems which a government confronts each day.

But can we not agree that there is one area of foreign policy in which moral principles should prevail and in which they have not? And that is in relation to the settlement of disputes within nations and among nations without resort to violence. If so, three specific steps are required:

1. We should reduce the risk of conflict within and among nations by establishing a system of collective security[5] which would have two objectives: the prevention of war and the termination of conflict in the event deterrence fails.

2. The system of collective security should place particular emphasis on limiting the risk of war between or among great powers.

3. To avoid the risk of destruction of nations, in the event collective security breaks down, we should redouble our efforts to eliminate weapons of mass destruction, particularly nuclear weapons.

The collective security regime should:

(1) Provide all states with collective guarantees against external aggression—frontiers would not be changed by force.

(2) Codify the rights of minorities and ethnic groups within states—the rights of Muslims in Bosnia, for example—and provide a process by which such groups, who believe their rights have been violated, may seek redress without resort to violence.

(3) Establish a mechanism for resolution of both regional conflicts, and conflicts within nations, without unilateral action by the great powers. Military force, other than in defence of national territory, would be used only multilaterally in accordance with agreed-upon norms.

In sum, I believe we should strive to move toward a world in which relations among nations would be based on the rule of law, a world in which conflict-resolution and peace-keeping functions necessary to accomplish these objectives would be performed by multilateral organizations—a reorganized and strengthened United Nations and new and expanded regional organizations. That is my vision of a system of collective security for the twenty-first century.

Such a vision is easier to articulate than to achieve. The goal is clear; but how to get there is not. And I have no magic formula, no simple road map to success. I do know that such a vision will not be achieved in a month, a year, or even a decade. It will be achieved, if at all, slowly and through small steps by leaders of dedication and persistence. So I urge that we begin that process now. Such a world will need leaders. The leadership role may shift among nations depending on the issue at hand. But more often than not, no nation other than the USA will be capable of filling that role.

However, we cannot succeed in such an endeavour without the co-operation of other nations. And we will not receive that co-operation if we continue to act as though we were omniscient. We are not. And yet over and over again—as with respect to Vietnam, Cuba, Iran, and Iraq—we act as though we think we are. Failing to obtain the endorsement of other nations, we have applied our power unilaterally. My belief is that the USA should never apply its economic, political, or military power other than in a multilateral context. The single exception would be in the highly unlikely case of a direct threat to the security of the continental USA, Alaska or Hawaii.

Whenever the USA accepts leadership in such a multilateral context, it must accept collective decision-making—a concept our people are neither accustomed to nor comfortable with. And other nations—certainly including Japan—must accept a sharing of the risks and costs: the political risks, the financial costs, and the risks of casualties. If the casualities in the Gulf War had been as great as the US Joint Chiefs of Staff originally forecast, 90 per cent of the 'blood cost' would have been borne by the USA while by far the greater part of the benefits—in the form of assured petroleum supply—would have accrued to other nations.

Had the United States and other major powers made clear their commitment to such a system of collective security, and had they stated they would protect nations against attack, the 1990 Iraqi invasion of Kuwait might well have been deterred. Similarly, had the United Nations or NATO taken action, when conflict in the former Yugoslavia erupted in the early 1990s, the ensuing slaughter of tens of thousands of innocent victims might have been prevented.

In the post-cold-war world, operating under a system of collective security, nations—and, in particular, the great powers—should be clear about where, and how, they would apply military force. They clearly cannot and should not intervene in every conflict involving the slaughter of innocent civilians. More than a dozen wars currently rage throughout the world. And other serious conflicts may soon break out elsewhere. Where, if at all, should the great powers and/or the United Nations be involved? Neither the United States nor any other great power has a clear answer to that question. The answers can be developed only through intense debate, over a period of years, within our own nation, among the other great powers, and in the councils of international organizations.

The rules governing response to aggression across national borders can be relatively simple and clear. But those relating to attempts to maintain or restore political order and to prevent wholesale slaughter within nations as, for instance, within Rwanda or Burundi, are far less so. The criteria determining the use of US military forces should be derived from a precise statement of US foreign-policy objectives. For forty years our objective remained clear: to contain an expansionist Soviet Union. But that can no longer be the focus of our efforts. We have lost our enemy. What will we put in its place? President Clinton told the UN General Assembly on 27 September 1993: 'Our overriding purpose must be to expand and strengthen the world's community of market-based democracies.' Anthony Lake, the national security adviser, echoed this a short time later when he stated that 'the successor to a doctrine of containment must be a strategy of enlargement—enlargement of the world's free community of market democracies'. Such a general formulation of our objectives is not sufficient.

The United States cannot and should not intervene in every conflict arising from a nation's attempt to move towards capitalist democracy. For example, we were surely correct not to support with military force Eduard Shevardnadze's attempt to install democracy in Georgia. Nor can we be expected to try to stop by military force every instance of the slaughter of innocent civilians.

10.1. *The Question of Military Intervention*

Several crucial questions must be faced. To what degree of human suffering should we respond? Under a UN convention, formalized in a global treaty in

1989, the United States agreed to join in stopping genocide. But what constitutes genocide? In June 1994, the US government, while recognizing the killing of over 200,000 Rwandans as 'acts of genocide', refused to state that the killing fell under the treaty's provisions.[6] And would there not be other cases, short of genocide, that would also justify intervention? At what point should we intervene—as preventive diplomacy fails and killing appears likely, or only when the slaughter is increasing? How should we respond when nations involved in such conflicts, as was the case in the former Yugoslavia, claim that outside intervention clearly infringes on their sovereignty? We have seen regional organizations—in particular, the Organisation of African Unity and the Organisation of American States—time and time again fail to support such intervention.

Above all else, the criteria governing intervention should recognize a lesson we should have learnt in Vietnam: external military force has only a limited capacity to facilitate the process of nation-building. It should be made clear to our people that such questions will, at best, require years to answer. But we should force the debate within our own nation and within international forums. Some of the issues may never be resolved. There may be times when we must recognize that we cannot right all wrongs. If we are to achieve the objective of avoiding in the twenty-first century the tragic loss of life we have just lived through, above all else, special emphasis must be placed on avoiding conflict among the great powers.

10.2. *Relations between the Great Powers*

Excluding the end of the cold war, I believe the two most important geopolitical events of the past fifty years have been the reconciliation between France and Germany, after centuries of enmity, and the establishment of peaceful relations between Japan and the USA, after one of the bloodiest conflicts in the modern era. It is inconceivable today that either Germany or Japan would engage in war with any of the great powers of the Western world. Can we not move to integrate both Russia and China into the family of nations in ways that make war between them and the other great powers equally unlikely? We have not done so.

The expansion of NATO is viewed by many Russian leaders as a threat to their security. At a time when the nation's military forces—both conventional and nuclear—have been severally weakened, they see NATO planning to move its forces to their western borders. This has strengthened the position of their hard-line nationalists, increased their feelings of xenophobia, and, with the scrapping of their doctrine of 'no first use', led to a more aggressive nuclear policy. George Kennan has stated NATO expansion will prove to be one of the greatest foreign-policy mistakes made by the West since the end of the Second World War. I agree with him.

Similarly, China has viewed the action taken in 1997 by Japan and the USA to extend—and, in the words of the Chinese, 'to expand'—the US–Japan Security Treaty as a hostile act. In 1997, Prime Minister Li Peng stated very emphatically to me and my associates, during a visit to his country, that whereas, initially, the treaty might have been directed against the Soviet Union, with the end of the cold war it could have no purpose other than to contain and, ultimately, threaten China. He supported his argument by emphasizing that, unlike Germany, Japan had never admitted or accepted responsibility for its role in the Second World War. He claimed—perhaps with exaggeration—that Japan was responsible for 20 million Chinese dead. And he said he observed continuing signs of militarism in Japanese society.

Dangerous frictions also exist between China and the USA arising from divergent policies toward Taiwan, North Korea, and the east Asia region. My associates and I were shocked by the vehemence with which the Chinese stated their views. I mention them here to illustrate how far both we and the Japanese have to go before we can establish a pattern of relations with China comparable to those which exist between France and Germany and between the USA and Japan.

10.3. *Weapons of Mass Destruction*

I turn now to the third of the three actions to which I urge immediate attention be directed: action to avoid the risk of destruction of nations, through the use of weapons of mass destruction, in particular, nuclear weapons, in the event that collective security breaks down.

Today, nine years after the end of the cold war, there are approximately 40,000 nuclear warheads in the world with a destructive power more than 1 million times greater than the bomb that flattened Hiroshima. We in the USA—and all other inhabitants of our globe—continue to live with the risk of nuclear destruction. US war plans provide for contingent use of nuclear weapons just as they did when I was Secretary of Defence thirty-seven years ago in the 1960s. But I do not believe that the average American recognizes this fact. No doubt, he or she was surprised and pleased by the announcement of the START I nuclear arms control treaty, which was signed by the USA and Russia in 1991. When finally implemented it will reduce the arsenal to approximately 20,000 weapons. In June 1992, Presidents Bush and Yeltsin agreed to Start II which would further reduce the total to 10,000. In March 1997, Presidents Clinton and Yeltsin spoke of going still lower to a level of 6,000. But Start II has not been and may never be ratified.

Moreover, even if it, and the further reductions discussed in 1997, were to be approved by the Congress and the Duma, the risk of destruction of societies across the globe, while somewhat reduced, would be far from eliminated. I doubt that a survivor—if there was one—could perceive much difference between a world in which 6,000 nuclear warheads had been exploded and one subject to attack by 40,000. So the question is, can we not go further? Surely the answer must be yes. The question points to both the opportunity and the urgency with which the nuclear powers should re-examine their long-term nuclear force objectives. We should begin with *a broad public debate over alternative nuclear strategies*. I believe such a debate should open with a discussion of the moral issues relating to the use of nuclear weapons by the seven declared nuclear powers.

As I stated earlier, most political scientists and most security experts oppose introducing moral considerations into discussions of international relations and defence policy. And I will admit that in many situations they provide ambiguous guidance at best. But surely the human race should be prepared to accept that it is totally immoral for one nation, no matter what the provocation, to believe it—through its leader, acting alone—has the right to initiate action that will destroy another nation. And would it not be even more morally unacceptable if such action by one belligerent would destroy not only the other belligerent, but—through the spread of radioactive fallout—non-belligerent nations across the globe as well. Yet that would have been the result if either Russia or the USA had implemented the nuclear strategy which each nation followed for forty years and continues to follow today.

The debate should then move beyond moral considerations to a detailed examination of the military utility of nuclear weapons and of the offsetting military risks of their use. I believe it would support the conclusion that we should move back to a non-nuclear world. In support of my position, I will make three points:

1. The experience of the Cuban Missile Crisis in 1962—and, in particular, what has been learnt about it recently—makes clear that so long as we and other great powers possess large inventories of nuclear weapons, we will face the risk of their use and the destruction of our nation.

2. That risk is no longer—if it ever was—justifiable on military grounds.

3. In recent years, there has been a dramatic change in the thinking of leading Western security experts—both military and civilian—regarding the military utility of nuclear weapons. More and more of them, although certainly not yet a majority, are expressing views similar to those I have stated.

10.4. *The Lessons of the Cuban Missile Crisis*

It is now widely recognized that the actions of the Soviet Union, Cuba, and the United States in October 1962 brought the three nations to the verge of war. But what was not known then, and is not widely understood today, was how close the world came to the brink of nuclear disaster. Just a few months ago, the Kennedy Library released heretofore highly classified tapes[7] which provided new insights into the near catastrophe from a US point of view. A few months before that, a similar account of Khrushchev's state of mind was published.[8] Both accounts are frightening. Neither the Soviet Union nor the United States intended, by its actions, to create the risks they both incurred.

You may recall that the crisis began when the Soviets moved nuclear missiles and bombers to Cuba—secretly and with the clear intent to deceive—in the summer and early fall of 1962. The missiles were to be targeted against cities along America's East Coast. On Sunday, 14 October 1962 the deployments were brought to President Kennedy's attention. He and his military and civilian security advisers believed that the Soviets' action posed a threat to the West. Kennedy therefore authorized a naval quarantine of Cuba to be effective from Wednesday, 24 October. Preparations also began for air strikes and an amphibious invasion. The contingency plans called for a 'first-day' air attack of 1,080 sorties, a huge attack. An invasion force totalling 180,000 troops was assembled in south-eastern US ports. The crisis came to a head on Saturday, 27 October, and Sunday, 28 October. Had Khrushchev not publicly announced on that Sunday that he was removing the missiles, I believe that on the Monday a majority of Kennedy's military and civilian advisers would have recommended launching the attacks.

To understand what caused the crisis—and how to avoid similar ones in the future—high-ranking Soviet, Cuban, and American participants in the decisions relating to it met in a series of conferences beginning in 1987. The meetings extended over a period of five years. One chaired by Fidel Castro in Havana in January 1992 was the fifth and last. By the conclusion of the third meeting in Moscow, it had become clear that the decisions of each of the three nations, before and during the crisis, had been distorted by misinformation, miscalculation, and misjudgement. I shall cite only four of many examples:

1. Before Soviet missiles were introduced into Cuba in the summer of 1962, the Soviet Union and Cuba believed the United States intended to invade the island in order to overthrow Castro and remove his government. But we had no such intention.

2. The United States believed the Soviets would never move nuclear warheads outside the Soviet Union—that they never had—but in fact they did. In Moscow, in 1989, we learnt that by October 1962, although the CIA at the time was reporting no nuclear weapons on the island, Soviet nuclear warheads had, indeed, been delivered to Cuba. As I have said, they were to be targeted on US cities.

3. The Soviets believed that nuclear weapons could be introduced into

Cuba secretly, without detection, and that the USA would not respond when their presence was disclosed. There, too, they were in error.

4. Finally, those who were prepared to urge President Kennedy to destroy the missiles by a US air attack which, in all likelihood, would have been followed by an amphibious invasion, were almost certainly mistaken in their belief that the Soviets would not respond militarily. At the time, the CIA reported 10,000 Soviet troops in Cuba. At the Moscow conference, we learned there were in fact 43,000 Soviet troops on the island, along with 270,000 well-armed Cuban troops. Both forces, in the words of their commanders, were determined to 'fight to the death'. The Cuban officials estimated they would have suffered 100,000 causalities. The Soviets—including long-term Foreign Minister Andrei Gromyko and former Ambassador to the USA Anatoly Dobrynin—expressed utter disbelief that we would have thought that, in the face of such a catastrophic defeat, they would not have responded militarily somewhere in the world. Very probably, the result would have been uncontrollable escalation.

By the end of that meeting in Moscow, we had agreed we could draw two lessons from our discussions:

(1) In the face of nuclear weapons, crisis management is inherently dangerous, difficult, and uncertain; and

(2) Due to misjudgement, misinformation, and miscalculation of the kind I have referred to, it is not possible to predict with confidence the consequences of military action between great powers armed with such weapons. Therefore, we must direct our attention and energies to crisis avoidance.

In 1962, during the crisis, some of us—particularly President Kennedy and I—believed the United States faced great danger. The Moscow meeting confirmed that judgement. But during the Havana conference, we learnt that both of us—and certainly others—had seriously underestimated those dangers. While in Havana, we were told by the former Warsaw Pact Chief of Staff, General Anatoly Gribkov, that, in 1962, Soviet forces in Cuba possessed not only nuclear warheads for the intermediate-range missiles targeted on US cities, but nuclear bombs and tactical nuclear warheads as well. The tactical warheads were to be used against US invasion forces. At the time, as I mentioned, the CIA was reporting no warheads on the island.

In November 1992—thirty years after the event—we learnt more. An article appeared in the Russian press which stated that, at the height of the missile crisis, Soviet forces on Cuba possessed a total of 162 nuclear warheads, including at least 90 tactical warheads. Moreover, it was reported that, on 26 October 1962—a moment of great tension—warheads were moved from their storage sites to positions closer to their delivery vehicles in anticipation of a US invasion.[9] The next day, Soviet Defence Minister Malinovsky received a cable from

General Pliyev, the Soviet commander in Cuba, informing him of this action. Malinovsky sent it to Khrushchev. Khrushchev returned it to Malinovsky with 'Approved' scrawled across the document. Clearly, there was a high risk that in the face of a US attack—which, as I have said, many in the US government, military and civilian alike, were prepared to recommend to President Kennedy—the Soviet forces in Cuba would have decided to use their nuclear weapons rather than lose them.[10]

We need not speculate about what would have happened in that event. We can predict the results with certainty. Although a US invasion force would not have been equipped with tactical nuclear warheads—the President and I had specifically prohibited that—no one should believe that, had American troops been attacked with nuclear weapons, the US would have refrained from a nuclear response. And where would it have ended? In utter disaster.

10.5. *Nuclear Weapons and Risk*

Human beings are fallible. We know we all make mistakes. In our daily lives, mistakes are costly, but we try to learn from them. In conventional war, they cost lives, sometimes thousands of lives. But if mistakes were to affect decisions relating to the use of nuclear forces, there would be no learning period. They would result in the destruction of nations. I believe, therefore, it can be predicted with confidence that the indefinite combination of human fallibility and nuclear weapons carries a very high risk of a potential nuclear catastrophe.[11]

Is there a military justification for continuing to accept the risks inherent in nuclear use? The answer is no. Proponents of nuclear weapons have produced only one plausible scenario for initiating their use: a situation where there is no prospect of retaliation. That means either against a non-nuclear state or against one so weakly armed as to permit the user to have full confidence in his nuclear forces' capability to achieve a totally disarming first strike. But even such circumstances have not, in fact, provided a sufficient basis for the use of nuclear weapons in war. For example, although American forces were in desperate straits twice during the Korean War—first immediately following the North Korean attack in 1950 and then when the Chinese crossed the Yalu—the United States did not use nuclear weapons. At that time, North Korea and China had no nuclear capability and the Soviet Union only a negligible one.

The conclusion is clear the military utility of nuclear weapons is limited to deterring one's opponent from their use.[12] Therefore, if our opponent has no nuclear weapons, there is no need for us to possess them.

10.6. *Contemporary Changes in Thinking about Nuclear Weapons*

Partly because of the increased understanding of how close we came to disaster during the missile crisis, but also because of a growing recognition of the lack of military utility of the weapons, there has been a revolutionary change in thinking about the role of nuclear forces. Much of this change has occurred in the past five years. Many military leaders are now prepared to go far beyond the Bush–Yeltsin agreement. Some go so far as to state, as I have, that the long-term objective should be a return to a non-nuclear world.[13]

That is, however, a very controversial proposition. A majority of Western security experts—both military and civilian—continue to believe that the threat of the use of nuclear weapons prevents war. Zbigniew Brzezinski, President Carter's national security adviser, has argued that a plan for eliminating nuclear weapons 'is a plan for making the world safe for conventional warfare. I am therefore not enthusiastic about it.' A report of an advisory committee, appointed by former Defence Secretary Richard Cheney and chaired by former Air Force Secretary Thomas Reed, made essentially the same point.[14] Clearly the current Administration supports that position.[15] However, even if one accepts that argument, it must be recognized that the deterrent to conventional force aggression carries a very high long-term cost: the risk of a nuclear exchange.

It is that risk—which to me is unacceptable—that is leading prominent security experts to change their views. I doubt that the public is aware of these changes. They have been reflected in numerous unclassified, but not widely disseminated, statements. I will cite only a few. Four recent reports, three of which I referred to earlier, all recommend major changes in nuclear strategies and drastic reductions in nuclear force levels.

1. The spring 1993 issue of *Foreign Affairs* carried an article, co-authored by retired Chairman of the Joint Chiefs of Staff, Admiral William J. Crowe, Jr., which concluded that, by the year 2000, the USA and Russia could reduce strategic nuclear forces to 1,000–1,500 warheads each. The article was later expanded into a book which added; 'Nor is 1,000–1,500 the lowest level obtainable by the early 21st Century.'[16]

2. In December 1995, the Stimson Center Report, signed by four recently retired four-star officers, recommended moving through a series of four steps to the goal of 'elimination' of nuclear weapons.[17]

3. The Canberra Commission, which was appointed by Prime Minister Keating of Australia, recommended in 1996 'a program to achieve a world totally free of nuclear weapons' (p. 7). The Commission members included, among others: Michel Rocard, the former prime minister of France; Joseph

Rotblat, the 1995 Nobel Laureate and one of the designers of the original nuclear bomb; Field Marshal Lord Carver, former Chief of the British Defence Staff; General Lee Butler, former commander of the US Strategic Air Command; and myself. The Commission's recommendations were unanimous. They were presented without any qualification or even the slightest note of dissent among the seventeen members of the commission.

4. The National Academy of Sciences Report (1997) stated that reductions by the US and Russia, within a few years, to a level of 2,000 warheads each 'should be easily accommodated within the existing and anticipated strategic force structures of both sides' (p. 59). It then recommended moving to 1,000 warheads each and later to 'roughly 300 each' (p. 80).

These four reports should not have come as surprises. For nearly twenty years, more and more Western military and civilian security experts have expressed doubts about the military utility of nuclear weapons. This is what they have said:

- By 1982, five of the seven retired Chiefs of the British Defence Staff expressed their belief that initiating the use of nuclear weapons, in accordance with NATO policy, would lead to disaster. Lord Louis Mountbatten, Chief of Staff 1959 to 1965, said a few months before he was murdered in 1979: 'As a military man I can see no use for any nuclear weapons.' And Field Marshal Lord Carver, Chief of Staff 1973–6, wrote in 1982 that he was totally opposed to NATO ever initiating the use of nuclear weapons.[18]
- Henry Kissinger, speaking in Brussels in 1979, made quite clear he believed the US would never initiate a nuclear strike against the Soviet Union, no matter what the provocation. 'Our European allies', he said, 'should not keep asking us to multiply strategic assurances that we cannot possibly mean or if we do mean, we should not execute because if we execute we risk the destruction of civilization.'[19]
- Melvin Laird, President Nixon's first Secretary of Defence, was reported in *The Washington Post* of 12 April 1982 as saying: 'A worldwide zero nuclear option with adequate verification should now be our goal . . . These weapons . . . are useless for military purposes.'
- Former West German Chancellor Helmut Schmidt stated in a 1987 BBC interview: 'Flexible response [NATO's strategy calling for the use of nuclear weapons in response to a Warsaw Pact attack by non-nuclear forces] is nonsense. Not out of date, but nonsense . . . The Western idea, which was created in the 1950s, that we should be willing to use nuclear weapons first, in order to make up for our so-called conventional deficiency, has never convinced me.'[20]
- Admiral Noel Gaylor, former Commander-in-Chief of US air, ground, and sea forces in the Pacific, remarked in 1987: 'There is no sensible

military use of any of our nuclear forces. The only reasonable use is to deter our opponent from using his nuclear forces.'

- General Larry Welch, former US Air Force Chief of Staff and previously Commander of the Strategic Air Command, recently put the same thought in these words: 'Nuclear deterrence depended on someone believing that you would commit an act totally irrational if done.'[21]
- In July 1994, General Charles A. Horner, then Chief of the US Space Command, stated: 'The nuclear weapon is obsolete. I want to get rid of them all.'[22]
- On 5 December 1996, nineteen senior retired US military officers and forty-two senior admirals and generals from other nations across the world stated their support for complete elimination of nuclear weapons.
- On 2 February 1998, 119 present and former heads of state and other senior civilian leaders—including, for example, Helmut Schmidt, Michel Rocard, James Callaghan, Jimmy Carter, and six former prime ministers of Japan—endorsed a similar statement.

10.7. *Conclusion*

In the early 1960s, I had reached conclusions similar to those which I have cited. In long private conversations, first with President Kennedy and then with President Johnson, I had recommended, without qualification, that they never initiate, under any circumstances, the use of nuclear weapons.[23] I believe they accepted my recommendations. But neither they nor I could discuss our positions publicly because they were totally contrary to established NATO policy.

In truth, for over thirty years, with respect to our stated nuclear policy, it could have been said 'The Emperor has no clothes'. I do not believe that after 1960, by which time the Soviets had acquired a survivable retaliatory force, any one of our presidents—Eisenhower, Kennedy, Johnson, Nixon, Ford, Carter, Reagan, Bush, or Clinton—would ever have initiated the use of nuclear weapons. Nor would our allies have wished them to do so. To initiate a nuclear strike against a comparably equipped opponent would have been tantamount to committing suicide. To initiate use against a non-nuclear opponent would have been militarily unnecessary, politically indefensible, and morally repugnant. It was the acceptance of that judgement that led the Canberra Commission to recommend the complete elimination of nuclear weapons.

But the Commission went further. It accepted the evidence that the current nuclear posture of both Russia and the USA poses a totally unacceptable danger to the two countries and indeed to the peace of the world. A report by Bruce G. Blair of The Brookings Institution graphically describes the danger.[24]

Blair states that both the USA and Russia keep thousands of nuclear warheads on 'hair trigger' alert, poised for launch before the opposing side's missiles reach their targets. The 'launch on warning' doctrine requires that in less than fifteen minutes a missile attack be detected and analysed, the decision to retaliate made, and orders to do so disseminated to hundreds of weapons sites. The risk of accidental, inadvertent, or unauthorized launch would exist under the best of conditions. But today, according to Russia's own commanders, their country's alert position is particularly vulnerable. Their command posts will not survive attack, much of their early-warning network is not functioning; safeguards against unauthorized use of nuclear forces are ineffective, large numbers of both their land-based and sea-based forces are inoperative; and the majority of the remainder would not survive a US counter-force attack. The situation, in Blair's words, is 'extremely dangerous'. Both the USA and Russia, while seeking to deter a vanishing risk of deliberate nuclear aggression, are running a growing risk of stumbling into an inadvertent nuclear war.

The Canberra Commission came to the same conclusion. Therefore, with the strong support of its two military chiefs (Field Marshal Lord Carver and former US Strategic Air Command Commander General Lee Butler), it urged that the five declared nuclear powers at that time—China, Russia, Britain, France, and the United States—not only state their unequivocal political commitment to the elimination of nuclear weapons, but accompany that commitment with three immediate steps consistent with fulfilling it:

(1) the removal of all nuclear weapons from alert status;
(2) the separation of all nuclear warheads from their launch vehicles;
(3) a declaration of 'no first use' of nuclear weapons against nuclear states, and 'no use' against non-nuclear nations.

Years will pass before the Commission's recommendations are fully implemented. But we are beginning to break out of the mindset that has guided the strategy of the nuclear powers for over four decades. More and more political and military leaders are coming to understand two fundamental truths: (1) we can indeed 'put the genie back in the bottle'; (2) if we do not, there is a substantial and unacceptable risk that the twenty-first century will witness a nuclear holocaust.

In sum, with the end of the cold war, if we act to establish a system of collective security, and if we take steps to move to a non-nuclear world, the twenty-first century, while certainly not a century of tranquillity, need not witness the killing, by war, of another 160 (or even 300) million people. Surely that must be not only our hope, not only our dream, but our steadfast objective. I know that some—perhaps many—may consider such a statement so naïve, so simplistic, and so idealistic as to be quixotic. But as human beings, citizens with power to influence events in the world, can we be at peace with ourselves if we strive for less? I think not.

11

At the End of a Journey: The Risks of Cold-War Thinking in a New Era

Lee Butler

It is distressingly evident that, for many people, nuclear weapons retain an aura of utility, of primacy, and of legitimacy, that justifies their existence well into the future, in some number, however small. The persistence of this view, which is perfectly reflected in the modifications of US nuclear-weapons policy in recent years, lies at the core of the concern that moves me so deeply. This abiding faith in nuclear weapons was inspired and is sustained by a catechism instilled over many decades by a priesthood who speak with great assurance and authority. I was for many years among the most avid of these keepers of the faith in nuclear weapons, and for that I make no apology. Like my contemporaries, I was moved by fears and fired by beliefs that date back to the earliest days of the atomic era. We lived through a terror-ridden epoch punctuated by crises whose resolution held hostage the saga of humankind. For us, nuclear weapons were the saviour that brought an implacable foe to his knees in 1945 and held another at bay for nearly a half-century. We believed that superior technology brought strategic advantage, that greater numbers meant stronger security, and that the ends of containment justified whatever means were necessary to achieve them.

These are powerful, deeply rooted beliefs. They cannot and should not be lightly dismissed or discounted. Strong arguments can be made on their behalf. Throughout my professional military career, I shared them, I professed them, and I put them into operational practice. And now it is my burden to declare with all of the conviction I can muster that in my judgement they served us extremely ill. They account for the most severe risks and most extravagant costs of the US–Soviet confrontation. They intensified and prolonged an already acute ideological animosity. They spawned successive generations of new and more destructive nuclear devices and delivery systems. They gave rise to mammoth bureaucracies with gargantuan appetites and global agendas. They incited primal emotions, spurred zealotry and demagoguery, and set in motion forces of ungovernable scope and power. Most importantly, these enduring beliefs, and the fears that underlie them, perpetuate cold-war policies and practices that make no strategic sense. They continue to entail enormous costs and expose all humankind to unconscionable dangers. I find that intolerable. Thus I cannot stay silent. I know too much of these matters, the frailties, the flaws, the failures of policy and practice.

At the same time, I cannot overstate the difficulty this poses for me. No one who ever entered the nuclear arena left it with a fuller understanding of its complexity nor greater respect for those with whom I served its purposes. I struggle constantly with the task of articulating the evolution of my convictions without denigrating or diminishing the motives and sacrifice of countless colleagues with whom I lived the drama of the cold war. I ask them and you to appreciate that my purpose is not to accuse, but to assess, to understand, and to propound the forces that birthed the grotesque excesses and hazards of the nuclear age. For me, that assessment meant first coming to grips with my experience and then coming to terms with my conclusions.

I knew the moment I entered the nuclear arena I had been thrust into a world beset with tidal forces, towering egos, maddening contradictions, alien constructs, and insane risks. Its arcane vocabulary and apocalyptic calculus defied comprehension. Its stage was global and its antagonists locked in a deadly spiral of deepening rivalry. It was in every respect a modern-day holy war, a cosmic struggle between the forces of light and darkness. The stakes were national survival, and the weapons of choice were eminently suited to this scale of malevolence.

The opposing forces each created vast enterprises, each giving rise to a culture of messianic believers infused with a sense of historic mission and schooled in unshakeable articles of faith. As my own career progressed, I was immersed in the work of all of these cultures, either directly in those of the Western world, or through penetrating study of communist organizations, teachings, and practices. My responsibilities ranged from the highly subjective, such as assessing the values and motivation of Soviet leadership, to the critically objective, such as preparing weapons for operational launch. I became steeped in the art of intelligence estimates, the psychology of negotiations, the interplay of bureaucracies, and the impulses of industry. I was engaged in the labyrinthine conjecture of the strategist, the exacting routines of the target planner, and the demanding skills of the aircrew and the missilier. I have been a party to their history, shared their triumphs and tragedies, witnessed heroic sacrifice and catastrophic failure of both men and machines. And in the end, I came away from it all with profound misgivings.

Ultimately, as I examined the course of this journey, as the lessons of decades of intimate involvement took greater hold on my intellect, I came to a set of deeply unsettling judgements. That from the earliest days of the nuclear era, the risks and consequences of nuclear war have never been properly weighed by those who brandished it. That the stakes of nuclear war engage not just the survival of the antagonists, but the fate of mankind. That the likely consequences of nuclear war have no politically, militarily, or morally acceptable justification. And, therefore, that the threat to use nuclear weapons is indefensible.

These judgements gave rise to an array of inescapable questions. If this be so, what explained the willingness, no, the zeal, of legions of cold warriors, civilian and military, to not just tolerate but to multiply and to perpetuate such risks? By what authority do succeeding generations of leaders in the nuclear-weapons states usurp the power to dictate the odds of continued life on our planet? Most urgently, why does such breathtaking audacity persist at a moment when we should stand trembling in the face of our folly and united in our commitment to abolish its most deadly manifestation?

These are not questions to be left to historians. The answers matter to us now. They go to the heart of present-day policies and motivations. They convey lessons with immediate implications for both contemporary and aspiring nuclear states. As I distil them from the experience of three decades in the nuclear arena, these lessons resolve into two fundamental conclusions.

First, I have no other way to understand the willingness to condone nuclear weapons except to believe they are the natural accomplice of visceral enmity. They thrive in the emotional climate born of utter alienation and isolation. The unbounded wantonness of their effects is a perfect companion to the urge to destroy completely. They play on our deepest fears and pander to our darkest instincts. They corrode our sense of humanity, numb our capacity for moral outrage, and make thinkable the unimaginable. What is clear is that these fears and enmities are no respecters of political systems or values. They prey on democracies and totalitarian societies alike, shrinking the norms of civilized behaviour and dimming the prospects for escaping the savagery so powerfully imprinted in our genetic code. That should give us great pause as we imagine the task of abolition in a world that gives daily witness to acts of unspeakable barbarism. So it should compound our resolve.

The evidence to support this conclusion is palpable, but for much of my life I saw it differently. That was a product of both my citizenry and my profession. From the early years of my childhood and through much of my military service I saw the Soviet Union and its allies as a demonic threat, an evil empire bent on global domination. I was commissioned as an officer in the United States Air Force as the cold war was heating to a fever pitch. This was a desperate time that evoked on both sides extreme responses in policy, in technology, and in force postures: bloody purges and political inquisitions; covert intelligence schemes that squandered lives and subverted governments;

atmospheric testing with little understanding or regard for the long-term effects; threats of massive nuclear retaliation to an ill-defined scope of potential provocations; the forced march of inventive genius that ushered in the missile age arm in arm with the capacity for spontaneous, global destruction; reconnaissance aircraft that probed or violated sovereign air space, producing disastrous encounters; the menacing and perilous practice of airborne alert bombers loaded with nuclear weapons.

By the early 1960s, a superpower nuclear arms race was under way that would lead to a ceaseless amassing of destructive capacity, spilling over into the arsenals of other nations. Central Europe became a powder keg, trembling under the shadow of Armageddon, hostage to a bizarre strategy that required the prospect of nuclear devastation as the price of alliance. The entire world became a stage for the US–Soviet rivalry. International organizations were paralysed by its grip. East–West confrontation dominated the nation-state system. Every quarrel and conflict was fraught with potential for global war.

This was the world that largely defined our lives as American citizens. For those of us who served in the national security arena, the threat was omnipresent, it seemed total, it dictated our professional preparation and career progression, and cost the lives of tens of thousands of men and women, in and out of uniform. Like millions of others, I was caught up in the holy war, inured to its costs and consequences, trusting in the wisdom of succeeding generations of military and civilian leaders. The first requirement of unconditional belief in the efficacy of nuclear weapons was early and perfectly met for us: our homeland was the target of a consuming evil, poised to strike without warning and without mercy.

What remained for me, as my career took its particular course, was to master the intellectual underpinning of America's response, the strategic foundation that today still stands as the central precept of the nuclear catechism. Reassessing its pervasive impact on attitudes toward nuclear weapons goes directly to my second conclusion regarding the willingness to tolerate the risks of the nuclear age.

That also brings me to the focal point of my argument. For all of my years as a nuclear strategist, operational commander, and public spokesman, I explained, justified, and sustained America's massive nuclear arsenal as a function, a necessity, and a consequence of deterrence. Bound up in this singular term, this familiar touchstone of security dating back to antiquity, was the intellectually comforting and deceptively simple justification for taking the most extreme risks and the expenditure of trillions of dollars. It was our shield and by extension our sword. The nuclear priesthood extolled its virtues, and bowed to its demands. Allies yielded grudgingly to its dictates even while decrying its risks and costs. We brandished it at our enemies and presumed they embraced its suicidal corollary of mutual assured destruction. We ignored, discounted, or dismissed its flaws and cling still to the belief that it obtains in a world whose security architecture has been wholly transformed.

But now, I see it differently. Not in some blinding revelation, but at the end of a journey, in an age of deliverance from the consuming tensions of the cold war. Now, with the evidence more clear, the risks more sharply defined and the costs more fully understood, I see deterrence in a very different light. Appropriated from the lexicon of conventional warfare, this simple prescription for adequate military preparedness became in the nuclear age a formula for unmitigated catastrophe. It was premised on a litany of unwarranted assumptions, unprovable assertions, and logical contradictions. It suspended rational thinking about the ultimate aim of national security: to ensure the survival of the nation.

How is it that we subscribed to a strategy that required near perfect understanding of an enemy from whom we were deeply alienated and largely isolated? How could we pretend to understand the motivations and intentions of the Soviet leadership absent any substantive personal association? Why did we imagine a nation that had survived successive invasions and mind-numbing losses would accede to a strategy premised on fear of nuclear war? Deterrence in the cold war setting was fatally flawed at the most fundamental level of human psychology in its projection of Western reason through the crazed lens of a paranoid foe. Little wonder that intentions and motives were consistently misread. Little wonder that deterrence was the first victim of a deepening crisis, leaving the antagonists to grope fearfully in a fog of mutual misperception. While we clung to the notion that nuclear war could be reliably deterred, Soviet leaders derived from their historical experience the conviction that such a war might be thrust upon them and, if so, must not be lost. Driven by that fear, they took Herculean measures to fight and survive no matter the odds or the costs. Deterrence was a dialogue of the blind with the deaf. In the final analysis, it was largely a bargain we in the West made with ourselves.

Deterrence was flawed equally in that the consequences of its failure were intolerable. While the price of undeterred aggression in the age of uniquely conventional weaponry could be severe, history teaches that nations survive and even prosper in the aftermath of unconditional defeat. Not so in the nuclear era. Nuclear weapons give no quarter. Their effects transcend time and place, poisoning the earth and deforming its inhabitants for generation upon generation. They leave us wholly without defence, expunge all hope for meaningful survival. They hold in their sway not just the fate of nations, but the very meaning of civilization.

Deterrence failed completely as a guide in setting rational limits on the size and composition of military forces. To the contrary, its appetite was voracious, its capacity to justify new weapons and larger stocks unrestrained. Deterrence carried the seed, born of an irresolvable internal contradiction that spurred an insatiable arms race. Nuclear deterrence hinges on the credibility to mount a devastating retaliation under the most extreme conditions of war initiation. Perversely, the redundant and survivable force required to meet this exacting test is readily perceived by a darkly suspicious adversary as capable, even designed, to execute a disarming first strike. Such advantage can never be conceded between nuclear rivals. It must be answered, reduced, nullified. Fears are fanned, the rivalry intensified. New technology is inspired, new systems roll from production lines. The correlation of force begins to shift, and the bar of deterrence ratchets higher, igniting yet another cycle of trepidation, worst-case assumptions, and ever mounting levels of destructive capability.

Thus it was that the treacherous axioms of deterrence made seemingly reasonable nuclear weapon stockpiles numbering in the tens of thousands. Despite having witnessed the devastation wrought by two primitive atomic devices, over the ensuing decades the superpowers gorged themselves at the thermonuclear trough. A succession of leaders on both sides of the East–West divide directed a reckless proliferation of nuclear devices, tailored for delivery by a vast array of vehicles to a stupefying array of targets. They nurtured, richly rewarded, even revelled in the industrial base required to support production at such levels.

I was part of all of that. I was present at the creation of many of these systems, directly responsible for prescribing and justifying the requirements and technology that made them possible. I saw the arms race from the inside, watched as intercontinental ballistic missiles ushered in mutual assured destruction and multiple warhead missiles introduced genuine fear of a nuclear first strike. I participated in the elaboration of basing schemes that bordered on the comical and force levels that in retrospect defied reason. I was responsible for war plans with over 12,000 targets, many struck with repeated nuclear blows, some to the point of complete absurdity. I was a veteran participant in an arena where the most destructive power ever unleashed became the prize in a no-holds-barred competition among organizations whose principal interest was to enhance rather than constrain its application. And through every corridor, in every impassioned plea, in every fevered debate rang the rallying cry, deterrence, deterrence, deterrence.

As nuclear weapons and actors multiplied, deterrence took on too many names, too many roles, overreaching an already extreme strategic task. Surely nuclear weapons summoned great caution in superpower relationships. But as their numbers swelled, so mounted the stakes of miscalculation, of a crisis spun out of control. The exorbitant price of nuclear war quickly exceeded the rapidly depreciating value of a tenuous mutual wariness. Invoking deterrence became a cheap rhetorical parlour trick, a verbal sleight of hand. Proponents persist in dressing it up to court changing times and temperaments, hemming and rehemming to fit shrinking or distorted threats.

Deterrence is a slippery conceptual slope. It is not stable, nor is it static, its wiles cannot be contained. It is both master and slave. It seduces the scientist yet bends to his creation. It serves the ends of evil as well as those of noble intent. It holds guilty the innocent as well as the culpable. It gives easy semantic cover to nuclear weapons, masking the horrors of employment with siren veils of infallibility. At best it is a gamble no mortal should pretend to make. At worst it invokes death on a scale rivalling the power of the creator.

Is it any wonder that at the end of my journey I am moved so strongly to retrace its path, to examine more closely the evidence I would or could not see? I hear now the voices long ignored, the warnings muffled by the still lingering animosities of the cold war. I see with painful clarity that, from the very beginnings of the nuclear era, the objective scrutiny and searching debate essential to adequate comprehension and responsible oversight of its vast enterprises were foreshortened or foregone. The cold light of dispassionate scrutiny was shuttered in the name of security, doubts dismissed in the name of an acute and unrelenting threat, objections overruled by the incantations of the nuclear priesthood.

The penalties proved to be severe. Vitally important decisions were routinely taken without adequate understanding, assertions too often prevailed over analysis, requirements took on organizational biases, technological opportunity and corporate profit drove force levels and capability, and political opportunism intruded on calculations of military necessity. Authority and accountability were severed, policy dissociated from planning, and theory invalidated by practice. The narrow concerns of a multitude of powerful interests intruded on the rightful role of key policy-makers, constraining their latitude for decision. Many were simply denied access to critical information essential to the proper exercise of their office.

Over time, planning was increasingly distanced and ultimately disconnected from any sense of scientific or military reality. In the end, the nuclear powers, great and small, created astronomically expensive infrastructures, monolithic bureaucracies, and complex processes that defied control or comprehension. Only now are the dimensions, costs, and risks of these nuclear nether worlds coming to light. What must now be better understood are the root causes, the mindsets, and the belief systems that brought them into existence. They must be challenged, they must be refuted, but most importantly, they must be let go. The era that gave them credence, accepted their dominion and yielded to their excesses is fast receding.

But it is not yet over. Sad to say, the cold war lives on in the minds of those who cannot let go the fears, the beliefs, and the enmities born of the nuclear age. They cling to deterrence, clutch its tattered promise to their breast, shake it wistfully at bygone adversaries and balefully at new or imagined ones. They are gripped still by its awful willingness not simply to tempt the apocalypse but to prepare its way.

What better illustration of misplaced faith in nuclear deterrence than the persistent belief that retaliation with nuclear weapons is a legitimate and appropriate response to post-cold-war threats posed by weapons of mass destruction? What could possibly justify our resort to the very means we properly abhor and condemn? Who can imagine our joining in shattering the precedent of non-use that has held for over fifty years? How could America's irreplaceable role as leader of the campaign against nuclear proliferation ever be re-justified? What target would warrant such retaliation? Would we hold an entire society accountable for the decision of a single demented leader? How would the physical effects of the nuclear explosion be contained, not to mention the political and moral consequences? In a singular act we would martyr our enemy, alienate our friends, give comfort to the non-declared nuclear states, and impetus to states who seek such weapons covertly. In short, such a response on the part of the United States is inconceivable. It would irretrievably diminish our priceless stature as a nation noble in aspiration and responsible in conduct, even in the face of extreme provocation.

And as a nation we have no greater responsibility than to bring the nuclear era to a close. Our present policies, plans, and postures governing nuclear weapons make us prisoner still to an age of intolerable danger. We cannot at once keep sacred the miracle of existence and hold sacrosanct the capacity to destroy it. We cannot hold hostage to sovereign gridlock the keys to final deliverance from the nuclear nightmare. We cannot withhold the resources essential to break its grip, to reduce its dangers. We cannot sit in silent acquiescence to the faded homilies of the nuclear priesthood. It is time to reassert the primacy of individual conscience, the voice of reason, and the rightful interests of humanity.

12

Weapons of the Underdog

Robert O'Neill

My argument is that with the end of the cold war the utility of nuclear weapons has changed. Formerly they were the weapons of the top dogs: now they are becoming weapons of the underdogs. Let me explain.

The first book that I edited on nuclear weapons (in 1975)[1] was set in a context very different to that of the current work. The Vietnam War was in its final stages, the SALT I agreement was not long in place, and the Vladivostok agreement had been reached while the book was in progress. There was hope that the world was moving towards a more stable nuclear relationship through the process of superpower arms control diplomacy. The Nuclear Non-Proliferation Treaty was nearly due for review, and this was the occasion for the work which resulted in the book. The most serious cloud on the horizon was that created by India's nuclear explosion in 1974.

12.1. *The Five Original Nuclear Powers*

It was a time when the dangers of nuclear weapons were becoming more clearly and widely understood, not least in the defence communities of the superpowers. Unfortunately this official caution was not widely recognized outside these circles at the time. Nuclear strategists tended to be seen by non-specialists, particularly those who were radically opposed to United States policies in Vietnam, as being singlemindedly of a hawkish inclination. Such condemnation was, of course, wide of the mark in most cases. Four successive United States presidents, from Truman to Johnson, all had had occasion to examine the use of nuclear weapons in actual conflicts or crises, and all had concluded that such action would have been counterproductive. During the 1950s and 1960s experts both within Western governments and in the wider public domain warned of the dangers of crisis escalation, inadequate political control over the actual firing of nuclear weapons, and arms racing which would lead to increased hostility and instability. By the end of the 1960s it was clear to most who thought seriously about the utility of nuclear weapons that their only rational purpose was to deter the use of opposing nuclear weapons. They were simply too destructive to make their use profitable. Further debates began over the deployment of multiple warheads on intercontinental ballistic missiles. There was also a growing consensus that ballistic missile defences were, on the whole, undesirable.

In other words, by the mid-1970s nuclear weapons were recognized increasingly within official circles as causes of concern, even anxiety, rather than as unambiguous guarantors of security. They were useful to deter the use of the nuclear weapons of others, and thus they addressed a real need. But in terms of creating usable forces and effective security in any other sense they were an investment of very dubious value. This was certainly a central element in the research and debates of the International Institute for Strategic Studies. Informed concern regarding the problems of nuclear weapons is evident in its publications and debates over the forty years of its existence as the principal forum of debate for strategists, both official and non-official.

Twenty-four years on from 1975 where are we? For sixteen of those years the world was in the firm grip of the cold war. Command and control over nuclear weapons was very tightly held. Political leaders were rigorously advised by expert staffs who well understood the dangers of any use of nuclear weapons. Physical control of warheads was firm and effective on both sides but the 1970s and 1980s saw a steady build-up in the number and diversity of weapons in the opposing arsenals. Some progress in checking this process was made in the late 1980s, including agreement to eliminate all intermediate-range nuclear weapons, but a large number of nuclear strategic and arms control issues were yet to be resolved when the Soviet Union collapsed, and the cold war ended.

Since 1991 the world has been in a situation of having thousands of nuclear warheads, in five (or more) separate national arsenals, but the public justification for which, according to their owners, is simply to deter their use by others. At the same time all of the five nuclear great powers profess friendship for each other and are committed to avoid any relapse into a militarily intense rivalry which consumes resources fruitlessly and deflects all, particularly the weaker, from the path of progress. The five permanent members of the Security Council all support the development of a mutually beneficial international community governed by law not brute force. They want to decrease their defence budgets and disarm substantially.

Yet, despite a welcome reduction in warhead numbers, not much has changed regarding the prominence and deployment of nuclear weapons. Despite the negotiation of the START II agreement between the United States and the Soviet Union/Russia, ratification has not yet followed and nuclear warhead numbers remain at levels consistent with an early return to a new cold war. More than half of the world's remaining warheads are in the hands of a weak, internally divided Russia, whose parliament and some of its military leaders have come to see them as one of Russia's most important sources of security and leverage on the international community. The Duma therefore is determined in its refusal to ratify the START II agreement. There is insufficient desire on the parts of both Russia and the United States to press on immediately in the absence of such ratification with negotiation of a START III treaty, thereby undercutting many of the objections to the existing agreement. Russian critics, including some military leaders, have buttressed their arguments for greater reliance on nuclear weapons by pointing to the expansion of NATO and a growing need to offset its conventional force superiority. In the mean time Russia continues in a state of internal weakness, politically, economically, and socially. The 'loose nukes' problem is being addressed very gradually, and on the whole unconvincingly, in terms of preventing leakage from the Russian arsenal in the coming decade.

The strategic nuclear forces of all five great powers continue to be held in a high state of readiness. Despite the de-targeting agreements entered into by the United States with Russia and China, missiles can be unleashed in a matter of minutes should any of the five governments give its assent to military advice to do so. Nuclear weapons can also be used as a result of accident—an unlikely contingency, but not of zero probability given the state of affairs within Russia. Existing national control systems can also be divided, subverted, or simply torn apart. General Lebed may not have been entirely serious when he proposed in July 1998 that his part of Siberia should break away from Moscow's authority, taking with it a proportion of the Russian ICBM force, but the scenario is not wholly incredible. It will be a very long time before the danger of use or misappropriation of nuclear weapons from the Russian arsenal disappears. And are the arsenals of the other nuclear powers all perfectly secure from unauthorized penetration or the danger of accident?

Britain and France continue to retain their much smaller nuclear arsenals—both under very firm and effective political control—but their avowed arguments for retention of nuclear weapons nowadays are very thin. Whatever justification there was during the cold war for Britain and France to safeguard themselves against any American return to isolationism through having their own nuclear weapons has surely vanished. In the more interdependent context of the post-cold-war world the United States simply cannot retreat from any significant crisis (particularly one involving a nuclear-weapons state) and leave matters to resolve themselves. It has every incentive to remain closely engaged in the event of any flagrant breach of international order (particularly a nuclear threat to one or the other of its close allies, i.e. the only contingencies for which British and French nuclear weapons are supposedly relevant) and shows no signs of failure to recognize this condition of its own security and prosperity. The fact that hard-headed British and French politicians continue to devote scarce resources to the maintenance of nuclear-strike forces cannot be acceptably explained without reference to their status in the international pecking order, particularly to their right to continued membership of the United Nations Security Council, their standing in NATO (especially *vis-à-vis* Germany) and their perceived importance in the eyes of Washington.

China has nuclear weapons because the two other great powers with which it collided in the 1950s and 1960s had them. The Chinese nuclear force remains small by comparison with those of the United States and Russia, and it is well behind both of them technologically. The Chinese government has long professed willingness to disarm in a nuclear sense if the other nuclear powers did likewise. But until such agreement is reached, China will continue to develop its nuclear forces with determination despite their substantial cost in resources. If nuclear force is the currency of geostrategic power, China argues, then it intends to show that it is far from insolvent. China, of course, also has an eye to its position in the east Asian region. It has known for a very long time of India's nuclear research and development programme. Now south Asia has to be included in any broad international agreement to disarm if China is to feel free to embark on that journey.

All five of the long-standing nuclear-weapons states face a continuing need to maintain and modernize their forces. Most of us can recall the intensity of the debates which took place in the United States, Britain, and France during the 1980s, when the last great round of force modernization had to be agreed upon and financed by legislatures. The need for another major round of modernization is not imminent, but it cannot be held off forever. Russia will be in a particularly weak situation for financing a new family of major missiles and warheads, not to mention the command, control, and warning systems which are essential accompaniments. China, even assuming its economic development continues without major interruption, will not be able to close the gap with the United States in terms of effective nuclear forces. Britain and France will also find the marshalling of sufficient political will, security rationale, and money for a new generation of nuclear weapons extremely difficult. Only the United States has to hand the kind of resources necessary for its attainment, and there the future of nuclear weapons is a more contested issue than in any of the other four.

Would it be in the best interests of the United States to pursue its security interests by forging further ahead in terms of nuclear-weapons capabilities? What would the rest of the world, including the other four major nuclear powers, think about that prospect? Are there preferable options both from the perspective of US national security interests and that of the international system as a whole? These are questions to which I shall return later in the chapter.

12.2. *Five Lesser Nuclear Powers*

India and Pakistan accepted the costs of declaring possession of nuclear weapons with their tests of May 1998. The economic and technological pressures applied by the international community have been painful, particularly to Pakistan. The reasons for the open nuclearization of the subcontinent derive essentially from the frustrated and assertive nationalism which is inherent in the policies of the Bharatiya Janata Party. The Congress, when in power, could see that the demonstration of a full military nuclear capability would be counterproductive. The BJP, much less experienced in government and diplomacy, less sensitive to the views of the international community, and dependent for its political strength on keeping the Congress on the defensive, saw the balance of costs and gains differently. The popularity of its stance has been amply confirmed by the upsurge of rejoicing and national feeling which followed the tests and the subsequent international chastisement.

There can be little doubt that the Indian acquisition of nuclear weapons derives essentially from the refusal by most Indians to accept the two-tier status of nuclear haves and have-nots, and the determination of the BJP leadership to harness popular resentment in order to strengthen their position in the internal political battle. The Pakistani motivation must have been very similar, but as the smaller of the two powers, there is a more obvious security objective to be achieved in its case. At all events the nuclearization of south Asia in 1998 demonstrated that the mechanism of proliferation remains alive and powerful, and that one of its driving forces is the existence of other nuclear-weapon states. In this situation it is difficult to see how international sanctions against such proliferation can be effective. In the current context, if a state is reasonably robust and does not transgress international law by attacking its neighbours, it can get away with developing a nuclear force.

Israel is another example of proliferation in the face of a disapproving international community. Despite all the pressures that have been exerted to prevent proliferation in the context of the Arab–Israeli conflict by superpowers and others, it is almost certain that Israel has gone ahead and developed a secret nuclear force. The cloak of tight secrecy, lifted briefly by Mordechai Vanunu in the 1980s, has enabled Israel to escape the painful obloquy which would have followed any known testing or assembly of nuclear weapons. Israel's position has also been assisted by its avoidance of major offensive action across its borders since its failure in Lebanon in 1982. Although it has often initiated smaller scale military operations, Israel has not run the risks which Saddam Hussein accepted in invading Kuwait in 1990, and then losing the consequent trial of strength with the United Nations. Israel has not had to tolerate a highly intrusive, protracted international inspection aimed at the destruction of all weapons of mass destruction.

Had Saddam not invaded Kuwait (and had the cold war not been over and Kuwait not been the source of a vital international commodity), he probably would not have had to suffer this enforced disarmament and loss of sovereignty, and would have been able to continue to develop nuclear, biological, and chemical weapons. North Korea was able to go a long way down the path of nuclear-weapons development, despite acute tensions on the Korean Peninsula, because it had not crossed the line into overt aggression. Had North Korea been strong and prosperous, it might have continued with its nuclear programmes despite the evidence against it, and the condemnations of the United States, South Korea, and their allies. But it was hamstrung by acute shortages of foreign currency, home-grown food, and other essentials, and was in a poor position for withstanding international pressures directed at halting its nuclear-weapons programmes. North Korea chose the path of controlled disclosure of its nuclear activities, and acceptance of an extremely generous Western plan by way of compensation. The Korean Peninsula Energy Development Organisation will not only provide essential fuel oil for the generation of electricity and but also construct a nuclear power-generation system which is more compatible with non-proliferation than that which it will replace.

All five smaller powers have pursued serious nuclear weapons programmes. Only those of India and Pakistan have resulted in clear evidence of a developed nuclear weapons capability, but there can be little doubt that the other three, Iraq, Israel, and North Korea, have also made substantial progress in this direction. Other states such as Iran, Libya, and Syria are also referred to in expert debates as potential nuclear proliferators. Obviously they have some potential for undertaking weapons-development programmes but what are their incentives? First and most obvious is a possible need to balance and deter any Israeli use of nuclear weapons against them or (in the cases of Libya and Syria) against their Arab brothers in the event of another war in the Middle East. It can be countered that the probability of Israel making any threatening use of nuclear weapons other than to prevent Israeli territory from being overrun is extremely low. But what seems low to a distant observer in a relatively safe position does not necessarily seem low to someone living on a potential target for retaliation. In the case of Iran, the main motivation might have more to do with religion than support of the Palestinian cause, but this consideration would not make Israelis feel any more comfortable about the possibility of Iran's acquisition of nuclear weapons.

A second motivation for any of these three to develop nuclear weapons is to gain leverage on Israel's chief ally and protector, the United States. Radical Arab states might choose to use such influence on the US through nuclear deterrence, or through threatening to strike at key US interests in the Middle East, particularly those concerned with energy resources. Neither of these scenarios has great credibility because of the relative ease with which the

US could retaliate and defend its interests by use of modern conventional weapons, but that does not mean that they can be safely ignored. A third motive might lie in the taking of revenge through action against a key target or population centre in the United States itself. This contingency has obvious credibility, as is confirmed by US attempts to develop anti-missile defences for dealing with relatively isolated attacks. The extent to which these three states are mentioned in current public debate is further testimony to the credibility of a radical Arab or Iranian threat to Israel and/or the United States.

12.3. *The Possibility of Subnational Nuclear Actors*

One of the major differences between the nature of international order during the cold war and the current state of affairs is the implosion of states and empires which has resulted in bitter civil wars and the extension of anarchy in highly sensitive parts of the world: the Balkans, the Caucasus, and Central Asia. Participants in these conflicts have been known to be savage and ruthless in the extreme. They are capable of hating their opponents to the extent that they would be willing to use weapons of mass destruction, including nuclear weapons, against them.

To the best of our current knowledge, none of these groups has been able to build, buy, or steal a nuclear device. But there is ample evidence abroad that several have tried to obtain a warhead or fissile material from former Soviet sources. Who can say whether or not they have been successful? The prospect is sufficiently worrying for the Bush and Clinton administrations, supported by both Houses of Congress, to have voted substantial sums for improving the security of storage of former Soviet warheads, and the destruction of those made surplus under arms control treaty obligations. To prevent forever such weapon-grade material from falling into the hands of subnational groups, given the huge number of devices which are still in existence, or will be even when the START II treaty is ratified, will be an enormous challenge.

The severity of the internal problems facing Yeltsin's Russia is so acute that catastrophes of several kinds, all with implications for the security of nuclear weapons, cannot be ruled out. The social fabric may rupture, leaving the central government without effective authority. Parts may break away, taking elements of the nuclear forces with them. Important servants of the state, both civil and military, may be in such poverty that they are willing to connive at illegal sales of fissile material. Dissident groups, either associated with regions which want to break away or with political causes which are implacably opposed to the central government, may acquire their own nuclear weapons. Criminal groups may seek to acquire nuclear weapons to further their own interests in any of several ways. Or individual fanatics, simply bent on revenge, may seek to settle scores with the Russian or other local leaderships. The range of credible scenarios of this kind is vast.

It should not be thought that Russia is the only possible source of leakage of nuclear weapons or fissile material. The arsenals of all of the nuclear powers have a new attractiveness as targets for penetration, theft, or bribery in a way in which they were not during the cold war. The relative degree of balance between the two sides and the massive size of the opposing nuclear forces then meant that the misappropriation of a single warhead would achieve relatively little, and the major actors then did not attempt to steal each other's nuclear warheads in order to use them. In today's more anarchical situation, acquisitive eyes are much more likely to be turned towards the weapons stocks of all the other nuclear powers than during the cold war. The more arsenals there are the easier it will be for a determined group or individual to penetrate one of them. The attempts to penetrate can come from many directions and be that much more difficult to counter or frustrate.

12.4. *The Future Relevance of Nuclear Weapons*

This then is the situation in which we find ourselves. What is the relevance of nuclear weapons to national and international security in future? Essentially nuclear weapons are relevant in five ways: to maintain deterrence (and hopefully peace) between the great powers of the world; to reinforce the general international status of the powers possessing them; to preserve stability in tense regional rivalries; to instil in the minds of the leaders of rogue or potential rogue states a respect for international law and restrain them from some of the worst acts of which they are capable; and for subnational actors to use in venting their anger against the international community or its leaders, particularly the United Nations and the United States.

How strong is each of these cases? What conclusions can be drawn regarding the relevance on nuclear weapons in the future? The first of these purposes, deterrence at the great-power level, is obviously still thought to be relevant to the security of all five by their political leaders and their national security advisers. But in their private thinking they are almost certainly much less sure than they sound in public. Some, such as former US Defence Secretary Robert McNamara and General Lee Butler, former Commander-in-Chief, US Strategic Command, have already gone so far as to argue publicly, and in this volume, that the retention of nuclear weapons is not in the security interests of the United States. Those who know the history of decision-making in the cold war are aware that nuclear weapons achieved very little in a positive, demonstrable sense. The negative argument that they prevented a Third World War is unprovable because we do not know whether anyone intended to start such a war. To date no historical researchers have found concrete evidence of either side planning to launch a war with the same ambitious aims as those of Adolf Hitler. Even Stalin was very cautious in facing the risks of war with the United States because the Soviet Union had taken such a beating during the Second World War. The more we know of US war plans during the cold war, particularly those relating to the use of nuclear weapons, the more we see the role of nuclear weapons being restricted in the minds of political and military leaders.

Whatever people may argue about the role of nuclear weapons during the cold war, the five major nuclear powers agree that their essential purpose now is to deter the use of nuclear weapons by other states. This suggests that there would be no effective loss of security to any of them if all five nuclear great powers were to agree to eliminate their nuclear weapons. In effect their security would be enhanced because of the elimination of the risk of occurrence of accidents involving nuclear weapons and their theft. The fact that there is so little acceptance of the desirability of eliminating nuclear weapons among four of the five powers suggests that they, and possibly the fifth, China, have other reasons for retaining nuclear weapons.

Chief of these, and never publicly admitted, is status. This reason is particularly important for Britain and France, whose international influence has waned considerably since they were major allies of the United States in 1945. If a new UN Security Council with five permanent members were to be put together today, it is arguable that the five would be the United States, Russia, China, Japan, and Germany, with Nigeria, India, and Brazil also in the frame for consideration. Britain and France may, in fact, do a little better in the international status competition than that, but one of the thoughts which really worries their political leaders and diplomats is that Britain and France are in danger of being relegated on several scales. Hence they are all the more determined to cling to marks of status which might assist in keeping their toehold.

The status issue is also extremely important for Russia. Many years ago the Soviet Union was dismissed as being 'Upper Volta with missiles'. How much more is this the case for Russia? Take away its nuclear weapons and what is left? Actually quite a lot remains, including the world's largest reserves of natural gas, but to Russian officials and leaders under challenge at home, elimination of their nuclear weapons would unacceptably reduce their country's status both domestically and internationally.

China does not seem to have the same anxieties. Chinese people have always been confident that they have a special status which rests on the size, population, resources, civilization, and cohesion of the country. Nuclear weapons are marginal to China's standing. They put China on an inside track in relations with the United States and Russia. They give China an edge over Japan, which also makes many Chinese feel better. But a China without nuclear weapons (in a world in which all nuclear powers have disarmed) is not going to look very different in the eyes of the world to the China which has them today, and that is very much the way its officials approach the question.

A second power whose status is less dependent on nuclear weapons is the United States. It derives its standing much more from its capacity to generate ideas which take hold in the global system and shape it. The USA has unparalleled economic power. Its capital resources and technology create enormous strength both at home and abroad. Its dynamism, the openness of its society, and its particular form of idealism are challenges to all other nations. Its conventional military power is now unsurpassed. Its media and the outward orientation of its culture give the USA a unique presence in the domestic debates of virtually every country and society around the world. In a world without nuclear weapons the United States would still be the supreme power by a long way. In such a world the USA would also be more secure from attack by disgruntled opponents, particularly rogue state leaders and subnational actors, because there would also be in effect a much stronger non-proliferation regime, for reasons that I shall soon come to.

If a decision to eliminate nuclear weapons is ever to be taken, it will require the United States to take a strong lead, supported by China, in reaching out to Russia to reduce the inevitable short-term loss of status that Russians would feel before gaining the real benefits of not having to face a new round of weapons modernization, and of enjoying a more secure international environment. Britain and France would probably be very obstructive, but if the United States believed that a nuclear-weapons-free world was in its own interest, it would have sufficient leverage to complicate severely the development by either Britain or France of a competitive new generation of nuclear weapons. Irrespective of the stance taken by the United States, the preferences of the British and French electorates will ultimately be decisive. In a world in which the possibility of major war has receded considerably since the end of the cold war, public opinion is unlikely to be willing to pay out billions of pounds, francs, or euros for a new generation of nuclear weapons.

Nuclear weapons are also relevant to regional rivalries, as we have seen from their original deployment in Europe at the most intense phase of the cold war. While the security problems of Europe have changed dramatically following the removal of the east–west dividing line through Germany, there are several other regions which remain divided and unstable, particularly the Middle East, south Asia, and north-east Asia. There probably are nuclear weapons in the Middle East. We know that both sides have them in south Asia. And there remain concerns as to whether North Korea has or might not acquire such weapons. These regional nuclear rivalries complicate the problems of proliferation control far beyond the fact that they are worrying examples of the regime's erosion. There are so many more nuclear actors who have to be persuaded to join the regime and keep strictly to its terms. There are many more independent centres of decision which can release nuclear weapons—not all of which are well supported by expert staffs whose members have the benefit of many years of managing a tense nuclear relationship. And there are so many more systems that can suffer accidents, theft, or misuse through impoverished, venal, or disloyal guardians.

Given the examples that have been set by the five nuclear great powers, it is very difficult to insist effectively that regional powers alone should eliminate their nuclear weapons unless, as in the case of North Korea, they are in a situation of great weakness. It is extremely hard to see what would be the logic of a case which would persuade India and Pakistan, or Israel, to disarm and open themselves fully to international inspection while at the same time permitting Britain, France, and China (not to mention the United States and Russia) to retain theirs. Given that the NPT regime has been eroded to this point, we must expect other infringements to occur, unless all nuclear weapons powers agree to denuclearization as part of a global process. The more the NPT regime frays, the more difficult will become the task of convincing every nuclear power to disarm in a fully authenticated way which permits other powers to feel that their security is not being undermined. The more the credibility of the NPT is brought into question, the greater will be the incentives for other states and groups who would normally not wish to have nuclear weapons to acquire their own before they are isolated and defenceless in an increasingly nuclearized world.

Seasoned outsiders who observe regional rivalries with an experienced eye may shake their heads and dismiss the claims of the local governments that nuclear weapons improve their security. They may point to the harmful wider effects that such proliferation will have on international security in general, and use moral arguments to shame the offending governments. The fact remains, however, that in these situations it is the local governments which are in control—unless they become very weak economically or transgress international law to a point at which the UN Security Council is prepared to authorize the use of force against them.

These local governments may also be driven by concerns other than security, especially that of status. In the case of India this factor has been particularly important. India, as a proud nation with an ancient civilization, has not taken kindly to being lectured by the West and China. In many ways, and certainly in the field of nuclear physics, India is an advanced nation. Indian public opinion therefore rejoices when its government shows such disregard for the displeasure of the top dogs of international society that it has chosen to join them at their own game. Many Pakistanis think similarly, although Pakistan's position is complicated by its greater exposure to international economic forces. But given the example of India, the Pakistani government and people seem likely to be prepared to endure hardships for the sake of security and status in their relationship with India.

Israel, if Israel has nuclear weapons, is a special case all of its own. The

Holocaust has left a legacy of insecurity of such intensity that it is very difficult for any non-Israeli to comprehend. This experience has been reinforced
by the savagery of Israel's long struggle for the right to exist since 1948. It will
be a long time before any Israeli government opens the country up to international inspection of the kind that would be necessary to establish quite
clearly that there were no nuclear weapons in its arsenal. These regional
nuclear proliferators have put very formidable obstacles in the path of all who
believe that proliferation should be contained, but they can no longer be dealt
with as if they were simply part of a regional problem. They are now part of
the global class system of nuclear haves and nuclear have-nots.

The relevance of nuclear weapons to regional rivalries extends beyond the
bounds of the troubled regions. There are members of the international security communities in the five major nuclear powers who argue for the retention of their systems on the ground that they have an overshadowing or
coercive effect on rogue states. A case which is frequently used in support of
this view is that Saddam Hussein was deterred from the use of biological or
chemical weapons against the United Nations allies, and Israel, in 1990–1 by
the fact that the US had nuclear weapons. This implies that Saddam thought
that the US was ready to break the nuclear taboo that it had observed since
1945 in order to deal with his use of chemical or biological weapons. If he
thought this way regarding use of biological and chemical weapons, why then
was he not deterred from the more flagrant offence of invading a neighbouring country? To rely on a dubious case such as this is tantamount to advocating the legitimation of the use of nuclear weapons against states which are
not known to have nuclear weapons. Quite apart from the unacceptability of
such a policy to most people, it raises the potential level of destructiveness of
regional conflicts and creates another incentive for regional powers to develop
nuclear weapons. Overshadowing of regional aggressors is more easily and less
damagingly to be achieved by a combination of conventional military force
and economic, technological and political measures.

There is a third set of actors to whom nuclear weapons are relevant in the
post-cold-war world, namely subnational groups. Given that most of the conflicts that have occurred since 1990 have been as a result of irreconcilable differences between groups which are not identifiable national governments, that
there is no sign that these conflicts will cease, and that organized international
criminals are also becoming an increasingly serious problem, it would be
foolish to continue to regard nuclear weapons solely in the context of their
employment by national governments. This change carries important complications for those who advocate continued retention of nuclear weapons by
states which currently have them, because deterrence is very hard to apply to
subnational groups. If there is no government, with a known seat, a known
set of leaders, known armed forces, known national territory, and known
national infrastructure to strike back at, what is there to exercise deterrence

against? How is deterrence to be offered? Even if the country from which a terrorist group is operating is identified, nuclear weapons are too destructive to be acceptable. The danger of killing large numbers of innocent people would be unacceptably high.

It is true that, eight years into the post-cold-war era, no subnational group has used or threatened to use a nuclear weapon. This is no ground, however, for imagining that the danger will never arise. As the Harvard study on the Russian 'loose nukes' problem stated:

It does not require a large step to get from terrorist acts like Oklahoma City and the World Trade Center to the first act of nuclear terrorism. Suppose that instead of mini-vans filled with hundreds of pounds of the crude explosives used in Oklahoma City and New York, terrorists had acquired a suitcase carrying one hundred pounds of highly enriched uranium (HEU), roughly the size of a grapefruit. Using a simple, well-known design to build a weapon from this material, terrorists could have produced a nuclear blast, equivalent to 10,000 to 20,000 tons of TNT. Under normal conditions, this would devastate a three-square-mile urban area. Much of Oklahoma City would have disappeared. The tip of Manhattan, including all of Wall Street reaching up to Grainercy Park, would have been destroyed.[2]

There are people who have crude and simple views of oppressed and oppressors, people who hate enough to want to maim and kill, not only political or military leaders who may be seen as the direct agents of injustice, but also their supporting staffs, and their military or police. Such terrorists may also be indifferent to killing large numbers of others who are in no way associated with their grievances just because they are reachable by such violence, they seem guilty by association, unsympathetic to the dissidents' concerns, or just suitable targets for obtaining publicity. The people who attempted to blow up the World Trade Center in New York in 1992 and those who killed 162 people and destroyed the Federal Office Building in Oklahoma City in 1995 were driven by these kinds of hatreds. Terrorism with weapons of mass destruction is, according to the FBI's assessment, the most severe risk to the security of the United States at present.

This is a problem for countries other than the United States, including the other nuclear-weapons states. But the USA is the most at risk because it has the highest international profile, it is easiest to blame for whatever seems wrong in the lives of aggrieved people, its culture is the most likely to be seen as threatening, and an attack in the United States will attract great attention from the media world-wide. Washington is one obvious target. New York is another, at risk on at least four counts: it is a major American city; Wall Street is the hub of American capitalism; New York contains the headquarters of many media groups; and it houses the headquarters of the United Nations, which can also serve at a focal point for revenge or protest for iniquities in the international system.

There are other targets for terrorism in the United States, as the Oklahoma

City bombing has demonstrated, and there are other US installations abroad against which attacks can be made. There are also many other countries in the world where terrorist incidents occur. None of the nuclear-weapons states can feel secure that it will not be the target for a terrorist incident which involves use or threatened use of a nuclear weapon. They all have a very strong interest in eliminating that danger to the greatest extent possible. But no other power is as exposed to nuclear terrorism as is the United States. It will have to be the United States which takes the lead in shaping an international policy for reducing the risk of nuclear terrorism. At present, because it has not happened, political and public opinion currently relegates this contingency to a low priority which does not justify any major change in national policies. But should a terrorist nuclear attack ever happen, there will be a landslide of public opinion demanding major changes, including reduction of the dangers of nuclear proliferation by moving to eliminate nuclear-weapons.

12.5. *Who Benefits Most from Nuclear Weapons in the Post-Cold-War Era?*

Given that none of the existing nuclear-weapons powers wishes to give them up, and that the number of these powers has increased by at least two in the past year, it is readily apparent that they all think that they benefit from possessing such weapons. The chief reason they all advance is the additional security they feel from being able thereby to deter the possible nuclear attacks of others. But there is a circular element in this justification: what if none of the nuclear powers intends to use nuclear weapons against any other of their number? What is the real gain here? And what is the real cost, in terms of resources, force structure for dealing with more frequent contingencies, political attention, risk of accidents, and impact on proliferation? How will the balance look when substantial resources have to be found to finance successive generations of new nuclear weapons (including their launch vehicles)? Clearly there is a balance here to be assessed, a balance in which, as world order changes, the possession of nuclear weapons will be seen as less desirable rather than as good value.

I have already referred to the status argument. There can be no denying that nuclear-weapons states have more clout in the international system just because they have nuclear weapons. They attract more attention, they take each other more seriously, their defence establishments think about each other in a more significant way, and they form an identifiable club, three or four of whose members are states that other nations wish most to have close relations with or gain the attention of. And it is a club whose membership is not controlled by those who already wear the tie. New members simply have to be willing to make their own tie and wear it. The other members then have to recognize them. This looks to be a situation in which club membership can only increase as time goes by.

The less powerful of the nuclear-weapons states derive the greater perceived benefit from membership. Belonging to the club is that much more a demonstrable asset for them. In states whose people feel that they are not given their due respect in international society, which make up most of the developing world, the status of having nuclear weapons has great significance in the context of internal politics. The application of sanctions by existing nuclear-weapons states in this situation is seen as provocative and tends to confirm domestic opinion in support of governments which unveil nuclear weapons programmes. This kind of domestic opinion greatly complicates any attempts at nuclear disarmament, or even arms control, unless is it approached on a universal basis. Even then it will be far from easy. The case of France and its relations with NATO over the past forty years indicates the difficulties in handling a nuclear-weapons state which is very sensitive regarding its status. Given the recent changes in status of India and Pakistan, why should others not seek to join them?

Another disadvantage of this situation is that expansion of the nuclear club cannot be restricted to national governments, any more than it can be limited to a certain small number of nations. Once subnational groups acquire nuclear weapons, the perceived balance of interest in retaining the two-tier international system will change. The strongest powers will become the most threatened, the United States in particular. The effectiveness of deterrence will diminish. Because a majority of American voters have not yet recognized that this change is likely, the world will continue much as it is, with a slow, steady expansion of the number of nuclear-weapons states, and a growing probability that one or more subnational groups will come to have their own nuclear weapons and one day use them.

12.6. *What is to be Done?*

In this situation the easiest course seems to be to leave matters very much as they are. There may be some gradual reduction in the numbers of weapons held by the five major states, particularly the United States and Russia, once the START II treaty is ratified by both sides, and the expense of maintaining a force leads the other three to reduce their own stocks somewhat. The difficulty in this option is that it will encourage proliferation of nuclear weapons, and a growing feeling that, even though they may not directly enhance a nation's security, they are a good way of commanding attention and gaining a lift in status. In the dog-eat-dog fraternity of sovereign states this option is both interesting and dangerous. The point is likely to be reached at some time when a significant number of middle powers feel that without nuclear weapons they just do not rate on the international scale, and are liable to be disadvantaged by the club of those who have them. At that stage international society can lurch into rapid proliferation, severe insecurity, and the attendant risk that nuclear war will occur. The dangers to civilized life do not need to be spelt out. A second difficulty in just letting the existing situation continue, as mentioned above, is the inevitable cost of modernization when it comes time to order a new generation of weapons

One option, proposed in this volume by John Baylis, Lawrence Freedman, and Michael Quinlan, is for the existing nuclear-weapons powers consciously and gradually to marginalize these systems. The difficulty in this approach is that it is very hard to distinguish from the first, apart from a change in rhetoric. The existing nuclear-weapons states would continue to have their forces, at lower levels, and with less prominence in their postures, but the two-tier system remains, with all its disadvantages. The idea of marginalization of nuclear weapons sounds to the non-nuclear states very much like children being told to run off and play, and leave the adults to handle serious matters. Alternately it seems like being told to shut up and stop complaining as if it were the complaints that are causing the problem, not nuclear weapons: just tiptoe around the arsenals of the nuclear-weapons states and almost treat them as if they were not there.

Marginalization will not be convincing to the non-nuclear states, and all the incentives for proliferation will continue to be in effect. Perhaps proliferation will be even easier if nobody is making a fuss about nuclear weapons. But marginalization is not likely to prove workable because the potential of nuclear weapons for causing death and destruction is simply too great. Nuclear-weapons crises will occur from time to time, resulting from a wide range of causes—accidents, defiance of international treaties, proliferation, and terrorism to name but a few—and people will call for their control, reduction, or elimination.

A third option is for the existing five major holders of nuclear weapons to recognize that their long-term security interests would be better served by ridding the world of nuclear weapons and begin to act on that basis. In other words they should be treated similarly to the other two major categories of weapons of mass destruction, biological and chemical weapons, and eliminated. The process of elimination could not be immediate. It would require a long series of gradual steps, each to be taken as confidence grows that security is actually being increased by a controlled passage towards elimination. There would not be any real loss of security. The international political climate would become much colder for proliferators. Much of the status argument would subside. The NPT regime could be tightened up considerably once it was clear that all powers were in it seriously. The effect of example and international agreement would be to raise the obstacles that proliferators would have to face.

Once the big five had agreed that their long-term goal was to eliminate nuclear weapons, the international community would be in a better position for dealing with the problems posed by India and Pakistan, and India would lose its rationale that China will always pose a nuclear threat. Other regional nuclear-weapons states could also be brought into the elimination dialogue, and if they refused to participate they could be isolated, sanctioned, and subjected to intense inspection. The pressures against having nuclear weapons would be much stronger than at present, and with the weight of international consensus, from great powers and small, and international public opinion all against them, it is hard to see what proliferators would gain from their actions.

If a government really decided to defy international opinion and develop (or expand) its own nuclear-weapons system, it could. Breaking out will always be possible. This is inherent in the nature of a system of sovereign states coexisting with one another. But just as in H. G. Wells's story, in the country of the blind the one-eyed man is not necessarily king. What would a break-out state be able to achieve, other than to unite the international community against itself? If it actually used a nuclear weapon it could be dealt with very firmly and effectively by modern conventional strike forces. A break-out state could not hope suddenly to gain the upper hand in a complex world in which power has very many dimensions. International surveillance systems may not be able to see into everything, but they can certainly tell when a sizeable nuclear force has been developed. They can identify strategic launch vehicles. They can identify a major problem once it exists, and then it can be dealt with.

A world in which nuclear weapons are outlawed, and in which the current large stocks are being eliminated, will be much less open to the possibility of subnational groups acquiring nuclear weapons. There will be fewer sources of supply. There will be stricter international surveillance and control. This does not mean that a terrorist threat to, say, New York or Washington will become impossible. It does mean that such action will be far more difficult in the long term than in a world where nuclear weapons are coming into the hands of more and more governments, and kept under control systems of unknowable effectiveness.

The process of moving from the current situation towards elimination has been analysed and set forth in some detail in the *Report of the Canberra Commission on the Elimination of Nuclear Weapons.*[3] Space does not permit me to do more than refer to this more extensive work. Suffice it for me to emphasize its conclusion that movement towards elimination can be self-reinforcing once it begins, like the process which brought to an end the Warsaw Pact and the cold war. Once international public opinion sees that the governments of the five major nuclear-weapons states are seriously committed, a landslide of support for elimination is likely to develop. National governments and the United Nations will be able to act much more firmly in support of a nuclear-weapons-free world. There will be a wide recognition that nuclear weapons do very little for the top dogs of international society and essentially serve the purposes of aggrieved and violent underdogs.

NOTES

Notes to Introduction

1. There are two main schools of thought in the contemporary debate: the 'traditionalist' school which argues that nuclear weapons have utility in international politics and the 'abolitionist' school which argues that they do not. A third school, the 'marginalist' school, straddles both of the main schools. All 'marginalists' wish to downgrade the significance of nuclear weapons. However, some see marginalization as an end in itself, while others see it as a step on the way to total elimination.

Notes to Chapter 1

1. Michael Quinlan, *Thinking about Nuclear Weapons* (London: Royal United Institute for Defence Studies, 1997), 28.
2. Patrick M. Morgan, *Deterrence: A Conceptual Analysis* (Beverly Hills, Calif.: Sage, 1977), ch. 2.
3. One telling indication of this political and military fact is the cumulative demotion of 'Strategic Nuclear Forces' in the *Annual Reports* of the Secretary of Defense to the point where, in 1998, those forces appear under chapter 5, following chapters on conventional, and special operations forces. William S. Cohen, Secretary of Defense, *Annual Report to the President and the Congress* (Washington, DC: Government Printing Office, Apr. 1998), ch. 5. This admittedly somewhat 'Kremlinological' point is checkable for accuracy with the relative positioning of the chapter-length discussion of the strategic nuclear forces in the *Annual Reports* for, say, 1990 and 1991.
4. See Carl Sagan and Richard Turco, *A Path Where No Man Thought: Nuclear Winter and the End of the Arms Race* (London: Century, 1990), 54.
5. Richard Price and Nina Tannenwald argue that '[t]he drive to create "smart" bombs and other high-tech options *so that* leaders will not have to resort to nuclear weapons is indicative of the special status of nuclear weapons'. 'Norms and Deterrence: The Nuclear and Chemical Weapons Taboos', in Peter J. Katzenstein (ed.), *The Culture of National Security: Norms and Identity in World Politics* (New York: Columbia University Press, 1996), 140–1. Emphasis added. The causal connection asserted by Price and Tannenwald is rather too simple and direct for my taste.
6. For discussion of this matter in a period classic with some lasting merit, see Lewis A. Dunn, *Controlling the Bomb: Nuclear Proliferation in the 1980s* (New Haven: Yale University Press, 1982), ch. 3, 'How Many Countries Will Get the Bomb?'

7. Mitchell Reiss, *Bridled Ambition: Why Countries Constrain their Nuclear Capabilities* (Washington, DC: Woodrow Wilson Center, 1995).
8. I equivocate a little here because the explosion of criminal and inter-tribal violence in the new South Africa has led to a marked deterioration in the personal security of all citizens.
9. Martin van Creveld, 'New Wars for Old', in *The Economist: The World in 1997* (London: 1996), 91.
10. Quinlan, *Thinking about Nuclear Weapons*, 1.
11. A strong argument for 'marginalization' is advanced in Lawrence Freedman, 'Nuclear Weapons: From Marginalisation to Elimination?', *Survival*, 39 (1997), 184–9.
12. Sun Tzu, *The Art of War*, trans. and ed. Ralph D. Sawyer (Boulder, Colo.: Westview, 1994), esp. 177.
13. H. R. Ellis Davidson, 'The Secret Weapon of Byzantium', *Byzantinische Zeitschrift*, 66 (1973), 61–74.
14. Michael J. Mazarr, 'Virtual Nuclear Arsenals', *Survival*, 37 (1995), 7–26; *Nuclear Weapons in a Transformed World: The Challenge of Virtual Nuclear Arsenals* (London: Macmillan, 1997).
15. Peter R. Lavoy, 'Nuclear Myths and the Causes of Nuclear Proliferation', in Zachary S. Davis and Benjamin Frankel (eds.), 'The Proliferation Puzzle: Why Nuclear Weapons Spread (and What Results)', *Security Studies*, 2 (1993), esp. 206, n. 7.
16. Abolitionist aspirations are demolished in Freedman, 'Nuclear Weapons', 184–9; Quinlan, *Thinking about Nuclear Weapons*; Keith B. Payne, *The Case Against Nuclear Abolition and for Nuclear Deterrence* (Fairfax, Va.: National Institute for Public Policy, 1997). Also, there is enduring merit in Patrick J. Garrity, 'The Depreciation of Nuclear Weapons in International Politics: Possibilities, Limits, Uncertainties', *The Journal of Strategic Studies*, 14 (1991), 463–514. Garrity concludes his lengthy review of nuclear matters by suggesting (p. 501) that '[i]t is possible to argue that officials and scholars have hitherto been overly fascinated with thinking about nuclear weapons, as opposed to understanding other outstanding political and military issues that are now coming to the forefront. Whatever the merits of this viewpoint, we should perhaps now be concerned that in the future there will be too little official academic interest in things nuclear. Nuclear weapons may now seem to be increasingly anachronistic and irrelevant. But if this attitude prevails, or if traditional concepts are applied unthinkingly to new circumstances, nuclear weapons could re-emerge on the scene in unexpected and dangerous ways.' Those are words of wisdom.
17. Jonathan Haslam, *The Soviet Union and the Politics of Nuclear Weapons in Europe, 1969–87* (Ithaca, NY: Cornell University Press, 1990); Beatrice Heuser, *NATO, Britain, France and the FRG: Nuclear Strategies and Forces for Europe, 1949–2000* (London: Macmillan, 1997).
18. For a brief sample of an extensive literature, abolitionist sentiment may be located in the following: Jonathan Schell, *The Abolition* (New York: Alfred A. Knopf, 1986); Regina Cowen Karp (ed.), *Security without Nuclear Weapons: Different Perspectives on Non-Nuclear Security* (Oxford: Oxford University Press, 1992); Joseph Rotblat, Jake Steinberger, and Bhalchandra Udgaonkar (eds.), *A Nuclear-Weapon-Free World: Desirable? Feasible?* (Boulder, Colo.: Westview, 1993); The Canberra Com-

mission on the Elimination of Nuclear Weapons, *Report of the Canberra Commission* (Canberra: Australian Department of Foreign Affairs and Trade, 1996); General Andrew Goodpaster and General Lee Butler, 'National Press Club Luncheon Address', transcript (Washington, DC, 4 Dec. 1996); General Lee Butler, 'Stimson Center Award Remarks', transcript (Washington, DC, 8 Jan. 1997); National Academy of Sciences, Committee on International Security and Arms Control, *The Future of U.S. Nuclear Weapons Policy* (Washington, DC: National Academy Press, 1997); Joseph Rotblat (ed.), *Nuclear Weapons: The Road to Zero* (Oxford: Oxford University Press, 1998).

19. Mazarr, 'Virtual Nuclear Arsenals'; 'The Notion of Virtual Arsenals', in Mazarr (ed.), *Nuclear Weapons in a Transformed World*, 3–29.

20. Mazarr, 'Notion of Virtual Nuclear Arsenals', 14.

21. Ibid.

22. Colin S. Gray, *House of Cards: Why Arms Control Must Fail* (Ithaca, NY: Cornell University Press, 1992), ch. 6, provides detailed justification for this claim.

23. Thomas C. Schelling, *The Strategy of Conflict* (Cambridge, MA: Harvard University Press, 1960), ch. 8.

24. David H. Dunn, *The Politics of Threat: Minuteman Vulnerability in American National Security Policy* (London: Macmillan, 1997), ch. 8.

25. Carl von Clausewitz, *On War*, trans. and ed. Michael Howard and Peter Paret (Princeton: Princeton University Press, 1976), 178.

26. Keith B. Payne, *Deterrence in the Second Nuclear Age* (Lexington, Ky.: University of Kentucky Press, 1996), 17.

27. Quinlan, *Thinking about Nuclear Weapons*, 16.

28. For reasons explained admirably in Barry D. Watts, *Clausewitzian Friction and Future War*, McNair Paper, 52 (Washington, DC, Oct. 1996).

29. Fred Charles Iklé, 'The Second Coming of the Nuclear Age', *Foreign Affairs*, 75 (1996), 119–28, is thoughtfully sceptical about our record of success with deterrence during the cold war. Iklé is nothing if not consistent; see his articles, 'Can Nuclear Deterrence Last Out the Century?', *Foreign Affairs*, 51 (1973), 267–85, and 'Nuclear Strategy: Can There Be a Happy Ending?', *Foreign Affairs*, 63 (1985), 810–26. In the growing library of post-cold-war histories of the first nuclear age, the following are prominent among those works that merit close attention: Christopher Andrew and Oleg Gordievsky, *Instructions from the Centre: The Secret Files on KGB Foreign Operations, 1975–1985* (London: Hodder & Stoughton, 1991); Marc Trachtenberg, *History and Strategy* (Princeton: Princeton University Press, 1991); James A. Nathan (ed.), *The Cuban Missile Crisis Revisited* (New York: St Martin's, 1992); Melvyn P. Leffler, *A Preponderance of Power: National Security, the Truman Administration, and the Cold War* (Stanford, Calif.: Stanford University Press, 1992); Scott D. Sagan, *The Limits of Safety: Organizations, Accidents, and Nuclear Weapons* (Princeton, NJ: Princeton University Press, 1993); Richard Ned Lebow and Janice Gross Stein, *We All Lost the Cold War* (Princeton: Princeton University Press, 1994); David Holloway, *Stalin and the Bomb: The Soviet Union and Atomic Energy, 1939–1956* (New Haven: Yale University Press, 1994); Vladislav Zubok and Constantine Pleshakov, *Inside the Kremlin's Cold War: From Stalin to Khrushchev* (Cambridge, Mass.: Harvard University Press, 1996); Helga Haftendorn, *NATO and the Nuclear Revolution: A Crisis of Credibility, 1966–1967*

(Oxford: Clarendon Press, 1996); Saki Dockrill, *Eisenhower's New-Look National Security Policy, 1953–61* (London: Macmillan, 1996); Vojtech Mastny, *The Cold War and Soviet Insecurity: The Stalin Years* (New York: Oxford University Press, 1996); John Lewis Gaddis, *We Now Know: Rethinking Cold War History* (Oxford: Clarendon Press, 1997); Aleksandr Fursenko and Timothy Naftali, *'One Hell of a Gamble': Khrushchev, Castro, Kennedy, and the Cuban Missile Crisis, 1958–1964* (London: John Murray, 1997); Ernest R. May and Philip D. Zelikow (eds.), *The Kennedy Tapes: Inside the White House during the Cuban Missile Crisis* (Cambridge, Mass.: Harvard University Press, 1997); Ben B. Fischer, *A Cold War Conundrum: The 1983 Soviet War Scare, CSI 97-10002* (Langley, Va.: CIA, Sept. 1997).

30. Janice Gross Stein, 'Deterrence and Compellence in the Gulf, 1990–91: A Failed or Impossible Task?', *International Security*, 17 (1992), 147–79, is excellent.

31. Michael Howard, 'Lessons of the Cold War', *Survival*, 36 (1994–5), 161–6.

32. Quinlan, *Thinking about Nuclear Weapons*, 16. Emphasis added.

33. Notwithstanding his focus upon irregular warriors, Ralph Peters offers a superb essay on the power of human motivation in 'Our New Old Enemies', in Lloyd J. Matthews (ed.), *Challenging the United States Symmetrically and Asymmetrically: Can America be Defeated?* (Carlisle Barracks, Pa: US Army War College, July 1998), 215–38.

34. For some arguably relevant theory, see Glenn E. James, *Chaos Theory: The Essentials for Military Applications*, Newport Paper, 10 (Newport, RI: Naval War College, Center for Naval Warfare Studies, Oct. 1996).

35. Peters, 'Our New Old Enemies'.

36. Suffice it for now to record that for centuries to come scholars will be arguing about 'the decline and fall of the Soviet Empire'. At the present time there is a short list of contending major explanations (most are predominantly deterministic, as scholars fall into the trap of rationalizing what was substantially highly contingent), but there is no dominant theory that commands near-universal respect.

37. In addition to James, *Chaos Theory*, see David Ruelle, *Chance and Chaos* (London: Penguin, 1993); Stephen H. Kellert, *In the Wake of Chaos: Unpredictable Order in Dynamical Systems* (Chicago: Chicago University Press, 1993); Roger Beaumont, *War, Chaos, and History* (Westport, Conn.: Praeger, 1994).

38. See Bert S. Hall, *Weapons and Warfare in Renaissance Europe: Gunpowder, Technology, and Tactics* (Baltimore: Johns Hopkins University Press, 1997), esp. ch. 2, 'Gunpowder's First Century, ca. 1325–ca. 1425'.

39. Michael Mandelbaum, 'Lessons of the Next Nuclear War', *Foreign Affairs*, 74 (1995), 22–37.

40. Freedman, 'Nuclear Weapons', 39.

41. Scott D. Sagan and Kenneth N. Waltz, *The Spread of Nuclear Weapons: A Debate* (New York: W. W. Norton, 1995), 17.

42. On taboo issues, see T. V. Paul , 'Nuclear Taboo and War Initiation in Regional Conflicts', *The Journal of Conflict Resolution*, 39 (1995), 696–717; Price and Tannenwald, 'Norms and Deterrence'.

43. Many of the most pertinent issues are discussed usefully in Dean Wilkening and

Kenneth Watman, *Nuclear Deterrence in a Regional Context* (Santa Monica, Calif.: RAND, Arroyo Center, 1994).

44. John Keegan, *The Face of Battle* (London: Jonathan Cape, 1976).

45. Michael Krepon, 'Are Missile Defenses MAD? Combining Defenses with Arms Control', *Foreign Affairs*, 74 (1995), 19–24; Payne, *Deterrence in the Second Nuclear Age*, 142–52.

46. The following sample from the large literature available covers all points of view: Ashton B. Carter and David N. Schwartz (eds.), *Ballistic Missile Defense* (Washington, DC: Brookings Institute, 1984); Keith B. Payne, *Strategic Defense: 'Star Wars' in Perspective* (Lanham, Md.: Hamilton, 1986); Zbigniew Brzezinski (ed.), *Promise or Peril: The Strategic Defense Initiative* (Washington, DC: Ethics and Public Policy Center, 1986); Herbert York, *Does Strategic Defense Breed Offense?* (Cambridge, Mass.: Harvard Center for Science and International Affairs, 1987); *The Concept of Defensive Deterrence: Strategic and Technical Dimensions of Missile Defense* (Washington, DC: George C. Marshall Institute, 1988); Antonia H. Chayes and Paul Doty (eds.), *Defending Deterrence: Managing the ABM Treaty Regime into the 21st Century* (Washington, DC: Pergamon-Brassey's, 1989); Keith B. Payne, *Missile Defense in the 21st Century: Protection Against Limited Threats, Including Lessons from the Gulf War* (Boulder, Colo.: Westview, 1991); Donald R. Baucom, *The Origins of SDI, 1944–1983* (Lawrence, Kan.: University of Kansas Press, 1992); Edward Reiss, *The Strategic Defense Initiative* (Cambridge: Cambridge University Press, 1992).

47. On 10 Nov. 1932, British Prime Minister Stanley Baldwin told the House of Commons in a phrase that has become cliché that 'the bomber will always get through'. For the context see Uri Bialer, *The Shadow of the Bomber: The Fear of Air Attack and British Politics, 1932–1939* (London: Royal Historic Society, 1980), ch. 1 (Baldwin's claim is quoted on p. 14).

48. The agreement laid out in the 'White House Press Release, Joint Statement Concerning the Anti-Ballistic Missile Treaty, Helsinki Summit, March 21 1997', is reprinted in *Comparative Strategy*, 16 (1997), 415–16. For the full political, legal, and strategic contexts, see Steven J. Lambakis and Colin S. Gray, *Political and Legal Restrictions on U.S. Military Space Activities* (Fairfax: National Institute for Public Policy, Dec. 1997).

49. Appropriately scathing comment upon this unfortunate and strategically imprudent development, is provided by David J. Smith, 'Missile Defense After Helsinki', *Comparative Strategy*, 16 (1997), 369–76.

50. It is the logic of asymmetrical strategy. See Matthews (ed.), *Challenging the United States Symmetrically and Asymmetrically*.

51. Ballistic missiles are the most militarily attractive delivery vehicles for nuclear weapons; they are good enough—though not ideal—for delivery of chemical agents that require carefully controlled dispersal if they are to be suitably promptly lethal; but they are far from ideal for exact delivery of the delicate living organisms that are the agents of biological warfare. See OTA, *Proliferation of Weapons of Mass Destruction*, 50–2; OTA, *Technologies Underlying Weapons of Mass Destruction*, esp. 32–6, 94–9.

52. Bruce G. Blair, *The Logic of Accidental Nuclear War* (Washington, DC:

Brookings Institute, 1993); Sagan, *Limits of Safety*; Fischer, *Cold War Conundrum*.

53. See Wilkening and Watman, *Nuclear Deterrence in a Regional Context*; John Arquilla, 'Bound to Fail: Regional Deterrence after the Cold War', *Comparative Strategy*, 14 (1995), 123–35.

54. On the basics, see Wolfgang K. H. Panofsky, 'The Mutual Hostage Relationship Between America and Russia', *Foreign Affairs*, 52 (1973), 109–18.

55. Price and Tannenwald, 'Norms and Deterrence', 140.

56. e.g. we recognize taboos against incest and cannibalism, while in addition there is a taboo against remaining seated during the playing of the national anthem.

57. Lewis A. Dunn, *Containing Nuclear Proliferation*, Adelphi Paper, 263 (London: IISS, Winter 1991), 69, 70. Emphasis added.

58. Ibid. 70.

59. John Mueller, *Retreat from Doomsday: The Obsolescence of Major War* (New York: Basic Books, 1989).

60. Quoted in Michael Walzer, *Just and Unjust Wars: A Moral Argument with Historical Illustrations* (New York: Basic Books, 1997), 240. The Chancellor's actual words were 'necessity knows no law'.

61. Clausewitz, *On War*, 605.

62. Hugh D. Crone, *Banning Chemical Weapons: The Scientific Background* (Cambridge: Cambridge University Press, 1992), is helpful.

63. Eliot Cohen, one among 'Three Comments' [on Heather Wilson, 'The Politics of Proliferation'], *The National Interest*, 34 (1993/4), 37.

64. Waltz in Sagan and Waltz, *The Spread of Nuclear Weapons*, 21, 22, 24; Quinlan, *Thinking about Nuclear Weapons*, 16.

Notes to Chapter 2

1. For arguments looking forward to a total elimination of nuclear weapons, see Michael Mazarr and Alexander T. Lennon (eds.), *Toward a Nuclear Peace* (New York: St Martin's, 1994), Joseph Rotblat, Jack Steinberger, and Bhalchandra Udgaonkar (eds.), *A Nuclear-Weapons-Free World: Desirable? Feasible?* (Boulder, Colo.: Westview, 1993), and Jonathan Schell, *The Abolition* (New York: Morrow, 1984).

2. A strong statement favouring extended nuclear deterrence can be found in Karl Kaiser, Georg Leber, Alois Mertes, and Franz-Josef Schulze, 'Nuclear Weapons and the Preservation of Peace', *Foreign Affairs*, 60/5 (Summer, 1982), 1157–70.

3. For an argument that the USA and the West should have lost interest in extended nuclear deterrence, see Committee on International Security and Arms Control (CISAC), *The Future of U.S. Nuclear Weapons Policy* (Washington, DC: National Academy of Sciences, 1997).

4. On the evolution of the Nuclear Non-Proliferation Treaty, see William B. Bader, *The United States and the Spread of Nuclear Weapons* (New York: Pegasus, 1968).

5. For an eloquent example, see K. Subrahmanyam (ed.), *Nuclear Proliferation and International Security* (New Delhi: Institute for Defence Studies and Analyses, 1985).

6. On this broader appeal of the NPT, see Tariq Rauf (ed.), *Extending the Non-Proliferation Treaty, Perpetuating the Global Norm* (Ottawa: Candian Centre for Global Security, 1995).

7. The Irish resolution for a 'non-nuclear club' is discussed in William Epstein, *The Last Chance* (New York: Freeman, 1976), 61–3. See also Harald Müller (ed.), *How Western Nuclear Policy is Made* (New York: St Martin's, 1991).

8. The text of the NPT can be found in United States Arms Control and Disarmament Agency, *Documents on Disarmament: 1968* (Washington: USGPO, 1969), 461–5.

9. Thomas C. Schelling and Morton Halperin, *Strategy and Arms Control* (New York: Twentieth Century Fund, 1961).

10. On the inherent fears and temptations of cheating here, see John W. Spanier and Joseph L. Nogee, *The Politics of Disarmament* (New York: Praeger, 1962).

11. For an earlier analysis stressing such possibilities of good example, see Epstein, *Last Chance.*

12. On the risks of a spread of non-nuclear 'weapons of mass destruction', see John F. Sopko, 'The Changing Proliferation Threat', *Foreign Policy*, 10/5 (Winter, 1996–7), 3–20.

13. On the alleged power of revolutionary applications of computers to the conventional battlefield, see David Alberts and Daniel S. Papp (eds.), *The Information Age* (Washington, DC: National Defense University Press, 1997).

14. Such a criticism of the American failure to shift to 'no-first-use' can be found in George Bunn, 'Expanding Nuclear Options: Is the U.S. Negating its Non-Use Pledges?', *Arms Control Today*, 26/4 (May/June 1996), 7–10.

15. The Israeli approach to nuclear weapons is outlined in Louis Rene Beres (ed.) Security or Armageddon (Lexington, Mass.: D. C. Heath, 1986).

16. South Korean preparations for acquiring nuclear weapons are noted in Leonard Spector, *Nuclear Ambitions* (Boulder, Colo.: Westview, 1990), 121–6.

17. On Taiwan's latent nuclear option, see Lincoln Kaye, 'Atomic Intentions', *Far Eastern Economic Review* (3 May 1990), 9.

18. On the Russian new interest in 'flexible response', see Wolfgang Panofsky and George Bunn, 'The Doctrine of the Nuclear Weapons States and the Future of Non-Proliferation', *Arms Control Today*, 24/6 (July/Aug. 1994), 7.

19. For provocative examples, see John Mearsheimer, 'Back to the Future', *International Security*, 15/1 (Summer 1990), 5–86, and 'The Case for a Ukrainian Deterrent', *Foreign Affairs*, 78/3 (Summer 1993), 50–66.

20. For a statement of British arguments favouring retention of nuclear weapons, see Michael Quinlan, 'British Nuclear Weapons Policy: Past, Present and Future', in John C. Hopkins and Weixing Hu (eds.), *Strategic Views from the Second Tier* (San Diego: University of California Institute on Global Conflict and Cooperation, 1994), 125–40.

21. On the concerns about the control over nuclear weapons after the break-up of the Soviet Union, see James Blaker, 'Coping wih the New "Clear and Present Danger" From Russia', *Arms Control Today*, 25/3 (Apr. 1995), 13–16.

22. North Korean nuclear possibilities are discussed in Michael Mazarr, *North Korea and the Bomb* (New York: St Martin's, 1995), and Leon Sigal, *Disarming Strangers* (Princeton: Princeton University Press, 1998).

Notes to Chapter 3

1. See my monograph, *Thinking about Nuclear Weapons* (London: Royal United Services Institute for Defence Studies, 1997), 50–4.
2. Ibid. 54–6
3. See Michael J. Mazarr (ed.), *Nuclear Weapons in a Transformed World: The Challenge of Virtual Nuclear Arsenals* (London: Macmillan, 1997).
4. See Stansfield Turner, *Caging the Nuclear Genie* (Boulder, Colo.: Westview, 1997).

Notes to Chapter 4

1. For an excellent history of the anti-nuclear movement over this period see Lawrence S. Wittner, *Resisting the Bomb: A History of the World Nuclear Disarmament Movement, 1954–1970* (Stanford, Calif.: Stanford University Press, 1997).
2. I discuss this in Lawrence Freedman, *The Evolution of Nuclear Strategy*, 2nd edn. (London: Macmillan, 1989).
3. The contrasting views can be found in Hedley Bull, *The Control of the Arms Race* (London: Weidenfeld & Nicolson, 1961) and Philip Noel-Baker, *The Arms Race* (London: John Calder, 1958).
4. Regina C. Karp, *Security without Nuclear Weapons? Different Perspectives on Non-Nuclear Security* (Oxford: Oxford University Press, 1992); Joseph Rotblat, Jack Steinburger, and Bahalchandra Udgaonkar, *A Nuclear-Weapon-Free World: Desirable? Feasible?* (Boulder, Colo.: Westview, 1993).
5. The Court took the view that 'the threat and use of nuclear weapons would generally be contrary to the rules of international law applicable in armed conflict, and particularly the principles and rules of humanitarian law'. The word 'generally', however, provides a sufficient get-out for powers claiming that they have no interest except in deterrence of extreme acts against them.
6. The Gorbachev, Rajiv Gandhi and Rockefeller Foundations, as well as the Carnegie Corporation, backed the project on the elimination of nuclear weapons of the State of the World Foundation. http://www.arq.co.uk/worldforum.
7. Schell acknowledges that many are rather old. Jonathan Schell, *The Gift of Time: The Case for Abolishing Nuclear Weapons* (New York: Metropolitan Books and Henry Holt & Company, 1998).
8. Cathleen Fisher, preface to Steve Fetter, *Verifying Nuclear Disarmament*, Occasional Paper, 290 (Washington, DC: The Henry L. Stimson Center, Oct. 1996). See *An Evolving US Nuclear Posture: Second Report of the Steering Committee: Project on Eliminating Weapons of Mass Destruction* (Washington, DC: Henry L. Stimson Center, Dec. 1995).
9. Schell, *Gift of Time*, 13.
10. *Report of the Canberra Commission on the Elimination of Nuclear Weapons* (Canberra: Australian Department of Foreign Affairs and Trade, Aug. 1996), 24.
11. Ibid. 10.
12. J. M. Keynes, *Essays and Sketches in Biography* (New York: Meridian Books, 1956), 255.

13. Sir Michael Quinlan, 'The Future of Nuclear Weapons in World Affairs', *The Atlantic Council of the United States Bulletin*, 7/9 (20 Nov. 1996). Quinlan is a target of the disarmament movement because of his readiness to make the case for a continuing, though low salience, role for nuclear deterrence in terms of a 'non-specific concept of helping to underpin world order in whatever context it might be threatened, and to help reduce the risk of major war wherever it might occur'. 'The Future of Nuclear Weapons: Policy for Western Possessors', *International Affairs*, 69/3 (1993); For a critique see Michael MccGwire, 'Is there a Future for Nuclear Weapons?', *International Affairs*, 70/2 (Apr. 1994).

14. *Canberra Commission*, 15.

15. Thus the State of the World Foundation describes its objectives as bringing 'pressure to bear on the United States and Russia to reduce their existing nuclear stockpiles to 500 apiece and, once that is accomplished bring in the 3 remaining declared nuclear powers to commit a process of mutual reduction which would bring all their stockpiles to 200 each'.

16. Michael Mazarr, 'Virtual Nuclear Arsenals', *Survival* (Autumn 1995).

17. These issues are thoroughly discussed in Scott Sagan and Kenneth N. Waltz, *The Spread of Nuclear Weapons: A Debate* (New York: W. W. Norton, 1995).

18. Responsible dismantling of nuclear weapons requires consideration of the proper disposal and storage of the plutonium and highly enriched uranium. For a useful discussion of the problems of disposal see 'Costing a Bomb', *The Economist* (4 Jan. 1997).

Notes to Chapter 5

1. For a discussion of the process of marginalizing nuclear weapons in the 1990s see G. Allison *et al.*, *Cooperative Denuclearization: From Pledges to Deeds* (Cambridge, Mass.: Center for Science and International Affairs, 1993).

2. See M. MccGwire, 'Deterrence: The Problem—Not the Solution', *International Affairs*, 45/1 (1986).

3. It is estimated that by 1950 over 340,000 had died as a result of the two bombs. See Committee for the Compilation of Materials on Damage Caused by the Atomic Bombs in Hiroshima and Nagasaki, *Hiroshima and Nagasaki: The Physical, Medical and Social Effects of the Atomic Bombings* (London: Hutchinson, 1981).

4. Assumptions of moral neutrality were an important feature of the early strategists who wrote about nuclear weapons. See J. C. Garnett, 'Strategic Studies and its Assumptions', in J Baylis, Ken Booth, John Garnett, and Phil Williams, *Contemporary Strategy: Theories and Concepts*, i (New York: Holmes & Meier, 1987).

5. For a discussion of this debate see D. Lackey, 'Immoral Risks: A Deontological Critique of Nuclear Deterrence', in Ellen Frankel Paul, Fred D. Miller, Jeffrey Paul, and John Ahrens (eds.), *Nuclear Rights and Nuclear Wrongs* (Oxford: Blackwell, 1983).

6. J. McMahon, 'Deterrence and Deontology', in Russell Hardin, John J. Mearsheimer, Gerald Dworhin, and Robert E. Goodwin (eds.), *Nuclear Deterrence: Ethics and Strategy* (Chicago: University of Chicago Press, 1985), 158.

7. For a discussion of this argument see J. Nye, *Nuclear Ethics* (London: Macmillan, 1986).

8. M. Walzer, *Just and Unjust Wars: A Moral Argument with Historical Illustrations* (New York: Basic Books, 1992).

9. J. Mueller, *Retreat from Doomsday: The Obsolescence of Major War* (New York: Basic Books, 1989).

10. J. Gaddis, *The Long Peace: Inquiries into the History of the Cold War* (New York: Oxford University Press, 1987).

11. See Malcolm Rifkind, 'UK Defence Strategy: A Continuing Role for Nuclear Weapons', in *The Framework of United Kingdom Defence Policy: Key Speeches on Defence Policy by the Rt. Hon. Malcolm Rifkind QC MP, 1993–95* (London: Brassey's, 1995).

12. See N. Lebow and J. Stein, *We All Lost the Cold War* (Princeton: Princeton University Press, 1994).

13. R. Falk, 'Nuclear Weapons and the End of Democracy', *Praxis International*, 2/1 (Apr. 1982).

14. S. Lee, *Prudence, Morality and Nuclear Weapons* (Cambridge: Cambridge University Press, 1993).

15. B. Blair, *Strategic Command and Control: Redefining the Nuclear Threat* (Washington, DC: Brookings, 1985) and *The Logic of Accidental Nuclear War* (Washington, DC: Brookings, 1993).

16. C. Flavin, *Reassessing Nuclear Power: The Fallout from Chernobyl* (New York: Worldwatch Institute, 1987).

17. See S. Sagan, 'The Perils of Proliferation Organization Theory, Deterrence Theory, and the Spread of Nuclear Weapons', *International Security*, 18/4 (Spring 1994).

18. M. Evans, 'False Alarm Took Russia to the Brink of Nuclear War', *The Times* (13 July 1998).

19. S. Sagan, *The Limits of Safety: Organizations, Accidents, and Nuclear Weapons* (Princeton: Princeton University Press, 1993).

20. See also Sagan, 'Perils of Proliferation'.

21. See K. N. Waltz, *The Spread of Nuclear Weapons: More May Be Better*, Adelphi Paper, 171 (London: IISS, 1981); John Mearsheimer, 'The Case for a Ukrainian Nuclear Deterrence', *Foreign Affairs*, 72/3 (Summer 1993); and David Karl, 'Proliferation Pessimism and Emerging Nuclear Powers'. *International Security*, 21/3 (Winter 1996/7).

22. One of the UN inspectors is reported to have commented: 'I wouldn't want to be around if it fell off the edge of the desk.' See G. Milhollin, 'Building Saddam Hussein's Bomb', *New York Times Magazine* (8 Mar. 1992).

23. *Report of the Canberra Commission on the Elimination of Nuclear Weapons* (Canberra: Australian Department of Foreign Affairs and Trade, 1996).

24. See R. O'Neill, 'Britain and the Future of Nuclear Weapons', *International Affairs*, 71/4 (Oct. 1995).

25. See George Lee Butler, 'Time to End the Age of Nukes', *The Bulletin of the Atomic Scientists* (Mar./Apr. 1997).

26. Statement on Nuclear Weapons by International Generals and Admirals, 6 Oct. 1996. See P. Taylor, 'Generals who Learnt to Hate the Bomb', *The Sunday Times* (8 Dec. 1996).

27. P. Nitze, 'A Conventional Approach', UN Naval Institute Proceedings, May 1994, and 'Is it Time to Junk our Nukes?' *The Washington Post* (16 Jan. 1994).

28. F. Ikle and S. Karaganov, *Harmonizing the Evolution of US and Russian Defense Policies* (Washington, DC, and Moscow: Center for Strategic and International Studies and the Council on Foreign and Defense Policy, 1993).

29. For a discussion of American nuclear policies in the 1990s see S. A. Cambone and P. J. Garrity, 'The Future of US Nuclear Policy', *Survival*, 36/4 (Winter 1994–5).

30. 'Department of Defense Briefing on the Nuclear Posture Review', 22 Sept. 1994, in Federal News Service Transcript, p. 2.

31. See Address by Secretary of Defense William Perry, 'United States Relationship with Russia', George Washington University DC, 14 Mar. 1994, in Federal News Service transcript, p. 8.

32. See 'Nuclear Weapons Testing: A New Era of Non-Proliferation and its Impact on the Public's Opinion of Nuclear Energy', *The Nuclear Review* (Mar. 1996) and 'Virtual Testing with the Paragon Supercomputer and Sandia Codes Helps Ensure Nuclear Weapons Integrity', *Sandia LabNews* (9 June 1995), http:/www.sandia. gov/LabNews/LN06-09-95/virtual.html. It is not clear whether the US has given any assistance to China in terms of helping to maintain the safety of its nuclear weapons.

33. See *The Economist* (6–12 June 1998).

34. For a discussion of the nuclear capabilities of Israel see L. S. Spector, M. G. McDonough, and E. S. Medeiros, *Tracking Nuclear Proliferation* (Washington, DC: Carnegie Endowment for International Peace, 1995).

35. For a very critical role of the record of arms control see C. Gray, *House of Cards: Why Arms Control Must Fail* (Ithaca, NY: Cornell University Press, 1992).

36. This agreement, however, was dependent on the implementation of START II which is currently being held up in the Russian Duma.

37. See Robert A. Manning, *Back to the Future: Toward a Post-Nuclear Ethic—The New Logic of Nonproliferation* (Washington, DC: The Progressive Foundation, Jan. 1994).

38. 'Retrospective on the Cuban Missile Crisis', 22 Jan. 1983, Atlanta, Ga. Participants: Dean Rusk, McGeorge Bundy, Edwin Martin, Donald Wilson, and Richard E. Neustadt.

39. R. N. Lebow and J. G. Stein, *We All Lost the Cold War* (Princetion: Princeton University Press, 1994), 368.

40. J. Schell, *The Abolition* (New York: Alfred Knopf, 1984).

41. R. C. Molander and P. A. Wilson, 'On Dealing with the Problem of Nuclear Chaos', *The Washington Quarterly*, 17/3 (1994) and *The Nuclear Asymptote: On Containing Nuclear Proliferation*, MR-214-CC (Santa Monica, Calif.: The RAND Corporation, 1993).

42. See Manning, *Back to the Future*, and M. Mazarr, 'Virtual Nuclear Arsenals', *Survival*, 37/3 (Autumn 1996).

43. S. Turner, *Caging the Nuclear Genie: An American Challenge for Global Security* (Boulder, Colo.: Westview, 1997), 65–73.

44. The term 'existential deterrence' was coined by McGeorge Bundy.

45. M. Brown, 'Nuclear Doctrine and Virtual Nuclear Arsenals', in M. Mazarr (ed.), *Nuclear Weapons in a Transformed World* (London: Macmillan, 1997).

46. See B. Blair, 'Command, Control, and Warning for Virtual Arsenals', in Mazarr, *Nuclear Weapons in a Transformed World*.
47. G. Perkovich, 'A Nuclear Third Way in South Asia', *Foreign Policy*, 91 (Summer 1993).
48. See Cambone and Garrity, 'Future of US Nuclear Policy'.
49. Just as NATO emphasized nuclear weapons to make up for its conventional inferiority during the cold war so Russian generals have argued that Russia will have to put more emphasis on nuclear weapons to compensate for growing conventional inferiority in the post-cold-war era. See 'Russia Needs Policy of First-Use Nuclear Strike', *The Times* (12 Feb. 1997).
50. Hearing before the Subcommittee on International Security, Proliferation, and Federal Services, 'The Future of Nuclear Deterrence', 12 Feb. 1997 (Washington, DC: US Government Printing Office, 1997).
51. Plans to reduce the number of missiles to 300 were rejected in favour of a ceiling of 450/500.
52. Attempts to reduce US ICBMs in the Nuclear Policy Review to 300 missiles were thwarted by objections from members of the Senate. As a result the number was increased to 500. See 'Department of Defense Briefing on the Nuclear Posture Review', 22 Sept. 1994.
53. See *The Economist* (6–12 June 1998).
54. D. Kay, 'The Challenge of Inspecting and Verifying Virtual Nuclear Arsenals', in Mazarr, *Nuclear Weapons in a Transformed World*.
55. Mazarr, *Nuclear Weapons in a Transformed World*.
56. K. Waltz, 'Thoughts on Virtual Nuclear Arsenals', in Mazarr, *Nuclear Weapons in a Transformed World*.
57. See Y. Evron, *Israel's Nuclear Dilemma* (Ithaca, NY: Cornell University Press, 1994).
58. See Cambone and Garrity, 'Future of US Nuclear Policy'.
59. US officials have argued that, for the foreseeable future, the US 'will continue to need a reliable and flexible nuclear deterrent, survivable against the most aggressive attack, under highly confident constitutional command and control, and assured in its safety against both accident and unauthorized use'. Hearing before the Subcommittee on International security, Proliferation, and Federal services, 12 Feb. 1997, p. 4.
60. Even 'traditional' thinkers like Richard Perle have argued that: 'I want a minimum nuclear force not because nuclear weapons are inherently dangerous and should be eliminated, but because they can serve our security interests if they are deployed in numbers and according to a doctrine that is realistic and carefully conceived.' Ibid. 41. What is not agreed is how low the numbers can fall before nuclear deterrence is undermined.

Notes to Chapter 6

1. For the Shah's 'nuclear vision', see e.g. Mohammed Reza Pahlavi, *Answer to History* (New York: 1980), ch. 8; Marvin Zonis, *Majestic Failure: The Fall of the Shah* (Chicago: Chicago University Press, 1991), 79–80.
2. Sermons delivered by Ayatollah Ruhollah Khomeini on 2 Nov. 1979 and 11 Feb.

1980, as brought in F. Rajaee, *Islamic Values and World View: Khomeini on Man, the State, and International Politics* (Lanham, Md.: University Press of America, 1983), 31, 48, 82–3.

3. See e.g. *Sunday Times, Sunday Telegraph* (27 Aug. 1995).
4. Cited in Leonard Spector, 'Nuclear Proliferation in the Middle East: The Next Chapter Begins', in Efraim Karsh, Martin Navias, and Philip Sabin (eds.), *Non-Conventional Weapons Proliferation in the Middle East: Tackling the Spread of Nuclear, Chemical, and Biological Capabilities* (Oxford: Clarendon Press, 1993), 143. For further details of Iran's nuclear programme see Frank Bamaby, 'Capping Israel's Nuclear Volcano', in the same volume; Geoffrey Kemp, *Forever Enemies? American Policy and the Islamic Republic of Iran* (Washington, DC: Carnegie Endowment, 1994); Shabram Chubin, *Iran's National Security Policy: Capabilities, Intentions, and Impact* (Washington, DC: Carnegie Endowment, 1994).
5. For Saddam's mindset and the nature of his personal rule see Efraim Karsh and Inari Rautsi, *Saddam Hussein: A Political Biography* (New York: The Free Press, 1991).
6. See e.g. *Ha-aretz* (13 Aug. 1992); *Maariv* (14 July 1995).
7. For Israel's nuclear programme see e.g. Shlomo Aronsohn (with the assistance of Oded Brosh), *The Politics and Strategy of Nuclear Weapons in the Middle East* (Albany, NY: State University of New York Press, 1992); idem, 'The 1967 Six Day War Thirty Years After: An Israeli Perspective', *King's College Mediterranean Papers* (Dec. 1998); Avner Cohen, *Israel and the Bomb* (New York: Columbia University Press, 1998).
8. *Sunday Times* (27 Aug. 1995).
9. *Washington Post* (4 Apr. 1995).
10. 'Secret Weapon', *Newsweek* (4 Sept. 1995), 14–15; *Sunday Times* (27 Aug. 1995); *Yediot Aharonot* (27, 28 Aug. 1995).
11. Revelations made by former UN arms inspector Scott Ritter in an interview with *Ha-aretz*. See David Makovsky, 'Hide and Seek with the Palace Guard', *Ha-aretz: English Internet Edition* (29 Sept. 1998).
12. *The Times* (17 June 1992).
13. Makovsky, 'Hide and Seek'.
14. See e.g. Rolf Ekdus, 'Iraq: The Future of Arms Control', *Security Dialogue*, 25/1 (1994), 7–16.

Notes to Chapter 7

1. Other countries with comparable ambiguities in their nuclear postures include Iran, Iraq, Israel, North Korea, and South Africa. The last signed the NPT in 1992. On 24 Mar. 1993, President F. W. de Klerk said in parliament that South Africa had indeed possessed six nuclear bombs, but that these had been dismantled by his administration since coming to power in 1989. For the story of the transition of South Africa from a clandestine NWS to the key signatory of the African nuclear-weapon-free zone, see Julius O. Ihonvbere, 'Africa: The Treaty of Pelindaba', in Ramesh Thakur (ed.), *Nuclear-Weapon-Free Zones* (London: Macmillan, 1998), 93–116.

2. Neil Joeck, 'Pakastani Security and Nuclear Proliferation in South Asia', *Journal of Strategic Studies*, 8/4 (Dec. 1985), 86–7.

3. Tim Weiner, citing US officials and declassified US government documents, in 'U.S. and Chinese Aid was Essential as Pakistan Built Bomb', *International Herald Tribune* (2 June 1998).

4. Quoted in Dilip Bobb and Raminder Singh, 'Pakistan's Nuclear Bombshell', *India Today* (31 Mar. 1987), 12.

5. Kuldip Nayar, 'We have the A-Bomb, Says Pakistan's "Dr Strangelove"', *The Observer* (London, 1 Mar. 1987).

6. *Asian Defence Journal* (Jan. 1988), 102.

7. Seymour M. Hersh, 'On the Nuclear Edge', *New Yorker* (29 Mar. 1993), 56–73. The article is unusual both for its details and also for the number of senior former officials—including CIA director Robert M. Gates—who were prepared to be interviewed on the record.

8. Salamat Ali and Frank Tatu, 'Pakistan: Nuclear Fallout', *Far Eastern Economic Review* (25 Oct. 1990), 11–12.

9. *Statesman Weekly* (Calcutta, 30 Sept. 1989), 4.

10. The long term political changes in India are discussed in Ramesh Thakur, 'A Changing of the Guard in India', *Asian Survey* 38/6 (June 1998), 603–23.

11. The four options are examined in Ramesh Thakur, 'The Nuclear Option in India's Security Policy', *Asia Pacific Review* 5/1 (Spring/Summer 1998), 39–60.

12. The Western scientific and intelligence communities remain sceptical of the numbers and yields of the tests. The veracity of the claims made by both governments on these two points is not relevant to the analysis of this chapter.

13. The poll was conducted by the Indian Market Research Bureau on 12 May in Mumbai, Delhi, Calcutta, Chennai, Bangalore, and Hyderabad; *Hindu* (Chennai, 13 May 1998).

14. K. Subrahmanyam, 'Politics of Shakti: New Whine in an Old Bomb', *Times of India* (Delhi, 26 May 1998).

15. Jaswant Singh, 'Against Nuclear Apartheid', *Foreign Affairs* 77/5 (Sept./Oct. 1998), 49.

16. *The Economist* (23 May 1998), 27; Christopher Thomas, 'Bhutto Adds to Pressure for Pakistan Nuclear Test', *The Times* (London, 21 May 1998).

17. Benazir Bhutto, 'Perspective on South Asia; Punishment: Make it Swift, Severe . . .', *Los Angeles Times* (17 May 1998).

18. Harish Khare, 'Roll Back Proxy War, Pak. told', *Hindu* (19 May 1998). Advani's remarks were widely condemned in the Indian media: if the BJP government wished to be treated with the respect due to a nuclear power, it could begin by behaving like a responsible nuclear power, was the general tenor of the advice offered to him. See e.g. the editorial 'Need for Caution' in *Hindu* (22 May 1998).

19. For details, published before the tests of May, see 'China's Missile Exports and Assistance to Pakistan', and 'China's Nuclear Exports and Assistance to Pakistan', Center for Non-proliferation Studies, Monterey Institute for International Studies, Apr. 1998 and Jan. 1998 respectively, at: http://cns.miis.edu.

20. Pakistan is also working on another missile named Ghaznavi. Both missiles carry powerfully belligerent connotations from Indian history. Mahmud of Ghazni (AD 971–1030) 'led no fewer than seventeen bloody annual forays into India . . . zeal-

ously smashing countless Hindu temple idols . . . and looting India's cities of as many of their jewels, specie, and women as he and his horde of Turkish cavalry could carry back across the Afghan passes'. Stanley Wolpert, *A New History of India* (New York: Oxford University Press, 1977), 107. And these are the words of an American historian. His sacking of the temple town of Somnath became part of Hindu folklore for centuries. His exploits were repeated a century and a half later by Muhhamad of Ghur (hence Ghauri), who led his first raid into India in 1175. The great university at Nalanda, home to over 10,000 monks, was sacked around 1202. 'The severity of the Turko-Afghan persecution directed against centers of Buddhist monasticism was so unrelenting that the religion of Buddha was now sent into exile from the land of its birth, never to return again in any significant numbers'; ibid. 108. By contrast, the Indian missiles are named after the elements of nature: Prithvi (earth), Agni (fire), Akash (sky).

21. Weiner, 'U.S. and Chinese Aid was Essential'.
22. Ibid.
23. *Defense News* (14–20 Apr. 1997), 3, 26.
24. The phrase is from K. Subrahmanyam, 'An Indian Perspective on International Security', in D. H. McMillen (ed.), *Asian Perspectives on International Security* (London: Macmillan, 1984), 165.
25. Western intelligence experts believe that Pakistan can produce smaller, more sophisticated, missile-deliverable warheads that can be mounted on ballistic missile systems acquired from China and North Korea. India must still rely on warplanes for delivery. *Japan Times* (30 May 1998). On the other hand, the conduct of three different types of warhead explosions by India on 11 May, within a fleeting timespan, required a very sophisticated level of nuclear management skills.
26. See Ramesh Thakur, 'The Desirability of a Nuclear Weapon Free World', in Canberra Commission on the Elimination of Nuclear Weapons, *Background Papers* (Canberra: Department of Foreign Affairs and Trade, 1996), 74–88.
27. *Report of the Canberra Commission on the Elimination of Nuclear Weapons* (Canberra: Department of Foreign Affairs and Trade, 1996), 18–22.
28. As an editorial in the *Japan Times* put it, 'Nuclear stockpiles must be reduced and then eliminated . . . As the cycle of action and reaction in South Asia has proven, nuclear stockpiles feed on themselves'; 'South Asia's Nuclear Chain Reaction', *Japan Times* (30 May 1998).
29. Singh, 'Against Nuclear Apartheid', 41–2; or 'India, through a limited series of tests, has only reasserted that either the international nuclear security paradigm be reviewed or that it be made inclusive'; Jaswant Singh, 'For India, Disarmament or Equal Security', *International Herald Tribune* (5 Aug. 1998). Singh is also the person conducting negotiations with US Deputy Secretary of State Strobe Talbott on how to bridge India's security needs and global non-proliferation concerns.
30. Ramesh Thakur, 'Nuclear India Needs Coaxing, Not Coercion', *Australian* (Sydney, 6 Sept. 1996). The UN General Assembly vote on the CTBT was held on 10 Sept. 1996.
31. K. Sundarji, 'India's Best Option', *Hindu* (17 Sept. 1996). The call for 'a few more underground nuclear tests' was repeated a fortnight later; K. Sundarji, 'India's Post-CTBT Strategy', *Hindu* (30 Sept. 1996).

32. K. Subrahmanyam, 'The World After CTBT', *Economic Times* (Delhi, 19 Sept. 1996).

33. K. K. Katyal, 'Gujral Defends Pokhran Tests', *Hindu* (26 Sept. 1998). Similarly Jaswant Singh, the principal architect of nuclear security policy in the BJP government, writes that 'When the international community approved the coercive CTBT, India's security environment deteriorated significantly'; Singh, 'Against Nuclear Apartheid', 46.

34. Kenneth N. Waltz, *The Spread of Nuclear Weapons: More May Be Better*, Adelphi Paper, 171 (London: IISS, 1981).

35. S. Rashid Naim, 'Asia's Day After: Nuclear War between India and Pakistan?', in Stephen P Cohen (ed.), *The Security of South Asia: American and Asian Perspectives* (Urbana, Ill.: University of Illinois Press, 1987), 260–9.

36. For the most sophisticated presentation of this case, see Devin Hagerty, *The Consequences of Nuclear Proliferation: Lessons from South Asia* (Cambridge, Mass.: MIT Press, 1998).

37. Singh, 'Against Nuclear Apartheid', 49.

38. News accounts used this phrase *ad nauseam* in discussing the nuclear developments.

39. This provoked almost uncontrolled fury among Indian commentators: 'The President of the world's most powerful democracy has spent a remarkable nine days prostituting himself in the world's most powerful autocracy.... When he is not coddling young women, he is coddling dictators. Mr Clinton's escape from Monicaland to dragonland helped put his character on public display: Not only did he coddle, he kowtowed and fawned...'; Brahma Chellaney, 'Dealing with Beijing–Washington Axis', *Pioneer* (Delhi, 8 July 1998). For a more measured critique, see Michael Yahuda, 'Unrealistic Premises will Sink this "Beijing-Washington Axis"', *International Herald Tribune* (4–5 July 1998).

40. See Ramesh Thakur, 'From National to Human Security', in Stuart Harris and Andrew Mack (eds.), *Asia–Pacific Security: The Economics–Politics Nexus* (Sydney: Allen & Unwin, 1997), 52–80.

41. A senior Pakistan government official quoted in Christopher Thomas, 'Nuclear Power Forced to Rattle its Begging Bowl', *The Times* (26 Aug. 1998). See also Paula R. Newberg, 'Putting a Halt to Pakistan's Descent toward Default', *Japan Times* (13 Aug. 1998).

42. Two weeks after the Indian tests, a US Senate panel released CIA analysis linking the sale of US high technology exports to China to long-range Chinese nuclear missiles, thirteen of which are targeted at US cities; *Japan Times* (23 May 1998). House Speaker Newt Gingrich commented that 'as the Indians watch the Clinton administration sell missile technology to the Chinese, it should not shock us that the Indians want to protect themselves'; *CNN* on the Internet: http://www.cnn.com, 19 May 1998.

43. Reports of the speech can be found in the *Hindu* and the *Times of India* (29 Sept. 1998).

44. However, for a cautionary note on US denial mode in the past about Pakistan-based terrorism in the region, see Prem Shankar Jha, 'Supping with the Devil', *Hindu* (7 and 8 Sept. 1998).

45. In my view, any solution to Kashmir will have to find a balance between four propositions: (1) Kashmir is not simply a territorial dispute between two states;

rather, it is a symbol of three competing nationalisms: the territorial nationalism of the Kashmiris, the Islamic nationalism of Pakistan, and the secular nationalism of India; (2) Pakistan has no interest in a bilateral solution if it can succeed in internationalizing the dispute; (3) India can retain Kashmir indefinitely against the force of Pakistan; but (4) it cannot do so forever against the wishes of the Kashmiri people. See Ramesh Thakur, *The Politics and Economics of India's Foreign Policy* (London: C. Hurst, 1994), 48–61.

46. In many ways the short- and long-term repercussions for Israel will be the most interesting to watch. Israel maintained a low profile in international reactions to the twin series of tests. To the extent that Israel's security is assured by a threshold posture which no other country in the region has, Israel was bound to be unhappy at the breach of the non-proliferation barrier. It was therefore in Israel's interest to ensure that substantial costs were inflicted upon the transgressors. Nor would Israel have been happy at perceptions among people in surrounding countries that now there is an 'Islamic bomb' (a term popularized by Prime Minister Zulfikar Ali Bhutto of Pakistan), Islamabad's protestations to the contrary notwithstanding. On the other hand, the manner in which India's tests caught the vast apparatus of the US intelligence community off guard strengthens the Israeli argument that no non-proliferation regime is proof against break-outs, and that Israel just does not have the margin of comfort to react to a breakout after the fact. There are also many rumours and suspicions in Pakistan of collusion between India and Israel, the spreading of which would help to isolate and delegitimise India in the Arab–Islamic world. See Gerald M. Steinberg, 'Assessing the Impact of the Indian and Pakistani Nuclear Tests on the Middle East', *Jerusalem Letter/Viewpoints*, 386 (15 July 1998).

47. See Ramesh Thakur, 'A Nuclear-Weapon-Free Zone for Central Asia', *Trends* (Singapore), 88 (27–8 Dec. 1997).

48. Robert McNamara in *Disarmament Diplomacy*, 4 (Apr. 1996).

49. For an account of just how unprepared India is with regard to the infrastructure of nuclear weapons and the panoply of nuclear doctrines, see Manoj Joshi, 'Nuclear Weapons: In the Shadow of Fear', *India Today* (Delhi, 21 July 1997), 62–5.

50. Against this, it might be argued that neither India nor Pakistan possesses the infrastructure of sophisticated targeting and precision delivery systems to provide credible first-strike capability.

51. Stephen I. Schwartz (ed.), *Atomic Audit: The Costs and Consequences of Nuclear Weapons since 1940* (Washington, DC: Brookings, 1998).

52. Figures cited in C. Rammanohar Reddy, 'The Wages of Armageddon', *Hindu* (31 August, 1 and 2 Sept., 1998). The crore is an Indian unit of measurement; 1 crore = 10 million; as of Sept. 1998, US$1.00 = Indian Rs 42.50. The figure of 150 warheads is arrived at as follows. To inflict unacceptable damage, India would need to destroy five cities in Pakistan and ten in China with three bombs each. With an estimated 70% success rate for a first strike by an enemy, this works out to an arsenal of 150 bombs.

53. Reddy, 'The Wages of Armageddon-III', *Hindu* (2 Sept. 1998).

54. Ramesh Thakur, 'India in the World: Neither Rich, Powerful, nor Principled', *Foreign Affairs*, 76/4 (July/Aug. 1997), 15–22.

55. Kanti P. Bajpai, *Nuclear Weapons and the Security of India: Giving up the Bomb*, Working Paper, 161 (Canberra: Peace Research Centre, Sept. 1996), 13–18.

56. See Ramesh Thakur, 'The Last Bang before a Total Ban: French Nuclear Testing in the Pacific', *International Journal*, 51/3 (Summer 1996), 466–86.

57. For the argument why NAM is an anachronism, see Ramesh Thakur, 'India after Nonalignment', *Foreign Affairs*, 71/2 (Spring 1992), 165–82.

58. In the case of India, the strongest reaction came from the USA, Australia, Canada, Japan, and New Zealand. Russia resisted US pressure to terminate long-established defence links with India. By Sept., France was ready to initiate a 'strategic dialogue' with India; C. Raja Mohan, 'India, France to Start Strategic Dialogue', *Hindu* (30 Sept. 1998).

59. Thus an editorial in the *Japan Times* noted that Japan 'lived in peace under the U.S. nuclear umbrella: This might be called a sort of nuclear hypocrisy'; 'Leading the Non-Nuclear Movement', *Japan Times* (8 Aug. 1998). See also the sampling of comments from the vernacular press published in the *Japan Times* on 30 Aug. 1998, especially the excerpts from *Chunichi-Tokyo-Hokuriku Chunichi, Niigata Nippo, Nagasaki Shimbun, Kahoku Shimpo, Nishi Nihon Shimbun, Mainichi Shimbun*, and *Ryukyu Shimpo*. Many criticized their government's initial one-sided condemnations of India and Pakistan without due linkage to the refusal of the five NWS to engage in nuclear disarmament. For example the *Kahoku Shimpo* declared that 'If Japan is to deal squarely with the "India-Pakistani shocks," it has no choice but to lead an international movement toward complete elimination of nuclear weapons'; *Japan Times* (their translation, 30 Aug. 1998). Indian commentators of course were quick to brand Japan's reactions as hypocritical; see e.g. C. Raja Mohan, 'Japan's Nuclear Hypocrisy', *Hindu* (6 August, Hiroshima Day 1998).

60. In an interview with *Newsweek* (14 Sept. 1998), 58.

61. This is probably an exaggerated argument. Well after the tests, on 14 July 1998, Brazil signed the NPT and ratified the CTBT; *Japan Times* (19 July 1998).

62. Thomas C Schelling, 'Thinking About Nuclear Terrorism', *International Security*, 6 (Spring 1982), 76.

63. I first argued this in Ramesh Thakur, 'Into the Security Council, Out of the Nuclear Trap', *International Herald Tribune* (1 Feb. 1993).

64. Singh, 'For India, Disarmament or Equal Security'.

65. *Japan Times* (28 Sept. 1998).

66. Andrew Mack, 'Five Nuclear Blasts and a Possible Silver Lining', *International Herald Tribune* (18 May 1998).

67. K. K. Katyal, 'India Foils Concerted Move on Nuclear Tests', *Hindu* (5 Sept. 1998).

68. The eight countries are Brazil, Egypt, Ireland, Mexico, New Zealand, Slovenia, South Africa, and Sweden. See David Andrews and Lena Hjelm-Wallen (the foreign ministers of Ireland and Sweden), 'Revive the Drive Against Nuclear Weapons Now', *International Herald Tribune* (22 June 1998).

69. E.g. on 6 Aug. (Hiroshima Day), *c.*400,000 people marched on the streets of Calcutta in an anti-nuclear rally; *Hindu* (7 Aug. 1998). On 10 Aug. a forum organized in Chandigarh urged India to destroy its nuclear weapons, arguing that the capability had not provided any defence superiority, nor diplomatic leverage to Pakistan. Instead, it was merely a burden on the national exchequer; *Hindu* (12 Aug. 1998). After the Indian tests, even before the Pakistan riposte, a cross-section of scientists from some of India's most prestigious institutions issued a joint press

statement expressing 'deep dismay and unhappiness' at India's nuclear tests; *Hindu* (19 May 1998). The debates in parliament too turned out to be surprisingly robust, with many MPs questioning the need for the tests and rebuking the government for having needlessly damaged India's relations with China, Pakistan, and the USA.

70. See Kim Richard Nossal, *Rain Dancing: Sanctions in Canadian and Australian Foreign Policy* (Toronto: University of Toronto Press, 1994), ch. 10.

71. Thus Jasjit Singh, Director of the Institute for Defence Studies and Analyses and co-convenor of the national security task force: 'The Americans shouldn't waste time telling us to get rid of nuclear weapons. That decision has been made. The issue now is what kind of nuclear power we are going to be.' Quoted in John F. Burns, 'In Nuclear India, Small Stash Does Not a Ready Arsenal Make', *New York Times* (26 July 1998).

72. Paper tabled in Parliament of India on 'Evolution of India's Nuclear Policy', Government of India, 27 May 1998, paragraph 14. See also Singh, 'Against Nuclear Apartheid', 49–52, for a reiteration and elaboration of this argument.

73. Singh, 'Against Nuclear Apartheid', 52.

74. *Times of India* (22 Sept. 1998).

75. Office of the Press Secretary, the White House, 28 May 1998.

76. India government paper, 'Evolution of India's Nuclear Policy', 27 May 1998, paragraph 18.

77. This statement, along with other official Indian pronouncements since the tests of May, can be found on the Internet at: http://www.meadev.gov.in

78. http://www.meadev.gov.in

Notes to Chapter 8

1. *Livre Blanc sur la Défense 1994. La Documentation française* (Paris: Collection des Rapports Officiels, 1994); Pascal Boniface, *Contre le révisionnisme nucléaire* (Paris: Ellipses, 1994); *Strategic Assessment 1996: Instruments of U.S. Power* (Washington, DC, Institute for National Strategic Studies, National Defence University, 1996), ch. 16.

2. Yuri Fyodorov, 'Prospects and Conflicts of Russian Nuclear Deterrence', *Yaderni Kontrol*, 1 (Spring 1996), 12–15.

3. John Mearsheimer, *Conventional Deterrence* (Ithaca, NY: Cornell University Press, 1983).

4. Jonathan Schell, *Die Abschaffung: Wege aus der atomaren Bedrohung* (Munich: Piper, 1984).

5. Significantly, while the USA does not explicitly rule out the use of nuclear weapons against other weapons of mass destruction, its counter-proliferation initiative tries to develop a variety of conventional measures to cope with this threat. Cf. Office of the Secretary of Defense, *Proliferation: Threat and Response* (Washington, DC, Apr. 1996).

6. cf. Jayantha Dhanapala (ed.), *Regional Approaches to Disarmament, Security and Stability* (Dartmouth: Aldershot, 1993).

7. cf. Virginia Foran (ed.), *Security Assurances. Implications for the NPT and Beyond* (Washington, DC: Carnegie Endowment for International Peace, 1995).
8. Hans J. Morgenthau, *Politics Among Nations* (New York: Knopf, 1968); Kenneth Waltz, *Theory of International Relations* (New York: Random House, 1979).
9. Michael W. Doyle, 'Liberalism and World Politics', *American Political Science Review*, 80/4 (1986).
10. Harald Müller, 'Maintaining Non-Nuclear Weapon Status', in Regina Cowen Karp (ed.), *Security with Nuclear Weapons? Different Perspectives on National Security* (Oxford: Oxford University Press, 1991), 301–39.
11. There exist now several excellent studies trying to develop a viable path towards this end: Joseph Rotblat, Jack Steinburger, and Bhachandra Udgaonhar (eds.), *A Nuclear-Weapons Free World: Desirable? Feasible?* (Boulder, Colo.: Westview, 1993); Regina Cowen Karp, *Security without Nuclear Weapons? Different Perspectives in Non-Nuclear Security* (Oxford: Oxford University Press, 1992); Henry L. Stimson Center, *Beyond the Nuclear Peril: The Year in Review and the Years Ahead* (Report of the Steering Committee, Project on Eliminating Weapons of Mass Destruction, Report, 15, Washington, DC, Jan. 1995); Henry L. Stimson Center, *An Evolving US Nuclear Posture* (Second Report of the Steering Committee, Project on Eliminating Weapons of Mass Destruction, Report 19, Washington, DC, Dec. 1995); Andrew J. Goodpaster, *Tighter Limits on Nuclear Arms: Issues and Opportunities for a New Era* (Washington, DC: Consultation Paper, The Atlantic Council of the United States, May 1992); Andrew J. Goodpaster, *Further Reins on Nuclear Arms: Next Steps for the Major Nuclear Powers* (Washington, DC: Consultation Paper, The Atlantic Council of the United States, Aug. 1993).

Notes to Chapter 9

1. Sir Michael Quinlan posed these alternatives in 'The Future of Nuclear Weapons: Policy for Western Possessors', *International Affairs*, 69/3 (1993), 485–596. The qualifiers 'firm and serious' were needed to distinguish this policy-goal from long-standing but empty governmental pronouncements on this issue.
2. The British Trident SSBN programme is a good example. It is justified by the need 'to deter', without specifying who is to be deterred from doing what.
3. This syllogism was first articulated by Robert McMamara.
4. *Thinking about Nuclear Weapons* (London: Royal United Services Institute, 1997). Quinlan was the senior permanent official in the British Ministry of Defence (1988–92). He spent thirty-one of his thirty-eight-year career in defence-related posts, including service with NATO's Nuclear Planning Group.
5. *Thinking*, 13.
6. Scott B. Sagan, *Moving Targets: Nuclear Strategy and Nuclear Security* (Princeton: Princeton University Press, 1989); Bruce G. Blair *The Logic of Accidental Nuclear War* (Washington, DC: Brookings Institution, 1991); Peter Douglas Fever, *Guarding the Guardians: Civilian Control of Nuclear Weapons in the United States* (Ithaca, NY: Cornell University Press, 1992); S. D. Sagan, *The Limits of Safety: Organizations, Accidents, and Nuclear Weapons* (Princeton: Princeton University Press, 1993). For a review article of the three later books, see Bradley A. Thayer, 'The

Risk of Nuclear Inadvertence', *Security Studies*, 3/3 (Spring 1994). This touches on earlier work by Ashton Carter, Paul Bracken, and John Steinbruner.

7. *Thinking*, 35.
8. Ibid.
9. See Ch. 10 by Robert McNamara's in this volume; the words cited are his own.
10. Paul B. Stares talks of 'the largely unappreciated danger of inadvertent war'. *Command Performance: The Neglected Dimension of European Security* (Washington, DC: Brookings Institution, 1991), 11, 121–5. Discussing the first half of the 1980s he notes that 'the possibility of inadvertent escalation leading to spontaneous combustion between two well-primed and heavily armed adversaries grew very real.'
11. For an overview of this incident see MccGwire, *Perestroika and Soviet National Security* (Washington, DC: Brookings Institution, 1991), 387–92. American talk about the inevitability of war and the first Reagan administration's confrontational policies and operational deployments led to a serious debate within the Soviet political-military establishment in 1983–4 about the imminence of war (ibid. 118–23). By Dec. 1981, US behaviour had already generated enough uncertainty to justify instituting special measures to provide strategic early warning of plans to attack the Soviet Union. East–West tension rose steadily in 1983, fuelled by high-profile events such as the 'Evil Empire' speech, the Strategic Defence Initiative, the increasingly acrimonious dispute over the deployment of Euromissiles, and the downing of KAL-7 in Sept. In the West, repercussions of the latter obscured the importance of the 'Declaration' by General Secretary Yuri Andropov on 28 Sept. This was to the effect that the USA had launched a crusade against socialism and was bent on military domination; Andropov declared that the Soviet Union would respond as necessary to any attempt to disrupt the existing military balance (ibid. 117).
12. *Thinking*, 20.
13. Remarks at the National Press Club, Washington, DC, 2 Feb. 1998, reproduced as Ch. 11 in this volume.
14. I had some sense of this, having been a NATO war planner in the 1960s and having spent a sabbatical at the US National War College in the 1970s. During my time at Brookings in the 1980s, I participated in the ten-day Global War Games at the US Naval War College and one year ran the 'Soviet' side.
15. *Thinking*, 30–2.
16. Ibid. 34.
17. e.g. the 688 class of US attack submarine (authorized in FY 1969) was intended to seek out and kill Soviet SSBNs, which at that time constituted the primary Soviet second-strike capability. The Strategic Defence Initiative (1983) was explicitly intended to restore US invulnerability to strategic attack, invalidating the concept of Mutual Assured Destruction, which lay at the heart of Western deterrence doctrine.
18. *Thinking*, 32.
19. See MccGwire, *Perestroika*, 24–44. This summarizes the detailed analysis of Soviet strategy in the event that world war was deemed inescapable, as set out in MccGwire, *Military Objectives in Soviet Foreign Policy* (Washington, DC: Brookings Institution, 1987).

20. This was a copybook example of the *colonel's fallacy*, whereby the worst-case analysis that is appropriate for contingency planning at the military/tactical level is applied at the foreign-policy/strategic level.

21. For a powerful critique, see Ch. 11 by Lee Butler in this volume.

22. R. Ned Lebow and Janice G. Stein note that 'the history of the cold war provides compelling evidence of the pernicious effects of the open-ended quest for nuclear deterrence'; this is one conclusion of 375 pp. of empirical analysis backed by 250 pp. of interview and source notes: *We All Lost the Cold War* (Princeton: Princeton University Press, 1994), 367. In an earlier collection drawing on psychological findings as well as empirical political analysis, the general opinion of those who studied conventional deterrence as a strategy was that it was based on a deficient model of interaction, analytically weak, politically crude, and normatively biased. George Levinger (ed.), *Beyond Deterrence*, special issue of *Journal of Social Issues* 43/4 (New York, 1987).

23. In Lebow's judgement, as a general principle, the strategy of deterrence was a primary cause of crisis instability, whether it stemmed from the doctrinal need to demonstrate resolve, or from the use of preprogrammed (and sometimes automated) decisions. The strategy served as a catalyst for very accurate missiles capable of destroying the opponent's command and control, should war seem unavoidable. It encouraged both sides to adopt a high state of alert early in a serious crisis to discourage adversarial pre-emption, thereby increasing the risk of accidental war. R Ned Lebow, *Nuclear Crisis Management* (Ithaca, NY: Cornell University Press, 1987), chs. 2 and 3. This judgement is supported by the findings of Blair's analysis in *Logic of Accidental Nuclear War*.

24. The USA consistently led the arms race. In 1959, when the Soviets still lacked an effective means of delivering weapons on North America, the US Strategic Air Command had 1,750 bombers and was beginning to deploy ICBM. Ten years later, the Soviet ICBM force still lagged the US force in numbers, accuracy, reliability, and response time. The USA was the first to diversify into multiple independently targeted re-entry vehicles (MIRV), followed by strategic cruise missiles (SLCM, ALCM), and in 1983 embarked on the Strategic Defence Initiative that would take the arms race into space. As late as the START negotiations in Feb. 1990, the Soviets wanted counting rules for ALCM that would limit numbers, while the USA pushed for large numbers.

25. This was set out in Jimmy Carter's Presidential Directive 59, leaked in July 1980.

26. Richard Nixon and Ronald Reagan both ran for president on a platform of restoring US military superiority, something America had never relinquished. The requirement for 'preponderant power' goes back to 1950 and NSC-68.

27. See *Perestroika*, 110–14. A major theme of the contemporary rhetoric was that Soviet communism was a political aberration, an evil that was not only destined to fail but should be made to fail. Richard Pipes, senior Soviet specialist on the NSC, had asserted (Mar. 1981) that the Soviet leaders would have to chose between peacefully changing the system or going to war; Secretary of State Shultz was reported as saying (June 1983) that changing the Soviet system was a US objective. The Defence Plannning Guidance for 1984–5 (leaked May 1982) spoke of developing a decapitating strategy aimed at Soviet political and military C3.

The Soviets saw the Pershing II, with its short time of flight and 30 metre accuracy, as having this potential.

28. A few weeks after Andropov's 'Declaration' (n. 11 above), Minister of Defence Dmitri Ustinov, addressing a special gathering of senior officers, gave a structured analysis of US policies. Those policies included a sustained US effort to achieve military superiority, including the capability for a disarming first strike on the USSR. See 'For High Combat Readiness', *Krasnaya Zvezda* (12 Nov. 1983), 3; *Perestroika*, 115–18. The East German archives include minutes of Warsaw Pact meetings at this period. Forthcoming research by Beatrice Heuser shows that in 1982–3, the Soviet High Command was comparing the current situation with that in 1940–1, prior to the German assault on the Soviet Union.

29. A very senior State Department official made that claim in 1983 at a closed seminar of specialists on the Soviet Union. He argued that the Soviets, recognizing that the international arena was more dangerous, would become more cautious. They would refrain from initiatives that the USA would have to counter with military force, leading to conflict. War was therefore less likely. The Reagan administration was not finally persuaded of the Soviet concern about the imminence of war until they read a report by Oleg Gordievskiy on 'Soviet Perception of Nuclear Warfare' written after he defected in mid-1985. Gordon Brook-Shepherd, *The Storm Birds: Soviet Postwar Defectors* (London: Weidenfeld and Nicolson, 1989), 129–31.

30. The 'holding to ransom' incentive is dealt with here. 'The great equaliser' (to use Richard Bett's term) is covered by a different line of argument; see the discussion by Robert O'Neill in Ch. 12 below.

31. For a discussion, see Andrew Mack, 'Nuclear Breakout: Risks and Possible Responses', in *Background Papers for the Canberra Commission on the Elimination of Nuclear Weapons* (Canberra: Australian Department for Foreign Affairs and Trade, Aug. 1996); Tom Milne and Joseph Rotblat, 'Breakout from a Nuclear Weapons Convention', in J. Rotblat (ed.), *Nuclear Weapons: The Road to Zero* (Boulder, Colo.: Westview Press, 1998).

32. See the discussion by Robert O'Neill in Ch. 12 below.

33. Between 1979 and 1985, Henry Kissinger, Samuel Huntingdon, and Robert McNamara all went on record to the effect that the USA would not have initiated the use of nuclear weapons in defence of NATO, if such action would have threatened nuclear strikes on the USA.

34. *Thinking*, 17.

35. Others include the close marking of US carrier groups by Soviet warships; the KAL-7 heading for Vladivostok, which would not have posed a threat were it not for the possibility it was carrying a nuclear device; and the Able Archer CPX in Nov. 1983. With regard to Cuba, the deployment of Soviet regional-range missiles in 1962 was an expedient element of the overall Soviet response to the US Minuteman programme (authorized in 1961), which would place 1,000 ICBMs in hardened silos in the American mid-West. Those missiles would be safe from the projected Soviet capability for area devastation against soft targets, which was scheduled to deploy 1961–75. Minuteman necessitated a radical restructuring of Soviet missile programmes (*Perestroika*, 49–51), the 'initial' response being to take

over the regional-range production facilities for the hurriedly adapted SS-11 ICBM programme, which would not, however, begin to enter service until 1966. 'Pipeline-inertia' yielded some forty of the original regional-range missiles. Given the Soviets' pre-emptive strategy at this period and their extremely limited capability to strike at North America, the opportunity to emplace these forty missiles within range of the US bomber bases and surface-positioned intercontinental missiles was hard to forgo, particularly since forty-five Jupiter missiles (targeted on the Soviet Union) had been deployed in Italy and Turkey that spring–summer.

36. For a full exposition of the argument, see MccGwire, 'Deterrence: The Problem—not the Solution', *International Affairs* (London, Winter 1985/6); and more recently 'Nuclear Deterrence', in Canberra Commission, *Background Papers*, 229–39.

37. Henry Kissinger favoured escalating 'rapidly and brutally to a point where the opponent can no longer afford to experiment': *White House Years* (Boston, Mass.: Little, Brown, 1979), 622. Discussing the nuclear alert he ordered during the Arab–Israeli War in Oct. 1973, Kissinger noted that 'the Soviets subsided as soon as we showed our teeth. We were thus able to use the crisis to shape events and reverse alliances in the Middle East in defiance of the pressure of our allies, the preferences of the Soviets, and the rhetoric of Arab radicals.' *Years of Upheaval* (Boston, Mass.: Little, Brown, 1982), 980.

38. Lt. Gen. William Odom, USA, quoted by Lebow and Stein, *We All Lost the Cold War*, 256, 285.

39. They were not shared by Andropov, who accused the USA of having a flippant attitude to peace and war. *Pravda* (27 Mar. 1983), 1. For an impression of how outside observers would have perceived the policies of the first Reagan administration, see Alexander Dallin and Gail W Lapidus, 'Reagan and the Russians: United States Policy towards the Soviet Union and Eastern Europe', in Kenneth A. Oye, Robert J. Lieber, and Donald Rothschild (eds.), *Eagle Defiant: United States Foreign Policy in the 1980s* (Boston, Mass.: Little, Brown, 1983), 191–236. For an overview of US policy and behaviour towards the Soviet Union during both administrations, see *Perestroika*, 110–14, 186–204, 382–92.

40. The advent of rough strategic parity at the end of the 1960s removed this concern, but as developments in the Third World seemed to be moving their way, the Soviets continued with existing policies, adding the use of proxies (Cubans, Vietnamese, North Koreans) to their repertoire. *Perestroika*, 133–6. The 'war-related' task of close-shadowing US naval strike forces deployed within range of the Soviet Union (notably the Sixth Fleet) was not affected by these considerations.

41. The more assertive policy was one of the decisions emanating from the 1983–4 policy review, by which time there was substantial evidence supporting the conclusion that Washington would not initiate a strategic strike on Russia, even in defence of Europe (ibid. 136–47). The policy was reversed following the 27th Party Congress at the end of Feb. 1986, which saw the consolidation of Gorbachev's power. This meant that Soviet naval forces were not involved in the second, violent stage of the US-Libyan confrontation (23 Mar.–15 Apr.).

42. *The Communist Manifesto* was published in 1848; 1848–9 was the year of revolutions.

43. In Russia's case this was evidenced by her withdrawal from the Balkans in 1828 after victory in a war that ranged her with France and Britain against Turkey, and effected the liberation of Greece. Russia also withdrew on her eastern front with Turkey, to the distress of the Armenians living south of the border.

44. Karl Marx was one of those who sensed this at the time. A practical indicator was the adoption of free trade as government policy by Britain (1846–60).

45. Martin Walker, *The Cold War* (London: Fourth Estate, 1993), 336–8, 348. There will, of course, continue to be bitter local disputes between rival claimants to particular territories, to critical resources such as water, and to other contested assets. But during the last fifty years, resort to war has rarely succeeded in resolving such disputes in the initiator's favour. Meanwhile, from the viewpoint of the two superpowers, the utility of coercive military force *outside their national security zones* steadily declined, while the costs of projecting such force (political as well as financial) rose exponentially.

46. See *Perestroika*, 80–3, which draws on the work of Margo Light, Allen Lynch, and Michael J. Deane.

47. The great majority were in the Western alliance, including Italy, Japan, and the best part of Germany, the expansionist powers that brought about the Second World War.

48. As late as 1984, Secretary of Defence Casper Weinberger was still repeating his claim that the Soviets were set on military world domination. *Washington Post* (11 Apr. 1984).

49. *Perestroika*, 281–91, 306–17. Some have argued that it was the politically assertive and militarily confrontational nature of American policy (particularly during the first Reagan administration) that brought about the change in Soviet policy, by playing on their dread of war. Whatever its merits, the argument undermines Quinlan's claim of increased caution and exemplifies the kind of 'brinkmanship' thinking induced by the false confidence of deterrence theory. For a refutation of the claim, see ibid. 381–93, summarizing Soviet policy responses during 1985, which were clearly against Western interests. Those Soviet responses highlight how fortunate we were that Gorbachev was chosen as General Secretary in 1985, and not one of the other aspirants.

50. John L. Gaddis, *The United States and the Origins of the Cold War* (New York: Columbia University Press, 1972), 229, 245, 318–23, 388–9; Daniel Yergin, *Shattered Peace: The Origins of the National Security State* (Boston, Mass.: Houghton Mifflin, 1978), 5, 249; D. F. Fleming, *The Cold War and its Origins, 1917–60*, i (New York: Doubleday, 1961), 486; Peter Calvocoressi, *Survey of International Affairs 1947–48* (London: Oxford University Press, 1952), 60. Trachtenberg notes that in the late 1940–early 1950s preventive war thinking was surprisingly common on the American side and was (e.g.) the prevailing philosophy at the Air War College. Marc Trachtenberg, 'Strategic Thought in America 1952–66', *Political Science Quarterly* 104/2 (1989), 314–15, 308–9.

51. Melvyn P. Leffler, 'The American Conception of National Security and the Beginning of the Cold War 1945', *International Security Studies Working Paper*, 48 (Washington, DC: The Wilson Center, May 1983), 27–8, 36.

52. This was the conclusion of the 'Clifford Memorandum' commissioned by Truman

and reflecting the views of senior officials throughout the administration. Gaddis, *Origins*, 318–23; Yergen, *Shattered Peace*, 241–5.

53. General Carl Spaatz, just retired as Chief of Staff of the US Air Force spoke of destroying 'a few hundred square miles of industrial area in a score of Russian cities'. *Life Magazine* (5 July 1948), 34–44; (16 Aug 1948), 99–104.

54. By the time of the Hungarian uprising in Nov. 1956 the Soviets had a limited nuclear delivery capability against regional targets, using medium-range bombers. Their ground–air forces lacked a nuclear capability.

55. Vietnam provides another example of the threat of conventional war deterring military action. Although the USA enjoyed an effective nuclear monopoly in the area in 1965–72, it refrained from deploying its troops north of the 14th Parallel, for fear of drawing Chinese ground forces into the war.

56. e.g. forces that, in the process of driving back the Germans, had advanced about 250 miles into Norway. Why did the Soviet Union withdraw from Finland, Yugoslavia, Czechoslovakia, and the strategically located island of Bornholm in the Baltic? Why agree to four-power control over Berlin, a city captured by the Soviets at great cost and well behind their lines? And why, in 1944, did the Soviet Union insist that the Bulgarians withdraw their army from Thrace and the Aegean coast, so that British forces could take over, and refuse help to the communist insurgency in Greece that was positioned to seize power? In the 1950s: withdrawing from Austria; relinquishing military bases in Porkala, Finland, and Port Arthur, China; and failing to occupy Afghanistan in 1958 when the formation of CENTO linked Iran and Pakistan in an anti-Soviet alliance, which could be seen as breaching the Soviet–Iranian treaty of 1921. The absence of any urge to move into Afghanistan is particularly telling, since it was at this time that America and Britain intervened militarily in Lebanon and Iraq. In Dec. 1979, when the Soviets reluctantly moved forces into Afghanistan, the situation (internal and international) was very different. See *Perestroika*, 223–5; Raymond L. Garthoff, *Detente and Confrontation: American–Soviet Relations from Nixon to Reagan* (Washington, DC: Brookings Institute, 1985), 895–915, 925–36.

57. The Allies had agreed to Poland's physical displacement westwards, aligning the Polish–Soviet border with the 1919 Curzon line. The priority of Soviet interests in Poland and the Balkans had been acknowledged by the Allied leaders. As the course of war brought Soviet troops into Eastern Europe, Stalin was in a position to establish a buffer of amenable states between the USSR and the resurgent Germany that was expected to emerge in fifteen to twenty years' time.

58. This was a time when it had been announced by Stalin and (confirmed by US intelligence) that it would take at least fifteen years to overcome wartime losses in manpower, industry, and infrastructure. Leffler, *Beginning of the Cold War*, 26–45.

59. In 1947–8, the relatively reassuring view of Germany as the main but future threat was replaced with the assessment that by 1953, the Soviet Union would face the very real threat of a premeditated attack by a capitalist coalition. Its objective would be to oust the communists from Eastern Europe, to destroy the Soviets nascent nuclear capability, and to overthrow their system of government. *Perestroika*, 17–18.

60. For an overview of the new strategy and its implications see *Perestroika*, 24–9.

61. The analyses underlying this conclusion were set out in MccGwire, *Military Objectives*, and summarized and extended in *Perestroika*. The Soviet archives were opened to Western research in 1992–3 and this explanation (hypothesis) has yet to be disproved.

62. In 1993, Quinlan noted that 'if France and Britain were now facing the question of whether to incur from a zero base the costs (political as well as financial) of acquiring nuclear armouries, the strict security case for doing so might well seem inadequate'. 'Future of Nuclear Weapons', 492–3.

63. Peter Rodman, special assistant to Henry Kissinger in Oct. 1973 (Yom Kippur War), quoted by Lebow and Stein in *We All Lost the Cold War*, 256.

64. While 'explicit' knowledge can be conveyed and preserved in publications and certain machines, 'tacit' knowledge, reflecting personal experience, judgement, intuition, etc. is hard to pass on and decays with lack of use. Tacit knowledge is seen as essential to the design and construction of sophisticated nuclear systems. David MacKenzie, 'Theories of Technology and the Elimination of Nuclear Weapons' (unpublished paper, Edinburgh University, Sept. 1995).

65. Quinlan, 'Future of Nuclear Weapons'. The validity of the five tasks was assessed in MccGwire, 'Is there a Future for Nuclear Weapons?' *International Affairs*, 70/2 (1994), 211–28. In his recent monograph, Quinlan clearly implies that, given sufficient provocation, nuclear weapons could be used against non-nuclear states (*Theory*, 19), but he no longer claims this as a requirement.

66. See *Perestroika*, 179–86, 204–39, 253–7.

67. See the select bibliography at the end of this volume.

68. The Henry L. Stimson Center 'Project on Eliminating Weapons of Mass Destruction' posits preconditions; see the Steering Committee's second report, *An Evolving US Nuclear Posture* (Dec. 1995), with Robert McNamara dissenting. For a review of several different proposals and a justification of the Stimson position see Catherine Fisher (director of the project), 'Phased Elimination of Nuclear Weapons', in Rotblat, *Road to Zero*, 39–69.

Notes to Chapter 10

1. Carnegie Commission on Preventing Deadly Conflict, *Preventing Deadly Conflict, Final Report* (New York: Carnegie Corporation, Dec. 1997), 12.

2. *New York Times*, (31 Dec. 1989).

3. Henry Kissinger, *Diplomacy* (New York: Simon & Schuster, 1994), 805.

4. Carl Kaysen, 'Is War Obsolete?', *International Security*, 14/4 (Spring 1990), 63.

5. I have included in my concept of 'collective security' elements of what Janne Nolan refers to as 'Cooperative Security': see John Steinbrunner, Ash Carter, Bill Perry, and Janne E. Nolan, *Global Engagement: Co-operation and Security in the Twenty-First Century* (Washington, DC: Brookings Institution, 1994), 3–18. Ms Nolan states, 'one strategy does not preclude the other and both are, in fact, initially reinforcing'.

6. See *Washington Post* (11 June 1994).

7. Emest R. May and Philip D. Zelikow, *The Kennedy Tapes* (Cambridge, Mass.: Harvard University, 1997).

8. Aleksandr Fursenko and Timothy Naftali, *One Hell of a Gamble* (New York: Norton, 1997).

9. General Gribkov elaborated on these points at a meeting in the Wilson Center, Washington, DC, on 5 Apr. 1994.

10. See Anatoly Dokochaev, 'Afterword to Sensational 100 Day Nuclear Cruise', *Krasnaya Zvezda* (6 Nov. 1992), 2; and V. Badurikin interview with Dimitri Volkogonov in 'Operation Anadyr', *Trud* (27 Oct. 1992), 3.

11. Both the Canberra Commission and the Carnegie Commission came to the same conclusion: 'The position that large numbers of nuclear weapons can be retained in perpetuity and never used—accidentally or by decision—defies credibility.' Canberra, p. 22, and Carnegie, p. 70.

12. This statement was endorsed by the US National Academy of Science in 1991 in a report signed by eighteen security experts including David C. Jones, former Chief of Staff of US Air Force: *The Future of the US Soviet Nuclear Relationship* (Washington, DC: National Academy Press), 3; by the Stimson Center's Panel on Nuclear Forces chaired by the former Saceur, General Andrew Goodpaster, *An Evolving Nuclear Posture* (Washington, DC: Stimson Center, Dec. 1995), 15, and by the Report of the Canberra Commission on the Elimination of Nuclear Weapons (Canberra: Australian Department of Foreign Affairs and Trade, 1996), 18.

13. I recognize, of course, that the abolition of nuclear weapons would not be possible without development of an adequate verification system. Are acceptable verification regimes feasible? The decision point on whether verification is adequate for complete elimination (as opposed, for example, to reductions to a level of say 100 warheads), is not likely to be resolved for some time. In the end, comparative risks must be evaluated. The Canberra Commission (to which I will refer later), which also recommended abolition, concluded that the risk of use of the weapons far exceeds the risks associated with whatever nuclear force a cheating state could assemble before it was exposed.

14. See John J. Fialks and Frederick Kemps, 'U.S. Welcomes Soviet Arms Plan, But Dismisses Pact as Propaganda', *Wall Street Journal* (17 Jan. 1986).

15. See William Perry's statement to the Stimson Center 20 Sept. 1994; and Department of Defence briefing, 22 Sept. 1994.

16. McGeorge Bundy, William J. Crowe, Jr., and Sidney O. Drell, *Reducing Nuclear Danger: The Road Away from the Brink* (New York: Council on Foreign Relations Press, 1993), 100.

17. *An Evolving Nuclear Posture* (Washington, DC: The Stimson Center, Dec. 1995).

18. See Solly Zuckerman, *Nuclear Illusions and Reality* (New York: Viking, 1982), 70; and *Sunday Times* (London, 21 Feb. 1982).

19. Henry Kissinger, 'NATO Defense and the Soviet Threat', *Survival* (Nov.–Dec. 1979), 266.

20. BBC Radio interview with Stuart Simon, 16 July 1987.

21. Larry Welch to Adain Scheirunan, 21 Mar. 1994.

22. *Boston Globe* (16 July 1994).

23. Robert S. McNamara, 'The Military Role of Nuclear Weapons', *Foreign Affairs* (Fall 1983), 79.

24. 'De-alerting Strategic Nuclear Forces', a preliminary draft of a study of nuclear forces presented by Blair, on 29 Jan. 1998, to The Independent Task Force on Reducing the Risk of Nuclear War.

Notes to Chapter 12

1. Robert O'Neill (ed.), *The Strategic Nuclear Balance* (Canberra: Strategic and Defence Studies Centre, 1975).
2. Graham T. Allison, Owen R. Cote, Jr., Richard Falkenrath, and Steven E. Miller, *Avoiding Nuclear Anarchy*, CSIA Studies in International Security, 12 (Cambridge, Mass.: The MIT Press, 1996).
3. *Report of the Canberra Commission on the Elimination of Nuclear Weapons* (Canberra: Department of Foreign Affairs, 1996).

APPENDIX 1

Prepared Statement on the 'Future of Nuclear Deterrence'

Under Secretary of Defense, Walter B. Slocombe

Introduction

Nuclear deterrence has been the subject of much debate over the decades, and appropriately, this debate has been resumed after the end of the Cold War. Most recently, the nuclear question has been given prominence by respected individuals and committees who advocate a radical change—setting as a policy goal the complete abolition of nuclear weapons.

Indeed, such calls underscore the continuing American and global interest in a deliberate process to further reduce—and ultimately eliminate—nuclear weapons. The US has embraced this commitment for many years. When the Nuclear Non-proliferation Treaty was signed in 1968, we signed on to Article VI of the NPT, which calls for the parties to undertake 'to pursue negotiations in good faith relating to cessation of the nuclear arms race at an early date and to nuclear disarmament, and on a treaty on general and complete disarmament under strict and effective international control'. In 1995, when the NPT was indefinitely extended, we reiterated this pledge to work toward the complete elimination of nuclear weapons in the context of general and complete disarmament. President Clinton, in a speech to the United Nations this past September, said he looks forward to a new century 'in which the roles and risks of nuclear weapons can be further reduced, and ultimately eliminated'.

The United States has made remarkable progress in fulfilling our NPT Article VI commitment. The nuclear arms race has, in fact, been halted. The United States has been reducing its nuclear stockpile in a consistent fashion through both its unilateral and bilateral initiatives. For example, the 1987 Treaty on Intermediate-Range Nuclear Forces eliminated an entire category of US and Russian nuclear weapons. In 1991, we and our NATO allies decided to retire all nuclear artillery shells, all nuclear warheads for short-range ballistic missiles, and all naval nuclear anti-submarine warfare

This is a slightly abridged version of a statement made by Walter B. Slocombe to the Hearing before the Subcommittee on International Security, Proliferation, and Federal Services of the Committee on Governmental Affairs United States Senate, One Hundred Fifth Congress, 12 February 1997. The editors are grateful to Walter Slocombe and the Printing Office for permission to reprint this statement.

weapons. None of these weapons is deployed today, and the majority of them have been destroyed.

Over the past four years, the Clinton Administration has worked hard to secure de-targeting of US and Russian strategic missiles; the entry into force of the START I Treaty; the complete denuclearization of Ukraine, Belarus and Kazakstan; the indefinite extension of the NPT; Senate ratification of START II; and negotiation of the Comprehensive Nuclear Test Ban Treaty. And we have made clear that, once START II enters into force, we are prepared to work on further reductions in strategic nuclear arms as well as limiting and monitoring nuclear warheads and materials. Thus, lifting the threat of nuclear weapons destruction and limiting their spread has been and remains at the top of President Clinton's foreign policy agenda.

However, we are not yet at the point where we can eliminate our nuclear weapons. For the foreseeable future, we will continue to need a reliable and flexible nuclear deterrent—survivable against the most aggressive attack, under highly confident constitutional command and control, and assured in its safety against both accident and unauthorized use.

We will need such a force because nuclear deterrence—far from being made wholly obsolete—remains an essential ultimate assurance against the gravest of threats. A key conclusion of the Administration's National Security Strategy is that the United States will retain strategic nuclear forces sufficient to deter any future hostile foreign leadership with access to strategic nuclear forces from acting against our vital interests and to convince it that seeking a nuclear advantage would be futile.

To summarise the argument I will develop in more detail:
We have already made dramatic steps in reducing US, and Russian, and other, nuclear arsenals and potentials. We have also taken important steps to ensure safety, security—and non-diversion. We can and should do more on both the reduction and safety/security fronts. None the less, nuclear weapons remain essential to deter against the gravest threats, actual and foreseeable. Abolition, if understood as a near-term policy, rather than, as President Clinton has stated, an ultimate goal, is not a wise and surely not a feasible focus of policy. Therefore, assuring the reliability of our nuclear forces and the nuclear stockpile remains a high national security priority.

Let me turn to the rationale behind our nuclear forces, how and why we have been able to reduce our dependence on them in recent years, and then address why abolition in the near future is not a good idea. I should note that while there is a good deal that cannot be said in an unclassified session, the broad outlines of our nuclear policies have been available for years.

Nuclear Deterrence: The Cold-War Experience

Because the past has lessons for the future, let me review briefly how our nuclear forces have strengthened our security. First, they provided a principal means by which the United States deterred conventional and nuclear aggression by the Soviet Union and Warsaw Pact against itself and its allies. Second, the extension of the US nuclear umbrella allowed many of our allies to forego their own nuclear weapons, even though they had the technological know-how to develop them. Third, although the East–West competition spilled over into numerous regional conflicts during the Cold War, the nuclear capabilities possessed by the superpowers instilled caution, lest the United States and the Soviet Union be brought into direct, and possibly nuclear, confrontation.

It is a remarkable fact that for almost half a century, the US and its allies faced the USSR and its coerced auxiliaries in a division over ideology, power, culture, and the very definition of man, the state, and the world, and did so armed to the greatest extent huge sacrifice would afford, and yet did not fight a large-scale war. No one can say for sure why that success was achieved for long enough for Communism to collapse of its own internal weakness. But can anyone really doubt that nuclear weapons had a role?

Some argued, even in the Cold War, that the danger of a nuclear holocaust was so great that the risk of possessing these weapons far outweighed their benefits. I do not agree. Nuclear deterrence helped buy us time, time for internal forces of upheaval and decay to rend the Soviet Union and the Warsaw Pact and bring about the end of the Cold War.

The US nuclear deterrent has been transformed in the post-Cold War period. But the Cold War is over, and it is important to recognise the great degree to which our nuclear deterrent and indeed that of Russia has been transformed from that period. The role of nuclear weapons in our defence posture has diminished—we welcome this trend and expect it will continue in the future. US spending on strategic forces has declined dramatically from Cold War levels—from 24 per cent of the total DoD budget in the mid-1960's, to 7 per cent in 1991, to less than 3 per cent today. Moreover, we currently have no procurement programs for a next generation bomber, ICBM, SLBM or strategic submarine. The programs we do have are designed to sustain the effectiveness, safety and reliability of remaining forces, and to ensure the continued high quality of our people.

Russian spending on strategic forces has also declined substantially. The Russian Federation has some strategic systems under development—for example, a new single warhead ICBM (the SS-X-27) and a new strategic ballistic missile submarine but these programs are fewer in number (and their development pace slower) than at the height of the Cold War. These systems will replace deployed systems that will reach the end of their service lives over the next decade; or that would be eliminated under START II.

Stabilising agreed reductions in nuclear forces have been, and continue to be, a primary objective of the United States. The US and Russia have taken great strides in this regard in recent years. START I will reduce each side's deployed strategic weapons from well over 10,000 to 6,000 accountable weapons. Russia, like the US, is actually somewhat ahead of schedule in meeting the START I reduction requirements. START II, when it is ratified by the Russian Duma and enters into force, will further reduce to 3,000–3,500 each side's weapons. Following START II's entry into force, we are prepared to engage in negotiations further reducing strategic nuclear forces.

Meanwhile, the US has unilaterally reduced its non-strategic nuclear weapons (NSNF) to one-tenth of Cold War levels. While Russia pledged in 1991 to make significant cuts in its non-strategic nuclear forces and has reduced its operational NSNF substantially, it has made far less progress thus far than the US, and the Russian non-strategic arsenal (deployed and stockpiled) is probably about ten times as large as ours.

In addition to START reductions, there have been qualitative changes in our nuclear arsenal. There used to be nuclear landmines, artillery, infantry weapons, surface-to-surface missiles, surface-to-air weapons, air-to-air weapons, depth-charges, and tor-pedoes; all these have gone. In 1991 and 1992, the US unilaterally eliminated several nuclear weapons systems (e.g., Lance, FB-111, SRAM-A), halted a number of planned or on-going development programs (e.g., Small ICBM, Peace-keeper Rail Garrison, Lance Follow-on), took nuclear bombers off alert, and removed from alert, well ahead of the required schedule, those ICBMs and strategic missile submarines planned for elimination under START I. In 1994, further reflecting the changed international situation, the US and Russia agreed to no longer target their ballistic missiles against each other on a day-to-day basis.

Nor is the non-proliferation picture all bleak. No nation has openly joined the nuclear club since China in 1964. There are only three unacknowledged nuclear powers. South Africa has abandoned its capability, as Ukraine, Belarus and Kazakstan have theirs. Argentina and Brazil have renounced the option, as Sweden and Canada did long ago. North Korea's program is frozen. Iraq is under a special and highly intru-sive UNSCOM regime. The vast majority of countries support a permanent Non-Proliferation Treaty—mostly a benefit which non-nuclear countries confer on one another, not a favour they do for the nuclear powers. We have negotiated an end to nuclear testing.

Why Nuclear Deterrence?

The question, however, is rightly asked: Granted all these reductions, with the end of the Cold War, why do we continue to maintain a nuclear deterrent at all?

In September 1994, the Clinton Administration answered this question in its Nuclear Posture Review, the first comprehensive post-Cold War review of US nuclear policy. The NPR recognised that with the dissolution of the Warsaw Pact, the demise of the Soviet Union, and the embarkation of Russia on the road to democracy and a free market economy, the strategic environment has been transformed. Conventional forces therefore, could and should assume a larger share of the deterrent role. We con-cluded, nonetheless, that nuclear weapons continue to play a critical role in deterring aggression against the US, its overseas forces, its allies and friends. This conclusion is entirely consistent with NATO's Strategic Concept, adopted in 1991 after the end of the Cold War, which states that the fundamental purpose of NATO's nuclear forces is to preserve peace and prevent coercion and any kind of war.

Why did we reach this conclusion? Most importantly, because the positive changes in the international environment are far from irreversible. There are broadly, two classes of threats to which nuclear weapons remain important as deterrents.

First, Russia has made great progress and we do not regard it as a potential military threat under its present, or any reasonably foreseeable government. We wisely invest substantially in the Co-operative Threat Reduction program, in future arms control—and we share with the current Russian leadership (and most of their opponents) a determination not to let our relations return to a state of hostility in which these weapons would be a threat.

All that said, Russia continues to possess substantial strategic forces and an even larger stockpile of tactile nuclear weapons. And because of deterioration in its con-ventional military capabilities, Russia may be placing even more importance and reliance on its nuclear forces. We cannot be so certain of future Russian politics as to ignore the possibility that we would need again to deter the Russian nuclear force.

Second, even if we could ignore the Russian nuclear arsenal entirely, there are unfortunately a range of other potential threats to which nuclear weapons are a deterrent. One cannot survey the list of rogue states with potential WMD programmes and conclude otherwise. I do not, by the way, regard such states as undeterrable, either in the long-run sense of the incentives to acquire WMD capability, or the short-run sense of incentives to use such a capability. Indeed, the knowledge that the US has a powerful and ready nuclear capability is, I believe, a significant deterrent to proliferators to even contemplate the use of WMD. That this is so will, I think, be clear if one thinks about the proliferation incentives that would be presented to the Kaddafis and Kim-Chong-Ils of the world if the US did not have a reliable and flexible nuclear capability.

In view of this, it would be irresponsible to dismantle the well-established—and much reduced—system of deterrence before new and reliable systems for preserving stability are in place. What about the argument that our weapons promote proliferation, that states seek to acquire nuclear weapons in response to possession by nuclear weapons states? A more compelling case to me is that proliferant states acquire nuclear weapons not because we have them but for reasons of their own—to counter regional adversaries, to further regional ambitions, and to enhance their status among their neighbours. And, insofar as our nuclear capability is an issue, if a successful proliferator knew he would not face a nuclear response by the US, it would scarcely reduce his incentives to acquire a WMD capability. The incentives to proliferate would hardly be reduced if a rogue state would, through a successful nuclear weapons program, acquire a nuclear monopoly, not a token capability facing far stronger forces possessed by the US and other world powers.

Some people claim that once proliferation does occur, US nuclear forces lack any utility in deterring rogue leaders from using nuclear weapons because those leaders will not regard the costs, even of nuclear retaliation, as sufficiently great. But experience suggests that few dictators are indifferent to the preservation of key instruments of state control, or to the survival of their own regimes (or, indeed, their own persons). Thus, I believe the reverse is true—our nuclear capabilities are more likely to give pause to potential rogue proliferants than encourage them.

The important role of US nuclear capability in preventing the spread of nuclear weapons often goes unnoticed. The extension of a credible US nuclear deterrent to allies has been an important non-proliferation tool. It has removed incentives for key allies, in a still dangerous world, to develop and deploy their own nuclear forces, as many are technically capable of doing. Indeed, our strong security relationships have probably played as great a role in non-proliferation over the past 40 years as has the NPT.

Argument: Nuclear Weapons Should be Eliminated because they are Dangerous and Unsafe

Of course, nuclear weapons are dangerous; they contain high explosives and fissile material. But they are not unsafe in the sense that they are susceptible to accidental or unauthorised use. Our nuclear weapons meet the highest standards of safety, security, and responsible custodianship. Moreover, we place high priority on maintaining and improving stockpile safety. Our nuclear safety record is extraordinary. Although a few accidents involving nuclear weapons have occurred, no accident has ever resulted in a nuclear detonation and the last accident of any kind was almost twenty years ago.

We believe the likelihood of accidents has been dramatically reduced since the end of the Cold War. Our strategic bombers are no longer on alert; our surface ships and attack submarines no longer carry nuclear weapons. The Army and Marines have eliminated their nuclear weapons. Older weapons with less modern safety features have been removed from the stockpile. Technical safety mechanisms have been improved. De-targetting means that the missiles, even if somehow launched in error, would no longer be aimed at targets in Russia. The number of nuclear weapon storage sites have been decreased by 75 per cent and weapons consolidated. As a result of all these changes our weapons are much less exposed to accident environments.

In addition, nuclear weapons security has been a key element of DoD's Co-operative Threat Reduction Program with Russia from the beginning. A total of up to $101 million in CTR assistance has been made available under these CTR agreements for projects to enhance security of nuclear weapons under MoD control. In addition to agreements already signed on armoured blankets and security upgrades to nuclear weapons railcars, other nuclear weapons transportation and storage security projects are underway or being developed.

On balance, the safety risks of maintaining a smaller nuclear arsenal are far outweighed by the security—and non-proliferation—benefits that we continue to derive from nuclear deterrence.

The Bottom Line on Abolition

I would summarise the case for retaining nuclear weapons for the foreseeable future as follows:
There is no reasonable prospect that all the declared and de facto nuclear powers will agree in the near term to give up all their nuclear weapons. And as long as one such state refuses to do so, it will be necessary for us to retain a nuclear force of our own. If the nuclear powers were, nevertheless, to accept abolition, then we would require—and the Congress would rightly demand—a verification regime of extraordinary rigor and intrusiveness. This would have to go far beyond any currently in existence or even under contemplation. It would have to include not merely a system of verification, but what the international generals statement calls 'an agreed procedure for forcible international intervention and interruption of current efforts in a certain and timely fashion'.

The difficulties with setting up such a system under current world conditions are obvious. Such a regime would have to continue to be effective in the midst of a prolonged and grave crisis—even during a war—between potentially nuclear-capable powers. For in such a crisis, the first question for all involved would be that of whether—or when—to start a clandestine nuclear program. For the knowledge of how to build nuclear weapons cannot be abolished.

Finally, we who are charged with responsibility for national security and national defence must recall that we are not only seeking to avert nuclear war—we are seeking to avert major conventional war as well. As I indicated earlier, during the Cold War nuclear weapons played a stabilising role in that they made the resort to military force less likely. The world is still heavily armed with advanced conventional weapons and will increasingly be so armed with weapons of mass destruction. The existence of nuclear weapons continues to serve as a damper on the resort to the use of force.

Need to Maintain Safe and Reliable Nuclear Weapons Stockpile

Because nuclear deterrence is to remain part of our national security policy for the foreseeable future, the US nuclear deterrent must remain credible—weapon systems must be effective and their warheads safe and reliable. The quality, reliability, and effectiveness of the forces themselves (including their communication and command systems) and the people who operate them, is one of our top priorities in DoD. With respect to the nuclear devices themselves, DoE has an aggressive, well-funded, program designed to ensure our weapons remain safe and reliable in the absence of nuclear testing. The Department of Defence fully supports this program. Today, we have high confidence in the safety and reliability of our nuclear deterrent force; the stockpile stewardship and management program is designed to provide the tools to assure this in the future.

Summary

Our objective is safe, stable world. But we must develop our national security policy with the undertaking that nuclear weapons and the underlying technical knowledge cannot be disinvented whether or not the US retains its weapons. In this connection, the US will continue to lead the way to a safer world through the deep reductions in nuclear forces undertaken in START and through Nunn-Lugar co-operative threat reduction and other actions. At the same time, we will maintain a smaller nuclear force as a 'hedge' against a future that is uncertain and in a world in which substantial nuclear arsenals remain.

Successive US administrations have embraced the objective of nuclear disarmament as our ultimate goal. Two years ago at the NPT Review and Extension Conference, the US reaffirmed its commitment to this goal in the Conference's statement of principles and objectives. In an uncertain world, however, the path to this goal is not clearly marked. What is clear is that the ultimate goal will be reached only through realistic moves forward, as genuine security permits, with each step building on those before it.

We will continue to strive to make the world a safer place for our children and grandchildren. In this regard, the United States is committed to Article VI of the NPT which calls for the complete elimination of nuclear weapons in the context of general and complete disarmament. Until these conditions are realised, however, I believe that nuclear weapons will continue to fulfil an essential role in meeting our deterrence requirements and assuring our non-proliferation objectives.

A further problem is that among some military colleagues, there is deeply felt concern that by urging nuclear arsenal reduction we are somehow denigrating the important—indeed vitally important—role that these nuclear-armed military forces successfully served during the Cold War. It would be a regrettable mistake to be drawn into such a view. During that time our very survival was at stake. Our nuclear weapons served their Cold War purpose, and served successfully. Security was successfully preserved, and war with the Soviets successfully avoided. I at least, and many others who served in the military forces—including notably our highly-trained, highly-skilled nuclear forces—have no doubt that our nuclear forces played a central, crucial, indispensable role in that process. I myself was drawn into the argument 'Better Red than dead'. My response was always 'Better neither than either', and that in fact was the outcome, thanks in crucial part to our highly capable nuclear weapons and forces.

But the Cold War is gone. And now it is time to look at the new possibilities and new era.

APPENDIX 2

Legality of the Use by a State of Nuclear Weapons in Armed Conflict

The International Court of Justice, The Hague, 8 July 1996

The Court

Replies in the following manner to the question put by the General Assembly:

A. Unanimously: there is in neither customary nor conventional international law any specific authorisation of the threat or use of nuclear weapons;

B. By eleven votes to three: there is in neither customary nor conventional international law any comprehensive and universal prohibition of the threat or use of nuclear weapons as such;

C. Unanimously: a threat or use of force by means of nuclear weapons that is contrary to Article 2, paragraph 4, of the United Nations Charter and that fails to meet all the requirements of Article 51, is unlawful;

D. Unanimously: a threat or use of nuclear weapons should also be compatible with the requirements of the international law applicable in armed conflict particularly those of the principles and rules of international humanitarian law, as well as with specific obligations under treaties and other undertakings which expressly deal with nuclear weapons;

E. By seven votes to seven [carried by the President's casting vote]: it follows from the above-mentioned requirements that the threat or use of nuclear weapons would generally be contrary to the rules of international law applicable in armed conflict, and in particular the principles and rules of humanitarian law. However, in view of the current state of international law, and of the elements of fact at its disposal, the Court cannot conclude definitively whether the threat or use of nuclear weapons would be lawful or unlawful in the extreme circumstance of self-defence, in which the very survival of a State would be at stake;

F. Unanimously: there exists an obligation to pursue in good faith and bring to a conclusion negotiations leading to nuclear disarmament in all its aspects under strict and effective international control.

APPENDIX 3

Nuclear Weapons: The ICJ 1996 Pronouncement

Sir Michael Quinlan

1. The ICJ pronouncement is an advisory opinion, not an authoritative determination. It cannot create binding international law.

2. The opinion contains six statements. The first four were described in the written contribution of the Court's own Vice-President, later its President, as 'anodyne asseverations of the obvious'. That may be over-severe, since there are within them some restatements or clarifications that may be found useful; but they cannot be supposed to be of major new importance.

3. The fifth statement—reached by the narrowest possible margin and by means, unusually in an advisory opinion, of a casting vote—is on the legality of the use or threat of nuclear weapons. It says that this would be 'generally' illegal. But the use of nuclear weapons is not addressed to any generality of situations; it would arise only in (and its threat would relate only to) exceptional and extreme circumstances. The qualification 'generally' therefore largely deprives the sentence of practical application. The statement goes on to indicate that the Court cannot make up its mind on whether use by a state would be legitimate 'in an extreme circumstance of self-defence, in which its very survival would be at stake'. 'Survival' is a term not defined—does it refer to averting physical extinction? or political annexation? or massive loss of territory, population or other key resources?—the Court does not say. And whose is the survival in question? The natural meaning is just that of the state itself possessing the weapons; but that would imply that it was illegal to extend to others, or to receive from others, nuclear-deterrent protection as in the NATO or US–Japan alliances. Such an implication would be an open incitement to proliferation; and that cannot be sensible, or what the Court really intended. In brief, this fifth statement is both inconclusive and unclear.

4. The sixth statement—not made in response to any question put to the Court, and so strictly *obiter dictum*—is about the obligation to negotiate nuclear disarmament. The statement neither adds to nor strengthens that obligation; it merely recalls what is already present in Article VI of the NPT. Article VI sets nuclear disarmament close alongside general and complete disarmament, and it is understood that the Court fully recognized this even though making no mention of it. One may wonder what are the current prospects, conditions and time-scale of general and complete disarmament, and what steps towards it are being proposed by any party. Yet nothing in the ICJ statement, or in the NPT, places the two obligations on a different footing one from the other. Most of the nuclear signatories have done considerably more about

nuclear disarmament than other signatories have about general and complete disarmament, an obligation resting equally on them.

5. In summary, the ICJ pronouncement will not bear the weight which anti-nuclear comment often seeks to place upon it as altering the status of nuclear weapons in international law, or as requiring dramatic new action by the nuclear powers.

A Nuclear-Weapon-Free Zone in Central Europe?

Public discussion of the idea of a NWFZ in Central Europe is, at the present writing, not yet highly developed. This note offers initial reflections; given the immaturity of the debate, it does not seek to indicate a fully settled conclusion.

Two background considerations:

1. The NWFZ concept has in the past been used as a valuable device to help prevent nuclear weapons needlessly becoming part of the regional security landscape in areas where they have not hitherto been so. That is not the situation in Central Europe.

2. The limitations of the concept, even where it is useful, need to recognized. With modern delivery systems nuclear weapons can reach every corner of the world, and their shadow therefore extends everywhere. Declaring an area a NWFZ does not render it immune from nuclear threat. The people of Hiroshima would no doubt, given the chance, have gladly declared their city a NWFZ.

There are at present, so it is understood, no nuclear weapons deployed in Central Europe (assuming that region to be defined for this purpose as essentially comprising the independent ex-communist states west of Russia and as excluding Germany—the inclusion of Germany, in whole or part, would raise further and more awkward issues not addressed here). NATO has indicated clearly and publicly that it has no need and no intention to alter this situation, regardless of membership expansion. That is a matter of political choice and political assurance, not international legal requirement, and so is in theory readily reversible. But the same is true of the non-deployment of nuclear weapons in Norway and Denmark; that has held for over forty years, and is as dependable and permanent a reality as could reasonably be wished for.

Any NATO deployment of nuclear weapons into Central Europe would require the agreement, at minimum, of both the sending state—in practice, the United States—and the recipient. This would be a big political decision for each of them, and the only conceivable scenario in which their combined agreement might be forthcoming would be a change gravely for the worse in the character and behaviour of Russia itself.

The objective reality which the declaration of a NWFZ in Central Europe would be intended to create is accordingly already securely in existence. The case for a declaration can therefore relate to little more than psychology and symbolism.

Russia would doubtless welcome a NWFZ. That is natural, since for Russia there is no disadvantage; it is virtually impossible to imagine any plausible scenario in which Russia would want, or be willingly allowed, to deploy its own nuclear armoury into the territory of its sovereign neighbours to the west, so no genuine option would be foregone. For Russia, the only effect of a NWFZ would be to alter a 99.8 per cent likelihood of no NATO deployment into a 99.9 per cent likelihood. But there can be no rational basis for significant Russian fears of a new NATO nuclear deployment eastward unless Russia herself does something grave to provoke it.

From the NATO standpoint the effect would be in some degree simply the converse—a NWFZ would make the nuclear-deployment option rather more difficult politically as a possible response (and so, in latent prospect, as a contributory deterrent) to a severe deterioration in the external behaviour of a changed Russia. This looks today no more than a theoretical possibility; but security policy is a long-term business, concerned to seal off risks in advance even if they seem remote.

There is on the NATO side a further point, albeit of a more symbolic character. The essence of the NATO Alliance is agreement, encapsulated in Article V of the 1949 Treaty, to regard the territories of all its members as constituting ultimately a single homogeneous security space. Any new Central European members will sign up, as all existing members have, to a common Alliance-wide strategic concept in which nuclear weapons continue to feature as a last-resort underpinning. To import an external legal constraint limiting what NATO is entitled to do in the territory of some of its members, but not of others, would be a crack in the formal integrity of this edifice. (For similar reasons the Federal Republic of Germany during the cold war was wont firmly to resist any measure that might appear to 'singularise' it.)

In practical terms it is probable that neither of the above NATO-related points matters greatly. But given that a NWFZ would not actually alter objective reality—the desired reality exists already, and is under no threat of alteration—there seems no adequate reason why NATO should incur these disadvantages even if at present they seem small, and no sufficient justification for expending political and diplomatic effort upon securing agreement to the project from all the relevant states (some of which, like Poland, show no sign of welcoming it).

APPENDIX 4

Executive Summary

The Canberra Commission on the Elimination of Nuclear Weapons

The Canberra Commission is persuaded that immediate and determined efforts need to be made to rid the world of nuclear weapons and the threat they pose to it. The destructiveness of nuclear weapons is immense. Any use would be catastrophic.

The proposition that nuclear weapons can be retained in perpetuity and never used—accidentally or by decision—defies credibility. The only complete defence is the elimination of nuclear weapons and assurance that they will never be produced again.

The end of the bipolar confrontation has not removed the danger of nuclear catastrophe. In some respects the risk of use by accident or miscalculation has increased. Political upheaval or the weakening of state authority in a nuclear weapon state could cripple existing systems for ensuring the safe handling and control of nuclear weapons and weapons material, increasing the odds of a calamity. The same fate could befall other states or sub-state groups with a less developed nuclear weapon capability or those that seek to develop such a capability in the future.

Nuclear weapons have long been understood to be too destructive and non-discriminatory to secure discrete objectives on the battlefield. The destructiveness of nuclear weapons is so great that they have no military utility against a comparably equipped opponent, other than the belief that they deter that opponent from using nuclear weapons.

Possession of nuclear weapons has not prevented wars, in various regions, which directly or indirectly involve the major powers. They were deemed unsuitable for use even when those powers suffered humiliating military setbacks.

No nuclear weapon state has been or is prepared to declare as a matter of national policy that it would respond to the use of chemical or biological weapons with nuclear weapons. The solution to these concerns lies in the strengthening and effective implementation of and universal adherence to the Chemical Weapons Convention and Biological Weapons Convention, with particular emphasis on early detection of untoward developments. The response to any violation should be a multilateral one.

The Canberra Commission on the Elimination of Nuclear Weapons was established as an independent commission by the then Australian Government in November 1995 to propose practical steps towards a nuclear-free world including the related problem of maintaining stability and security during the transitional period and after this goal is achieved. The Report was published in 1996.

Thus, the only apparent military utility that remains for nuclear weapons is in deterring their use by others. That utility implies the continued existence of nuclear weapons. It would disappear completely if nuclear weapons were eliminated.

A New Climate for Action

Nuclear weapons are held by a handful of states which insist that these weapons provide unique security benefits, and yet reserve uniquely to themselves the right to own them. This situation is highly discriminatory and thus unstable; it cannot be sustained. The possession of nuclear weapons by any state is a constant stimulus to other states to acquire them.

In the 1960s, the world looked at the prospect of dozens of nuclear weapons states, recoiled and rejected it. The result was the Treaty on the Non-Proliferation of Nuclear Weapons (NPT) of 1968 with its promise of a world free of these weapons. The overall success of the NPT and other nuclear non-proliferation regimes has been gratifying, but it has been hard won, and is by no means guaranteed. The prospects of a renewal of horizontal proliferation have become real. The proliferation of nuclear weapons is amongst the most immediate security challenges facing the international community. Despite the impact of the international nuclear non-proliferation regime, the disconcerting reality is that several states have made, and some continue to make, clandestine efforts to develop nuclear arsenals. The possible acquisition by terrorist groups of nuclear weapons or material is a growing threat to the international community.

The end of the Cold War has created a new climate for international action to eliminate nuclear weapons, a new opportunity. It must be exploited quickly or it will be lost.

The elimination of nuclear weapons must be a global endeavour involving all states. The process followed must ensure that no state feels, at any stage, that further nuclear disarmament is a threat to its security. To this end nuclear weapon elimination should be conducted as a series of phased verified reductions that allow states to satisfy themselves, at each stage of the process, that further movement toward elimination can be made safely and securely.

Immediate Steps

The first requirement is for the five nuclear weapon states to commit themselves unequivocally to the elimination of nuclear weapons and agree to start work immediately on the practical steps and negotiations required for its achievement. This commitment should be made at the highest political level. Non-nuclear weapon states should support the commitment by the nuclear weapon states and join in cooperative international action to implement it. This commitment would change instantly the tenor of debate, the thrust of war planning, and the timing or indeed the necessity for modernisation programs. It would transform the nuclear weapons paradigm from the indefinite management of a world fraught with the twin risks of the use of nuclear weapons and further proliferation, to one of nuclear weapons elimination.

Negotiation of the commitment should begin immediately, with the aim of first steps in its implementation being taken in 1997.

The commitment by the nuclear weapon states to a nuclear weapon free world must be accompanied by a series of practical, realistic and mutually reinforcing steps. There are a number of such steps that can be taken immediately. They would significantly reduce the risk of nuclear war and thus enhance the security of all states, but particularly that of the nuclear weapon states. Their implementation would provide clear confirmation of the intent of the nuclear weapon states to further reduce the role of nuclear weapons in their security postures. The recommended steps are:

1. Taking nuclear forces off alert.
2. Removal of warheads from delivery vehicles.
3. Ending deployment of non-strategic nuclear weapons.
4. Ending nuclear testing.
5. Initiating negotiations to further reduce United States and Russian nuclear arsenals
6. Agreement amongst the nuclear weapon states of reciprocal no first use undertakings, and of a non-use undertaking by them in relation to the non-nuclear weapon states.

Nuclear weapon states should take all nuclear forces off alert status and so reduce dramatically the chance of an accidental or unauthorised nuclear weapons launch. In the first instance, reductions in alert status could be adopted by the nuclear weapon states unilaterally.

The physical separation of warheads from delivery vehicles would strongly reinforce the gains achieved by taking nuclear forces off alert. This measure can be implemented to the extent that nuclear forces can be reconstituted to an alert posture only within known or agreed upon timeframes.

The nuclear weapon states should unilaterally remove all non-strategic nuclear weapons from deployed sites to a limited number of secure storage facilities on their territory.

Pending universal application of the Comprehensive Test Ban Treaty all states should observe at once the moratorium it imposes on nuclear testing.

The United States and Russia must continue to show leadership in reversing the nuclear accumulations of the Cold War. Their purpose should be to move toward nuclear force levels for all the nuclear weapon states which would reflect unambiguously the determination to eliminate these weapons when this step can be verified with adequate confidence.

The nuclear weapon states should agree and state that they would not be the first to use or threaten to use nuclear weapons against each other and that they would not use or threaten to use nuclear weapons in any conflict with a non-nuclear weapon state. Such an agreement should be brought into operation as soon as possible.

Reinforcing Steps

The following steps would build on the solid foundation of commitment, accomplishment and goodwill established through implementation of the steps recommended for immediate action:

1. Action to prevent further horizontal proliferation.
2. Developing verification arrangements for a nuclear weapon free world.
3. Cessation of the production of fissile material for nuclear explosive purposes.

The problem of nuclear proliferation is inextricably linked to the continued possession of nuclear weapons by a handful of states. A world environment where proliferation is under control will facilitate the disarmament process and movement toward final elimination, and vice versa. The emergence of any new nuclear weapon state during the elimination process would seriously jeopardise the process of eliminating nuclear weapons. Action is needed to ensure effective non-proliferation controls on civil and military nuclear activities, and to press for universal acceptance of non-proliferation obligations.

Effective verification is critical to the achievement and maintenance of a nuclear weapon free world. Before states agree to eliminate nuclear weapons they will require a high level of confidence that verification arrangements would detect promptly any attempt to cheat the disarmament process whether through retention or acquisition of clandestine weapons, weapons components, means of weapons production or undeclared stocks of fissile material. Formal legal undertakings should be accompanied by corresponding legal arrangements for verification. To maintain security in a post-nuclear weapon world the verification system must provide a high level of assurance as to the continued peaceful, non-explosive use of a state's nuclear activity. A political judgement will be needed on whether the levels of assurance possible from the verification regime are sufficient. All existing arms control and disarmament agreements have required political judgements of this nature because no verification system provides absolute certainty.

A key element of non-proliferation arrangements for a nuclear weapon free world will be a highly developed capacity to detect undeclared nuclear activity at both declared and undeclared sites. Progressive extension of safeguards to nuclear activity in the nuclear weapon states, the undeclared weapon states and the threshold states will be needed with the end point being universal application of safeguards in all states. Systems will be needed to verify that nuclear warheads are dismantled and destroyed, and their fissile material content safeguarded to provide maximum confidence that such material cannot be reintroduced to weapons use.

The political commitment to eliminate nuclear weapons must be matched by a willingness to make available the resources needed for nuclear disarmament including effective verification. States must also be confident that any violations detected will be acted upon. In this context, the Security Council should continue its consideration of how it might address, consistent with specific mandates given to it and consistent with the Charter of the United Nations, violations of nuclear disarmament obligations that might be drawn to its attention. This should demonstrate that the collective security system enshrined in the Charter will operate effectively in this field.

Further United States/Russian Strategic Arms Reduction Treaties (START) and nuclear confidence building measures should establish a receptive international climate for negotiations on global reduction of nuclear arms. The United States and Russia could commence a process for bringing the United Kingdom, France and China into the nuclear disarmament process. Further early steps could be for the US and Russia to prepare the ground for verification of nuclear weapon states reductions by sharing information and expertise on START verification, on weapons dismantlement and on verification and control of fissile material from dismantled weapons. US/Russian experience on nuclear confidence building might be extended to the other nuclear weapon states and new measures developed which involve them.

The Future Environment

Concurrent with the central disarmament process, there will be a need for activity supported by all states, but particularly the nuclear weapon states, to build an environment conducive to nuclear disarmament and non-proliferation.

It will be extremely important for the pursuit of the elimination of nuclear weapons to protect fully the integrity of the Anti-Ballistic Missile Treaty.

Nuclear weapon free zones are part of the architecture that can usefully encourage and support a nuclear weapon free world. The spread of nuclear weapon free zones around the globe, with specific mechanisms to answer the security concerns of each region, can progressively codify the transition to a world free of nuclear weapons.

At the level of national action, states have the fundamental obligation, under a variety of treaties, and in moral terms, to ensure that sensitive nuclear material, equipment and technology under their jurisdiction and control do not find their way into the hands of those who would misuse them.

The Commission noted with satisfaction the response of the International Court of Justice made in July 1996 to a request from the General Assembly of the United Nations for an advisory opinion on the legality of the threat or use of nuclear weapons. The Court's statement that there existed an obligation to pursue in good faith and bring to a conclusion negotiations leading to nuclear disarmament in all its aspects under strict and effective international control is precisely the obligation that the Commission wishes to see implemented.

The Commission considered carefully the merits of setting out a precise timeframe for the elimination of nuclear weapons, but elected not to do so. However, this does not imply that it accepts the extended timelines imposed by such current constraints as limited warhead dismantlement facilities. Those constraints could be relieved by political decisions and the allocation of resources required to advance dismantlement. In addition, another limiting factor may prove to be establishing the necessary confidence in the verification regime which would be required to take the final step to complete elimination. In this context, the Canberra Commission remains convinced of the basic importance of agreed targets and guidelines which would drive the process inexorably toward the ultimate objective of final elimination, at the earliest possible time.

SELECT BIBLIOGRAPHY OF
RECENT SOURCES

Allison, G. T., Carter, Ashton, B., Miller, Steven, E., and Zelikow, Philip, *Cooperative Denuclearization: From Pledges to Deeds* (Cambridge, Mass.: Center for Science and International Affairs, 1993).
——Cote, Owen, R., Falkenwrath, Richard, A., and Miller, Steven, E., *Avoiding Nuclear Anarchy: Containing the Threat of Loose Russian Nuclear Weapons and Fissile Material* (Cambridge, Mass.: Center for Science and International Affairs, John F Kennedy School of Government, Havard University, 1996).
Arkin, W., and Kristensen, H., 'Dangerous Directions', *Bulletin of the Atomic Scientists* (Mar. 1998).
——Norris, R., and Handler, J., *Taking Stock: Worldwide Nuclear Deployments 1998* (New York: Natural Resources Defense Council, 1998).
Betts, R. K., 'The New Threat of Mass Destruction', *Foreign Affairs* (Jan./Feb. 1998).
Blair, B., Feiveson, H., and Von Hippel, F., 'Taking Nuclear Weapons off Hair-Trigger Alert', *Scientific American* (Nov. 1997).
Brown, M., *Phased Nuclear Disarmament and US Defense Policy* (Washington, DC: Henry L. Stimson Center, 1996).
Bunn, G., and Holloway, D., *Arms Control without Treaties? Rethinking US-Russian Strategic Negotiations in light of the Duma-Senate Slowdown in Treaty Approval* (Stanford, Calif.: Stanford University, Center for International Security and Arms Control, 1998).
Canada and the Nuclear Challenge: Reducing the Political Value of Nuclear Weapons for the Twenty-First Century (Ottawa: Standing Committee on Foreign Affairs and International Trade, Dec. 1998).
Chellaney, B., 'After the Tests: India's Options', *Survival,* 40/4 (1998/9).
Cockburn, A. and L., *One Point Safe* (New York: Doubleday, 1996).
Delpech, T., 'Nuclear Weapons and the "New World Order": Early Warning from Asia?', *Survival,* 40/4 (1998/9).
Graham, T., 'South Asia and the Future of Nuclear Non-Proliferation', *Arms Control Today* (May 1998).
Goodpaster, A., *Shaping the Nuclear Future: Toward a More Comprehensive Approach,* Occasional Paper (Washington, DC: The Atlantic Council of the United States, Dec. 1997).
Hanson, M., and Ungerer, C., 'Promoting an Agenda for Nuclear Weapons Elimination: The Canberra Commission and Dilemmas of Disarmament', *The Australian Journal of Politics and History,* 44/4 (1998).

Heisbourg, F., 'The Prospects for Nuclear Stability between India and Pakistan', *Survival*, 40/4 (1998/9).

Jones, R. W., McDonough, Mark, Dalton, Toby, F., and Koblentz, Gregory, D., *Tracking Nuclear Proliferation: A Guide in Maps and Charts 1998* (Washington, DC: The Carnegie Endowment for International Peace, 1998).

McWhinney, E., *Nuclear Weapons and Contemporary International Law* (Dordrecht: Martinus Nijhoff Publishers, 1989).

Mattoo, A., 'India's Nuclear Status Quo', *Survival*, 38/3 (1996).

Mazarr, M. (ed.), *Nuclear Weapons in a Transformed World: The Challenge of Virtual Nuclear Arsenals* (New York: St Martin's, 1997).

'Nuclear Weapons: The Abolitionist Upsurge', *Strategic Survey* 1997/98 (London: International Institute for Strategic Studies, 1998).

Panofsky, W. K., 'Dismantling the Concept of "Weapons of Mass Destruction"', *Arms Control Today* (Apr. 1988).

Quester, G., *International Safeguards for Eliminating Weapons of Mass Destruction*, Occasional Paper, 31 (Washington, DC: Henry L. Stimson Center, 1996).

Quinlan, M., *Thinking about Nuclear Weapons*, RUSI Whitehall Paper Series (London: Royal United Servicas Institute for Defence Studies, 1997).

Report of the Canberra Commission on the Elimination of Nuclear Weapons (Canberra: Department of Foreign Affairs and Trade, Aug. 1996).

Schell, J., *The Gift of Time: The Case of Abolishing Nuclear Weapons* (New York: Metropolitan Books, 1998).

Simpson, J., 'Smoke and Mirrors', *The World Today* (July 1998).

Turner, S., *Caging the Nuclear Gene: An American Challenge for Global Security* (Boulder, Colo.: Westview, 1997).

Turner, S., 'The Specter of Nuclear Proliferation', *Security Dialogue* (Sept. 1998).

United States Senate, *The Future of Nuclear Deterrence*, Hearing before the Subcommittee on International Security, Proliferation, and Federal Services of the Committee on Governmental Affairs United States Senate, 105th Congress, First Session (Washington, DC: Government Printing Office, Feb. 1997).

Walker, W., 'International Nuclear Relations after the Indian and Pakistani Test Explosions', *International Affairs*, 74/3 (1998).

Yost, D., 'The New NATO and Collective Security', *Survival*, 40/2 (1998).

INDEX

Algeria 89
Argentina 34, 35, 51, 65, 89, 128
arms control 33, 44, 58–60, 77–8, 90–1,
   94–6, 99–100, 128, 138, 174–5
   see also Comprehensive Test Ban Treaty;
   INF; Partial Test Ban Treaty; START

ballistic missile defence 19–24, 28, 30, 93,
   192
   ABM Treaty 21, 24
   SDI 60, 149
   see also theatre missile defence
Baruch Plan 57
Ben-Gurion, David 90
Bhutto, Zulfikar Ali 102
biological/chemical weapons 7, 8, 23, 29,
   35–6, 45–6, 49, 68–9, 84, 85, 88–9,
   92, 95–6, 99, 137–8, 161, 162, 202,
   206
Blair, Bruce 73, 74, 181–2
Brazil 34, 35, 51, 66, 88, 128
Britain:
   CND in 57–8
   and nuclear weapons 40, 48, 118, 127,
   193–4, 199, 200
Bull, Hedley 59
Butler, Lee 63, 74, 146, 147

Canberra Commission 2, 62, 64, 65–7,
   69, 78, 109, 167, 179–80, 181, 182,
   207–8
Chernobyl 73
China 14, 20, 23, 38, 40, 47, 48, 65, 69, 88,
   89, 104, 106, 107, 108, 163, 168, 170,
   194, 199–200, 201
Clausewitz, Carl von 11, 27
Clinton, Bill 172
cold war 31, 38, 153–8
   see also nuclear weapons, deterrence
Comprehensive Test Ban Treaty 1, 60, 76,
   99, 101, 103, 105, 109, 110, 115, 120,
   122, 162, 164

conventional warfare 35–7, 38, 39, 75,
   138–9, 154, 156–7, 179
Cuba 43, 51, 52, 170
Cuban Missile Crisis 79, 112, 146, 153,
   175–8

deterrence, conventional 133–5
deterrence, nuclear 5, 33, 36, 37, 65–6, 71,
   112–13, 145–7, 149–50, 153, 160,
   202–3
   in cold war 31, 59–60, 62, 65, 71–2, 73,
   147, 153–4, 157–8, 186–90, 198
   extended 37
   minimum 53, 78–81, 82, 85, 86
   stability of 12–16, 23, 71–2, 73–4,
   146–50, 159, 182, 188–9
   see also nuclear weapons
disarmament movement 56, 57–8, 63
   see also nuclear weapons (abolition)
Dunn, Lewis A. 26

Egypt 87, 91, 92
ethnocentrism 28

Falk, Richard 72
Fissile Material Production Program 78
France:
   and nuclear weapons 40, 47–8, 61–2,
   65–6, 127, 193–4, 199, 200, 205

G7 23, 120
Gaddis, John L. 72
Gaylor, Admiral Noel 180–1
Germany 40
Gorbachev, Mikhail 15, 60, 155, 162
Gulf War 7, 13, 31, 36, 65, 75, 89, 91, 93,
   96, 98, 130–1, 134, 162, 171–2, 195,
   196, 202
   Desert Storm 31, 36
Gujral, I. K. 110

Horner, Charles A. 181

IAEA 52, 53, 89, 97, 102, 132
Iklé, Fred 75
India 6, 40, 118–19
  BJP in 103, 104, 195
  nuclear test of 1, 6, 9, 10, 39, 40, 51, 62, 68, 74, 76, 78, 79, 84, 101–21, 126, 195
  and nuclear weapons 25, 48, 51, 66, 82, 102, 121–4, 191, 196, 201, 205, 207
INF Treaty 1, 9, 162
International Court of Justice 52
intervention 172–3
Iran 6, 87–8, 88–9, 91, 92, 95, 98, 106, 196
Iraq 6, 35, 39, 49, 51, 61, 64, 65, 74, 84, 88, 89, 91, 92–3, 95, 96–8, 163, 196
  see also Gulf War; Saddam Hussein
Ireland 32, 33
Israel:
  and nuclear weapons 1, 6, 9, 10, 25, 37, 48, 51, 65, 66, 84, 89–90, 92, 93–4, 98, 127, 195, 196, 201–2

Japan 40, 116, 151, 171
Jordan 91, 92, 95

Kaysen, Carl 169
Kennan, George 173–4
Kennedy, John F. 176, 177
Khan, Abdel Qadir 102–3
Khomeini, Ayatollah Ruhollah 88
  see also Iran
Kissinger, Henry 71, 153, 168–9, 180
Korea, North 6, 43, 49, 51, 65, 88, 106, 115, 129, 132, 196, 201
Korea, South 37, 43, 115
Korean War 65, 157–8
Kruschev, Nikita 176, 178
Kuwait 39
  see also Gulf War

Laird, Melvyn 180
Lebow, Ned and Stein, Janice Gross 72, 79
Lee, Steven 72
Libya 6

McMahon, Jefferson 71
Mazarr, Michael 84
Missile Technology Control Regime 52, 53
Mountbatten, Lord Louis 180
Mueller, John 72

NATO 9, 36, 38, 64, 83, 139, 150, 158, 163, 173–4
flexible response 158
Nasser, Gamal Abdel 87
  see also Egypt
Nitze, Paul 74–5
Non-Aligned Movement 104, 115–16, 120
Non-Proliferation Treaty 1, 5, 6, 26, 27, 32–3, 43, 47, 49, 51, 52, 59, 76, 89, 90, 96, 101, 103, 108, 119, 122, 151, 161, 162, 191, 201, 206
  extension of (1995) 5, 32, 61, 103, 125, 126, 164
  see also nuclear proliferation
nuclear proliferation 4–7, 29–30, 32–5, 44, 50–2, 59, 61, 62, 74, 75, 78, 93, 110, 136, 160–1, 195
  see also Canberra Commission; Non-Proliferation Treaty; nuclear weapons
nuclear weapons:
  abolition of 7–9, 31, 43–4, 45, 46–51, 54–5, 56–8, 62–5, 66–8, 74, 75, 85, 117–18, 120, 125, 126, 128–33, 139–43, 144–5, 159–66, 178, 179–82, 201, 204, 206–8
  benefits of 126–9, 146, 147, 152–3, 198, 204–5
  'break-out' 129–33, 150–2, 160, 207
  and cold war 45, 46, 65, 71, 72, 152, 154–9, 166, 182, 183–6, 191–2
  and conventional warfare 36–7, 45–6, 49, 50, 64, 133–5
  de-alerting 53–4
  and democracy 141
  limited wars and 16–19, 33–4, 150
  marginalization of 7, 60–2, 68–9, 70, 75, 82, 83–4, 85, 86, 125, 159, 165, 206
  morality of 70–2, 153, 175, 125
  myths 8
  no first use of 53
  nuclear weapons free zones 54
  and subnational groups (nuclear terrorism) 197–8, 202–4, 205, 207
  taboos on 16, 24–9, 202
  virtual arsenals 8, 9–11, 53–4, 67, 70, 81–4, 135–6
  see also ballistic missile defence; Canberra Commission; deterrence; nuclear proliferation

O'Neill, Robert 63, 161

Pahlavi, Shah Muhammad Reza 87–8
  see also Iran
Pakistan:
  nuclear test 1, 6, 9, 10, 39, 40, 51, 62,
    74, 76–7, 78, 79, 84, 101–4, 105–6,
    110–21, 126, 195
  and nuclear weapons 6, 25, 48, 51, 66,
    68, 82, 102, 121–4, 127, 151, 196, 205,
    207, 210
Partial Test Ban Treaty 58
Payne, Keith B. 12
Perry, William 76
post-cold war 167–72, 173–4, 192–3
  collective security in 170–2

Quinlan, Michael 12, 13, 67, 145, 146,
  147, 152–3, 154, 156

Reagan, Ronald 60
realism 39, 71, 140, 144, 168–9
Revolution in Military Affairs (RMA) 36,
  75
rogue states 12, 14, 23–4, 28, 33–4, 35–6,
  129–33, 138–9, 150, 198, 200, 202
Rotblat, Joseph 61, 180
Russell, Bertrand 58, 66
Russia:
  post-cold war 1, 20, 21, 31, 35, 38, 41,
    42, 49, 64, 65, 94, 139, 173, 199
  and nuclear weapons 37, 47, 68, 73–4,
    75, 77, 83, 108, 174, 180, 192–3, 194,
    197–8, 200, 205
Rwanda 173

Sandel, Michael 168, 169
Saudi Arabia 91
Saddam Hussein 35, 88, 89, 96, 97, 202
  see also Gulf War, Iraq
Sagan, Scott 74
SALT agreement 59
Schell, Jonathan 63, 64, 67, 81, 135–6
  see also nuclear weapons (virtual
    arsenals)
Schelling, Thomas 11, 33

Schmidt, Helmut 180
Sharif, Nawaz 105, 106
  see also Pakistan
Slocombe, Walter 83
South Africa 6, 51, 66, 127–8
Soviet Union 31, 36–7, 57, 65, 127, 146,
  147, 153, 155–6, 157–9, 162, 163
  former Soviet republics 38, 42, 51, 61,
    66, 80
START agreements 1, 47, 60, 64, 77–8, 82,
  83, 163, 174, 192–3, 197, 205
  see also arms control
Stimson Center 63
Syria 65, 89, 91, 92, 95, 196

Taiwan 38
theatre missile defence 21, 23
  see also ballistic missile defence
Tokyo Forum 2
Turkey 91

United Nations 49, 57, 118–19, 139, 155,
  171, 172, 208
  Security Council 40–1, 96, 97, 118, 119,
    123
United States 21, 36, 105, 139, 196–7,
  203–4
  and cold war 35, 57, 146–7, 155, 156–7,
    168
  and deterrence 14–15, 153–4
  and nuclear weapons 1, 5, 7, 11, 20–2,
    23, 24, 30, 31, 37, 48, 75–6, 77–8, 83,
    120, 156, 162–3, 164–5, 174–5, 180,
    191, 197, 199, 202, 205
  post-cold war 12–13, 41, 43, 87, 92, 94,
    99, 103, 108, 109, 111–12, 168

Vajpayee, Atal Behari 111
Van Creveld, Martin 6–7

Waltz, Kenneth 17, 110
Waltzer, Michael 71
Welch, Larry 181

Yeltsin, Boris 73
Yugoslavia 172, 173

Printed in the United Kingdom
by Lightning Source UK Ltd.
130478UK00002B/136-144/A